SELECT DOCUMENTS ON
JAPANESE FOREIGN POLICY

1853–1868

SELECT DOCUMENTS ON

JAPANESE

FOREIGN POLICY

1853–1868

TRANSLATED AND EDITED

BY

W. G. BEASLEY

Professor of the History of the Far East
University of London

LONDON
OXFORD UNIVERSITY PRESS
NEW YORK   TORONTO

Oxford University Press, Ely House, London W.1

GLASGOW NEW YORK TORONTO MELBOURNE WELLINGTON
CAPE TOWN SALISBURY IBADAN NAIROBI LUSAKA ADDIS ABABA
BOMBAY CALCUTTA MADRAS KARACHI LAHORE DACCA
KUALA LUMPUR HONG KONG TOKYO

FIRST EDITION 1955

REPRINTED 1960 AND 1967

PRINTED IN GREAT BRITAIN

ACKNOWLEDGEMENTS

Much of the preparatory work for this volume was carried out during a visit to Japan in the academic year 1950–1. I would like to express my gratitude to the authorities of Tōkyō University for their generosity in granting facilities for my work; and especially to the Director of the Shiryō-hensanjo for permission to use and make translations from the archives and publications of his department. Many individual members of the university gave ungrudgingly of their time to discuss my problems and offered invaluable advice. I must particularly mention Professor Iwao Seiichi of the Department of History; Professor Enoki Kazuo of the Tōyo Bunko; and Mr. Morisue Yoshiaki, Mr. Konishi Shirō, and Mr. Yoshida Tsunekichi of the Shiryō-hensanjo. Mr. Numata Jirō (now also of the Shiryō-hensanjo), to whom my special thanks are due, gave constant assistance in the tracing of material and advice on its interpretation. Without his help my work could never have been completed in the time at my disposal.

I wish also to record my thanks to colleagues at the School of Oriental and African Studies, University of London, whom I have consulted on various points of detail; especially to Mr. R. P. Dore, who has read most of the typescript and made many valuable suggestions, and to Mr. S. Yanada who has written the Japanese characters reproduced in Appendixes A and B. To the School itself I am indebted both for making possible my visit to Japan and for the grant which has financed the publication of this book.

W. G. B.

LONDON 1954

CONTENTS

ACKNOWLEDGEMENTS   v

LIST OF DOCUMENTS   ix

NOTE ON JAPANESE NAMES, TITLES, AND DATES   xii

INTRODUCTION

1. THE BACKGROUND OF IDEAS   3

2. THE FORMULATION OF BAKUFU POLICY   18

3. COURT AND BAKUFU: THE STRUGGLE FOR CONTROL OF POLICY   35

4. THE OPENING OF THE PORTS   47

5. THE YEARS OF CRISIS, 1863–4   58

6. 'A STICK TO BEAT THE BAKUFU': FOREIGN AFFAIRS IN 1865–7   77

7. CONCLUSIONS   91

SELECT DOCUMENTS

I. THE PERRY CONVENTION, 1853–4 (DOCUMENTS 1–9)   97

II. THE DUTCH SUPPLEMENTARY TREATY OF 1857 (DOCUMENTS
10–18)   128

III. THE AMERICAN COMMERCIAL TREATY OF 1858 (DOCUMENTS
19–30)   156

IV. THE KAZUNOMIYA MARRIAGE AND THE LONDON PROTOCOL,
1860–2 (DOCUMENTS 31–38)   195

V. EXPULSION AND THE NAMAMUGI INDEMNITY, 1862–3 (DOCU-
MENTS 39–49)   222

VI. THE PARIS CONVENTION AND THE SHIMONOSEKI INDEMNITY,
1863–4 (DOCUMENTS 50–59)   257

VII. IMPERIAL RATIFICATION OF THE TREATIES, 1865 (DOCU-
MENTS 60–67)   290

VIII. THE OPENING OF HYŌGO, 1867 (DOCUMENTS 68–77)   306

APPENDIX A. GLOSSARY OF ADMINISTRATIVE AND OTHER TECH-
NICAL TERMS   321

APPENDIX B. BIOGRAPHICAL NOTES   331

BIBLIOGRAPHY   343

INDEX   349

LIST OF DOCUMENTS

Section I. The Perry Convention, 1853–4

1. President of the United States to the Emperor of Japan, 13 November 1852   99
2. Commodore Perry to the Emperor of Japan, 7 July 1853   101
3. Tokugawa Nariaki to Bakufu, 14 August 1853   102
4. Jisha-bugyō, machi-bugyō, and kanjō-bugyō to Rōjū, 26 August 1853   107
5. Shimazu Nariakira to Bakufu, 2 September 1853   112
6. Matsudaira Keiei to Bakufu, 9 September 1853   114
7. Ii Naosuke to Bakufu, 1 October 1853   117
8. Text of the Perry Convention, 31 March 1854   119
9. America ōsetsu-gakari to Rōjū, 2 April 1854   122

Section II. The Dutch Supplementary Treaty of 1857

10. Rōjū to other senior officials, 19 March 1857   130
11. Hotta Masayoshi to the officials responsible for the study of foreign trade, March/April 1857   131
12. Kaibō-gakari ōmetsuke and metsuke to Rōjū, April/May 1857   134
13. Kaibō-gakari kanjō-bugyō to Rōjū, April/May 1857   137
14. Mizuno Tadanori, Arao Narimasa, and Iwase Tadanari to Rōjū, 20/28 August 1857   139
15. Same to same, 29 August 1857   142
16. Same to same, 22 September 1857   144
17. Mizuno Tadanori to Kawaji Toshiaki and Toki Tomoaki, 14 October 1857   146
18. Text of Additional Articles to the Dutch Treaty of 1856, dated 16 October 1857   149

Section III. The American Commercial Treaty of 1858

19. Statement made by Townsend Harris at his interview with Hotta Masayoshi, 12 December 1857   159
20. Memorandum by Hotta Masayoshi, late December 1857   165
21. Tokugawa Nariaki to Rōjū, 30 December 1857   168
22. Mizuno Tadanori to Rōjū, 2 January 1858   170
23. Iwase Tadanari to Rōjū, c. 4 January 1858   174
24. Daimyō of the Tamari-no-ma to Rōjū, 10 January 1858   176

25. Matsudaira Keiei to Rōjū, 10 January 1858　　　　　179
26. Imperial Court to Hotta Masayoshi, 3 May 1858　　　180
27. Journal of Utsuki Roku-no-jō, 29 July 1858　　　　181
28. Text of Commercial Treaty with the United States, 29 July 1858　　183
29. Manabe Akikatsu to Kujō Naotada, 21 December 1858　　189
30. Imperial Court to Manabe Akikatsu, 2 February 1859　　193

SECTION IV. THE KAZUNOMIYA MARRIAGE AND THE LONDON
PROTOCOL, 1860–2

31. Iwakura Tomomi to Emperor Kōmei, July/August 1860　　198
32. Rōjū to Imperial Court, 14 September 1860　　　200
33. Rōjū to Kyōto-shoshidai, 21 December 1860　　　204
34. Kyōto-shoshidai to Kampaku, c. 8 January 1861　　206
35. Kuze Hirochika and Andō Nobumasa to Rutherford Alcock, 30 May
1861　　　　　　　　　　　　　　　　　208
36. Memorandum by Rutherford Alcock, 14 February 1862　　211
37. Text of the London Protocol, 6 June 1862　　　216
38. Gaikoku-bugyō to Bakufu, October/November 1862　　218

SECTION V. EXPULSION AND THE NAMAMUGI INDEMNITY, 1862–3

39. Matsudaira Katamori to Bakufu, 8 November 1862　　225
40. Matsudaira Keiei to Bakufu, 4 December 1862　　　227
41. Hitotsubashi Keiki and others to Imperial Court, 29 March 1863　234
42. Jisha-bugyō, machi-bugyō, and kanjō-bugyō to Bakufu, April 1863　234
43. St. John Neale to Japanese Ministers for Foreign Affairs, 6 April 1863　236
44. Mizuno Tadanori to Inoue Masanao, 20 April 1863　　240
45. Ogasawara Nagamichi to Bakufu, May 1863　　　243
46. Hitotsubashi Keiki to Rōjū in Edo, 12 June 1863　　246
47. Jisha-bugyō, machi-bugyō, and kanjō-bugyō to Bakufu, 21 June 1863　248
48. Hitotsubashi Keiki to Kampaku, 9 July 1863　　　250
49. Ogasawara Nagamichi to Bakufu, 27 July 1863　　254

SECTION VI. THE PARIS CONVENTION AND THE SHIMONOSEKI
INDEMNITY, 1863–4

50. Ikeda Nagaaki and colleagues to Bakufu, 19 January 1864　260
51. Emperor Kōmei to Shōgun Iemochi, 28 February 1864　263
52. Same to same, 5 March 1864　　　　　　　264
53. Shōgun Iemochi to Emperor Kōmei, 21 March 1864　　266

54. Hara Tadanari to Minobe Matagorō and Nomura Teijitsu, 25 March 1864   268
55. Shōgun to Imperial Court, 26 March 1864   272
56. Text of the Paris Convention, 20 June 1864   273
57. Ikeda Nagaaki and colleagues to Bakufu, *c.* 18 August 1864   274
58. Minutes of conference at Yokohama, 18 September 1864   282
59. Text of Shimonoseki Indemnity Convention, 22 October 1864   288

Section VII. Imperial Ratification of the Treaties, 1865

60. Memorandum by the Ministers in Japan of Britain, France, America, and Holland, 30 October 1865   293
61. Uchita Naka-no-suke to Kampaku, 16 November 1865   296
62. Shōgun Iemochi to Emperor Kōmei, 18 November 1865   297
63. Sir Harry Parkes to Shōgun Iemochi, 21 November 1865   299
64. Senior Bakufu officials to Imperial Court, 22 November 1865   301
65. Ōkubo Toshimichi to Saigō Takamori and Minoda Dembei, 24 November 1865   301
66. Imperial Court to Bakufu, 22 November 1865   304
67. Bakufu to British Minister in Japan, 24 November 1865   304

Section VIII. The Opening of Hyōgo, 1867

68. Shōgun Keiki to Imperial Court, 9 April 1867   308
69. Imperial Court to Shōgun, 23 April 1867   310
70. Shōgun Keiki to Imperial Court, 26 April 1867   310
71. Imperial Court to Shōgun, 3 May 1867   311
72. Ōkubo Toshimichi to Konoe Tadahiro, May 1867   311
73. Ōkubo Toshimichi to Shimazu Hisamitsu, May 1867   312
74. Diary of Saga Sanenaru, 25 and 26 June 1867   314
75. Diary of Prince Asakiko, 25 and 26 June 1867   316
76. Imperial Court to Bakufu, 26 June 1867   319
77. Date Muneki, Shimazu Hisamitsu, Yamanouchi Toyoshige, and Matsudaira Keiei to Imperial Court, 28 June 1867   319

NOTE ON JAPANESE NAMES, TITLES
AND DATES

Names and titles. Japanese names are usually given in the order: family name, followed by given name (e.g. Ii Naosuke, where Ii is the family name). This order is observed here. Where a feudal title is included, however, the Japanese would insert it between the family and given names, e.g. Ii Kamon-no-kami Naosuke. Since this might be misleading to Western readers, the feudal title is here given last, e.g. Ii Naosuke, Kamon-no-kami.

For convenience, brief biographical accounts of the more important people mentioned in the text are given separately (Appendix B). Explanations of their status or official position, therefore, are not usually given in footnotes. However, where references to them are made in the text of a document (and these are often by title rather than by name) sufficient information is interpolated in square brackets to enable the reader to find the appropriate entry in this appendix. As far as is possible, changes of name and variant readings of names are also shown in this appendix.

The names of administrative offices mentioned in the notes or in the text are explained in Appendix A.

Dates. Dates in the documents are usually given in Japanese in the form: *year*, according to year-period (*nengō*) or by reference to the sexagenary cycle; *month and day*, according to the lunar calendar. In the translations these have all been converted to Gregorian calendar equivalents. Thus Bunkyū 2 (or, the Year of the Dog), 10th month, 13th day, is given simply as 4 December 1862. Where the day is not included the date is usually rendered here in the form Gregorian year, followed by lunar month (e.g. 1862, 10th month), the Gregorian equivalents for the first and last days of that month then being added in brackets, e.g. 1862, 10th month (22 November–20 December).

The same conventions, wherever applicable, are observed in the introduction.

INTRODUCTION

THE translation of mid-nineteenth-century Japanese documents is a task
that presents many problems. In the first place, most documents of
interest to the historian are written in the literary style known as *sōrōbun*,
perhaps the least precise of all forms of Japanese expression. Verbs in
sōrōbun, for example, have no tense. It is true that there are other devices
by which past, present, and future time can be expressed, but these are not
always used, at least in this period; while the rarity of personal and
possessive pronouns, the prevalence of verbs of wide and often indefinite
application, and the general unwieldiness of the prose (which is usually
unpunctuated), all contribute to a state of affairs in which it is easier to
understand the general drift of an argument than to produce an exact
rendering of any part of it. The translator is often faced with passages
that can only be interpreted in the light of context or of events. Sometimes
not even this will make the meaning clear. In fact, every translation
included in this collection contains passages which offer ground for difference or debate.

Were this volume intended primarily as an aid to language study it
would have been necessary to discuss these problems at length. This
would have necessitated a multiplicity of footnotes dealing with points of
detail—points which would not for the most part, even collectively, greatly
affect the meaning of the whole. Their value in a book designed for
historians seems open to question. Those who can will wish to consult the
Japanese text for themselves; for them this book will chiefly be a means of
saving time and labour. Those who know no Japanese—and it is hoped
that there will be some among them who may find the book of use—are as
likely to be inconvenienced by the critical paraphernalia as to be helped
by the discussion. Such discussion, therefore, has generally been avoided.
Only where the problems of language seem sufficiently important to affect
the sense and meaning of the text as a whole have I indicated the points
at issue.

Then again, wherever the intention of the original text has thereby been
made clearer, use has been made of English words of a kind for which mid-
nineteenth-century Japanese had not in fact developed a specialized term.
For instance, most Japanese did not at this time distinguish verbally
between 'a treaty' and 'the ratifications of a treaty'. Yet there are occasions on which it would confuse the chronology of events not to differen-
tiate them in English, and I have preferred to do so in the translation
rather than by footnote. Similarly, nouns and proper names, omitted but
implicit in the original, have been interpolated wherever their insertion

makes the text easier to follow. In such respects the translations are more precise than the Japanese. It is felt that the advantages of this to the reader outweigh the theoretical objections to it; but it is necessary to emphasize that the result is sometimes a translation that renders the sense rather than the exact form of the original. Indeed, the differences between modern English and the *sōrōbun* style of Japanese are such that an exact rendering would be unintelligible. I have also omitted, as a rule, the formal greetings at the beginning of a document, where such exist; especially in private letters, where they usually take the form of comments on the weather or inquiries about the health of the recipient. Such omissions are not normally indicated. Where a document is shortened by the omission of redundant or irrelevant passages, however, the fact is always noted.

There are other matters in which accuracy is essential. The translation of technical terms, especially administrative terms, is often more misleading than helpful. To translate *kanjō-bugyō* as 'Finance Magistrate', for example, would admittedly convey an idea of the primary function of the office, but it would not make any clearer its importance in the administration of foreign affairs. To devise new translations of such terms might well be confusing to those already familiar with the old. I have therefore preferred to use the Japanese word and refer the reader for an explanation of it to the Glossary (Appendix A).

A further difficulty is presented by the frequent occurrence of words and phrases that have an emotional impact on the reader. The translation of the Chinese and Japanese term *i*, literally 'barbarian', has been a source of disagreement ever since the nineteenth century. It was used both in China and Japan as the general designation for 'foreigner' and can be so translated, though by long association it had undoubtedly come to carry a connotation of dislike and contempt. It was from about 1860 that some Japanese began to seek alternative expressions, which suggests that they were aware of these connotations. On the other hand, no other word was at this time in common use.[1] I have therefore chosen to translate it as 'foreigner', in the belief that constant repetition of the word 'barbarian' would heighten the effect unduly and that the general tone of the documents can be made sufficiently evident in other ways.

Other such expressions fall into a rather different category. They are used to appeal to the prejudices of the reader and so incline him to support the line of policy being advocated. Their meaning is never precise (and it may vary from time to time), but their connotations are invariably favourable, usually in the context of national pride or tradition. *Kokutai*, for example, which appears again and again in the political debates of the twentieth century—where it is usually translated rather vaguely as

---

[1] Except the term *ban* (in the expressions *namban, banjin,* &c.), which was if anything less complimentary still.

'national polity'—also occurs in the Bakumatsu period.[1] Here it seems to mean 'national prestige', as it often does also in Chinese (*kuo-t'i*). Such terms cannot be explained by mere translation. Nor is their immediate context always of the kind to make their significance clear. They can be understood only in the wider context of ideas current in society, in this case of ideas concerning foreigners and foreign relations generally. It is one function of this introduction to provide the background against which such expressions—and, indeed, the documents as a whole—can be set.

1. *The background of ideas*

In the seventeenth century, after nearly a hundred years of intercourse with the outside world, Japan had closed her doors to all but Dutch and Chinese, and even they were confined to the single port of Nagasaki, where they found themselves hedged about with restrictions of every kind. The reasons for this step were many and the relative weight we should give to each is still a matter of debate. Of greater importance to us here are those which the Japanese themselves regarded, or came to regard, as the motive for their actions, for by the nineteenth century these had become, for the majority, articles of faith.

The founders of the Tokugawa line had created a form of government, the Tokugawa Bakufu, which was designed to confirm and perpetuate the authority of their successors. The generations that followed came to regard its preservation as the primary object of administration, seeing their own function as that of stewards who had received the system intact and must pass it on equally undamaged and unchanged.[2] This attitude of conservatism, by extension, came to be applied to all existing institutions. It applied not least to the policy of national seclusion. As tradition had it, Tokugawa Ieyasu and his grandson Iemitsu, in their wisdom, had perceived that Japan was in danger from foreign attack. All foreigners, they knew, came with hostile intent, seeking territorial aggrandizement; while foreign trade and the Christian religion were not only tools to serve that end but were also things harmful in themselves. They had therefore taken steps to avert the danger by expelling foreigners from Japan. It followed that seclusion was a fundamental law of the Tokugawa house, which it was the duty of all officials to maintain, for only thus could their country be preserved from corruption and defeat. National seclusion, in fact, was enjoined alike by the dictates of patriotism and by the sanctions of ancestral law.

The importance of this tradition can easily be overlooked. The debates that raged after 1853 were conducted by a small minority, a minority even

---

[1] Bakumatsu, literally 'late-Bakufu', is the term used by Japanese historians to describe the closing years of Tokugawa rule, roughly the period 1840–68.

[2] For an interesting example of this point of view see Document 13, pp. 137–9.

of those who possessed social and political power, but they took place in a society which for the most part accepted it as axiomatic that foreign intercourse was dangerous and undesirable. It was to this tradition that many of the contestants appealed. It was against it that others fought. Its existence does much to explain both the language and the arguments that they found it necessary to use.

It would be totally misleading, however, to suggest that the leaders themselves based their views on an unthinking acceptance of ideas inherited from the seventeenth century. Even those most bitterly opposed to the opening of the country advanced more modern—and more cogent —reasons. They argued, in fact, from the events of recent history. By about 1800 some Japanese were becoming aware of a renewed European interest in their country. Russian explorers and trading-posts were beginning to appear in the Kurile Islands to the north of Ezo (Hokkaidō), where Japanese influence and administration had never been firmly established, while on two occasions Russians actually came to Japan itself in search of trading privileges. The second of these missions, that of Rezanov in 1804, was treated with scant courtesy. In revenge, Rezanov ordered local attacks on Japanese settlements in the northern islands, and though the incidents themselves were insignificant they served to confirm Japanese suspicion of foreign designs. The motives that had formerly been attributed to Portugal and Spain were now transferred to Russia and gained added strength from the knowledge that Russian territory already extended to the shores of the Pacific. Despite the fact that Russia remained inactive for some forty years thereafter, Japanese writers continued to urge the danger of Russian attack. By the middle of the century the idea was firmly established.

Meanwhile fear of Britain was being added to suspicion of Russia. It was a duty of Dutch and Chinese traders coming to Japan to keep the Tokugawa Bakufu informed about developments in the outside world. They did not fail to describe—and in the most unfavourable terms—the growing power of Britain in Asia. The effect was heightened by the high-handed actions of a British frigate which visited Nagasaki in 1808 and by a series of clashes with British whaling-vessels in the years that followed. Even so, the warning voices were comparatively few until after 1840. It was the Opium War in China, presented as evidence both of British strength and British aggression, that finally persuaded Japanese that an attack on their own country was not only possible but even imminent. Some believed that Britain would fight to extend her trade and others that trade was a pretext for acquiring territory, but almost all were now convinced that it was only a matter of time before Japan herself became an object of British greed.[1]

[1] For the influence of British and Russian actions on Japanese thinking about foreign affairs

Thus when Commodore Perry reached Uraga in 1853 many Japanese were already giving serious thought to the international position of their country. Their thinking was dominated by the threat from Russia in the north and that from Britain in the south; and these two Powers continued to play a vital, if unwitting, role in Japanese diplomacy even when they were not directly engaged in negotiations. Moreover, they had established in Japanese minds a lasting connexion between the problems of foreign policy and those of defence. To a minority it was obvious from the beginning that the West had made vast strides in the development of weapons and military science during the centuries of Japan's national seclusion. General acceptance of this fact had to wait until it had been conclusively demonstrated by the operations against Kagoshima and Shimonoseki in 1863–4; but it is with the active leaders of thought that we are here concerned, and they were virtually unanimous on the point even before 1853. Japan was in danger of attack and she could best be defended by weapons of the Western type, which, they said, she must therefore buy and if possible build. This assumption underlies every pronouncement on foreign policy in the Bakumatsu period. Frequently it is explicit. And when there first emerges among Bakufu officials a group primarily concerned with the problems of foreign relations, it is significant that they are designated *kaibō-gakari*, 'in charge of maritime defence'.

The need for strengthening defences to meet the threat of foreign attack was the one subject on which unanimity could be achieved. On other questions of foreign policy Japan's leaders were sharply divided. The active minority, comprising a number of Bakufu officials and feudal lords, together with several groups of scholars and pamphleteers, are usually regarded as falling into two main schools, the advocates of *jōi* ('expel the barbarians') and *kaikoku* ('open the country') respectively. A clear understanding of these is indispensable to any study of Bakumatsu history, for the relationship between them is more complex than the somewhat forthright labels might lead one to expect.

The *kaikoku* school is closely connected with the Rangakusha,[1] whose study of the West gave them a greater knowledge of world conditions than that possessed by most of their contemporaries. With greater knowledge came a more vivid realization of Japan's military weakness, and it was this that was the distinguishing feature of their thought. Like others, they acknowledged the existence of a threat to Japan's independence. They

in the first half of the nineteenth century see especially Inobe, 'Mito gakuha no jōi-ron', *Shirin*, v (1920), pp. 126–32; Tsuchiya, 'Bakumatsu shishi no mita Shina mondai', *Kaizo*, xx (July 1938), pp. 154–67; and R. H. van Gulik, '*Kakkaron*, a Japanese Echo of the Opium War', *Monumenta Serica*, iv (1939–40), pp. 481–511. I have also discussed the subject at somewhat greater length in *Great Britain and the Opening of Japan 1834–1858* (London, 1951), pp. 32–42.

[1] The Rangakusha or 'Dutch scholars' were so called because they studied the science and learning of the West through books which they obtained from the Dutch traders at Nagasaki.

admitted the urgent need to improve defences. They took the argument a stage farther, however, and asserted that without Western weapons and techniques Japan was quite incapable of defending herself and must therefore avoid war, even at the cost of acceding to foreign demands for the opening of ports. Indeed, the opening of ports seemed to some of them desirable as well as unavoidable. It would make much easier the adoption of Western military science and auxiliary techniques by enabling Japan to hire foreign instructors and send her own students abroad to study.

If this was the central theme of *kaikoku* argument, it was by no means all that has to be included under that heading. One must beware of assuming the existence of a *kaikoku* party in the sense of an organized body pressing for the adoption of a single and specific line of policy, for the label is applied to men who approached the problem in a variety of different ways. Some went much farther than others in admitting the need for concession to the West and some even managed to rid themselves of the inherited tradition that things foreign were necessarily evil. On the subject of trade, for example, there was considerable variation. There were a few who advocated it as the basis of national wealth and therefore, indirectly, of national strength. These were the men who rejected current theories about economic self-sufficiency and urged the Bakufu to grant the widest possible facilities for foreign commerce in Japan. The majority, of course, were not prepared to go so far. They argued the inevitability rather than the desirability of trade, pointing out that in the existing state of Bakufu finances it was extremely doubtful whether the enormous cost of defence preparations could be met without finding some new source of revenue. Trade seemed to them to offer useful opportunities for government profit. They envisaged it as being virtually a Bakufu monopoly (as indeed was most of the existing trade at Nagasaki) and therefore as contributing directly to a solution of the financial problem. Yet they remained reluctant to abandon long-standing economic theories derived from Japan's agrarian background and many of them urged that while ships should be sent to trade overseas, foreigners should not be permitted to come to Japan itself.[1]

The nature of what we call *kaikoku* thought did not only vary from individual to individual. In that it depended not so much on theory as on a reaction to concrete situations, it changed also with the progress of

[1] The views here outlined as those of the *kaikoku* school found expression, as one might expect, among those Bakufu officials most closely concerned with foreign affairs. See especially the documents given in Section II (pp. 128–55), which are discussed below on pp. 23–24, 28–30. Some general material on this subject will be found in Honjō, *Nihon keizai shisōshi gaisetsu* (Tōkyō, 1946), pp. 111–14, 142–3; Kanno, 'Shokō to gaikoku bōeki', in *Bakumatsu keizaishi kenkyū*, ed. Honjō (Tōkyō, 1935), pp. 386–8; D. C. Greene, 'Osada's Life of Takano Nagahide', *Trans. Asiatic Soc. Japan*, xli (1913), pp. 427–9; and D. Keene, *The Japanese Discovery of Europe: Honda Toshiaki and Other Discoverers 1720–1798* (London, 1952).

events. This can perhaps best be seen in the ideas expounded by Sakuma Shōzan, one of the most famous of the Rangakusha and a teacher of considerable influence.[1] At the time of the Opium War Sakuma became convinced, like many others, of the danger of attack by Britain. At this period, however, he was strongly opposed to granting trade or to making any concession at all under threat of military action. Trade was useless if not harmful, he said, while merely to submit to the threat of force would destroy national morale. He was, in fact, much more *jōi* than *kaikoku*. Yet by 1850 he was arguing that China's collapse had followed inevitably from her failure to study Western techniques, a task which he regarded as the modern equivalent of the traditional military maxim that one must 'know one's enemy'.[2] Japan must not make the same mistake. She must take every opportunity to increase her knowledge of the West, adopting not only Western weapons but also Western ideas of any kind that would contribute to her own wealth and strength. Until this policy had reached fruition, to open hostilities would be to invite disaster. Only if attacked was she to have recourse to war. Yet this did not mean that Sakuma would accept any policy that sacrificed Japanese interests as he defined them, and in 1854 we find him a bitter critic of the convention concluded with Perry. In the first place, the agreement was premature, he said. Japan must not enter upon any extensive relations with the West until study of Western ideas had put her in a position to profit by the change. Then again, to open the country from fear of foreign guns was mere capitulation, inviting dishonour. Finally, there was a specific objection to the choice of Shimoda as a port: it was too remote to be kept under proper supervision, whereas in Yokohama the foreigners could have been subjected to more effective control. These were criticisms of the timing, motive, and detail of Bakufu action, however, and did not make Sakuma any the less an advocate of *kaikoku*. Primarily, as he saw it, this was for the purpose of gaining the knowledge and training without which Japan would never be able to assert her independence, but he even came to urge the financial advantages of trade—provided always that it be conducted by sending Japanese ships abroad, not by admitting foreigners to Japan. To Sakuma, in fact, foreign intercourse might be distasteful, but it was necessary to national survival.

Sakuma Shōzan thought of the opening of Japan almost entirely in the

---

[1] For Sakuma's views see Inobe, 'Sakuma Shōzan no taigai iken', *Kokugaku-in Zasshi*, xxx (1924), pp. 455–86, 608–37.

[2] The maxim *kare wo shiri, onore wo shire* (literally, 'know the other man and know oneself') was frequently used by advocates of *kaikoku* in this period. In Chinese it is sometimes given more fully as *chih pi chih chi po chan po shêng* ('to know one's own and the enemy's plans brings constant victory') and as such it could be cited as justification for the study of Western ideas, even for their adoption. There were also times when it was used in the sense that policy must be framed in the light of a realistic appreciation of the situation, i.e. of Japanese weakness and foreign strength. In this sense it could be used to justify a temporary submission to foreign demands pending the completion of defence preparations that would enable Japan to resist successfully.

context of defence. Foreign trade, foreign books, and foreign teachers were to be welcomed not as good in themselves but as a means to an end, the end being the creation of a strong and independent Japan. In this he was typical of the great majority of *kaikoku* thinkers. There were some, it is true, who regarded this limited programme as insufficient to cure the deep-rooted social and economic ills of Japanese society, but these were never really influential in the period before 1868. Men in authority, in fact, were rarely willing to go beyond the views expressed by the *fudai daimyō* Ii Naosuke. When the Bakufu called for the advice of feudal lords concerning negotiations with Perry in 1853, Ii was at first non-committal; and it was only after some prompting that he revealed himself as being in favour of extending relations with the West.[1] Like those of Sakuma, his views sprang from a consciousness of Japan's danger. They did not depend on abstract theories about progress and the benefits of trade. In the changed conditions of the nineteenth century, he argued, the policy of national seclusion was no longer an effective means of attaining the object for which it had been devised. Japan must take more positive action, even for defence. In particular, she must revive the seventeenth-century practice of sending licensed trading-vessels to Batavia and elsewhere, thereby providing the training in navigation and seamanship which would make it possible to create a modern navy and acquiring the funds to pay for the purchase and construction of Western-style ships and guns. This was the immediate task. Only when it was completed would Japan regain her freedom of action in foreign affairs.

The advocates of *kaikoku*, then, sought something less than the 'opening' of Japan as it would have been defined by a Western diplomat or trader. Their opponents are equally misrepresented by the simple and uncompromising label 'expel the barbarians'. The policy of *jōi*, like that of *kaikoku*, had its roots in the warnings about Russian expansion sounded at the end of the eighteenth century[2] and it accordingly shared the general preoccupation with problems of defence. Gradually, however, it became recognizable as a distinct line of thought and the centre of opposition to the treaties concluded with the West. Initially this was the work of the Mito school,[3] notably of Aizawa Seishisai (also known as Aizawa Hakumin) and Fujita Tōko, but the impact of the Opium War, in particular,

[1] His memorandum is translated as Document 7, pp. 117–19. On Ii Naosuke's views generally see below, pp. 42–44.

[2] In this connexion the writings of Hayashi Shihei were especially important. A brief account is given in Keene, *The Japanese Discovery of Europe*, pp. 48–55.

[3] The best account is to be found in Inobe, 'Mito gakuha no jōi-ron', *Shirin*, v (1920), pp. 125–53, on which I have based much of the outline given here. The town of Mito, about 70 miles north-east of Edo (Tōkyō), was the castle-town of the fief held by one of the three senior branch houses of the Tokugawa. As early as the seventeenth century Mito scholars had become leading critics of the Confucian theories that were officially supported by the Bakufu, and even after the abolition of feudalism Mito itself remained a centre of ultranationalism and right-wing radicalism.

helped to spread their ideas throughout Japan. The development of *jōi* as a political movement will need to be considered separately and at some length. However, it is necessary here to remove some misconceptions about the nature of its ideas.

In economic terms the *jōi* leaders can be associated with ideas of much earlier provenance. Like the Confucian scholar Arai Hakuseki,[1] they accepted the view that foreign trade was of itself harmful to the State. Of foreign goods brought to Japan only medicines could be regarded as valuable, they said, while in return for useless woollens and other materials Japan was exporting gold, silver, and copper, metals that were the very substance of her wealth. An expansion of trade, therefore, would bring not wealth but impoverishment. Indeed, the ideas that lay behind the imposition of restrictions on the bulk and nature of Dutch trade at Nagasaki led men like Aizawa Seishisai to demand its total abolition. It was an attitude that accounted for much of the opposition to the inclusion of commercial privileges in the treaties of 1854–8.[2]

In a wider perspective, *jōi* was linked with cultural as well as economic prejudice. The concepts of Chinese moral and political philosophy had long been dominant in Japanese society and they were upheld, moreover, by Confucian scholars firmly entrenched in positions of influence and authority. It is true that since the eighteenth century they had been attacked with increasing virulence by the Kokugakusha, or 'national scholars', who maintained the validity of an older Japanese tradition, but both groups were equally hostile to the culture of the West. That the West had achieved technical superiority they were ready to admit. Indeed, China's collapse sprang in some measure from her failure to recognize this fact. Yet this was not all. To them, China's defeat was also attributable to the corruption of her society by the penetration of Western customs and religion, itself due to negligence in allowing the foreigners a foothold at Canton. Western religion, they said, was a false and alien doctrine which undermined the whole ethical basis of society. Western trade brought wealth to townsmen and merchants, which in its turn brought laxity and corruption. China had succumbed to these influences and must now be accounted 'barbarian'; and it was clear that Japan could escape a similar fate only by preventing the foreigner from securing entry to her ports.[3]

This appeal to the traditions of a Confucian philosophy and an agrarian economy accorded well with the inherited policy of national seclusion. It

[1] See Keene, op. cit., pp. 133–6.
[2] On this point generally see Kanno, 'Shōkō to gaikoku bōeki', pp. 382–9, and Tabohashi, *Kindai Nihon gaikoku kankei-shi* (rev. ed. Tōkyō, 1943), pp. 535–6.
[3] Such views were expressed, for example, by Ōhashi Totsuan in his book *Byakuja kogoto* (1852); see Tsuchiya, 'Bakumatsu shishi no mita Shina mondai', pp. 162–3. On the reactions of Confucian scholars see van Gulik, '*Kakkaron*', pp. 481–5. The influence of the Kokugakusha on the *jōi* movement is treated at greater length below, pp. 36–38.

undoubtedly does much to explain the popularity of *jōi* views in the
Bakumatsu period. Yet it would be altogether wrong to dismiss the *jōi*
movement and the attacks on foreigners as no more than an expression of
conservatism or blind reaction. The *jōi* leaders, at least, were no less
reformers than their opponents.

The essential argument for the policy of expulsion (by which was understood, before 1853, resistance of all foreign attempts to secure admittance
to Japan) was presented in two important books: Aizawa Seishisai's *Shinron*, written in 1825, and Fujita Tōko's *Hitachi-obi*, written twenty years
later.[1] Since their viewpoint differed little in substance they can in practice be treated together. Both rejected as demonstrably untrue the idea
that trade could be a thing useful or desirable in itself. For Japan, after
all, it had always involved the export of valuable metals in exchange for
valueless luxuries. Deserving of more serious attention, they thought, was
the suggestion that trade with the outside world could provide the money
and technical knowledge necessary to equip Japan's defences with modern
weapons of the Western type. Certainly such weapons were necessary, for
without them no final victory could be achieved. On the other hand,
weapons themselves were of no avail without the will and sense of purpose
that would make it possible to use them effectively; and this raised the
questions of national unity and morale that to *jōi* thinkers were central to
the whole problem. As they saw it, two centuries of peace and idleness
had already in great part destroyed the habits of discipline and frugality
on which Japan's strength traditionally depended—and, indeed, they
could point to changing economic and social conditions which seemed to
provide evidence for this assumption. Japanese society, they felt, was
already threatened with disintegration. If it were at this point to be
exposed, through trade, to the contamination of Western culture and
religion, collapse would be inevitable. Long before the new defences were
prepared the will to use them would have vanished. Thus it was essential
that Japan's entry into world affairs be preceded by creation of the unity
and consciousness of danger which would enable her people to adopt such
Western ideas as could be made to serve them, while firmly rejecting all
those that threatened the national ethos. This could not be achieved by
mere exhortation. The Bakufu would have to make its sincerity plain by
effecting thorough reform of the economy and administration. It must
also announce publicly a policy of expulsion, affirming that all foreign
demands would be refused even at the risk of war. Indeed, war itself
would play a part in achieving the desired end. Only the sound of cannon
could rouse Japan from her lethargy.

If one can accept its assumptions, this argument is not without coherence. To the Western mind, however, it involves one logical contradiction

[1] These books are summarized and discussed in Inobe, 'Mito gakuha no jōi-ron', pp. 129–44.

that cannot be dismissed without further examination. If Aizawa and Fujita recognized the inevitability of defeat in any immediate conflict with the West, that is, before Japan had modernized her military establishment, how could they reconcile this with a policy that would court and even welcome the risk of war as a means of achieving national unity? To this question no very clear answer emerges.[1] In some writings of the period one finds the suggestion that Western threats were but 'the art of subjugating by intimidation',[2] which implies that the West did not necessarily envisage full-scale hostilities and that a resolute demeanour might itself be enough to call the bluff. Rather more frequent was a partial denial of the inevitability of defeat. The West's strength lay in naval warfare, and in this Japan could not possibly hold her own for some time to come. Yet invasion of Japan could not be accomplished by naval victory alone; and if foreign troops attempted to penetrate the interior, Japanese skill and valour in land warfare would ensure success in the resulting campaign. Thus naval defeat, which could not be avoided, need not lead automatically to surrender.

These theories, which were in any case subject to changes of emphasis from time to time, were still further modified when it became necessary to apply them in the realm of practical politics. This can best be seen in the career of Tokugawa Nariaki, who was until shortly before his death in 1860 the active leader of the *jōi* movement. Nariaki derived much of his prestige from his position as head of the senior Tokugawa branch house of Mito, but even after a clash with Bakufu officials had brought his enforced retirement (in 1844) he remained one of the most influential men in Japan. Partly this was because of his reputation as a man of ability. Partly it was because of the size of his family, for through the marriage or adoption of his children he was connected with the two great Court families of Nijō and Takatsukasa, the Tokugawa branch house of Hitotsubashi, and several of the great fiefs, including those of Tottori, Okayama, Uwajima, and Sendai.[3] But largely his influence depended on being the patron and defender of the Mito scholars and hence a focus for the loyalties of *jōi* adherents throughout Japan.

Underlying Nariaki's attitude to foreign policy one can detect a strain of sheer xenophobia. This appears, for example, at the beginning of 1855, when Poutiatine's flagship the *Diana* was wrecked in Shimoda harbour and Nariaki recommended that the entire Russian crew be put to death. Nevertheless, hatred of foreigners did not lead him to urge a policy of

[1] The difficulty is discussed in Tokushige, 'Bakumatsu no taigai sensō shōri-ron', *Rekishi to Chiri*, xxxiii (1934), pp. 257–65, 347–57, though no very satisfactory conclusions are reached.

[2] See van Gulik, '*Kakkaron*', pp. 487–8.

[3] Thus three leading figures of the 1860s—Hitotsubashi Keiki, who became Shōgun as Tokugawa Keiki in 1866; Tokugawa Yoshiatsu of Mito; and Ikeda Yoshinori of Inaba (Tottori)—were in fact natural brothers, all being sons of Nariaki.

seclusion in the strictest sense of the term. In military matters, at least, he knew that Japan had much to learn from the West. As early as 1846 we find him urging the Bakufu to import foreign books on gunnery and similar subjects, while his later proposals included plans for the use of Western drill and military training and even the employment of Western instructors—though he was careful to enter a warning against letting this become an excuse for the study of Western languages and customs generally. 'My view is', he wrote to Abe Masahiro in 1854, 'that without abandoning Japanese ways we should adopt the best of foreign methods and join them to the best of our own'.[1] For the most part, of course, these were ideas to which many leaders of the day, *kaikoku* as well as *jōi*, would have subscribed.

At one time or another in his career Tokugawa Nariaki advanced most of the arguments for expulsion that have been outlined above, and they were already familiar by the time he repeated them in a long memorandum which he prepared for the Bakufu in August 1853.[2] However, the document affords a convenient summary of his views. In it he again insisted on the need to strengthen Japan's defences. He denied the value of trade and reminded the Bakufu that both trade and Christianity were instruments of Western aggression. Above all, he dwelt on the question of morale. Guns, he wrote, could not of themselves bring victory. Without resolution and high morale they were so much ornament; and however much the government laboured to complete its military preparations, no successful defence of Japan could be achieved unless a clear and decisive lead were given to national opinion. The Bakufu must make unmistakable its willingness to fight. To announce a policy of peace and the acceptance of American demands would destroy morale and hence bring ultimate catastrophe, though it might postpone that result for a time. To choose war would raise morale and so bring final victory, even if it meant a series of defeats at first.

Ostensibly, then, Nariaki was an advocate of the so-called 'war' policy of the *jōi* party. It is important to realize, however, that the official memoranda of this period are not of themselves a sufficient guide to policy, for their authors had to steer a course amidst a maze of intrigues, conflicting interests, and violent emotions. Some opinions were too dangerous to be set down on paper, except in a garbled form. Others were exaggerated or understated, according to the effect it was desired to produce on opponents or supporters. Almost all need to be interpreted in the light of private letters or events. This test can more aptly be applied to a man like Tokugawa Nariaki, who was actively engaged in the formulation of

---

[1] This letter is quoted in Akao, 'Perry torai zengo ni okeru taigai kokumin shisō no kōsatsu', *Shirin*, xxii (1937), p. 774. See also ibid., pp. 532, 779; and Tokushige, op. cit., pp. 263–4.

[2] The first part of this memorandum is translated as Document 3, pp. 102–7 below.

Bakufu policy, than to men whose main contribution to events was through the influence of their lectures and writing; nor need we be surprised to find that he sometimes failed to insist in practice on the execution of all that he had recommended on paper. It is true that he consistently urged the need for a firmer attitude than that adopted by most Bakufu officials. Yet it is also true that in private consultations with Rōjū and others he several times accepted, tacitly and even explicitly, the argument that recourse to war was impossible in the existing state of Japan's defences.[1] This is confirmed by his private correspondence. At the time of Perry's arrival in 1853, for example, he wrote to Matsudaira Keiei that expulsion would not be immediately practicable. In February of the following year he was even more convinced of this. Since his own warnings of the last twenty years had gone unheeded, he said in another letter, there was nothing else to be done but seek to gain time, as much as might be necessary for taking appropriate measures in Japan's defence.[2] This, one supposes, would entail concessions of some kind to the foreign envoy.

Had Nariaki maintained this attitude in his later public statements one might reasonably conclude that contact with hard reality had induced a change of heart. To some extent, indeed, this may be so. Openly, however, he remained an advocate of immediate expulsion, even war; and the key to this disparity between his public and his private views is to be found rather in his original motives than in any modification wrought by time. To say that he was stubborn and fanatical, though basically correct, is not of itself a satisfactory explanation. In his hatred of foreigners and his determination to resist their encroachment on Japan, Nariaki was a man of his age. He was not therefore necessarily a fool. Nor does fanaticism preclude political ability. A clue to the solution of this difficulty can be found in another of his letters to Matsudaira Keiei, written in September 1853. There his policy is described in the phrase *naisen gaiwa*, which can be translated 'war at home, peace abroad'.[3] Keiei took this to mean that Nariaki would continue to advocate an official announcement within Japan of the necessity and inevitability of war, since this was the only means of ensuring a proper emphasis on defence, but that Japan in her dealings with foreigners should adopt a conciliatory tone which would avert hostilities altogether or at least lay the responsibility for initiating them on the Western Powers. It was clear from the letter that Nariaki

[1] See especially *Ishin-shi* (Ishin Shiryō Hensan Jimukyoku, 6 vols., Tōkyō, 1939–41), i. 562–3; Tabohashi, *Kindai Nihon gaikoku kankei shi*, pp. 506–7, 509–11, 546–7.

[2] For these two letters to Matsudaira Keiei see respectively *Ishin-shi*, ii. 77, and *Sakumu kiji* (Nihon Shiseki Kyōkai series, 4 vols., Tōkyō, 1920–1), i. 105–6. Matsudaira Keiei's own *jōi* views are given in a memorandum to the Bakufu translated as Document 6, pp. 114–7 below.

[3] The text of this letter, dated Kaei 6.viii.11 (13 September 1853), is given in *Sakumu-kiji*, i. 82–84. Keiei's reply is also given, ibid. i. 84–85. See also Tokushige, 'Bakumatsu no taigai senso shōri-ron', pp. 264–5, and Akao, 'Nichi-bei kari tsūshō jōyaku chōin mondai wo meguru Ii Tairō to Mito-han ippa to no kōsō', *Shirin*, xxvi (1941), at p. 427.

came to this conclusion only with the utmost reluctance; and it became clear later that he did not even now envisage any major concessions, certainly not that of trade. It did, however, represent a modification of his earlier unyielding stand. It also throws some light on his attitude towards war. In view of Japan's unpreparedness—despite Nariaki's own past warnings that such a crisis was bound one day to arise—she could not afford to take the first step in opening the struggle. She must be prepared to defend herself, of course, if foreign intransigence forced her to do so, and must not in any case concede anything of substance. But even this degree of moderation, small as it was, must not be communicated to the country at large. The people must be told to be ready to fight, not that the government hoped to avoid the necessity. The 'choice of war', in fact, which Nariaki continued to urge upon the Bakufu, was not a foreign but a domestic policy. It was for internal consumption, directed towards raising morale and inducing a sense of urgency that would ensure the maximum of readiness should it happen that negotiations did in the end break down.

While we can accept this interpretation of Nariaki's policy as valid for the winter of 1853-4, we must be careful not to apply it too widely. His subsequent actions were influenced by many considerations that did not directly relate to foreign affairs. Moreover, the *jōi* party as a whole bore less responsibility and did not necessarily view the situation in the same way. The great majority of those who later attacked foreigners in the streets of the treaty ports undoubtedly acted out of a blind acceptance of tradition, and many more were convinced that such attacks would in the long run contribute to the preservation of national independence. Expulsion to them was not merely a call to arms intended as a means of securing unity within Japan. It was a duty they must perform, with or without the Bakufu's approval.

Yet against this we must set the evidence of later developments within the *jōi* movement. By 1867, at the latest, most of the leaders no longer regarded the expulsion of foreigners as either practicable or desirable, despite their continued and vehement arguments in its favour. Nor, when they had seized power, did they attempt to put expulsion into practice. On the contrary, they were the very men who in the Meiji period carried out the complex series of political, social, and economic changes which are summed up in the phrase 'the westernisation of Japan'. This is partly explained by the events of 1863-4 and by the sobering effect of responsibility, but it also serves to underline the fact that from the beginning there had existed a certain distinction between what was advocated and what was intended. Not all the arguments can be taken at their face value. This is seen in the general recognition that it was necessary to emulate Western technical superiority, with the consequent avowal that expulsion was a policy designed to meet the exigencies of an immediate situation; it did not rule out the possibility of later intercourse with the West, provided always that this could be achieved on terms of equality. In large measure this divorce between statement and intention sprang from the relationship between foreign policy and domestic politics.[1] Despite its obvious roots in chauvinism and xenophobia, the *jōi* movement became more and more preoccupied with political disputes in which advocacy of expulsion—regardless of whether it were possible or desirable in itself—proved an invaluable weapon against the Tokugawa Bakufu. It was on this account argued by many who did not in fact believe in it. At what stage this became a matter of calculated policy it is difficult to say, but it is certain that as early as 1853 men like Tokugawa Nariaki were thinking as much in terms of domestic reform as of foreign policy. The documents of the period must be read with this in mind.

It should now be possible to attempt a comparison of the rival policies of *kaikoku* and *jōi*. In the first place, it is clear that advocates of both recognized in the activities of the Western Powers a threat to the independence of Japan and were primarily concerned to combat this danger. Both agreed that to achieve this it would be necessary to adopt at least the military techniques developed by the West. In other words, both acted from the same motives and towards the same objective. They differed, in fact, not about the end but about the means of attaining it. Faced with the arrival of an American squadron demanding conclusion of a treaty, the *kaikoku* party argued as follows: the Americans will fight if their demands are refused, but Japan is neither financially nor militarily capable of offering effective resistance and will not be until her defences are strengthened and modernized; since this will take time, time must be bought by a policy of immediate (though temporary) concession. With some of these statements the *jōi* leaders could also agree. They objected, however, that it would be fatal to admit Western influences to a Japan psychologically unprepared to cope with them, however honourable the motives for so doing—and hence the necessity for reform at home as a preliminary to opening the ports. Even if the delay meant war, the risk of defeat was less great and less terrifying than the certainty of corruption.

Not all members of the two groups, of course, contented themselves with these arguments alone. There were *kaikoku* men who added that only by trading with the West could Japan obtain and pay for the weapons she required or learn the skills which the West had to teach. A few even maintained the value of trade as a source of national wealth in a wider sense. Similarly, there were those in the *jōi* party who argued that war, or the threat of war, was necessary to stimulate changes within Japan itself.

[1] This is discussed more fully below, pp. 36 ff.

This attitude merges gradually into the later practice of using *jōi* as a political weapon, 'a stick to beat the Bakufu'. It none the less remains substantially true that the differences between *jōi* and *kaikoku* were much smaller than the extravagance of their language and the bitterness of their recriminations would lead one to expect. This is borne out by the frequency with which writers of the period seem to change their allegiance, or rather, one should say, the retrospective difficulty of applying consistent labels to them. Satō Shinen, for example, is normally regarded as an exponent of *kaikoku* ideas. Yet in 1838, in a book called *Yume Yume Monogatari*, he was advocating the expulsion of Dutch and Chinese from Nagasaki, as well as the need for war as a means of rousing the country to a sense of its danger and preventing the hated foreigner from setting foot on the shores of Japan.[1] In the same way, Yoshida Shōin is usually classified as *jōi*; and properly so for the first part of his career, despite the fact that he was a pupil of Sakuma Shōzan. On the other hand, after Perry's arrival in 1853 we find him advocating a limited policy of intercourse with the outside world.[2]

Mention of Yoshida Shōin brings us to a further problem that arises in discussing the ideas of the Bakumatsu period. From time to time, in the writings of *jōi* or *kaikoku* leaders, one encounters phrases which seem to imply that their ultimate aim was something more than the purely negative one of maintaining Japan's independence. Nariaki, for example, talks of it becoming possible eventually 'to go out against foreign countries and spread abroad our fame and prestige'.[3] Ii Naosuke foresees the day when 'we can act so as to make our courage and prestige resound beyond the seas'.[4] Still more explicitly, in December 1857, Hotta Masayoshi argues that Japan must 'gradually subject the foreigners to her influence until in the end all the countries of the world know the blessings of perfect tranquillity and our hegemony is acknowledged throughout the globe'.[5] The language used in these expressions is evocative rather than precise, but it does raise the question whether one can legitimately take them as evidence that the active political leaders of the day looked forward to a time when Japan could take the offensive against the West. It is tempting to do so, especially in view of later Japanese history. Moreover, there was undoubtedly a strain of expansionist thought among scholars and writers generally. In 1823 Satō Shinen had advocated a Japanese invasion of China. Yoshida Shōin regarded it as necessary for Japan's own defence

---

[1] Inobe, 'Mito gakuha no jōi-ron', pp. 134–6.

[2] Tokutomi, *Yoshida Shōin* (rev. ed., Tōkyō, 1934), pp. 157–60; H. E. Coleman, 'The Life of Shoin Yoshida, being a Translation from the Japanese Life of Shoin Yoshida by Mr. Iichiro Tokutomi', *Trans. Asiatic Soc. Japan*, xlv (1917), pp. 159–61. [This book omits some passages given in the Japanese version.] Also Tsuchiya, 'Bakumatsu shishi no mita Shina mondai', p. 166.

[3] See Document 3, at p. 104.   [4] See Document 7, at p. 118.

[5] See Document 20, at p. 167.

that she should expand into such neighbouring territories as Kamchatka, Korea, Manchuria, and Taiwan. On a less grandiose scale, several Bakufu officials were in favour of annexing at least a number of small islands to serve as defence posts, and an attempt was actually made to occupy the Bonin group in 1862, though the party sent there was subsequently withdrawn.

Despite this, it would seem unlikely that the men who played an active part in determining Japanese policy had any precise plans for the more distant future. Like most statesmen—of whatever country—they were concerned with immediate problems, especially the problem of defence, and their approach to them was essentially practical. In discussing them, of course, they made use of an extremely emotional terminology. Their letters and memoranda are full of such phrases as 'maintaining our national prestige' and 'preserving our national laws', or 'disgracing our martial repute' and 'humbling ourselves before the might of the foreigners'. It was only natural, therefore, that they should express their objectives in language of the same kind. The objectives themselves were probably never thought out in concrete terms until after the Meiji Restoration had brought power and responsibility to a new group. Before that time national aspirations in the larger sense belonged to the realm of pious hopes and verbal flourishes, not to that of plans and action.

It would seem from this discussion that both *jōi* and *kaikoku* are misleading labels for the policies of those who dominated Japanese history in the years 1853–68. Still more misleading is the use of the English word 'expulsion'. When *kaikoku* leaders explained that trade and the opening of ports were mere temporary expedients, forced on Japan both by foreign threats and by the need to strengthen her economy and military establishment, they added that once this had been done Japan could assert her independence and 'expel the barbarian'. They did not mean by this a return to the policy of national seclusion. Instead, it became increasingly apparent after 1858 that 'expulsion' would mean abrogation of unequal treaties and the negotiation of new ones, by which Japan would enter into relations with the Great Powers on a footing of equality. The *jōi* party was no more anxious to revert to any strict interpretation of ancestral law. The assertion that 'expulsion' was a necessary preliminary to the adoption of Western ways, because it was the only means of ensuring that the process would be kept under proper control, did not always or necessarily imply that Japan must rid herself, by war, of all foreigners. It meant a firmer attitude to foreign demands, even at the risk of war. It meant preparations for war and a public announcement to the Japanese people themselves that the government was resolved to fight in Japan's defence. But to the few, at least, it was to be employed as a stimulus rather than as an imperative.

These remarks, of course, apply only to a very small minority. It is an important minority, both for its political influence in the period we are discussing and because it later provided the leadership for the new Japan. But it must not be taken as typical of the whole. Against the handful of leaders we must set the background of hundreds or even thousands of the rank and file who implicitly believed the catchwords and slogans of the age. Nor was the minority itself entirely unaffected by the emotional content of the expressions it habitually used. Only gradually did the idea of Japan as an active participant in world affairs win wider acceptance. More particularly, it took time and the pressure of events to remove the initial delusions and weld the varied and often conflicting elements of thought into what could be regarded as a national foreign policy. The working out of that process is in large part the theme of this book.

2. *The formulation of Bakufu policy*

It is now necessary that we should turn to the more practical aspects of policy-making and measure the impact of these ideas on the decisions of statesmen, for impact there most certainly was despite the fact that the Tokugawa Bakufu was in theory an autocracy. Not since the days of Yoshimune (1716–44) had the Shōgun in person controlled the activities of government. Indeed, the Bakufu of the nineteenth century can most aptly be described as authoritarian but oligarchic. Power was normally in the hands of four or five feudal lords, who as Rōjū comprised the Council of State in Edo and were responsible for an overall supervision of the administration, being assisted in this by a number of other senior officials of whom the most important were the *wakadoshiyori* (frequently described in English as members of the 'Second' or 'Junior' Council) and the *Kyōto-shoshidai* (whose function it was to keep a watchful eye on the political activities of the Imperial Court at Kyōto). All these were drawn from the ranks of the *fudai daimyō*, feudal lords whose ancestors had been the followers and comrades-in-arms of Tokugawa Ieyasu at or before the battle of Sekigahara in 1600. The *fudai daimyō*, therefore, as the only men entitled to fill high office, had a vested interest in the maintenance of the régime. By the same token they had a voice in the decisions of government even when not personally forming part of the administration, especially through the great families of Ii of Hikone and Sakai of Himeji, who by tradition had special privileges in the Tokugawa counsels and special responsibilities at times of crisis.

Another group whose views carried considerable weight were the branch families of the Tokugawa house, though they rarely held any official position. Of these the most important were the *sanke* (the 'Three Houses' of Mito, Kii, and Owari) and the *sankyō* (the 'Three Lords' of

Tayasu, Hitotsubashi, and Shimizu), from whose number the Shōgun was usually chosen if the direct line failed.[1] Less powerful individually, but influential collectively and sometimes personally, were the *kamon* (the 'Related Houses'), who bore the original family name of Matsudaira.[2] The most active representatives of these three groups in the politics of the Bakumatsu period were Tokugawa Nariaki of Mito, Hitotsubashi Keiki (son of Nariaki and later Shōgun), and the *kamon* Matsudaira Keiei of Fukui.

The lower ranks of officialdom were also filled by men of the samurai class, chiefly from the families of those who in one capacity or another were responsible for administering the Tokugawa estates. Unlike their seniors, however, whose influence depended largely on their hereditary status in society, these men derived their power from the office they held, appointment to which came partly from ability and partly from feudal connexions. There was for them, in fact, in some degree a career open to talent. A man of real ability, granted good fortune and the patronage of others more powerful, might rise to a position in which he could normally expect to be consulted about major questions of government policy and be accorded the dignity and respect due to a lesser feudal lord. There was a point, of course, beyond which he could not go. The ranks of *jisha-bugyō* and above could be held only by *daimyō*, lords whose fiefs had a rice revenue rated at 10,000 *koku* or more a year, and very rarely indeed was it possible to reach these heights from lower office. A few did so because, as younger sons, they unexpectedly succeeded to the family estates and so became *daimyō* in their own right. In the last years of the Tokugawa period, moreover, the rule was broken to allow the promotion of some men of outstanding merit, but this was a desperate move made by an administration bankrupt of power and prestige. In general it is true that for junior officials the top rung of the ladder was reached with appointment as one of the two *machi-bugyō*, whose chief duty it was to keep the peace in the Shōgun's capital of Edo.

Ranking with or slightly below the *machi-bugyō* were a number of officials who played an important part in the conduct of foreign affairs. These were the *ōmetsuke* and *metsuke*, whose task was supervision of the activities of officials and feudal lords, especially the detection of intrigue or disaffection; the *kanjō-bugyō*, initially responsible for revenue from the Tokugawa estates and hence for government finance; and the *bugyō* who governed the great ports, particularly Nagasaki, Hakodate, Shimoda, and Kanagawa (Yokohama). This specialization of function was not rigid, certainly

---

[1] Except that the Mito house was traditionally regarded as having a sort of tutelary position which removed it from the line of succession.

[2] Possession of the name Matsudaira did not necessarily imply relationship to the Tokugawa line. It was borne by a number of lesser Bakufu officials and was also used on many occasions by great feudal lords on whom it had been conferred as a mark of the Shōgun's favour.

not sufficiently so to prevent transfer from one to another of these posts or even at times concurrent tenure of more than one, but in so far as it existed at all it gave each of these officials a legitimate interest in the discussion of foreign affairs. One of the traditional reasons for rejecting foreign intercourse was the fear that the guns and wealth it would bring might make possible a successful revolt against Tokugawa rule. This brought it within the cognizance of *ōmetsuke* and *metsuke*. The cost of defence preparations and the raising of revenue from trade were obviously matters for the attention of the *kanjō-bugyō*. Indeed, one might reasonably conjecture that their consistent advocacy of *kaikoku* views was itself a function of office, reflecting detailed knowledge of the government's desperate financial straits. The *bugyō* of the ports, of course, were the men who had direct dealings with foreigners.

In addition to these, the years 1854–68 saw the creation of new specialist offices concerned chiefly with diplomacy and defence.[1] The term *kaibō-gakari*, 'in charge of maritime defence', had already been widely used as a prefix to official titles ranging from that of Rōjū down to *metsuke*, and this now became *gaikoku-gakari*, 'in charge of foreign relations'. In 1858 there appears the new office of *gaikoku-bugyō*, which took its place with *kanjō-bugyō* as one of the highest-ranking posts open to those who were not *daimyō*, and this was followed in the next ten years by others covering the fields of naval and military reorganization. After Keiki's succession as Shōgun in 1866 there was a regular spate of new creations and new appointments.

This development was paralleled by the emergence of men who themselves came to be regarded as specialists and were nominated to most of the new offices. It was from their ranks that the Bakufu usually selected the *ōsetsu-gakari* ('in charge of negotiations'), the commissioners appointed to conduct treaty negotiations with foreign envoys coming to Japan. They also provided the members of the diplomatic missions sent to Europe and America. One can even, in this brief period, see something resembling a diplomatic service taking shape. Not unnaturally, these were the officials who most consistently urged the necessity of compromise with the West. Not that they were unanimous. Their views ranged from a grudging acceptance of the inevitable, as represented by the memoranda of Kawaji Toshiaki and Mizuno Tadanori,[2] to advocacy of a complete revolution in Japan's approach to foreign relations, as argued by Iwase Tadanari and Ikeda Nagaaki;[3] but, on balance, they introduced a refreshing element of the rational into debates that were too often clouded by the language of prejudice and emotion.

[1] The impact of Western trade and diplomacy on the administrative structure of a largely feudal society would make an interesting study, which seems hitherto to have been neglected.

[2] See, for example, Document 13, pp. 137–9, and Document 22, pp. 170–4.

[3] See respectively Document 23, pp. 174–6, and Document 57, pp. 274–82.

The extent to which these men could influence policy is not easy to determine. They were dismissible at pleasure and were therefore dependent on the continued approval of their superiors. On the other hand, their ability and special knowledge were recognized as lending a good deal of weight to their advice; and if the accident of birth made them dependent on patronage, their patrons were likely to support them at the higher levels of government. Moreover, they were largely responsible for the detailed execution of policy. This enabled them not only to modify it in minor ways, but sometimes also to determine its whole course. When negotiations were being conducted in Edo, the Japanese plenipotentiaries were entirely subordinate to the Rōjū and reported to them for instructions on every detailed point that arose. Much the same was true when the foreign envoys went to Ōsaka in 1865 and 1867, for the Shōgun and most of his advisers were there and by this time the Rōjū were themselves taking a direct part in the discussions. The position was very different, however, when negotiations took place at some distance from the centre of government, especially when they were held in the capitals of Europe. On such occasions the exact supervision of events was impossible and the Japanese officials, who rarely had any precise written instructions from their government, often possessed or assumed a far wider discretion than was granted to diplomatic representatives of the West. The only real check on their actions was the possibility that they might be disavowed and punished. This happened, for example, to the Ikeda mission which negotiated the Paris Convention of 1864. Others were more fortunate. Mizuno Tadanori and Iwase Tadanari were sent to Nagasaki in 1857 as a commission of inquiry, to study the problem of foreign trade with a view to recommending plans for the future guidance of the Bakufu. Yet while there they not only drafted the terms of a commercial treaty with Holland, but also, without further instructions from Edo, signed both that and a similar agreement with Russia. These were accepted by the government and became the basis of Japanese foreign policy, which in this instance, therefore, had been formulated by two officials whose rank excluded them permanently from all senior posts in the administration.

In July 1853, when Perry's squadron entered Uraga Bay, the Bakufu did not have a foreign policy of any description. Neither the expedition nor its demands came as a surprise,[1] for warning of both had been received from the Dutch some time before, but no decision had been taken about what reply to make. The difficulty was that the oligarchy was sharply divided. Abe Masahiro, who had been head of the Rōjū since 1845, was a man of some ability but little force of character, hardly the man best fitted to meet a serious crisis. He himself had for some years favoured

[1] The letters embodying the American demands are given as Documents 1 and 2, pp. 99–102.

opening of the ports, largely on the grounds that to refuse would involve Japan in a catastrophic war, and he knew that he was supported in this by many of the officials—though a few of them hoped by tortuous diplomacy to avoid both war and concession.[1] Moreover, the head of the greatest of the *fudai* houses, Ii Naosuke of Hikone, favoured the conclusion of treaties with the West, in which he had the support of Hotta Masayoshi, the *fudai* lord of Sakura.[2] On the other hand, Abe had to set against this the attitude of some of the Shōgun's relatives. The *jōi* party was adamant in its opposition to such a policy and its case was energetically pressed by Tokugawa Nariaki and Matsudaira Keiei.[3] It seemed, therefore, that hasty action might easily precipitate a dispute in which officials and *fudai* would find themselves ranged against the branch families of the Tokugawa house.

The danger of such a split lay chiefly in its possible effect on the Bakufu's political position within Japan. Economic changes of the previous two hundred years had been gradually undermining the feudal basis of society and with it the structure of Bakufu authority and finances. The process was accompanied by considerable economic distress, which in its turn produced a growing demand for administrative reform and even, here and there, for the abolition of Tokugawa power and the restoration of direct Imperial rule. Faced with this challenge the Bakufu felt itself weaker than at any previous time in its history. The opposition, however, would only become of immediate danger if it gained the support of the *tozama daimyō*. These men, the 'outside feudatories', whose submission to Tokugawa rule in the seventeenth century had been no more than a grudging recognition of superior force, still governed huge fiefs in the north-east and south-west of Japan; and they had always been regarded by the Bakufu as potential leaders of disaffection. Their activities were subject to greater restrictions than those of the *fudai* and they were excluded from taking any part in the central administration. Yet they were, individually if not collectively, the most powerful of the feudal lords. Their reactions were therefore of prime concern to Edo. When Bakufu officials in the years 1853–68 spoke of the need for national unity, they were prompted, as often as not, by the fear that a crisis in foreign affairs might provide the *tozama* with opportunity to revolt. Thus from the beginning foreign policy decisions were strongly influenced by domestic

[1] Document 4, pp. 107–12, is an example of the tortuous thinking of some men of the period. For the views of other officials see also Akao, 'Perry torai zengo ni okeru taigai kokumin shisō', pp. 533–4, 550, and Honjō, *Nihon keizai shisō-shi gaisetsu*, pp. 142–3.

[2] For Ii Naosuke's views see Document 7, pp. 117–19. Those of Hotta Masayoshi are given in *Dai Nihon Komonjo—Bakumatsu Gaikoku Kankei Monjo* (22 vols. and 4-vol. appendix, Tōkyō, 1911– in progress), iii. 591–2.

[3] For the views of these two men see respectively Document 3, pp. 102–7, and Document 6, pp. 114–7.

politics. Specifically, in 1853, it seemed possible that a serious breach between officialdom and the Tokugawa branch houses might open the way for an attempt to overthrow the régime.

This situation does much to explain the desperate efforts made by Abe Masahiro to evolve a policy capable of general acceptance. His first action was to receive the letters brought by Perry and to promise that a reply would be given when the commodore returned in the spring of 1854. His second, in itself an unprecedented confession of Bakufu weakness, was to circulate copies of the letters to all *daimyō*—*tozama* and *fudai* alike—and to call on them to submit their views about the policy to be followed when negotiations were resumed.

The replies Abe received did little to reduce his difficulties, for they revealed only that the divisions within the Bakufu were reflected in the country as a whole. A few lords declined to express any opinion at all. There was a powerful minority which supported Nariaki in advocating a total rejection of American demands and the immediate adoption of measures to strengthen Japan's defences. Indeed, the emphasis on defence was general, as also was a distaste for trade. There were some, however, who regarded trade as either necessary or desirable, or who recognized the need to make concessions of some kind if Japan were not to be attacked and defeated. Between these two extremes lay a third group, accounting for about one-third of the replies that are still extant, composed of men whose instincts and background were all against concession made at the point of a gun, but whose reason rejected the possibility of immediate expulsion. They recommended the somewhat difficult course of avoiding both evils. This, as we have seen, was the plan preferred by some of the Bakufu officials—reduced to its simplest terms, the avoidance of war by adopting a conciliatory tone in dealings with the West without in fact making any concessions—while it received the powerful support of Shimazu Nariakira, head of the great *tozama* fief of Satsuma.[1] It had the advantage, moreover, of offering some hope of compromise between rival factions. Both the *jōi* and *kaikoku* parties, if confronted with the facts of the situation at home and abroad, might conceivably be brought to accept it, be it only as a *pis aller*. It was to this task, at least, that Abe Masahiro devoted his attention in the autumn and winter of 1853–4.

His first step was to conciliate the Mito party by making Tokugawa Nariaki formally a participant in the Bakufu counsels. In this he succeeded, despite considerable opposition from other officials, but did not seem thereby to bring a decision any nearer. There was one small but

---

[1] Shimazu's views are expressed in a memorandum translated as Document 5, pp. 112–4. The *daimyō* replies in general are very ably analysed in Inobe, 'Perry torai no sai ni okeru kokuron no kisū', *Shirin*, xiii (1928), pp. 348–54. See also Akao, 'Perry torai zengo ni okeru taigai kokumin shisō', pp. 546–9, and Kanno, 'Shokō to gaikoku bōeki', pp. 382–9.

important group within the administration that argued strongly against Nariaki's policy. It consisted of a number of able junior officials, led by the *ōmetsuke* Tsutsui Masanori and the *kanjō-bugyō* Kawaji Toshiaki, who owed their promotion largely to the influence of Abe himself and whose close connexion with him ensured that their views would get a hearing.[1] They regarded effective resistance to foreign attack as impossible, and wanted the Bakufu to adopt a policy which would postpone any conflict for five years or more until Japan's defences had been completed. Later in the autumn, with the arrival of the Russian admiral Poutiatine at Nagasaki, they even began to urge the advantages of a Russian alliance. Russia, they said, had of late years shown herself less dangerous than Britain, France, or America. She was none the less a great Power and would make an invaluable ally. Japan, therefore, should conclude a treaty of friendship with Poutiatine, granting him even the right to trade if necessary, and exact as her price for this concession a promise of Russian help against the other Powers.[2] This particular plan Nariaki was able to defeat. However, he could make little headway with his own proposals. His prime concern was to persuade the Rōjū to issue an announcement that the American demands would be rejected and force would be met with force, but he failed completely to carry his point, even though he explained that his purpose was to raise morale, not to provoke hostilities. After lengthy discussion a statement was in fact issued to the *daimyō* on 1 December 1853, but it represented a compromise between the two factions and was far from meeting Nariaki's wishes.[3] Japan, it said, would seek to avoid any definite reply to Perry, while doing all she reasonably could to preserve the peace; but since the foreigners might themselves act in such a way as to make war inevitable, preparations must be made and morale raised, that all might join in loyalty and resolution to prevent any stain on the national honour.

This announcement, despite its final note of defiance, was in effect a victory for the peace party in Japan. It accorded better with the ideas of the hesitant and uninformed majority than with those of the active (but conflicting) minorities, constituting as it did a rejection of both *jōi* and *kaikoku* views. To most men, after all, the former seemed too dangerous, the latter undesirable. Bakufu policy, therefore, as it had taken shape by the time of Perry's return in February 1854, was conceived entirely in

---

[1] This group included many of the junior officials who were of importance in foreign affairs in the period 1853-8. Apart from Tsutsui and Kawaji, one should mention in particular Inoue Kiyonao (true brother of Kawaji), Iwase Tadanari, and Nagai Naomune. See *Ishin-shi*, ii. 122-3.

[2] On the growth of a pro-Russian party among Bakufu officials see Tabohashi, *Kindai Nihon gaikoku kankei shi*, pp. 544-6; Akao, 'Perry torai zengo ni okeru taigai kokumin shisō', pp. 653-8; and Ōtsuka, *Bakumatsu no gaikō* (in Iwanami kōza, *Nihon rekishi*, Tōkyō, 1934), pp. 6-7.

[3] For the text of this announcement and a detailed account of the discussions preceding it see Tabohashi, *Kindai Nihon gaikoku kankei shi*, pp. 494-512.

negative terms. The demand for better treatment of American castaways could obviously be conceded without difficulty. Demands for trade and the opening of ports, however, ought properly to be refused—provided always that refusal proved to be consistent with the avoidance of hostilities. It was on this last point that the policy broke down. Perry's attitude, once negotiations began, quickly demonstrated that no such simple solution was possible. The conferences at Edo Castle in February and March, attended not only by officials but also by Nariaki and the leading *fudai* lords, learned that concessions must be more substantial if peace was to be preserved; and as a last resort the Japanese plenipotentiaries were instructed that the need to avoid war must triumph over all other considerations.[1]

The Perry Convention, signed at Kanagawa on 31 March 1854, made no clear provision for trade,[2] but it opened the ports of Shimoda and Hakodate to American ships in need of stores and repairs. It also contained a number of minor provisions that had never even been discussed in Edo. Questions like that of consular representation and the fixing of the boundaries within which Americans could travel from Shimoda had been decided by the Japanese negotiators entirely on their own responsibility, and they were very conscious of their temerity in so doing. Their report[3] was as much apologia as narrative. It rather obviously glossed over the point about consuls and even suggested that the whole agreement might be regarded as revocable, since it was not signed and sealed in due form. These excuses, however, did no more to avert criticism than its monotonous insistence that national prestige was unimpaired. Nariaki was horrified at the extent of the concessions made without his knowledge, and his strictures were soon followed by a flood of bitter comment from all parts of Japan. The *jōi* party became more than ever convinced that only drastic reform could make the Bakufu competent to handle the country's affairs. Not even the *kaikoku* party could accept the manner and motives of Bakufu action, however much the result might accord with their own views, and they hastened to dissociate themselves from a policy that had its roots in fear and hesitation. Nor were the foreigners satisfied, though Britain and Russia accepted similar agreements within the next few months. In his attempt to compromise with all, in fact, Abe Masahiro had succeeded in pleasing none. This he might well have expected.

One result of the Perry Convention was to weaken Abe's position as head of the administration. This made it more than ever necessary that

[1] *Ishin-shi*, i. 589–90, 600–3. See also the first paragraph of the negotiators' report, Document 9, at p. 123.
[2] Unless Article VII can be interpreted as doing so—though the Japanese negotiators certainly did not intend it to (see Document 9, at p. 124). The text of the convention is given as Document 8, pp. 119–22.
[3] Document 9, pp. 122–7.

Tokugawa Nariaki should be openly associated with the government's policies, and to secure his co-operation Abe now proposed to make extensive reforms, especially in matters of finance and military preparations. For the second of these Nariaki was himself made personally responsible. At the urging of Kawaji Toshiaki, moreover, a new office was established for the study and translation of Western books on such subjects as military science and technology, to be supervised by the 'specialists' in foreign affairs—Tsutsui Masanori, Kawaji Toshiaki, Mizuno Tadanori, and Iwase Tadanari. It seemed that the Bakufu was at last taking energetic steps to combat the foreign menace.[1] These changes were not universally welcomed, however. There had long existed among officials a group who suspected Nariaki of aiming at personal power and their suspicions were increased by his insistence on the need to promote 'men of ability'. If this meant throwing open the doors of office to those who would normally be excluded because of their feudal status, it looked very like an attack on the privileges of the *fudai daimyō*. Among the latter, therefore, there now emerged the *zokuron-ha*, or 'conventional party', whose object was to prevent any fundamental alteration in the structure of Bakufu administration. This group was led by two Rōjū, Matsudaira Tadakata (Tadamasa) and Matsudaira Noriyasu, and in the course of 1855 it opposed practically every suggestion made by Tokugawa Nariaki and Abe Masahiro. The inevitable crisis came in the autumn of that year. On 14 September Abe finally gave way to Nariaki's urging and dismissed the two Rōjū, and in the week that followed he made extensive changes among lesser officials.[2] To all appearances Nariaki had triumphed.

His success was short-lived. It was no more possible for the Bakufu to act against the wishes of the *fudai daimyō* than it was to ignore the influence of Nariaki. Abe, moreover, was weary of dispute and badly overworked. In November, without consulting any of the senior *daimyō*, he reversed his policy, appointing Hotta Masayoshi as Rōjū and resigning leadership to him. This meant in effect that the breach between Nariaki and the officials was openly avowed and that Abe had thrown in his lot with the traditional centres of power; and though Abe did not in fact relinquish his authority completely, from this time on the trend was away from Nariaki and towards Hotta Masayoshi.

It would be unreal to suggest that these disputes were motivated by differences over foreign policy, despite a general correspondence between the lines of division, but the increasing influence of Hotta Masayoshi during 1856 undoubtedly facilitated the appearance of a new policy towards the Western Powers. This was not merely because Hotta himself had long held *kaikoku* views. So also had Abe Masahiro, after all, and

[1] For these reforms see *Ishin-shi*, ii. 116–22.
[2] See *Ishin-shi*, ii. 107–15.

many of the Bakufu officials. It was rather that with the exclusion of
Tokugawa Nariaki from the inner councils there was no longer any
authoritative voice to argue the opposite case. There were, moreover,
new forces at work to effect a change. The Dutch minister in Nagasaki,
Donker Curtius, had already made some progress in removing restrictions
on the trade at Deshima when in the summer of 1856 he informed the
Bakufu that Sir John Bowring, British Superintendent of Trade at Hong-
kong, was planning to visit Japan and negotiate a commercial treaty; and
since Japan must sooner or later open her ports, Curtius added, it would
be in every way wiser to do so in amicable arrangement with the Dutch
instead of waiting till concessions were extorted by the guns of a British
fleet. Almost identical were the arguments of Townsend Harris, the new
American consul at Shimoda. He had established himself there despite a
deal of argument and opposition, and within a few weeks began to demand
an audience with the Shōgun as a preliminary to discussing 'a most important matter affecting Japan'. He, too, promised to reveal all he knew of
Bowring's plans.

The men now in power in Edo were extremely susceptible to arguments
of this kind. In September 1856 discussions were begun to determine what
steps should be taken in anticipation of Bowring's arrival and their general
tone made it clear that most were convinced of the inevitability of opening
trade. In November Hotta Masayoshi received the Shōgun's orders to
make himself personally responsible for the conduct of foreign affairs, a
step which finally confirmed his leadership and marked the official decision
to adopt a policy of more extended relations with the outside world.
Three days later came the appointment of commissioners for the study
of foreign trade (*gaikoku bōeki torishirabe-gakari*).[1] It was their function to
decide the nature of the regulations that must be imposed to prevent the
interests of Japan, and more particularly those of the Bakufu, from being
subordinated to European theories of unrestricted commerce.

The somewhat desultory discussions of this problem were suddenly
made urgent and precise in the spring of 1857. News reached Nagasaki
in February that a new war had broken out between Britain and China,
the so-called 'Arrow' war, and in notifying the Bakufu of this Curtius did
not fail to point the moral. Japan was pursuing the same sort of policy of
vacillation and delay that had brought China to what would inevitably
be a new defeat, he said, and only an immediate commercial agreement
with Holland could save her from a similar fate. The bogy of British naval
power, in fact, was now consciously being used to frighten the Bakufu into

---

[1] This group comprised all the most able and experienced of Edo officials, including Hotta
himself; the *ōmetsuke* Toki Yorimune; the three *kanjō-bugyō* Matsudaira Chikanao, Kawaji
Toshiaki, and Mizuno Tadanori; the two *metsuke* Iwase Tadanari and Ōkubo Tadahiro. The
bugyō of Shimoda, Nagasaki, and Hakodate also took part in the discussions. On this subject
generally see *Ishin-shi*, ii. 192–6, and Ishii, *Bakumatsu no gaikō* (Tōkyō, 1948), pp. 29–30.

compliance—and with prompt effect. On receipt of the news from Nagasaki, the Rōjū once again called for the views of officials concerning policy,
and followed this a little later with a memorandum setting out the questions to be considered by the *gaikoku bōeki torishirabe-gakari*.[1] A new note of
urgency can be detected in these documents, familiar as was the procedure
adopted. Their fundamental assumption was that Japan must abandon
the practice, pursued hitherto, of refusing foreign requests until threats of
force compelled her to grant them. Instead, she must decide in advance
exactly what she could safely refuse and what she must necessarily accept,
since the detailed investigations that this required could not be conducted
properly in a time of crisis; and the process must at all costs be completed
before the end of the China war left Britain free to turn her attention to
Japan. Only in this way would it be possible to avoid granting concessions
of the kind embodied in China's treaties with the West.

The debates that followed revealed the existence of disagreements even
among those whom one can describe as having *kaikoku* views. Toki Yorimune and Iwase Tadanari, for example, came down strongly on the side
of major concessions. They considered that several ports must be opened
if foreign desires were to be satisfied, including one that would be sufficiently acceptable to forestall any demand for the opening of Ōsaka, while
both the fiefs and private merchants must be admitted to the trade without
undue interference from Bakufu officials. Any financial loss entailed in
abandoning the practice of Bakufu monopoly, they claimed, would be
more than balanced by the yield from taxation.[2] By contrast, Kawaji
Toshiaki and Mizuno Tadanori were essentially conservative. To them
trade was only acceptable because it was an alternative to the greater evil
of war—as indeed was the whole idea of opening the country. It followed
that the Bakufu should proceed with the greatest care, opening Nagasaki
to trade at first and continuing gradually from there in the light of experience, for its whole policy, they thought, should be based on necessity
rather than on choice. The object was to identify the minimum that
would satisfy the foreigners and limit concession to it.[3]

These differences of emphasis had the effect of delaying a decision still
farther. In committing itself to any form of *kaikoku* policy at all the Bakufu
was bound to incur unpopularity, so the inability of officials to agree on
details was enough to prevent progress. It was true that the views of
Kawaji and Mizuno carried greater weight,[4] but the position was still not

---

[1] The two documents are translated below as Documents 10 and 11, pp. 130–4. See also
generally *Ishin-shi*, ii. 234–8.

[2] See Document 12, pp. 134–6; also a similar memorandum in *Bakumatsu Gaikoku Kankei
Monjo*, xv. 819–24.

[3] See Document 13, pp. 137–9.

[4] This appears particularly in the discussions concerning Harris's request to come to Edo, in
which the two groups adopted attitudes parallel to those described here. See especially a report

so urgent as to rule out the possibility of continuing the discussions in the hope of reaching agreement; and the Rōjū therefore took the now familiar step of ordering yet another investigation. In May, Mizuno Tadanori and Iwase Tadanari—a representative of each group—were sent to Nagasaki to discuss the whole question of trade with Donker Curtius.

The resulting conversations at Nagasaki continued throughout the summer of 1857. The recommendations made by Curtius, of course, followed most closely those already put forward by Toki and Iwase, which suggested that this was in fact the acceptable minimum in Western eyes and so strengthened Iwase's hand in attempting to overcome Mizuno's reluctance. Moreover, as time passed it became clear that too long a delay might be dangerous. Towards the end of August, therefore, Mizuno, Iwase, and the Nagasaki *bugyō* Arao Narimasa wrote jointly to Edo reporting the conclusions they had reached.[1] In brief, they declared themselves in favour of an immediate treaty with Holland. The Dutch seemed ready to trade on terms similar to those governing the 'private' trade at Deshima, which meant that sales would be conducted by local officials but would be open to private merchants, and would be content with the opening of only two ports, Nagasaki and Hakodate. Mizuno and his colleagues did not think it was enough, however, simply to regard this as a basis for further discussions in Edo. A treaty must be drawn up and signed at once, so that it could be used as a pattern for negotiations both with Harris and with Bowring. Otherwise the arrival of the English squadron would find Japan unprepared and the whole summer's work would have been wasted, for no plenipotentiary would accept as his model a treaty that was merely in the course of negotiation. This point they repeated with still greater urgency in another letter a few days later.[2] This time the report was accompanied by a draft treaty, worked out in consultation with Curtius, which was thought likely to prove acceptable to all parties, including the English. In seeking Bakufu approval of this document the three men stated, significantly, that if the English arrived before the receipt of instructions from Edo they would do their best to effect delay, but that if this proved impossible they would sign the Dutch treaty on their own responsibility and undertake negotiations with Bowring on the same basis.

In fact it was Poutiatine, not Bowring, who brought matters to a head. The Russian admiral arrived at Nagasaki on 21 September and on the following day the officials there sent another messenger post-haste to Edo,

by the Rōjū to the Shōgun, *c.* 7 August 1857, printed in *Bakumatsu Gaikoku Kankei Monjo*, xvi. 437–40.

[1] Document 14, pp. 139–42.

[2] Document 15, pp. 142–4. On the same date Arao and Mizuno wrote privately to Matsudaira Chikunao and Kawaji Toshiaki in Edo seeking their support for the proposals, a letter which reveals clearly how greatly Mizuno's point of view had changed during the summer; see *Bakumatsu Gaikoku Kankei Monjo*, xvi. 744–9.

explaining that Russian demands, if they were made, were as much a source of danger as those of Britain and would necessitate similar action. Moreover, there was also this to be said, that a treaty signed by both Holland and Russia would stand all the better chance of acceptance by the other Powers.[1] For these reasons Mizuno and Iwase were prepared to act independently if Russia demanded a new treaty. The necessity for such action did not immediately arise, for after a short stay Poutiatine went off on a visit to the China coast. By the time of his return to Nagasaki on 11 October, however, there was still no word from Edo. With no instructions, and faced with the crisis which he had all along feared, Mizuno could see only one solution. In the hope that Bakufu silence meant consent, if not approval, he signed the agreement that had been negotiated with Curtius.[2] A week later he concluded a treaty with Poutiatine on similar terms.

Edo's silence had indeed meant consent, though it was not given without a good deal of heart-searching. The draft treaty sent from Nagasaki at the end of August had, as one might expect, caused fresh disputes among the officials. The *ōmetsuke* and *metsuke* again revealed themselves the most progressive group, urging the full adoption of Mizuno's proposals. The *kanjō-bugyō*, on the other hand, were still reluctant to grant such sweeping concessions and took particular exception to the opening of Hakodate and the absence of any restriction on the total volume of trade, on the grounds that this would lead to a vast export of goods and hence to the impoverishment of Japan. The first draft of a reply for Nagasaki was drawn up in these terms, apparently by the *kanjō-bugyō* themselves.[3] Most other officials (apart from the *metsuke*) were conspicuously non-committal, so the final choice between conflicting views was left to the Rōjū, presumably to Hotta himself, and the second draft of instructions for Mizuno, though unsigned, is attributed to him. This document, drawn up about the middle of October, definitely accepted the views of Mizuno and the *metsuke*. It stated the objections made by the *kanjō-bugyō*, but rejected them because the restriction of trade was the one provision which neither Holland nor any other Power would be willing to accept. A third and final draft omitted these arguments and simply instructed Mizuno to proceed on the basis he had proposed, with some minor changes of detail, and to use the resulting agreement as his model for the negotiations with Russia and England. Before this could be sent off, news reached Edo that he had already taken action.

[1] Document 16, pp. 144–5. In this connexion it is worth bearing in mind the fact that these men belonged to the group which in 1854 had favoured an alliance with Russia.

[2] For Mizuno's explanations see Document 17, pp. 146–9. The text of the treaty is given as Document 18, pp. 149–55.

[3] The drafts and memoranda to which reference is made in this paragraph are printed in *Bakumatsu Gaikoku Kankei Monjo*, xvii. 466–502.

The importance of the Dutch supplementary treaty of 1857 does not only lie in the manner of its negotiation, with the insight which this can give into the way in which Bakufu policy was formulated. It also represents the maximum that the Bakufu was willing to grant. In large part, of course, it was an expression of the policy of a progressive minority, only grudgingly accepted by the rest, but by contrast with the treaties that followed it became a thing of virtue in itself, to which a return would be welcome. In this sense the 1857 agreement most fairly represents the continuing attitude of the Bakufu towards the Western Powers—if it is possible to identify a norm in a period of such bewildering changes and disputing factions. At least one can say that any further extension of Western privileges would only be achieved against the most stubborn opposition.

Throughout the early part of 1857 Townsend Harris had continued to urge his request for an audience with the Shōgun and permission to negotiate directly with the Rōjū in Edo. In June he concluded an agreement with the Shimoda *bugyō* Inoue Kiyonao, rectifying a number of minor American grievances, but this in no way altered his intention of going to the capital to discuss the terms of a full-scale commercial treaty. The officials, as ever, were divided on this issue. The *kanjō-bugyō* and many others hoped to postpone a decision until Mizuno and Iwase returned from Nagasaki with the results of their investigation of trade, and thereafter to hold negotiations with Harris at Shimoda. The *metsuke* preferred to negotiate at once and in Edo, since they suspected that this was what it would come to in the end. They were overruled, but they received strong support from the Shimoda *bugyō*. Once again the man on the spot was the leading advocate of concession and his views eventually prevailed. On 21 August the Rōjū gave its permission for the Edo visit to take place, though no date was set and the *bugyō* was warned against making any commitments at all unless they were absolutely unavoidable.[1]

It was still some weeks before the decision was officially communicated to Harris, and even after that the date was several times postponed, but on 1 October the Bakufu finally committed itself by an announcement to the feudal lords. On 23 November Harris left Shimoda, arriving in Edo a week later. On 7 December he had a formal audience with the Shōgun, at which he handed over a letter from the U.S. President, and all was now ready for negotiations to begin.

Harris had been long enough in Japan to become familiar with the arguments used by Japanese in their discussions of foreign affairs and this

---

[1] On this subject see generally *Ishin-shi*, ii. 253–8, and the relevant entries in *The Complete Journal of Townsend Harris* (ed. Cosenza, New York, 1930). Some of the more important documents are to be found in *Bakumatsu Gaikoku Kankei Monjo*, xvi. 437–40, 497–501, 506–11, 656–9, 659–61.

enabled him to frame his statements in such a way as to produce the
maximum effect. At a long interview with Hotta at the latter's residence
on 12 December 1857 his technique was masterly.[1] His remarks on trade
might almost have been drafted in answer to one of the memoranda from
the *kanjō-bugyō*, so carefully did they refute the assumptions on which such
documents had hitherto been based. Trade, he said, would bring wealth
both to people and to government, since the former would profit by their
participation and the latter by the increased yield from taxation. Nor
was there any danger that exports would drain the country's wealth and
rob it of daily necessities. Production would inevitably increase to keep
step with demand. In fact this part of Harris's diplomacy—as he wrote in
his journal later—might aptly be described as 'teaching the elements of
political economy to the Japanese'.[2] His reasoning was not wholly economic, however. He reinforced it with an appeal to political necessity. If
Japan were to refuse his terms, he stated, there was no doubt that Britain
would demand similar ones in a much more forceful manner. Whereas
America was willing that the opening of Japan should proceed gradually,
Britain would brook no delay, while Japan's strategic position in relation
to Anglo-Russian rivalries might even endanger her territory itself. When
the British fleet arrived Japan must yield or fight, and there could be no
question about the outcome of any hostilities. There was therefore much
to be gained by negotiating with America without the intervention of a
naval threat, for it would not only enable Japan to obtain a moderate
agreement which Britain would in all probability be willing to accept in
her turn, but would also thereby preserve both her own prestige and that
of her government. To sign at the point of foreign guns, on the other hand,
'would humiliate the Government in the eyes of all the Japanese people,
and thus actually weaken its power'[3]—a danger of which the Bakufu was
already sufficiently aware. By contrast, he said, peaceful commerce would
enable Japan to build a navy that could maintain the national honour.
So shrewd a reference to the Bakufu's political difficulties at home, coupled
with an appeal to the national prejudice which played so large a part in
Japanese thinking at this time, materially increased Harris's chances of
success.

The three main points on which Harris insisted as forming the substance
of any agreement were the opening of more ports (though this could if
necessary be a gradual process); permission to trade without any of that
official intervention which still existed under the terms of the Dutch and
Russian treaties; and the right to appoint diplomatic representatives to

[1] Harris's own description of what took place is given in Harris, *Complete Journal*, pp. 485–6.
For a rather longer Japanese account see Document 19, pp. 159–65. There is no essential contradiction between the two, though the latter is much more detailed.
[2] Harris, *Complete Journal*, p. 490, entry for 17 December 1857.
[3] Ibid., p. 485, 12 December 1857.

reside in the Shōgun's capital. These proposals became the subject of fresh discussions among the officials in Edo, the tone of which was once again set by Hotta Masayoshi. At the end of December he wrote a memorandum dealing with the question of policy in general terms,[1] though without committing himself on the specific issues raised by Harris, arguing in effect that an attempt at expulsion could end only in failure and national collapse, while merely to grant foreign demands as a recognition of superior force would not lead to any permanent improvement in Japan's position. There must be active steps to secure wealth and knowledge, he said, through which alone Japan could take her proper place in the world. This, of course, did not represent any advance on the decisions made concerning negotiations with Russia and Holland earlier in the year. Certainly it did not necessarily imply a willingness to grant the new demands made by America, which was the question now to be decided. On this last issue, Mizuno Tadanori and Iwase Tadanari still held opposing views. Mizuno, as before, was unwilling to admit foreigners to Edo either as traders or as diplomatic agents, and he urged strongly that every device of reasoning and persuasion be used to confine them to the more distant ports. In fact his memorandum[2] is a classic example of the methods of Bakufu diplomacy. It evoked from Iwase a response which is quite startling in the frankness of its attack on such 'trifling arguments about detail'.[3] Iwase's own concern was that the Bakufu should revise its whole attitude to foreign affairs, reasserting its leadership by a decision to conform in substance with Harris's views and confining its efforts to the discussion of points that had a real importance. Other officials found such suggestions difficult to stomach. On the other hand, they were convinced of the need to avoid war and were to some extent open to persuasion if it could be shown that this was the minimum the West was willing to accept.[4] The treaties of 1857 had been concluded in the belief that they were an effective compromise between Japanese reluctance and foreign ambition, a belief on which Harris had now cast some doubt. Further progress could only be made by testing the reactions of the American envoy.

By the middle of January Hotta had decided in favour of negotiation. In a further interview with Harris he told him that he would agree in principle to the opening of trade and the appointment of resident ministers, but that no more than three ports could be opened: Nagasaki, Hakodate, and some other instead of Shimoda, which had proved unsatisfactory. On the following day Inoue Kiyonao and Iwase Tadanari were appointed as Japanese plenipotentiaries, in itself evidence of the

---

[1] See Document 20, pp. 165–8.   [2] See Document 22, pp. 170–4.
[3] See Document 23, at p. 176.
[4] See, for example, *Bakumatsu Gaikoku Kankei Monjo*, xviii. 249–51, 345–6; and Kanno, 'Shokō to gaikoku bōeki', pp. 391–3.

choice that had been made. On 18 January Harris submitted a draft treaty for discussion, and a week later detailed negotiations were begun.

In the talks that followed during the next month[1] Harris found ample reason for exasperation. Inoue and Iwase, acting directly under instructions from the Rōjū, at first tried to secure his acceptance of the treaty pattern they had thought to establish in the previous autumn. When this proved impossible they turned to the task of identifying the minimum which Harris would accept. This meant refusing, modifying, or postponing each of his proposals in turn, a process accompanied by constant repetition and long delays for consultation, and ending nearly always in their accepting something very like the draft which had been put forward in the beginning. It was a technique that might well have been dangerous against an envoy backed by naval force. Against Harris it proved not so much dangerous as ineffective. By 25 February 1858, by a mixture of persuasion and firmness, he had gained his end. The treaty had taken final shape. America was to have the right of appointing a resident minister in Edo and consuls at all the treaty ports, who would have legal jurisdiction over American citizens, while trade was to be conducted without interference from officials. The scale of customs duties was fixed and moderate. The ports of Nagasaki, Hakodate, and Kanagawa (Yokohama) were to be open from the date the treaty came into force and others were to be opened at intervals thereafter: Niigata on 1 January 1860 and Hyōgo (Kōbe) on 1 January 1863. In addition, the cities of Edo and Ōsaka were to be opened to foreign trade on 1 January 1862 and 1 January 1863 respectively.[2]

The treaty was therefore agreed. But it was not signed. Signature was an irrevocable step; and before taking it the Bakufu had to ensure that it could enforce the policy it had now evolved. The concessions that had been made were welcomed by only a very small minority among Bakufu officials, being reluctantly accepted as inevitable by the rest. Yet these were the men who were best informed about foreign strength and Japanese weakness. In the country at large feeling ran as high as ever. Many were still blindly clinging to traditional prejudices about foreign relations; many were opposed to Bakufu foreign policy on grounds that had at least an appearance of logical reasoning; and many more opposed it simply because they opposed the Bakufu itself, for reasons that had little or nothing to do with foreign affairs. Without an understanding of this opposition it is impossible to follow the shifts and expedients of Japanese reactions to the West in the years 1858–68, for the formulation of policy turned as often on the identification of what was possible as on the recogni-

---

[1] For an account of these negotiations see *Ishin-shi*, ii. 267–71, and Harris, *Complete Journal*, pp. 505–35.
[2] The text of the treaty is given as Document 28, pp. 183–9.

tion of what was desirable. It is therefore to the problem of control that we must now turn.

3. *Court and Bakufu: the struggle for control of policy*

The Bakufu was fully aware that in the negotiations with Harris it had gone far beyond what was acceptable to opinion in Japan at large. Indeed, this was almost equally true of the treaties already concluded with Russia and Holland. The negotiations were therefore accompanied from the beginning by an attempt to rally support. This took the form of yet another reference to the *daimyō* on the lines of that made in 1853, though with the difference that it was now not so much a tentative sounding of views as a conscious effort to secure an appearance of unity. Nor was the step entirely without success. In the previous four years there had been some shift in the balance between *jōi* and *kaikoku* among those whose arguments carried greatest weight, while even men like Tokugawa Nariaki had changed their ground under the impact of events. Nariaki, in fact, now admitted that nothing could be done at once to close the three ports that had already been opened, despite his continued reluctance to open more, while in proposing that he should himself be sent abroad with a selected group of followers to act as intermediary in Japan's trade with the United States he was adopting a position not far removed from that of Ii Naosuke in 1853.[1] Ii Naosuke himself, to judge from a memorandum he submitted in January 1858 in conjunction with other lords of the *tamari-no-ma*,[2] still favoured some such course. Matsudaira Keiei, like Nariaki, had abandoned his former *jōi* policy and now acknowledged the need for active participation in world affairs.[3] All these recommendations were expressed in a highly coloured language that contrasts strongly with that of the more able Bakufu officials, but it is clear that the former deep divisions had almost disappeared. On the other hand, while the degree of agreement that had been achieved might conceivably have brought acceptance of the treaties of October 1857, it did not extend also to the proposals made by Townsend Harris. These were anathema not only to the relatively ill-informed majority of the *daimyō*[4] but even to those whose knowledge of events had led them into a grudging acquiescence in the need for concession; and the arguments that had brought the Bakufu itself to the point

[1] For this proposal see Document 21, pp. 168–9.
[2] Feudal lords were often ranked according to the chamber in Edo Castle to which they were admitted on formal occasions. The *tamari-no-ma* was the chamber used by some of the *kamon* and a few of the more important *fudai* lords. For the memorandum referred to here see Document 24, pp. 176–9.
[3] See Document 25, pp. 179–80.
[4] On the views of the *daimyō* generally see Akao, 'Harris raichō tōji ni okeru taigai shisō ni tsuite', *Shirin*, xxiii (1938), pp. 808–12; Kanno, 'Shokō to gaikoku bōeki', pp. 393–400; Honjō, *Nihon keizai shisō shi gaisetsu*, pp. 140–2.

of agreement had no such immediate impact on the feudal lords. Clearly something more was needed if the treaty were to be signed.

The course chosen by Hotta proved in the result an exceedingly dangerous one. In February 1858 he informed Harris that a majority of the *daimyō* were still opposed to the treaty which had just been agreed in Edo and asked that its signing be delayed until steps could be taken to silence criticism. To achieve this end he proposed to secure the promulgation of an Imperial decree endorsing the Bakufu's decision. The Japanese negotiators were confident, or so they told Townsend Harris, that such a decree could be obtained without difficulty and that once signed it would have the effect of convincing all those who, 'like the obstinate of more enlightened countries, refused to listen to a word of reason, argument or explanation'.[1] In fact, they proved wrong on both counts.

Hotta's decision to make the Imperial Court a party to the debate is sufficiently unusual to require comment. The Bakufu had traditionally exercised a complete control over all questions of national policy, by virtue of the powers delegated to the Shōgun by the Emperor, and had always taken the greatest care to ensure that the Court had no opportunity to interest itself in politics. It was more difficult, however, to prevent others from interesting themselves in the Court. During the eighteenth century there had emerged a group of scholars known as the Kokugakusha, leaders of the so-called Shintō Revival, who had gradually become associated with the slogan *sonnō* ('honour the Emperor') and a movement to restore to the Imperial line some part of its former prestige as the ruling dynasty of Japan.[2] This was not in origin an attack on the political authority of the Bakufu but a reaction against the prevailing influence of Chinese ideas in Japanese society. Yet study of the ancient chronicles of Japan led the Kokugakusha to a belief in the existence, in the past, of a golden age which owed its outstanding virtues to the benefits of Imperial rule. From this it was but a short step to advocating a return to the political conditions which had characterized this era, before a Shōgun had usurped the Imperial prerogatives. It was a step that was at first too dangerous to be avowed. But as the ideas of the movement spread, the insistence that respect was a quality to be shown by the Bakufu in its dealings with the Court became for a few the more radical belief that only by renouncing his special powers and restoring direct Imperial rule could the Shōgun demonstrate true sincerity.

The writings of the Kokugakusha undoubtedly influenced the ideas of many who took part in the political disputes of the mid-nineteenth century.

---

[1] Harris, *Complete Journal* (18 February 1858), p. 543. See also ibid., p. 539, and G. Wagener, 'Aus dem Tagebuche Hendrik Heuskens', *Mitteilungen der Deutschen Gesellschaft für Natur- und Volkerkunde Ostasiens*, iii (June 1883), pp. 387–8.

[2] See D. C. Holtom, *The National Faith of Japan: a Study in Modern Shintō* (London, 1938), pp. 44–53.

Yet *sonnō* only became of major importance when its ideas were adopted by men whose opposition to the Bakufu sprang from other causes, more particularly by the Mito leaders and the *jōi* party. We have already seen[1] that the policy of *jōi* owed many of its arguments to a belief in the need for a thorough reform of Japanese politics and society, which, it was said, must necessarily precede the opening of the ports. Reform, in fact, was widely regarded as inevitable. There were ample signs that it was needed —in the impoverishment of the samurai class and the growing wealth of townsmen, in the periodic famines and the flight of cultivators from the land, in the frequent outbreak of peasant revolts. It was more than ever desirable in view of the recurrent crises in foreign affairs that began with the arrival of Perry in 1853. The Bakufu, however, which was still at this time thought of by most as the proper authority to put reforms into effect, showed little signs of taking any decisive action. Its foreign policy was one of weakness and vacillation. Its domestic policy was one of conservatism. It made no effort to raise those restrictions on the activities of *daimyō* which prevented them from taking any steps to solve their own or the country's problems, preferring—as it seemed to those most influenced by a growing nationalism—to maintain its own power even at the cost of national misery. Thus distrust of Bakufu motives and Bakufu competence was added to the older causes of discontent. Those who had always been jealous of Tokugawa power were now joined by some who had for centuries profited by it, and all began increasingly to look towards the Emperor as an ally who could put the seal of legitimacy on actions which Edo would undoubtedly seek to brand as rebellious.

The appointment of Hotta Masayoshi as head of the Rōjū had signalled the failure of Mito's attempt to influence Bakufu policy from within. From the end of 1856 the *jōi* party, with the possible exception of Tokugawa Nariaki himself, turned to the Imperial Court as a means of bringing pressure to bear from without. Thus it reinforced its own popularity with the appeal of *sonnō* ideas. In the process the argument for expulsion became slightly modified. The leaders still believed that reform and national unity must come before Japan's ports could safely be opened, but they now added that unity and reform could themselves be achieved only under the aegis of the Imperial prestige. The greatest danger, they said, was that of disunity in face of foreign aggression. The threat was to the whole, not merely to the part, and could be averted only by the whole working together; and since the Bakufu had by its actions forfeited all claim to leadership, defence itself, to say nothing of future expansion, made necessary the restoration of Imperial power.[2] Thus there was

[1] Above, pp. 9–10. On the connexion between *sonnō* and *jōi* see a brief but penetrating analysis in Inobe, 'Mito gakuha no jōi-ron', pp. 149–53.

[2] Such views are expressed, for example, by Yoshida Shōin in his *Ryūkon-roku*, written in prison in 1859. See Coleman, 'Life of Shoin Yoshida', pp. 162–5.

established a connexion between the ideas of *sonnō* and *jōi*. The events of
1858 welded it into a firm alliance. This had yet to attract the support
of the powerful *daimyō* before it could hope for success, but already by the
beginning of the year the tendency in favour of the Court was sufficiently
strong, and by the same token the Court's prestige was sufficiently widespread, to make it logical for Hotta to seek an Imperial decree as a means
of quelling opposition to the Harris treaty.

Such was the importance of the matter that Hotta decided to go himself
to Kyōto. It was an unprecedented step, but it was one that might be
expected to bring the Court into accord with Bakufu wishes, despite the
fact that it was ignorant and prejudiced on the subject of foreign affairs.
Jōi views were prevalent among the lesser nobles, but those filling the
senior offices were more amenable to reason and had not shown any
marked inclination to rebel against Bakufu control. Only a handful were
of real importance.[1] These could be persuaded or coerced into providing
Hotta with the decree he wanted—or so he confidently assumed. He
proved to be wrong in this assumption. He was wrong because, as he had
hitherto failed to realize, he was no longer dealing with the Court alone
or with a straightforward issue of foreign policy. And his discussions in
Kyōto were complicated, and eventually made abortive, by a concurrent
dispute concerning the nomination of a successor to the childless Shōgun
Iesada, a dispute that involved most of the great feudal lords and produced
a major split even within the ranks of Bakufu officialdom.

On grounds of blood relationship the logical successor to Iesada in
normal times would have been Tokugawa Yoshitomi of Kishū (Kii).
Yoshitomi, however, was young and inexperienced and many thought
that in time of crisis the Bakufu needed the guidance of a stronger hand.
It was this that led Matsudaira Keiei to urge the nomination of Hitotsubashi Keiki, son of Tokugawa Nariaki and head (by adoption) of the
Hitotsubashi branch of the Tokugawa family. As well as that of Nariaki
he secured the support of a group of the most powerful among the *daimyō*:
Date Muneki of Uwajima, Yamanouchi Toyoshige of Tosa, and Shimazu
Nariakira of Satsuma. In addition he later succeeded in persuading to
his views a number of Bakufu officials, including Kawaji Toshiaki, Toki
Yorimune, and Iwase Tadanari—most of the men, in fact, whose influence
was greatest in the formulation of foreign policy. This powerful faction
found itself opposed by Ii Naosuke and a number of senior Bakufu officials.
This was not so much because of Yoshitomi's closer relationship with
Iesada, though that was the argument they advanced publicly, as because

---

[1] The *Kampaku*, or Chief Minister; the *sadaijin*, *udaijin*, and *naidaijin* (Ministers of the Left,
Right, and Centre respectively); and the *gisō* and *buke-densō* (whose duties centred on the conduct
of relations between Court and Bakufu). In addition to these, there were usually one or two
Imperial Princes and former *Kampaku* who took an active part in the councils.

they saw in the attempt to nominate Keiki a new move to establish Mito supremacy in Edo, the danger against which they had rallied once before in 1855–6. Hotta himself seems to have been inclined to favour the Kii claim, for it was supported by the men to whom he owed his rise to power, but when the Shōgun's failing health made the problem a pressing one in the beginning of 1858 he was preoccupied with questions of foreign policy and left for Kyōto in March without having committed himself finally to either side.

Hotta's departure transferred the centre of intrigue from the Shōgun's to the Emperor's capital and thereby widened its scope to embrace new groups and factions.[1] In the first place, all the leading figures in the dispute were linked by tradition or by marriage with senior members of the Imperial Court. The former *kampaku* Takatsukasa Masamichi was Nariaki's brother-in-law; the *naidaijin* Sanjō Sanetsumu was Yamanouchi Toyoshige's father-in-law; a similar connexion existed between the *sadaijin* Konoe Tadahiro and Shimazu Nariakira, whose families had traditional ties going back for several centuries. The *kampaku* himself, Kujō Naotada, was related by marriage to Ii Naosuke. The Bakufu was also able to exert pressure through the *Kyōto-shoshidai*, an office at this time held by the *fudai* lord Honda Tadamoto of Okazaki, as well as through Hotta and his personal entourage. Thus the divisions between the Hitotsubashi and Kii parties were soon reflected in the attitudes of influential men at Court.

On the other hand, Hotta was not on this account faced with any insuperable difficulties. As long as the discussions were confined to the inner circle it was possible to maintain some sort of distinction between the two issues of foreign policy and the succession, and on the former there was a wide measure of agreement. The Hitotsubashi party, after all, was in no sense committed to *jōi* views. In fact, with some expressions of reluctance and from a variety of different motives, its members urged on their allies in Kyōto the necessity of confirming the Bakufu's decision to conclude a treaty with America. Even Nariaki did so. And it seemed probable for a time that the result would be an Imperial decree expressing concern at the turn events had taken and enjoining the Bakufu to reconsider its policy in consultation with *sanke* and *daimyō*, but making it clear that in the last resort the decision would be left to Edo.[2]

Hotta's failure, in fact, was not due to the divisions existing within this unacknowledged and limited alliance between Bakufu, *daimyō*, and senior Court officials, except in the sense that these weakened its cohesion in the

[1] Detailed accounts of the succession dispute and events in Kyōto during the spring of 1858 are to be found in *Ishin-shi*, ii. 332–46, 362–73, 382–431; Inobe, 'Ansei jōyaku chokkyo sōsei ni kansuru ichi-kōsatsu', *Shigaku Zasshi*, xlii (1931), pp. 478–90; and Akao, 'Harris raichō tōji ni okeru taigai shisō', pp. 814–26. These form the basis of the account I give here.

[2] Such a decree was in fact drafted by Kujō and received the Imperial assent on 24 April, though it was never issued.

face of opposition. It was due rather to a concerted attack from other forces that were mobilized in Kyōto during the spring of 1858. It is here that lies the real importance of Kyōto as the scene of operations. In the existing state of Japanese society, channels for the dissemination of ideas were few and restricted. There were no newspapers, and the publication of books and pamphlets was closely supervised by the Bakufu, which was quick to punish anything that smacked of sedition. Many of the works that have been mentioned in this introduction were only circulated secretly in manuscript. To some extent their arguments were passed by word of mouth, through teachers and travelling scholars, but this was a means of communication better suited to a community living in a single city than to men scattered through the length and breadth of a land where travel was difficult and regarded with suspicion by the government. In a city, moreover, use could be made of broadsheets and handbills posted in the streets. Edo was too well policed and guarded to provide much chance for such activities, but in Kyōto the presence of the Imperial Court provided both cover and protection. Kyōto was therefore a possible sanctuary for the disaffected and a centre for the organization of opposition to the Tokugawa Bakufu; and once the Bakufu had by its own action made the city a venue for political decisions of major importance, there were many there who sought to create and mould a public opinion that would help them to achieve their ends.

Most of the great lords sent their own representatives to Kyōto at the time of Hotta's visit. Tokugawa Nariaki was represented by Ishikawa Tokugorō, Matsudaira Keiei by Hashimoto Sanai, and Ii Naosuke by Nagano Shuzen. Hotta was accompanied by Kawaji Toshiaki and Iwase Tadanari. All these men were active in persuading the *kuge*[1] to support the Bakufu request about the treaty, but outside the ranks of the great officers they could make little headway against the influence of former Mito leaders then in the capital. These men, Harikawa Seigan and Umeda Umpin, had not changed their views when Nariaki abandoned his advocacy of immediate expulsion. They had for some time past been in Kyōto, making full use of Mito connexions at Court. Even without the seal of Nariaki's approval the *jōi* arguments had proved convincing. Moreover, the increasing influence of the *sonnō* group and the disputes occasioned by the succession problem gave them more material on which to work, enabling them eventually to form a loose coalition of all the elements that had reason to oppose the Bakufu's policies. It included those who doubted the Bakufu's capacity for government and wanted to strengthen its leadership by forcing the appointment of Hitotsubashi Keiki; those who insisted on reform as a precondition of opening the

[1] The term *kuge* ('Court families') is used as a general description of the Court nobility, as distinct from *buke* ('military families'), which designates the feudal nobility.

country; those who associated the Bakufu with a policy of spineless sub-servience to the hated foreigner; and those who looked to the future restoration of Imperial rule, the whole being bolstered by the popular appeal of the traditional sentiments and prejudices with which various sections of the opposition were associated. To these men the discussion of Hotta's request was not simply an issue of foreign policy. It was an oppor-tunity to bring into question the Bakufu's whole conduct of national affairs and to urge that the request be refused *in toto* as a gesture of dis-approval.

Had this opposition been confined to the ranks of powerless samurai and the lesser *kuge* it would have been more vociferous than dangerous. It had, however, patrons of some consequence. In Iwakura Tomomi and Ōhara Shigenori it had allies of considerable influence at Court, while the *naidai-jin* Sanjō Sanetsumu was both older and more powerful. Sanjō, indeed, was so convinced a supporter that he resisted all the efforts of Yamanouchi Toyoshige and Matsudaira Keiei to convince him of the need to approve the Harris treaty and so diverted their energies into an attempt to secure the Hitotsubashi succession. What was more, the Emperor himself was secretly encouraging resistance to the treaty. He made it quite clear that he was opposed to the opening of more ports, especially those in the neighbourhood of the capital,[1] and on several occasions showed disappro-val of the actions of Kujō and Takatsukasa. His intervention was decisive when on 24 April he let it be known privately that it was only with the greatest reluctance that he had given his consent to the decree drafted by the inner circle of officials. This decree was the one to which we have already referred. It expressed dissatisfaction with Edo handling of foreign affairs, but left the final responsibility for decisions with the Bakufu. By implication, therefore, it was a grudging admission that the American treaty would have to be signed. As such it constituted a defeat for the anti-Bakufu forces; and by disavowing it the Emperor prompted them into making a further effort.

Once begun, the clash was surprisingly short-lived. On 25 April Iwakura and Ōhara arranged a gathering of *kuge* at the Palace and carried a resolution demanding the withdrawal and revision of the decree drafted the previous day. Kujō suddenly found himself almost without allies and under attack from all sides. On 26 April he bowed to the storm, announ-cing that the decree would be revised before being handed to Hotta, and this process was completed within the next few days in consultation with other senior officials. The changes made in the text were few but vital.[2] The Bakufu was still ordered to reconsider its policy, but this time the

---

[1] See, for example, a letter from the Emperor Kōmei to Kujō Naotada, 11 March 1858, in *Bakumatsu Gaikoku Kankei Monjo*, xix, Appendix, pp. 4–7.

[2] The final text is given as Document 26, pp. 180–1.

document omitted any suggestion that the Shōgun could act subsequently without further reference to Kyōto. In effect the decree as issued was a complete rejection of the Harris treaty.

Hotta left Kyōto in the middle of May convinced that only the nomination of Hitotsubashi Keiki as the Shōgun's successor would enable the Bakufu to win support for its policies in the Imperial capital. Before he could reach Edo, however, he had been robbed of any power to put this decision into practice. The Bakufu's prestige had suffered a severe blow by his failure and there was an increasing clamour in Edo for the appointment of a Tairō, or Regent, a measure resorted to only in times of grave crisis. Few men were eligible for such an appointment: the heads of the two leading *fudai* families of Ii and Sakai, or one of the Shōgun's relatives. The Hitotsubashi party, now joined by Hotta, urged the selection of Matsudaira Keiei. Their rivals, the former members of the *zokuron-ha* among *fudai* and Bakufu officials, saw in this a threat to their own power and new evidence of the existence of a Mito conspiracy. It was in this light that they presented the case to Ii Naosuke in a successful attempt to persuade him to accept the office. The public announcement of his appointment as Tairō was issued on 4 June 1858.

From this time on Ii Naosuke became both the nominal and the real arbiter of Bakufu policies. Within a week the succession dispute had been decided in favour of Tokugawa Yoshitomi of Kii, later Shōgun under the name of Iemochi, and Naosuke began the task of removing from positions of influence all the officials who had supported the Hitotsubashi claim.[1] The decision was announced only to the Rōjū, however, for it was feared that any public rejection of Keiki might seriously reduce the chances of settling the treaty question. Considerable pains were being taken to secure at least a superficial appearance of unity on this subject between the Bakufu and feudal lords. Most of the latter, when asked for their opinions (in accordance with the Imperial orders to Hotta), were soon persuaded by the reasoning of the officials that the Harris treaty was necessary, if unpalatable, and submitted memoranda which the Bakufu could use to justify a fresh appeal to Kyōto.[2] Yet Nariaki proved more stubborn. Before he would write the kind of report wanted by Naosuke he required concessions from the Bakufu on points of detail, and this prevented any rapid agreement between them. Nevertheless, by 11 July enough of the lords had replied to make it safe to proceed with the succession question. Without actually disclosing the name of the chosen candidate, it was announced that a decision had been made and would be notified publicly

---

[1] Toki Yorimune and Kawaji Toshiaki were among the earlier victims, being dismissed on 16 June.

[2] On *daimyō* replies at this time see the two articles by Akao, 'Nichi-bei kari tsūshō jōyaku chōin mondai', pp. 431–5, and 'Harris raichō tōji ni okeru taigai shisō', pp. 828–9.

as soon as formal approval had been received from the Emperor. It was while waiting for this to arrive that Naosuke was faced with a foreign crisis that upset all his plans.

Towards the end of July Townsend Harris received word from China that the fighting there was over and an Anglo-French expedition was shortly expected to leave for Japan to negotiate a commercial treaty. On hearing this he hastened to Kanagawa, where he was met by Inoue Kiyonao and Iwase Tadanari, and urged the Bakufu to fulfil its promise by signing the American treaty before the arrival of the French and British warships. Inoue and Iwase, it seems, welcomed this opportunity to get the treaty signed. Certainly they went at once to Edo, on the morning of 29 July, and made every effort to convince the council that this was a step that must be taken if Japan were to avoid catastrophe. Ii Naosuke would have preferred to wait until Imperial sanction had been obtained, but he received little support in this. Eventually he instructed the two negotiators that they were to sign the treaty if Harris refused to consider any further delay.[1] The same day the treaty was signed, with no apparent attempt by Inoue and Iwase to avoid such a conclusion.

The signature of the treaty with America provoked a chorus of disapproval. The *jōi* party, with some justice, regarded the act itself as a negation of all it stood for, while the *kaikoku* group recognized that the motive was necessity rather than choice and had no confidence in Naosuke as executant. The officials among them, moreover, had already been made aware that his approach to administration was authoritarian, for he brooked little interference from those whose positon was based on ability rather than power, and this made them uneasy about their influence in general. And as the Hitotsubashi party came to realize, from the nature of the dismissals and appointments for which the Tairō was responsible, that the succession dispute had been decided against them, their influence, too, was swung against the new administration. Naosuke, in fact, could make no appeal to any group outside the ranks of the more conservative *fudai*. He rejected the policy of expulsion because he recognized that it was impracticable. On the other hand, he made no attempt to encourage the adoption of Western ideas and techniques because the whole weight of his prejudices inclined him to avoid the 'contamination' of traditional Japanese society. He stood rather for the Bakufu's right to determine policy without outside interference, an attitude that led him to sign the treaty without Imperial approval, although reluctantly, and also to oppose Keiki's nomination as Iesada's heir—thereby alienating the Hitotsubashi party, which might otherwise have supported him on the

[1] The account given of the council meeting by Naosuke's secretary, translated as Document 27, pp. 181–3, makes it clear that some Rōjū (of the *zokuron-ha*) were prepared to sign the treaty as an assertion of the Bakufu's authority.

foreign issue. Attacked by the *kaikoku, jōi,* and Hitotsubashi parties, as well as by the advocates of *sonnō,* he depended on a ruthless exercise of the Bakufu's remaining authority to maintain himself in power.[1]

Where Naosuke differed most clearly from his predecessors was in his readiness to act promptly and with decision. Once the die was cast and the treaty signed he took immediate steps to silence opposition. He dismissed Hotta Masayoshi and Matsudaira Tadakata, the only two Rōjū likely to challenge his authority, and replaced them with men subservient to his own will, seeking in the process to shift responsibility for signing the treaty—and the consequent odium—to the shoulders of those whom he now repudiated. Protests from Matsudaira Keiei, Tokugawa Nariaki, and two of the *sanke* were met by an announcement of the Kii succession and the enforced retirement or even house arrest of those who had voiced objections. By 4 August 1858 Naosuke was virtually a dictator in Edo.

There remained the problem of securing Imperial approval of the American treaty and the other treaties with Russia, Britain, France, and Holland which soon followed it. The Tairō refused to go himself to Kyōto, despite an Imperial message demanding his presence there, and sent instead Manabe Akikatsu, one of his own nominees to the office of Rōjū. The problems he had to face were the same as those that had confronted Hotta in the spring, but the Bakufu had meanwhile demonstrated that its power was not entirely a thing of the past and the lesson had not been lost on the senior members of the Court. The Emperor was still opposed to many of the provisions of the treaties. Yet he was conscious that an open conflict between Court and Bakufu might prove as dangerous to Japan as admitting foreign traders. This, in the light of the Bakufu's evident determination, weakened his resistance to Manabe's persuasions and eventually deprived the opposition of that august approval which had hitherto made their activities respectable. It was not an immediate change, of course. On 13 December, nearly two months after Manabe's arrival in Kyōto, the Emperor still regarded the Shimoda treaty as the most that could be granted to the intrusive foreigner.[2] A week later, however, Manabe submitted a new memorial that seems to have had a decisive effect.[3] The document was a skilful blend of cogent reasoning, conciliation, and veiled threat. Manabe repeated the argument that signature of the treaty was the only means of avoiding war and that defeat in war would have led to the imposition of very much severer terms. He suggested that Kyōto opposition was rather to the Bakufu than to the treaty and hinted that if it persisted the Tairō would have to employ the same

[1] For a discussion of Ii Naosuke's attitude in 1858 see especially Ishii, 'Gokai saretaru Ii Naosuke', *Rekishigaku Kenkyū,* viii. 532–3, 556–7.

[2] See his letter to Kujō Naotada, 13 December 1858, in *Bakumatsu Gaikoku Kankei Monjo,* xxi. 702–4.

[3] See Document 29, pp. 189–93.

sort of methods that had already been used with effect in Edo. Finally, he asserted that the Bakufu was no more anxious than the Court to submit Japan to the full effect of foreign influence and had every intention, once the country had been united and military preparations had been completed, of taking steps to secure the withdrawal of foreigners. The promise was vague enough. It did not commit the Bakufu to carrying out expulsion by war or to a date for taking action, but it served to reassure those elements at Court whose suspicions of foreign intercourse were not accompanied by a desire to overthrow the Tokugawa. These already included most of the senior officials, and the addition of the Emperor to their number removed their greatest difficulty. Manabe still found it necessary to promise that efforts would be made to avoid the opening of Ōsaka and to revise those details of the treaties that aroused the greatest hostility, but in substance he gained his point. On 2 February 1859, after further lengthy discussions of detail, the Imperial reply was formally handed over.[1] It expressed concern at the form of the treaties, but acknowledged that they were unavoidable. It also recorded the Bakufu undertaking to overthrow them as soon as it had achieved parity with the West in military strength. The Bakufu was thereby publicly committed to a policy which it was quite unable to carry out and which was to prove a constant source of embarrassment, both in domestic and in foreign affairs, during the course of the next ten years.

The actions of Ii Naosuke in 1858 were of major importance in determining the future shape of Japanese politics. By signing new treaties with the West—however reluctant the decision and however suspect the motive—he had completed the association of the two expressions *sabaku* ('support the Bakufu') and *kaikoku* ('open the country'). This confirmed the *jōi* adherents in their position as an opposition party, challenging not merely a specific policy but the government itself. The trend was confirmed by the gradual transference of *jōi* leadership from Mito to the western fief of Chōshū. The outstanding apologist of expulsion in 1858–9 was Yoshida Shōin; and with the death of Nariaki in September 1860 the *jōi* party found a new patron and protector in Yoshida's lord, Mōri Yoshichika, *tozama daimyō* of Chōshū. At the same time the alliance with the *sonnō* groups was growing stronger. Both Hotta and Ii, by seeking Imperial sanction for their actions, had helped to raise the Court's prestige. On the other hand, the attempt to assert Bakufu privileges over the signing of the treaty and the dictatorial methods of Naosuke had alienated not only those who looked upon the Throne as a depository of political power but also many who did not. Thus increasingly the debates on domestic and on foreign affairs came together. Just as those who advocated opening of

[1] The text is translated as Document 30, pp. 193–4.

the country felt themselves bound to support the Bakufu, so the opposition increasingly adopted the slogan *sonnō-jōi* ('honour the Emperor, expel the barbarian') and looked to Kyōto as its stronghold. The debate over foreign policy was becoming merged in a struggle between Court and Bakufu.

This polarization, however, was by no means complete. The great *daimyō* (other than *fudai*) who had so far been most active in national affairs were not willing to throw in their lot completely with either side. These were the men who had been the main strength of the Hitotsubashi party—Matsudaira Keiei, Yamanouchi Toyoshige, Date Muneki, and the new leader of Satsuma, Shimazu Hisamitsu[1]—and their collective power was enough to give them a deciding voice in the conflict. For some years after 1858 they continued as a separate and intermediate grouping. In foreign affairs they resented the degree of concession made to the West but did not thereby abandon their essentially *kaikoku* views; and in domestic affairs they regarded respect for the Emperor as desirable in itself without in any way detracting from the Bakufu's responsibility for administration. They sought not to abolish the Bakufu but to reform it. And the change they wished chiefly to effect was that the Shōgun should share his power with the great feudal lords. It was the method of determining policy that was to be altered, not the structure of administration, and to this extent they were supporters of the Bakufu rather than of the Court. Yet as members of the Hitotsubashi party, now in disgrace, they no longer had access to the centres of power in Edo. They were therefore forced to use their connexions with the senior nobles in Kyōto as a means of influencing events, which brought them into alliance with the Imperial Court, or at least with certain elements in it. The result was what is known as the *kōbu-gattai* ('Court-Bakufu unity') movement. This cast back in some respects to the ideas concerning national unity expressed by Tokugawa Nariaki and the earlier *jōi* leaders, for it was based on the argument that the divisions within Japan, especially those between Court and Bakufu, would have to be healed if the threat from the Western Powers were to be met with any hope of success. But the new leaders saw themselves as mediators between Court and Bakufu, moderating the policies of both (and confirming their own position of influence in the process). The Bakufu, they felt, must accept the co-operation of the Court and the great lords in the determination of policy; the Court, in its turn, must accept the necessity of limited agreements with the West. Only in this way could Japan be united and her actions made effective.

Thus by 1859, when the new treaties came into force, the disagreements

---

[1] On the death of Shimazu Nariakira in August 1858 headship of the fief had passed to Shimazu Tadayoshi, son of Nariakira's brother Hisamitsu. After this time, however, Hisamitsu was for some years the effective leader of Satsuma in national affairs.

over foreign affairs had been aligned with definite political groupings. On one side stood the Bakufu, now committed to a *kaikoku* policy. At the opposite extreme stood a *sonnō-jōi* party, with its main strength drawn from the lower ranks of the samurai and Imperial courtiers, which advocated complete abrogation of the 1858 agreements. Between the two was a new *kōbu-gattai* group, consisting largely of former Hitotsubashi supporters, a loose but powerful alliance of senior Court officials, great *tozama* lords and members of the *kamon* houses, which was prepared to support Bakufu foreign policy in return for specific political concessions. It was the struggle for power between these three factions that chiefly determined Japanese foreign policy in the years 1860–8.

4. *The opening of the ports*

The opening of the ports in 1859 added appreciably to the Bakufu's difficulties in its handling of foreign affairs. In the first place, it brought a steadily increasing number of foreign merchants and diplomats to Japan and thereby opened the way for a series of incidents that exacerbated relations with the West. By the end of 1860 isolated attacks on foreigners in the treaty ports had already led to the death, among others, of a Russian naval officer, two Chinese in the service respectively of the British and French legations, and a Dutch merchant captain. To this was added in January 1861 the murder of Hendrik Heusken, secretary to Townsend Harris.[1] As a measure of protest the representatives of France, Britain, and Holland withdrew from the capital, but they returned a few weeks later when they found that the Bakufu showed pleasure rather than regret at a development which so conveniently removed the scene of discussions from the immediate neighbourhood of Edo Castle. In July, however, there came an incident much more serious in its repercussions. At the beginning of that month the British minister, Rutherford Alcock, returned from a visit to Nagasaki and took up residence in the temporary legation, the Tōzenji temple at Shinagawa. On the following night the building was attacked by a party of fourteen samurai, who succeeded in wounding two of the British staff before being driven off by the guards provided by the Japanese government. The incident initiated a dispute that was not settled until March of 1862, when the Bakufu finally agreed to pay an indemnity to the wounded men and to construct a new and defensible legation at its own expense.[2]

Foreigners tended to attribute these attacks to the activities of Mito. In this they were partly correct, for the men who made the Tōzenji attack all came from the Mito fief and most other incidents were inspired by the

[1] For an account of these attacks see generally Ōtsuka, *Bakumatsu no gaikō*, pp. 31–35.
[2] On this incident see Ōtsuka, *Bakumatsu no gaikō*, pp. 48–49, and Alcock, *The Capital of the Tycoon* (2 vols., London, 1863), ii. 151 ff.

arguments of the *jōi* school. On the other hand, it did not necessarily follow that they formed part of a conspiracy aimed at precipitating a clash between Japan and the West, though such suspicions undoubtedly existed at the time. Rather, they were evidence of a growing turbulence in Japanese society. The years after 1858 saw a marked increase in the use of violence in political disputes within Japan. It was manifested not only in attacks on foreigners but also in attempts to assassinate Bakufu leaders; in recurrent peasant revolts, often led by samurai; and in the appearance at Kyōto of armed bands of samurai and lordless *rōnin* who at times dominated the city and even attacked the Imperial palace in their efforts to control the decisions of the Court. Such things cannot satisfactorily be explained by a simple theory of conspiracy. Their roots lie deeper, notably in the economic changes that were sapping the strength of the entire régime.

Since the seventeenth century, feudal rule had become in many respects an anachronism in Japan. With the establishment of peace and stability the samurai class had lost its *raison d'être* and had simultaneously acquired habits of luxury that demanded for their maintenance an increasing proportion of the national wealth. Higher standards of living, however, were not matched by any comparable increase in agrarian production. It followed that exactions on the peasant grew heavier and riots more frequent. Yet despite all their efforts the feudal lords could not keep out of debt. By the nineteenth century their revenues were heavily mortgaged to the new class of *chōnin*, townsmen whose wealth, acquired through commerce and finance, had grown out of all comparison with their social and political status. Yet it was the lesser ranks of the samurai who suffered most conspicuously by the change. Their incomes depended as a rule not on the tenure of land but on stipends granted by their lords; and these stipends were often the obvious target for economies in expenditure. The result was a growing split within the feudal class, as the lesser samurai became conscious that their own interests were becoming more and more divorced from those of the great lords.

The arrival of the foreigners imposed new strains on an economy already near to dislocation. The Bakufu had long since dissipated the financial reserves built up by the early Tokugawa, and its currency manipulations, undertaken in a series of desperate attempts to reduce the annual deficit, had done nothing to improve the position in the country as a whole. After 1853 the cost of defence works increased by leaps and bounds. The opening of the ports, moreover, pushed government expenditure higher still. The revenue that could be raised through customs duties was limited by the restrictions embodied in the treaties and was more than balanced by the cost of importing foreign ships and guns.[1] In addition there was the

[1] On the financial results of the opening of the ports see Tsuchiya, 'Bakumatsu dōranki no keizaiteki bunseki', *Chūō Koron*, xlvii. 11 (October 1932), pp. 86–87; and, for its effects on the

cost of maintaining installations and officials at the ports, of sending embassies overseas, and (much the largest item of all) of indemnities for the attacks made on foreign ships, citizens, and legations. These new burdens brought the government to the point of bankruptcy. Nor were the feudal lords in much better case. They, too, felt the need to acquire Western weapons, while only a few found a solution for their financial difficulties by increasing production and engaging extensively in foreign trade.

The financial embarrassments of Bakufu and feudal lords, leading as they did to further debasement of the coinage and new issues of paper currency, were soon reflected in instability of commodity prices. This, in its turn, was accentuated by the direct effects of foreign trade.[1] In the early months of the new commerce, for example, foreign merchants found that the unusual gold : silver ratio in Japan enabled them to exchange foreign silver for Japanese gold at rates which furnished staggering profits. The consequent drain of gold, and no less the measures taken by the Bakufu to end it, increased the turmoil. So, too, did the demand for Japanese goods like silk, silkworm eggs, and tea, which were still not in sufficiently large-scale production to meet the needs of an international market. The total effect was a sharp rise in commodity prices within Japan. Between 1860 and 1867 the price of rice rose more than tenfold, while the prices of other daily necessities showed similar, though smaller, changes.

Economic distress resulting from these price movements had an important impact on the dispute between *jōi* and *kaikoku* schools.[2] The loyalty of the lesser samurai had already been weakened by the reduction of their stipends and by the knowledge that the rigidity and ossification of Tokugawa society left them little scope to improve their position within the existing framework. With the rapid deterioration of conditions after 1860 their livelihood seemed in greater danger than ever. It was easy for them to attribute this to the adverse effects of foreign trade, against which so many warnings had been sounded in recent years, and therefore to adopt *jōi* views with an immediacy and vehemence which stemmed directly from a feeling of insecurity. Their reasoning, certainly, was oversimplified.[3] Yet it was based on evidence that was convincing enough to contemporaries; and since the events of 1858 had associated the Bakufu in the

fiefs especially, Kanno, 'Shokō to gaikoku bōeki', pp. 402–13. It has to be borne in mind that Bakufu income, like that of medieval European monarchies, was derived principally from the yield from the ruler's personal estates.

[1] See generally Tsuchiya, 'Bakumatsu dōranki no keizaiteki bunseki', pp. 76–85, and Norman, *Japan's Emergence as a Modern State* (New York, 1940), pp. 40–43.

[2] See Tsuchiya, 'Bakumatsu dōranki no keizaiteki bunseki', pp. 87–89, and Ishii, *Bakumatsu no gaikō*, pp. 76–78.

[3] It was rare indeed for Japanese of this period to recognize that foreign trade was not the sole—or even the chief—cause of hardship, but it did occasionally happen: see, for example, Document 45, at p. 245.

popular mind with a policy of opening the country, it was only natural that the discontented should turn to Kyōto for support. By 1862–3, at the latest, the *sonnō-jōi* party had acquired a following that was still sectional but was no longer local or small in number. Much of the unrest, it is true, was not of a kind directly relevant to the discussion of foreign affairs. It included rice riots, for example, as well as sporadic attacks on merchants known to be trading with the West. But it meant that the anti-Bakufu leaders were now able to call upon a large, if ill-organized, body of armed and desperate men to back their arguments with force. Especially was this so in Kyōto. It was not until Chōshū challenged the Bakufu that the anti-Tokugawa forces could be said to have an army, but some years before that they had made the streets of the Imperial capital unsafe for the supporters of Edo policy. This was not without its influence on the Court, where the Bakufu found itself faced with growing stubbornness and resistance.

These changes, of course, did not follow immediately on the opening of the ports. They form, rather, a continuing and developing strand in the history of the last few years of Tokugawa rule. This is not to imply, however, that the settlement imposed by Ii Naosuke enjoyed in the interval a period of stability. Quite apart from the opposition it aroused within Japan, it proved from the beginning a source of conflict with the Western Powers, especially with Great Britain. It was not merely that personal attacks on foreigners gave rise to anger and recrimination. Of much wider implication were disagreements over the handling of trade. The treaties had laid it down that foreigners might 'freely buy from Japanese and sell to them any articles that either may have for sale, without the intervention of any Japanese officers in such purchase or sale, or in making or receiving payment for the same'.[1] It was an agreement, as we have seen, that the Bakufu had accepted only with the greatest reluctance. Few even of the *kaikoku* thinkers were convinced of the economic advantages of trade (as distinct from the financial benefits it might bring to the government or the possibilities it offered of strengthening Japan's military establishment), and these few were certainly in no position to control the official policy of the Bakufu. The majority still looked to the Dutch treaty of 1857 as the plan that was most acceptable. Their inclinations were towards restriction and monopoly, a fact which had been apparent, for example, to Laurence Oliphant when he accompanied Lord Elgin to Edo in 1858 to negotiate the British treaty.[2] Four years later the first British resident minister, Rutherford Alcock, described the attitude of the Japanese government as

---

[1] This wording is taken from Article III of the American treaty (Document 28, at p. 185). The other treaties were substantially the same.

[2] His remarkably accurate forecast of the difficulties to be expected is to be found in Oliphant, *Narrative of the Earl of Elgin's Mission to China and Japan* (2 vols., Edinburgh and London, 1859), ii. 243–53.

'a policy of negation, accepting the letter, but determined on resistance *à l'outrance* to the spirit of the treaties'.[1] It is a judgement that is confirmed by the record. From the beginning the Bakufu attempted to restrict trade by every means short of breach of treaty. It countenanced obstruction by customs officials, at one time imposed an embargo on silk exports, at another refused to supply the foreigners with Japanese currency. Yet these were only temporary expedients, adopted pending fuller consideration of the problem. Lengthy discussions between the *machi-bugyō* and *kanjō-bugyō* led finally to a decision that permanent control could most effectively be exercised by ensuring that all exports of certain selected goods (including silk thread, wax, and rape-seed oil) must pass through the hands of the great Edo wholesale houses, which were under Bakufu patronage and supervision. A decree to this effect was issued in May 1860.[2] It did not in fact achieve the desired measure of control, but this was in no way attributable to any change of heart by the officials. While Bakufu intentions remained restrictive, the attractions of wealth and profit proved stronger than the machinery of enforcement. Large-scale evasion made the regulations ineffective.

These manœuvres, though not always fully understood by the Western representatives, were recognized by them as attempts to prevent the development of a genuinely unrestricted commerce. Throughout 1860, therefore, their attitude was hardening. At the same time the Bakufu was discovering that the strong measures adopted by Ii Naosuke in 1858 had driven the domestic opposition not into submission but to violence. By signing the treaties without Imperial sanction and by his attacks on the Hitotsubashi party, he had outraged both the prejudices and the feudal loyalties of *jōi* adherents. The hatred so engendered sought revenge in assassination. On 24 March 1860 Naosuke was attacked and killed outside the gates of Edo Castle by a party of Mito samurai,[3] an event that had important repercussions on the administration. So much had come to depend on the personal decisions of the Tairō, who had himself dismissed many of the able men appointed by his predecessors—Hotta, Kawaji, Iwase, Nagai, and later Mizuno Tadanori—that his sudden removal from the scene left Edo with neither policy nor initiative. The new leaders had

---

[1] Alcock, *Capital of the Tycoon*, i, p. xvi.

[2] Bakufu attempts to restrict trade are briefly discussed in two works by Ishii, *Bakumatsu no gaikō*, pp. 46–47, 54–56, 107–8, and *Bakumatsu bōeki-shi no kenkyū* (Tōkyō, 1942), pp. 323–9.

[3] This is usually known as 'the Sakurada-mon incident' after the castle gate outside which it took place. Immediately after the attack the conspirators drew up a long memorandum explaining their action as a punishment for Naosuke's crimes in admitting the foreigners to Japanese soil and seeking to establish autocratic rule (i.e. seeking to free the Bakufu from the necessity of consulting the Imperial Court and great lords). It is interesting to note, however, that they advocated neither the overthrow of the Bakufu as such nor the immediate and forcible expulsion of foreigners, which suggests that Nariaki was still exerting a moderating influence on the movement. See *Ishin-shi*, ii. 716–23, and Akao, 'Harris raichō tōji ni okeru taigai shisō', pp. 839–42.

nothing like the same force of character. Andō Nobumasa, who had been appointed Rōjū by Naosuke and had been in charge of foreign affairs since the beginning of the year, represented the more conservative *fudai*. Kuze Hirochika, now restored to office as Rōjū, had previously been dismissed because of his association with Nariaki and the Hitotsubashi party, and his appointment reflected recognition of the need to restore unity among those groups traditionally linked with the fortunes of the Tokugawa house. Neither man could lay claim to much imagination, despite some degree of experience and administrative competence, but they were nevertheless to dominate Bakufu counsels for the next two years.

The most serious problem they faced was to find a policy that would prevent or postpone a crisis in Japan's relations with the West. In Kyōto the senior *kuge*, allies of the Bakufu, were only with difficulty able to hold in check the growing clamour for abrogation of the treaties. The foreigners, meanwhile, were insisting on full execution of the treaty stipulations. Andō and Kuze attempted the difficult task of reconciling these conflicting points of view without permitting the two antagonists to come into direct communication with each other. To the Court they explained that Japanese disunity made impossible any effective resistance to Western demands; to the foreigners that domestic opposition prevented them from carrying out the 1858 agreements. In this way, they hoped, the opposing forces could be made to cancel out and some sort of balance might be achieved.

It was this policy that provided the connexion between the Kazu-nomiya marriage proposals and Bakufu diplomacy. The plan to arrange a marriage between the Shōgun Iemochi and the Emperor Kōmei's sister, Princess Kazunomiya, had been discussed privately as early as 1858, when Manabe was in Kyōto, but it was not until May 1860 that the suggestion was made formally to the Court.[1] It was quickly refused, largely because of the Emperor's opposition. In July, however, the Bakufu renewed its request, urging the importance of making a public gesture of Court-Bakufu solidarity to demonstrate that recent differences had been settled and so unite the country in face of the foreign threat. This was an argument well calculated to appeal to Kōmei on political grounds, for his anti-foreign views had never led him to seek abolition of the Bakufu as an institution. None the less, the same was not true of members of his entourage. Iwakura Tomomi, for example, who for all his lack of senior office had now become accepted as one of the Emperor's personal advisers, wrote a memorandum on the marriage question which made it quite clear that he looked upon it as an opportunity to take the first step towards restoring the Imperial power.[2] The time for drastic action had not yet come, he thought, since

---

[1] The account of the marriage negotiations given here is based largely on *Ishin-shi*, ii. 755–87.
[2] Document 31, pp. 198–200.

an attempt to impose Kyōto's views on the Bakufu might well precipitate a civil war of which the result would be uncertain. On the other hand, the Bakufu's eagerness for the marriage could still be turned to good account. The Court should make its approval of the request conditional on Bakufu acceptance of a specific policy—expulsion of the foreigners—and so ensure its possession of real, if not of nominal, authority.

Iwakura's arguments may not have been entirely to the Emperor's taste, but the substance of his advice (so far as it applied to immediate action, at least) was adopted. The Bakufu was informed privately that the marriage could not be approved while the 1858 treaties remained in force, and this shifted the debate expressly to the subject of foreign affairs. In mid-September the Bakufu presented a written statement on foreign policy which reiterated many of the arguments used by Manabe two years earlier. It repeated, with emphasis, that the treaties had been signed not as a matter of choice but because of the need to gain time in which Japan's defences could be prepared for a trial of strength; that this could never be achieved while the country was torn by faction; and that the Kazunomiya marriage would provide the best means of uniting all parties behind the Court-Bakufu leadership. Where the *jōi* thinkers, in fact, argued that expulsion was a necessary preliminary to national unity, the Bakufu was now maintaining that unity was a precondition of expulsion. It did, however, make its promises more specific than before. It put a time-limit on the period of preparation. 'Within from seven or eight to ten years from now', it promised, 'action will certainly be taken either to cancel the treaties by negotiation or to expel the foreigners by force.'[1]

This promise, remote as was the date of its execution and doubtful as was the Bakufu's intention of redeeming it, was enough to overcome the Court's objections. By the beginning of October the marriage had been agreed. Subsequently, however, the accord was again disrupted, this time by a Bakufu attempt to regain some freedom of action in its handling of foreign affairs. In January 1861 the *Kyōto-shoshidai* presented to the Court a further letter from the Rōjū, together with an explanatory memorandum of his own,[2] the substance of which was that within the overall strategy of eventual expulsion it would be necessary from time to time to make concessions of various kinds to prevent any premature outbreak of hostilities. Immediately, this meant concluding treaties with more of the Western Powers: Prussia, Switzerland, and Belgium. The necessity could even be turned to tactical advantage, the Bakufu argued, for by restricting the privileges now to be granted Japan would strengthen her case for some revision of the treaties concluded in 1858, especially in terms of the number of ports to be opened, and might thus avoid the more extreme consequences

---

[1] Document 32, at p. 203.
[2] Documents 33 and 34, pp. 204–8.

of foreign intercourse. To the Court, as one might expect, this sounded very like tergiversation. Nor were such suspicions far from the truth. The *shoshidai*, however, succeeded in pacifying the *kuge* by agreeing to postponement of the Kazunomiya marriage (which eventually took place in January 1862) and by accepting an official but unpublished rebuke. A few weeks later he closed the dispute by writing again to the Court to reaffirm the Bakufu's promise to rid Japan of foreigners within ten years, but asserting that meanwhile there must be fluctuations in foreign policy as the needs and circumstances of the moment might dictate.

With this moderate success in Kyōto the Bakufu had to rest content. It had committed itself far more specifically than was desirable, but it had at least gained a breathing-space in which to seek means of escape from its difficulties. There remained the problem of persuading the foreigners, in their turn, to make similar concessions. This task had been begun the previous summer in discussions with the British, French, and American envoys in Edo, but their attitude had not been encouraging. In May 1861, therefore, the Bakufu announced its intention of sending a diplomatic mission to Europe, in the hope of meeting with a better reception from the governments themselves. The main object was to secure postponement of the opening of the ports of Hyōgo and Niigata and the cities of Edo and Ōsaka, known briefly as 'the two ports and two cities', to all of which foreigners were to be admitted (by the terms of the 1858 treaties) not later than 1 January 1863. The advantages to be gained from such a postponement were twofold. In the first place, it would help to limit the development of foreign trade, the economic effects of which were already causing the Bakufu some concern. In the second, it would provide evidence to the Court and opposition groups generally that the Bakufu was serious in its declarations of resistance to foreign encroachment. As presented to the foreigners, of course, the argument did not take quite this form. It ran, rather, that the rise in prices since the opening of trade had increased the prejudice against foreign intercourse to the point at which it threatened the treaty settlement as a whole. To open more ports at such a juncture would only increase the difficulties. Postponement, on the other hand, would give the Bakufu time in which to reconcile opinion to the step, so that when taken it would be regarded as welcome, not merely as necessary.[1] It is a question whether this statement, any more than that made to the Court, was intended seriously. More likely the Bakufu was simply using any means of persuasion that would serve its immediate ends, without overmuch thought about the possible consequences.

The mission to Europe, led by the two *gaikoku-bugyō* Takeuchi Yasunori and Matsudaira Yasunao, finally sailed from Nagasaki on 30 January

[1] See the Bakufu's letter to Rutherford Alcock on this subject, given as Document 35, pp. 208–11.

1862.[1] It was bound in the first instance for France. The envoys, however, soon realized that the key to their success lay in London, for Britain had much the largest stake in Japan's foreign trade and without her concurrence none of the other Powers would be willing to act. At the end of April, therefore, Takeuchi crossed to England. There he found fresh difficulties. News of the attack on the British legation at Tōzenji in the previous year had greatly influenced the attitude of the British government towards Japan. Russell, then Foreign Secretary, had refused at first to enter into any negotiations at all pending a settlement of this matter, and would not in any case act without the detailed advice of his representative in Edo. It seemed, despite the Bakufu's belief in the value of negotiating in Europe, that everything still depended on Rutherford Alcock in Japan.

Two considerations in particular disposed Alcock to accept the Bakufu's proposals when they were first explained to him in detail during 1861. The expansion of British trade would be severely handicapped if the opposition succeeded in provoking disturbance or civil war in Japan, for which reason any action that might strengthen the hand of the government could be justified as forwarding the economic interests of Great Britain. Secondly, it was desirable to support Japan against the encroachments of Russia, of which there had recently been ominous signs.[2] This, too, was an argument for fostering unity within Japan. On the other hand, his instructions from Russell made it clear that the Japanese proposals could on no account be accepted without satisfaction for the Tōzenji incident and some guarantee of future protection for British trade and citizens. In fact, the London dispatch had concluded, 'you will understand . . . that you are not to make concessions without equivalents; that so far from restricting or abandoning the trade of Japan, you are to maintain and, if possible, enlarge it; and that you are to preserve undiminished the reputation of the British name'.[3]

Alcock interpreted these instructions liberally. On 14 February 1862 he wrote a memorandum for the information of his Dutch and French colleagues in Edo[4] in which he described himself as agreeable to postponement of the opening of Edo and Niigata (though not of Ōsaka and Hyōgo) in return for (1) settlement of the Tōzenji affair, (2) the opening of Tsushima and a port in Korea, and (3) public recognition of the treaties by the Emperor or great lords. Alternatively, he thought, 'determined

[1] Japanese accounts of the mission are given in Ōtsuka, *Bakumatsu no gaikō*, pp. 44–47; Ishii, *Bakumatsu no gaikō*, pp. 76–90; and *Ishin-shi*, ii. 937–45. See also the documents printed in British *Parliamentary Papers, 1862*, vol. lxiv, and *1863*, vol. lxxiv.

[2] In April 1861 a Russian warship had arrived at the island of Tsushima, midway between Japan and Korea, and begun the erection of shore installations. It had only withdrawn, in September, after vigorous protests by the British and Japanese governments and threatening moves by the British fleet. See Ōtsuka, *Bakumatsu no gaikō*, pp. 43–44.

[3] See Russell to Alcock, 23 November 1861, in *Parliamentary Papers 1862*, vol. lxiv, pp. 74–75.

[4] Document 36, pp. 211–16.

action' by one or more of the Great Powers might solve the whole problem, though this involved a danger of hostilities and could be decided only by the governments themselves. In much of this Alcock had the support of both Dutch and French representatives. They differed slightly in their assessment of Japanese policy—de Wit seeing in it evidence that the Bakufu was 'yielding to an inimical party', whereas de Bellecourt was more inclined to suspect that this argument was being used as a cover for the Bakufu's own desires to restrict trade[1]—but they both agreed as to the impossibility of postponing the opening of Hyōgo and Ōsaka. All three men, in their memoranda, revealed a growing awareness of the complications of Japanese domestic politics.

The conditions Alcock wished to impose in return for concessions concerning Edo and Niigata, as well as his refusal to consider postponement of the opening of Hyōgo and Ōsaka, would, if carried through, have represented a major defeat for Bakufu policy. In the middle of March, however, he was persuaded to modify his stand. He had already been impressed by the promptness with which the Bakufu had acted to punish those responsible for the Tōzenji attack and was now further conciliated by promises of full recompense and future protection. This removed the main obstacle to agreement. The final step in his conversion was accomplished by Kuze Hirochika in two long interviews on the 12th and 16th of the month. In these Kuze at last succeeded in convincing him, in the words of his report to Russell, that 'the Government of the Tycoon has real difficulties of no ordinary kind and actual dangers to contend with, threatening the dynasty and the existence of the Government'.[2] From this it followed, in the interests of preserving law and order (and, by the same token, the opportunities for British trade), that the Bakufu proposals should be accepted even if the concessions so made were unilateral. All that could legitimately be exacted in return was full execution of the treaty provisions in the ports already open. It was not certain that the situation would improve even if delay were granted, Alcock thought,[3] but any other

[1] M. de Bellecourt's view was that 'les agents du Gouvernement Japonais paraissent invariablement attachés à suivre avec la plus stricte fidelité au programme consistant à ne tolérer dans les relations avec les étrangers que ce qui est rigoureusement indispensable pour prévenir, en sauvant les apparences, des complications intempestives et pourtant pour amoindrir en toutes circonstances la portée soit politique soit commerciale des stipulations des Traités ...'. This memorandum, together with those of Alcock and de Wit cited above, appears as an enclosure in Alcock to Russell, confidential, No. 23, 17 March 1862; see Foreign Office, General Correspondence, *Japan* (F.O. 46), vol. 21.

[2] Alcock to Russell, 17 March 1862 (F.O. 46/21). It might be remarked, as Alcock himself knew, that Andō Nobumasa had been attacked and wounded outside Edo Castle only a month before.

[3] Alcock to Russell, 17 March 1862 (F.O. 46/21): 'Whatever may be the amount of good faith with which they have conducted their policy in regard to foreigners (and in my opinion it has been little enough), and however doubtful may be their improvement under the reprieve thus earnestly desired (and doubtful it certainly must be considered), they feel at this moment so

policy would necessarily have to be supported by force, probably by Britain acting alone. In the circumstances he felt justified in recommending to the Foreign Office a delay of five years in the opening of the two ports and the two cities.

This recommendation he was able to make in person. It had previously been decided that he was to return home on leave, and Russell accordingly postponed all discussions with Takeuchi until Alcock should arrive. He came at the end of May, accompanied by the Bakufu's chief interpreter, Moriyama Takichiro, who brought fresh instructions for Takeuchi which had been drawn up as a result of the discussions between Alcock and Kuze. Since Alcock was appointed to conduct the talks on Russell's behalf it was not long before agreement was reached. The London Protocol was signed on 6 June 1862.[1] It provided for the postponement of the opening of Niigata (or some alternative port to be agreed meanwhile), Hyōgo, Edo, and Ōsaka until 1 January 1868, though this was conditional on full observance of the treaties at the remaining three ports. There was specifically to be redress of the existing grievances concerning conditions of trade. In addition, the Japanese envoys undertook to recommend to the Bakufu, on their return to Edo, the opening of Tsushima, the reduction of some customs duties, and the erection of bonded warehouses in Yokohama and Nagasaki. To them it seemed a small price to pay for such success. As the *gaikoku-bugyō* pointed out in their subsequent report[2]—a document full of the kind of verbal quibbling that was so dear to the hearts of Bakufu officials—no formal commitment had been made about Tsushima and it might yet prove possible to offer it as an alternative to Hyōgo and Ōsaka.

Having first obtained the consent of Britain it was not difficult to make similar arrangements with the other Treaty Powers. This Takeuchi did during September and October of 1862. To all appearances the Bakufu had been successful in its attempts to postpone a crisis. The Court had accepted the need for temporary concession and the foreigners had agreed not to insist on the opening of more ports during the next five years. In fact, however, the Bakufu's policy had sown the seeds of future danger. In the first place, it had made promises which it could never hope to fulfil. To the Court it had promised the eventual expulsion of foreigners, to the West it had promised a progressive expansion of trade. Both parties, moreover, had doubts about the Bakufu's sincerity and would watch closely for signs that they had been misled. Then, too, the very success that

vehemently pressed between two great dangers, the one from within, and the other from without, that their unwillingness to guarantee anything I think the best trait in the character of those at the helm I have known; for I am certain it arises from a conviction of utter powerlessness to answer for the future.'

[1] The text is given as Document 37, pp. 216–17.

[2] Document 38, pp. 218–21.

the London Protocol embodied was to prove a disadvantage of its own, for it convinced the officials, when they were confronted with similar problems thereafter, that they could continue to play off foreign demands against Kyōto reluctance without the necessity of committing themselves finally to either side. Events were rapidly to show that such a plan was quite impracticable.

5. *The years of crisis, 1863–4*

In the autumn of 1862 there began a series of political events within Japan that were to make apparent to all the fundamental weakness of the Bakufu's position. They were in origin more closely connected with the struggle for power than with foreign policy, but because the political groupings were by this time identified with varying attitudes towards 'expulsion' these events were to raise in an acute form the whole question of Japan's relations with the West. Broadly stated, the Bakufu (that is to say, the officials and most of the *fudai daimyō*) stood for opening of the ports and maintenance of the Tokugawa authority; the samurai, *rōnin*, and lesser *kuge* in Kyōto urged the expulsion of foreigners and the extension of the Imperial prerogatives; and a group of the great *tozama* lords, with the support of a number of the Shōgun's relatives, sought reform and a broadening of the basis of power in Edo, while continuing to uphold the necessity for trade and diplomatic relations with the outside world. It was the activities of the last two segments that tended to complicate the handling of foreign affairs.

Andō Nobumasa and Kuze Hirochika, during the two years they had been responsible for Bakufu policy, had sought to achieve a settlement of domestic disputes by agreement between Court and Bakufu. As they interpreted it, however, 'Court-Bakufu unity' did not constitute in any sense a broadening of the basis of power. It was rather an attempt to use the prestige of the Court to bolster the authority of the Bakufu, a change of form not of substance, which still left all real responsibility in the hands of the Shōgun's ministers. It was for this reason that they failed to secure the co-operation of those whom we have hitherto referred to as the *kōbu-gattai* party. It is true that they had announced the pardon of those chiefly concerned in the movement to secure the Hitotsubashi succession— including Keiki himself and Matsudaira Keiei—and that these men, together with Shimazu Hisamitsu of Satsuma and Yamanouchi Toyoshige of Tosa, formed the nucleus of the *kōbu-gattai* party; but they had not re-admitted them to the Bakufu's counsels. And as long as the great *tozama* lords were not represented in the formulation of national policy, either directly or through their allies among the *sanke* and *kamon*, they were unlikely to lend the weight of their influence to support the Bakufu in its dealings with Kyōto. On the contrary, they tried to use the growing Imperial prestige to further their own political ends.

For a brief period in the summer of 1862 it looked as if they might succeed. By bringing pressure to bear on the Bakufu they were able to secure the appointment of some of their own number to important offices in Edo. But in the process they left the way open for *sonnō-jōi* elements to secure an ascendancy at Court. Moreover, the differences among *kōbu-gattai* leaders, especially between Shimazu and the rest, quickly rendered their political action ineffective. By the spring of 1863 a somewhat uneasy alliance between Hitotsubashi Keiki, Matsudaira Keiei, and Bakufu officials was left almost unaided to face the renewed demand for expulsion emanating from Kyōto. And this they proved powerless to do. Public announcement of a date for expulsion, which soon followed, coincided with a fresh crisis in Japan's relations with Britain and resulted in something very near an outbreak of hostilities with the West.

These events rallied the *kōbu-gattai* party in another effort to assert its influence. This time the scene of action was Kyōto, where in September and October 1863, with the aid of troops from Satsuma and Aizu, steps were taken to exclude extremists from the Court and restore the authority of those *kuge* who favoured co-operation with the great lords. Yet the victory, if such it was, served only to renew the rivalry between Satsuma and Edo. Increasingly the *kōbu-gattai* party separated out into factions, each supporting one of the two antagonists, and the resulting split made nugatory all attempts to reach agreement on the subject of foreign affairs. The advocates of expulsion were relatively united in their demands. Their opponents, though more powerful, were divided. And as the deadlock persisted, during 1864, so did the danger mount, for the paralysis in Japanese policy was not matched by any similar inactivity on the part of the Western Powers. Indeed, the bombardment of Shimonoseki in September 1864 can be attributed in large part to the fact that Japanese leaders generally, both in the Bakufu and outside it, were preoccupied with the struggle for power to the virtual exclusion of all else.

The failure of the *kōbu-gattai* party to exploit its successes in these years sounded its death-knell as an independent element in Japanese politics. In and after 1865 there gradually emerged a new and simpler alignment of forces, in which Satsuma and Uwajima (Date Muneki) moved into alliance with Chōshū and the *sonnō-jōi* party, while Hitotsubashi Keiki became more closely associated with the Rōjū and *fudai*. Matsudaira Keiei and Yamanouchi Toyoshige, after some hesitation, eventually threw in their lot with Satsuma. At the same time the disputes over foreign policy were changing in character and purpose. Before continuing with a discussion of these later developments, however, it is necessary to examine in greater detail the events of 1862–4.

The political manœuvrings of 1862 were initiated by Shimazu Hisa-mitsu of Satsuma.[1] In the spring of that year he went to Kyōto and began to urge the dispatch of a special Imperial envoy to demand the adoption of new policies in Edo. Specifically, he sought the appointment of Hitotsu-bashi Keiki and Matsudaira Keiei to such offices as would give them a major voice in Bakufu decisions. To this another group, the *jōi* leaders, added a demand that the Shōgun should himself visit Kyōto to discuss 'affairs of state' (by which they meant steps to implement the expulsion policy), and within a few weeks the joint efforts of the two parties had secured the nomination of Ōhara Shigenori to perform the mission. He reached Edo at the beginning of July, escorted by Shimazu Hisamitsu and a force of Satsuma samurai.

A few days before this Kuze Hirochika had resigned, believing his position as head of the Rōjū to have been made untenable by the new developments. Andō had already been removed from office as a result of the wounds he had received in the Sakashita-mon attack earlier in the year. But many of the *fudai* and other officials proved more stubborn. In the proposed appointment of Hitotsubashi Keiki, especially, they saw a revival of the Mito plan to make him Shōgun, and this made them deaf to all Ōhara's arguments. Shimazu's entourage, however, led by Ōkubo Toshimichi and working closely with men from Owari, Mito, and Echizen, reinforced the appeal to reason by threats of assassination. This overcame all resistance—temporarily, at least. On 1 August Keiki was made *Shōgun-kōkenshoku* ('Guardian to the Shōgun'), an office usually filled only when the Shōgun was a minor, though Iemochi was now seventeen, and three days later Matsudaira Keiei was appointed *Seiji-sōsaishoku*, with powers equivalent to those of a Tairō. The changes were completed in the following month with the nomination of Matsudaira Katamori, the *kamon* lord of Aizu, to the post of *Kyōto-shugoshoku*. As such he was senior to the *Kyōto-shoshidai* and became responsible for the conduct of Bakufu relations with the Court.

When Ōhara departed, in mid-September 1862, the *kōbu-gattai* party seemed in a strong position. It had the co-operation of most of the senior Court nobles and the support of Satsuma, most powerful of the *tozama* fiefs. Its friends held new and responsible offices in Edo. Yet appearances were deceptive. Neither in Edo nor in Kyōto had the authority of the new leaders any stable foundation. Bakufu officials and anti-Bakufu extremists were alike in their reluctance to accept a compromise that put the reins of power in the hands of the great lords; and it needed only the defection of Shimazu to put the whole structure in danger.

---

[1] The narrative of political events in 1862–4 is given at length in *Ishin-shi*, vol. iii, and in somewhat less detail in *Gaikan Ishin-shi* (Mombushō, Tōkyō, 1944), pp. 406–606. Since both works are provided with an adequate index, detailed references to them will only be given where relevant to the discussion of particular problems.

Men like Iwakura Tomomi had never intended that the Ōhara mission should result in giving the *tozama* fiefs a preponderance of power.[1] Nor had most of the samurai in Kyōto. Their leaders, indeed, were drawn from the representatives of Chōshū, itself one of the great fiefs, but it did not therefore follow that they were in sympathy with the motives of the *kōbu-gattai* party. Its victory would bring them little benefit. In Chōshū, as previously in Mito, there was a growing division between the interests of the lord and those of his retainers. The latter were far more radical and sweeping in their plans.[2] Like others of the lesser samurai, they felt a bitter discontent at the conditions of their time—part economic and part political in its origins—which was directed against the régime as a whole, potentially even against the feudal basis of society, and manifested itself in a burning hatred of the Bakufu and of foreigners. To them, the results obtained by Ōhara were a gain for Satsuma, not for *jōi* policies. They wanted something more decisive. And since Shimazu's absence had enabled them to increase their influence at Court, they now began to prepare for a trial of strength.

It was these men, included among them some of his own retainers, that Shimazu found dominating Kyōto when he returned there from Edo at the end of September. He soon discovered that the senior *kuge* no longer had the means to hold them in check. He himself was preoccupied with other problems and could not afford to spend long in the capital.[3] For the time being, therefore, he abandoned the field, though before leaving for Kagoshima he warned the Court of the dangers that would attend any announcement of immediate expulsion. 'It is obvious', he wrote to the Kampaku, 'that the extremist samurai, on learning of such instructions, would become more and more active; and heedless of the fact that military preparations are yet incomplete, they would urge plans for a direct attack on such places as Yokohama and Nagasaki.'[4] To Shimazu such a policy seemed suicidal. To the samurai in Kyōto it seemed both desirable and necessary. Indeed, as soon as they were relieved once more of the restraining presence of Shimazu—whose troops, if not his arguments, were respected—they decided to press home their advantage. Early in November the Chōshū, Satsuma, and Tosa retainers still in the capital, apparently

[1] In the discussions at which Ōhara's instructions had been drawn up Iwakura had shown that while anxious to use the influence of Satsuma and Chōshū to overcome the Bakufu, he also wished to maintain some check on their growing power: see *Ishin-shi*, iii. 101–5. See also Document 31, pp. 198–200, in which he clearly shows his distrust of *tozama* ambitions.

[2] On the development of Chōshū policies in this period see especially Tokushige, 'Bakumatsu no taigai sensō shōri-ron', pp. 351–7, and Watanabe, 'Ishin no henkaku to Chōshū-han' (in *Meiji Ishin-shi kenkyū*, Shigakkai, Tōkyō, 1929), pp. 634–41.

[3] The prospects of a clash between Satsuma and Britain, due to the Namamugi incident (see below, pp. 64 ff.), made it highly desirable that he should return at once to his fief.

[4] Shimazu Hisamitsu to Konoe Tadahiro, 14 October 1862, in *Shimazu Hisamitsu Kō Jikki* (8 vols., Tōkyō, 1910), ii, ff. 50–56.

without the approval or authority of their lords, addressed a petition to the Court asking that decisive action be taken to ensure the immediate expulsion of foreigners. Almost at once it was announced that their chosen nominee, Sanjō Sanetomi, would be sent to Edo with orders to this effect. The step completed the discomfiture of the *kōbu-gattai* party by opening a rift between Hitotsubashi Keiki and Matsudaira Keiei and thereby increasing the difficulties with which they had already been faced in trying to carry out their policies.

The appointment of Keiki, Keiei, and Katamori had meant the promotion of some of the Shōgun's relatives to positions senior to any of those held by the *fudai*. Opposition to this had been overcome by threats of force from Satsuma, but suspicion and resentment had continued and were made manifest in the attempts of Bakufu officials to evade the logical consequences of the change. They hoped to make use of the *kōbu-gattai* party while denying it the reality of power. The Rōjū, especially, made this an opportunity to shift responsibility from their own shoulders to those of Keiki and Keiei; but although they consulted the two men on matters of day-to-day administration, they excluded them almost entirely from the secret discussions at which all important questions were decided. Some concessions they were compelled to make. The decision that the Shōgun must visit Kyōto was ratified and the date fixed for the spring of 1863. The *sankin-kōtai* regulations were revised to reduce the length of the periods which the great lords were required to spend in Edo and families of the *daimyō* were allowed to return to their fiefs. But beyond this they were not prepared to go. In particular, they were not willing to effect any fundamental change in the Bakufu's policy towards the Western Powers.

The attempt to formulate a new foreign policy was begun by Matsudaira Katamori on 8 November 1862. In a memorandum drawn up for discussion by the council[1] he pointed out that since hatred of foreigners was general, especially in Kyōto, any move to implement the rest of the 1858 treaties might well stir discontent to action. On the other hand, complete seclusion was undesirable and dangerous. It followed, he thought, that some measure of foreign intercourse must be maintained, for which purpose the ports of Nagasaki, Hakodate, and Yokohama should remain open; but a gesture must also be made to convince the Court of Bakufu sincerity in its protestations of a determination to effect foreign withdrawal. To accomplish this, all treaty stipulations that had not yet been carried out, including the promise to open Hyōgo, Ōsaka, and Edo and to permit foreigners to travel freely in Japan, must be publicly withdrawn.

This proposed compromise between *jōi* and *kaikoku* views was fiercely debated in Edo during the next few weeks. Matsudaira Keiei was for more drastic action still, urging that the treaties should be abrogated altogether, the ports closed, and the country put in a state of readiness for war. To him trade was best to be conducted by sending Japanese overseas. Most of the officials strongly disagreed. Led by the Rōjū Itakura Katsukiyo, they argued that to open the country was inevitable in face of foreign strength and was in any case a Bakufu responsibility to be decided without interference from the Court or *daimyō*. Keiki found himself isolated between the two factions. His own inclination was to accept Katamori's proposals and he succeeded after a time in persuading Keiei of the necessity of adopting a modified *kaikoku* policy in these terms. At this point, however, came news of Sanjō's mission and the instructions he would bring. Confronted with a choice between Imperial disapproval and foreign war, Keiei chose the latter as the lesser of two evils. He even threatened to resign if his recommendations were not followed.[1] Keiki, who lacked persistence for all his occasional stubbornness, attempted to do the same. Indeed, so great was the frustration and lack of self-confidence in Edo that both men began to talk of the Shōgun's resignation as being the only escape from an impossible dilemma.

The arrival of Sanjō in December did something to heal these divisions. His instructions, as a result of pressure from the Kampaku and Yamanouchi Toyoshige (of Tosa), now included a saving clause which provided that the methods and timing of carrying out 'expulsion' were to be left to Bakufu discretion. The Rōjū, moreover, rather than lose all support from Matsudaira Keiei, were willing to accept the Imperial commands as long as there remained a chance of evading their fulfilment. With some difficulty Keiki was persuaded to agree. On 24 January 1863, therefore, the Bakufu gave formal assent to the policy of expulsion, in a form of words sufficiently equivocal to gain at least the nominal support of all parties to the dispute.

The promises made to Sanjō were repeated and made more precise by Hitotsubashi Keiki when he went to Kyōto in February to make preparations for the Shōgun's visit. He arrived there very conscious of the weakness of his position. On the issue of foreign policy, as on much else, the Bakufu was itself divided, for the agreement of the previous month had been no more than a papering of the cracks. At the Court the *jōi* party was flushed with success, demanding an immediate announcement to fix the actual date of expulsion. The only hope of avoiding crisis, it was clear, lay in rallying the support of the *kōbu-gattai* lords. This proved impossible. Those closely associated with the Tokugawa family had already been summoned, but their disputes with the Rōjū made it difficult to secure concerted action, despite a common disapproval of the extremist views

---

[1] His letter of resignation, which contains a full account of his views and of the disputes with Keiki, is given as Document 40, pp. 227–34.

now dominant in the Imperial capital. Shimazu Hisamitsu, the one man capable of tipping the balance, had remained in Satsuma unwilling to risk another rebuff. He refused to move unless the Chōshū and Tosa leaders could first be expelled from Kyōto, which their influence with the *kuge* made unlikely, to say the least. Indeed, they not only maintained but even strengthened their position. In March their constant pressure and veiled threats secured the resignation of the Kampaku, Konoe Tadahiro, and his replacement by Takatsukasa Sukehiro, while by the end of the month Keiki and his colleagues had been forced to confess defeat and promise formally that negotiations to close the ports would be begun as soon as the Shōgun's visit had taken place.[1]

While foreign policy was thus becoming a symbol of the struggle for power in Kyōto, it was proving a very real and immediate problem to the officials left in Edo. Relations with Britain had deteriorated rapidly since the previous year and the two coutnries seemed to be moving towards open war. For the beginning of the dispute it is necessary to go back to June 1862, towards the end of which month the British legation at Tōzenji had again been attacked, this time by one of the samurai belonging to the guard. St. John Neale, chargé d'affaires in Alcock's absence, protested vigrously and withdrew from Edo, while the naval commanders prepared plans for a blockade and if necessary a bombardment of the Japanese coast.[2] Before any further action could be taken, however, the dispute became merged in yet another. On 14 September, as Shimazu Hisamitsu was returning to Kyōto after escorting the Ōhara mission, members of his escort attacked and killed an Englishman named Richardson near Namamugi on the Tōkaidō road. Neale's first step was to land troops to protect the settlement, meanwhile restraining the activities of the more revengeful foreign residents, but the situation became really serious when the Bakufu had to confess itself unable to punish or apprehend the murderers. The Satsuma men treated Bakufu demands with the utmost contempt. First they invented an imaginary attacker whom they claimed bore full responsibility and had subsequently escaped, then they insisted that the matter was one of feudal privilege in which the Bakufu had no right to interfere. In the circumstances Neale felt it best to await instructions from his government.

London's instructions concerning the Namamugi affair reached Yokohama in March 1863. They were much the most drastic ever sent to

---

[1] Document 41, p. 234.

[2] The plan was for demands on the Bakufu supported by the fleet, followed if necessary by direct negotiations with the Court; and were all this to fail, then the fleet would blockade Japanese ports on the Pacific seaboard and bombard coast batteries at selected points. See Ishii,' Bakumatsu ni okeru Eikoku kaigun no Nihon engan fūsa keikaku', *Rekishi Chiri*, lxxvi (1940), No. 1, pp. 35–44, and No. 2, pp. 111–23.

Japan.[1] From the Bakufu Neale was to demand a full formal apology and an indemnity of £100,000; and in the event of refusal the naval squadron was to take such measures 'of reprisal or blockade, or both' as seemed appropriate. This stemmed directly from the plans suggested to the Admiralty at the time of the second Tōzenji attack. Moreover, since the Bakufu seemed powerless against the defiance of Shimazu, Russell added, Neale was to treat directly with Satsuma in demanding from that fief an indemnity of £25,000 and the execution of the murderers in the presence of British officers. Once again naval action was to be the penalty for refusal.

With the last part of this plan Neale was in complete agreement, for he believed that by administering a sharp rebuke. to one of the great lords Britain would materially aid the Bakufu in its attempts to implement the treaties. On the other hand, he had less sympathy with the idea of blockading the Pacific coast ports generally. Such widespread operations, he thought, were likely to bring a disruption of trade that would more than outweigh the advantages to be gained. Still, it seemed probable that the Bakufu would in fact give way before threats and a show of force. If so, extreme measures would be unnecessary, and with this in mind he delayed his ultimatum until 6 April,[2] by which time Vice-Admiral Kuper had gathered a fleet of twelve ships at Yokohama.

Neale's uncompromising attitude did not come as a surprise to Satsuma or Edo. The possibility of a clash with Britain had been one of the factors contributing to Shimazu Hisamitsu's aloofness from the intrigues at Court, while the Rōjū had anticipated the demands early enough to advance the date of the Shōgun's departure for Kyōto and so ensure his absence when the crisis occurred. Nevertheless, the British ultimatum, coinciding as it did with the news that Keiki had already committed the Bakufu to a date for the expulsion of foreigners, widened the breach between the officials in Edo and those who were working on the Bakufu's behalf in the Imperial capital. The *jisha-bugyō*, *machi-bugyō*, and *kanjō-bugyō* submitted a joint memorandum criticizing the decision taken by Keiki about expulsion and urging the Shōgun to reverse it;[3] Mizuno Tadanori, now again retired after a brief period back in office, wrote to one of the Rōjū to recommend payment of the indemnity (for reasons that showed a remarkable blend of shrewdness and naïvety);[4] and the Rōjū Matsudaira Nobuyoshi and Inoue Masanao, in charge in Edo during the absence of the Shōgun and the rest of the council, sent post-haste to Kyōto for instructions. Meanwhile they persuaded Neale to extend the time limit set for their reply and

[1] Russell to Neale, 24 December 1862, printed in *Parliamentary Papers 1864*, vol. lxvi, pp. 179–80.

[2] See Neale to Bakufu, 6 April 1863 (Document 43, pp. 236–40).

[3] Document 42, pp. 234–6.

[4] Document 44, pp. 240–2.

issued orders to the fiefs that they were to make immediate preparations for hostilities.

Not unnaturally, news of these events gave added urgency to the negotiations then in progress at the Court. Matsudaira Keiei and Hitotsubashi Keiki had already appealed to the Kampaku to restrain the immoderate demands of the lesser *kuge*, only to be told, quite rightly, that the difficulties came not so much from the *kuge* as from the fiefs who backed them. At all events, an attempt to get a clear-cut confirmation of the Shōgun's authority ended in failure. At the beginning of May Shimazu Hisamitsu at last arrived in Kyōto and promptly rejected all the compromises made by other members of the *kōbu-gattai* party. When he found that they were unwilling to follow him in taking decisive action to crush the *sonnō-jōi* adherents, he informed both Court and Bakufu that their policies must lead inevitably to war and then departed once more to his fief. His action ended all pretence at unity. Within a few days Matsudaira Keiei, Date Muneki, and Yamanouchi Toyoshige had left the capital and Keiki was left alone to mediate between the *kuge* and Rōjū.

Nothing could now prevent the fixing of a date for expulsion. After some delay caused by unrest among the Bakufu officials, the day was fixed for 25 June and Keiki and the Rōjū thereafter concentrated on finding ways to avert the worst of the possible consequences. It is clear that they regarded the 'expulsion' of foreigners as something to be attempted in the first place by negotiation. It was to be accomplished by force only if all other measures failed. This had consistently been the Bakufu view ever since it had been so stated by the *Kyōto-shoshidai* in January 1861,[1] and it was implicit in the wording of the Bakufu's announcement of this new decision. The Bakufu statement to the feudal lords—unlike that made by the Court—implied that force was only to be used 'in the event of invasion',[2] while Keiki's instructions to the Rōjū in Edo followed the same pattern, despite an emphatic assertion that no delay or opposition would be tolerated from the reluctant officials.[3] Though direct evidence is lacking, indeed, this suggests that the Bakufu (and Keiki himself) still hoped to protract the negotiations until some more or less acceptable compromise could be worked out.

Support for this belief is to be found in the manœuvres leading up to payment of the Namamugi indemnity. The negotiation of this matter was entrusted not to the men left in Edo but to Ogasawara Nagamichi, who had risen to the rank of Rōjū largely by virtue of his loyalty to the *kōbu-gattai* party and whose presence in Kyōto during the discussions of

---

[1] See Document 34, at p. 207.

[2] The texts of both Court and Bakufu announcements (of 7 and 9 June 1863 respectively) are given in *Ishin-shi*, iii. 406.

[3] Keiki to Rōjū in Edo, 12 June 1863 (Document 46, pp. 246–8).

March and April made it certain that he would act in full knowledge of the political situation there. His views on foreign policy accorded closely with those of Matsudaira Katamori and Hitotsubashi Keiki. Expulsion, he thought, was dangerous and in the long run not to Japan's advantage. Full opening of the country, on the other hand, would be premature in the political and economic conditions then obtaining, which made it desirable that no more than three or four ports be opened for the time being. Yet he made it clear that he had little patience with the hesitation and vacillation being shown by his superiors. 'Simply to obey the Emperor's orders out of blind loyalty,' he wrote in May, 'making no attempt to assess their merits and demerits, would be the action of a woman.'[1] Since this statement was made immediately before his departure for Edo, his selection as the man to carry out the negotiations must cast some doubt on the sincerity of Keiki's protestations to the Court.

When Ogasawara reached Edo towards the end of May 1863 he found that the opposition of officials to the expulsion policy had in no way abated.[2] There were some, admittedly, who favoured both refusal of the indemnity and the initiation of expulsion negotiations, but these were largely to be found among the out-of-office, whose motives and attitudes were in many ways similar to those of the *rōnin* and the lesser samurai of the fiefs. They could without difficulty be disregarded. At the opposite extreme were the men who wanted not only payment of the indemnity but also rejection of the Imperial orders for expulsion, some even going so far as to suggest that the Shōgun should threaten resignation in an attempt to bring the Court to reason. To these Ogasawara pointed out that such a policy was as dangerous in its way as that of expulsion. If the Shōgun's resignation were accepted and the conduct of foreign affairs entrusted to the *tozama* lords the position would be worse than ever, for the Bakufu would lose all chance to exercise a moderating influence.[3] Yet a third group argued that independently of all other considerations it would still be best to pay the indemnity and so avert a clash with Britain. This done, the Bakufu could if necessary open negotiations with the foreigners on the wider issue, in the hope that an explanation of the political difficulties that had arisen would persuade them to accept peaceful withdrawal from the open ports. It was with this group that Ogasawara allied himself. On 7 June, when it became clear that Neale's patience was exhausted and no more delays would be permitted, he wrote jointly with the other Rōjū in Edo to promise that payment would begin on the 18th of the month. Shortly afterwards orders arrived from Keiki to the effect that the

[1] Document 45, at p. 246.
[2] On the views held by the officials at this time see *Ogasawara Iki-no-kami Nagamichi* (Tōkyō, 1943), pp. 166–7.
[3] See, for example, Document 47, pp. 248–50.

indemnity must not be paid, and these caused some confusion and misgivings, but on 24 June, now acting alone, Ogasawara went personally to
Yokohama and handed over the first instalment.

It is not easy to determine how far this step was really taken by Ogasawara on his own initiative. He himself asserted that it was,[1] and his
subsequent departure for Kyōto in July with a force of more than a thousand armed retainers, apparently in an attempt to strengthen the Shōgun's
hand at Court, bears witness that such resolution was by no means alien
to his character. Moreover, his claim that the decision was taken because
payment seemed a necessary preliminary to negotiations for closing the
ports is given some substance by the fact that immediately after handing
over the money to Neale he did try, though without success, to open discussions on the question of foreign withdrawal. On the other hand,
Ogasawara knew that his actions had powerful support. The senior Bakufu
officials, the *sanke*, and the *fudai* all regarded payment of the indemnity as
inevitable, despite their reluctance to associate themselves with its execution. There is even evidence that Keiki had foreknowledge of the course
that was to be followed.[2] As early as 6 May, while Ogasawara was still
in Kyōto, the matter had been discussed secretly with the Kampaku and
others at the Court and their approval obtained for making the payment.
In the light of this agreement Keiki's subsequent orders have been described by one Japanese historian as mere camouflage, 'donning a *jōi*
mask' for his own protection.[3] Certainly his report to Kyōto[4] must be
accounted more alibi than explanation. His journey from the capital was
suspiciously slow even for a man travelling in considerable state, which
suggests that he had no desire to arrive in Edo in time to assume personal
responsibility, while his actions on reaching there were not characterized
by any urgent efforts to prevent a contingency that must have seemed at
least a possibility. By his own account, after all, Keiki was in Kanagawa
on the day before payment was made.

Whether or not Keiki and Ogasawara were acting in collusion, the
incident does nothing to indicate that the Bakufu really planned to
present the foreigners with a clear-cut choice between negotiated withdrawal and open war. Rather, as events soon showed, the demand for the
closing of the ports rapidly became a plea for the closing of the one port
of Yokohama. Before that, however, two of the great fiefs had revealed
themselves as willing to act independently of the Bakufu in foreign affairs
and even to incur the risk of hostilities in so doing.

Because the Bakufu had capitulated to British demands for an in-

---

[1] The memorandum Ogasawara wrote to justify his actions is given as Document 49, pp. 254–6.
[2] See *Ishin-shi*, iii. 470. [3] Ōtsuka, *Bakumatsu no gaikō*, p. 61.
[4] Document 48, pp. 250–3.

demnity in the Namamugi dispute it did not follow that Satsuma would do the same. Its attitude throughout had been defiant, nor did it now show any signs of wavering. In August, therefore, having successfully carried out the first part of his instructions without precipitating war, St. John Neale turned his attention to this further problem. On the 6th he left Yokohama for Kagoshima, accompanied by the admiral and a squadron of seven ships, and on arrival there five days later he presented an ultimatum embodying the demands drawn up in London. The Satsuma reply was evasive and unsatisfactory. Neale at once ordered seizure of the three Satsuma vessels lying in the anchorage, the total value of which was considerably more than the indemnity demanded, but in moving to carry out these orders the squadron became involved in a gunnery engagement with the Kagoshima batteries. In the heavy firing that followed much damage was inflicted ashore as well as to the Satsuma ships. The squadron itself also suffered damage, however, enough to make repairs necessary, and on 17 August the force withdrew from Kagoshima Bay and returned to Yokohama to prepare for a second attack. This proved in the end to be unnecessary, for in November Satsuma opened negotiations through its Edo representative, Iwashita Sajiemon, and after some discussion agreed to pay the indemnity. Payment, in fact, was no great hardship. Shimazu was able to persuade (or coerce) the Bakufu into granting him a loan for the purpose, while in other respects the final agreement, concluded on 11 December 1863, was definitely advantageous to him. In return for a written undertaking that the Namamugi offenders, if and when found, would be punished in the presence of British officers,[1] Neale promised that his government would give favourable consideration to Satsuma's request for British help in buying foreign-built warships.

The fact that Satsuma had escaped so lightly (and despite the virtual destruction of Kagoshima could be popularly credited with a military victory in driving off the British squadron) did nothing to raise the Bakufu's prestige. Still more serious in its results, however, had been the action of Chōshū during the same period. On 25 June 1863, the date which had been fixed for the 'expulsion' of foreigners in the discussions between Keiki and the *jōi* party at Kyōto, two Chōshū steamers had fired on an American ship passing through the Shimonoseki Straits. In the weeks that followed there were similar incidents involving ships of France and Holland. In spite of small-scale punitive action by the French and American naval commanders, the Straits were for some months effectively

---

[1] No further steps to ensure their punishment appear to have been taken by either side. Indeed the offenders had actually taken part in the negotiations with Neale at Kagoshima that had preceded the bombardment in August! See Ōtsuka, *Bakumatsu no gaikō*, p. 64. An account of the Edo discussions will be found in *Ishin-shi*, iii. 504–9.

closed to foreign commerce; and since they formed the most direct route between Shanghai and Yokohama this produced immediate and threatening protests from the representatives of the Western Powers. The Bakufu had to confess itself helpless. Chōshū contended that it was only acting in accordance with the orders it had received from Edo and the Court, on the assumption that any negotiations thought necessary would already have been completed by the date fixed for expulsion.[1] This, of course, was untrue, since the whole incident was obviously designed to force the Bakufu's hand. But the Bakufu officials were only too conscious that their own actions during the Kyōto discussions would not bear much examination and they had no wish to explain them in detail to the foreign envoys. They therefore attempted to put the whole responsibility on the Imperial Court. The explanation they gave was hardly a satisfactory one—and its later repercussions on the question of Imperial prerogatives only added to the Bakufu's difficulties—but for the time an outbreak of hostilities was avoided, chiefly because Neale was still reluctant to take any action that might endanger the trade and the other Western diplomats were unwilling to risk war without specific instructions from their governments.

The events of July and August had an important effect on politics in the Imperial capital. The *sonnō-jōi* party rejoiced exceedingly at these 'victories' over the barbarian and both Satsuma and Chōshū were officially commended for their actions by the Court. On the other hand, the Chōshū leaders now became over-confident and thereby alienated many of their new-found allies. Satsuma had never been one of these, of course, but it was none the less unwise of Chōshū to use its influence with the *kuge* to exclude members of that fief from guard duties at the Palace. Such action could only embitter the existing rivalry between the two great western fiefs. Still more unwise was the plan for Imperial resumption of direct responsibility for the country's administration, active preparations for which were being pushed forward during September. The Emperor himself opposed it, and even appealed to Shimazu Hisamitsu for help in preventing it, while many of the lords who had favoured foreign withdrawal and administrative reform were still not willing to take part in the dissolution of the Bakufu. The result was that the *kōbu-gattai* party again began to rally. The lead was taken by the *Kyōto-shugoshoku*, Matsudaira Katamori of Aizu, and Prince Asahiko, a member of the Imperial family who had been playing an increasing part in discussions at the Court, and on 30 September these men, with troops from Satsuma and Aizu and the tacit support of the Emperor and senior nobles, carried out a *coup d'état*. In November the victory was confirmed by the arrival of Shimazu Hisamitsu at the head of 15,000 men.

[1] The text of the Chōshū report, dated 20 July 1863, together with a Bakufu minute thereon, is given in *Kawakatsu-ke Monjo* (Nihon Shiseki Kyōkai series, Tōkyō, 1930), pp. 278–81.

Although the Chōshū leaders had been driven from the capital, together with their chief allies among the *kuge*, power had not been seized by the Bakufu as such. Nor was there any immediate reversal of the Court's stand on foreign affairs. On the very day after the *coup d'état* an Imperial letter demanded explanations for the Bakufu's delay in carrying out expulsion, and the Rōjū Sakai Tadashige, sent to Kyōto to discuss this question during October, returned convinced that nothing less than the closing of Yokohama would satisfy the Emperor and his advisers. Yet this was none the less a gain of sorts. The idea of closing Yokohama was itself a Bakufu suggestion, formulated in Edo during the summer as an alternative to complete expulsion, and its acceptance by Kyōto might bring a fair measure of agreement. What was more, the fact that Yokohama was the channel for something like 80 per cent. of Japan's foreign trade meant that its closing would substantially reduce the impact of trade on the national economy, which had long been an important objective of Bakufu policy. Equally, of course, this circumstance ensured the hostility of the foreign envoys. The next step, therefore, was to find a way of circumventing the difficulty that this presented.

The Bakufu saw its solution in a repetition of the technique that had been so successful in 1862. The new *démarche*—though 'new' is perhaps a misleading description for something that bore all the hall-marks of earlier Japanese thinking on diplomacy—was to take the form of another embassy to Europe. The envoys, led by the *gaikoku-bugyō* Ikeda Nagaaki, were to exert themselves to secure consent for the closing of Yokohama by advancing arguments essentially similar to those used by Takeuchi in negotiating the London Protocol, though this time the scene of negotiations would be France, whose representatives in Japan seemed more disposed to listen than those of other countries. As many of the officials must have realized, of course, the prospects of success were not very great. Even France, reluctant as she was to undertake new burdens in the Far East at a time when her resources were already stretched to the utmost in Europe and elsewhere, was hardly likely to agree to such a proposal. Still less so were the other Powers. On the other hand, the prospect of failure did not necessarily make the attempt itself valueless. Such a mission would take time to complete whatever its results, and time above all things was what Edo sought to gain, especially since events seemed to be moving in its favour. The fact that envoys had been sent to Europe would justify the Bakufu in taking no further action until their return, which meant that there would be a lengthy interval to effect a settlement of outstanding problems with the more receptive leaders now in power in Kyōto. This was probably in large part the motive for the negotiations.[1]

[1] On the subject of Bakufu motives in this affair see *Ishin-shi*, iv. 223–6, and Ōtsuka, *Bakumatsu no gaikō*, pp. 68–69. Ikeda's memorial asking for instructions and the Bakufu reply to it do

It is not surprising to find, therefore, that February 1864 saw both the departure of Ikeda for France and that of the Shōgun for Kyōto. This time the Shōgun's visit was designed to exploit an advantage, not to stave off crisis, and some important preparatory work had already been completed in the Imperial capital by the *kōbu-gattai* lords, including the replacement of Takatsukasa by Nijō Nariaki as Kampaku and the dismissal of twenty-one Court officials who had been closely associated with Chōshū. The great lords themselves—Hitotsubashi Keiki, Matsudaira Keiei, Matsudaira Katamori, Yamanouchi Toyoshige, Date Muneki, and Shimazu Hisamitsu—had been admitted formally to participation in the Palace councils, a step entirely without precedent. The *tozama* members of the group also wished to take part in Bakufu discussions, on the grounds that this would make their mediation more effective. In fact the attempt proved a source of division rather than of unity. It was possible for Bakufu and feudal lords to work together against a common enemy, the *sonnō-jōi* extremists of Kyōto and Chōshū; but the move to force Edo into sharing its privileges and responsibilities revealed the existence of a deep rift between the two. Keiki himself suspected Shimazu of seeking something more than a mere share of power. So did the Rōjū. The latter, moreover, still retained their former doubts about Keiki and his presumed ambition to become Shōgun. The result was that they offered stubborn opposition to every change that was proposed, including that of admitting Satsuma to the Shōgun's council, and Keiki's failure to control them convinced Shimazu that Keiki had made common cause with the Rōjū in seeking to exploit the *kōbu-gattai* victory in the interests of Bakufu authority. It was in this atmosphere that the new discussions of foreign policy took place.

On 28 February, six days after the Shōgun's arrival in Kyōto, the Emperor handed him a formal statement of the Court's views on foreign affairs. This, together with a more detailed letter on the same subject on 5 March,[1] made it clear that there was no longer any insistence on immediate and forcible expulsion. The emphasis was on the completion of military preparations against the day when Japan would be able to manifest her independence of the foreigner. So great was the disparity between this and former announcements that it gave rise to widespread rumours that the letters did not in fact represent the wishes of the Emperor. Certainly there was evidence to show that they had been drafted under the influence of the Satsuma leaders,[2] an impression which was strengthened by Shimazu's attitude in the conferences that followed between the *kōbu-gattai* lords. In discussing the reply the Shōgun was to send, Shimazu

nothing to contradict the suggestion that the desire to gain time played an important part: see Document 50, pp. 260–3.

[1] The two letters are given as Documents 51 and 52, pp. 263–6.

[2] See, for example, the account of these events written by Hara Tadanari, one of Keiki's retainers: Document 54, at pp. 268–9.

argued that the time had come to drop all pretence that expulsion was possible and to withdraw the promises which had been made on this subject to the Court, even including the one about closing Yokohama. This accorded well enough with Satsuma's growing interest in foreign trade and was in any case the policy which Shimazu had advocated consistently since 1862. More surprising, at first sight, is the fact that Keiki objected. Formal adoption of such a policy, with the Court's approval, would have relieved the Bakufu of some of its most pressing difficulties. Granted always that the Bakufu idea of a *kaikoku* policy involved the limitation of trade to something like the scale envisaged in the Dutch treaty of 1857—and that the closing of Yokohama would substantially achieve that end—the difference of view between Keiki and Shimazu is still not sufficient to explain the dispute. Indeed, it can only be understood in the light of underlying motives of domestic politics. His resentment of Satsuma's dominant position in the Court led Keiki to resist Shimazu's assumption of leadership generally, while he apparently believed also that Bakufu prestige would suffer yet another set-back if, having given way to Chōshū insistence on expulsion one year, it reversed its policy at the behest of Satsuma the next.

Since Shimazu had not at this stage been admitted to the Shōgun's council, because of the opposition of the Rōjū, Keiki's view prevailed in the drafting of the Bakufu reply.[1] The reply took the form of an acceptance of the Imperial commands, emphasizing that expulsion would not be carried out by force and referring in rather vague terms to the possibility of closing Yokohama, and it was rather surprisingly challenged by the Court. The nature of the Court's objections suggests that Satsuma influence was less than Keiki had supposed, or at least that Shimazu's liaison with the *kuge* was extraordinarily bad. At all events the Court's action precipitated an open dispute. Keiki, perhaps because the meeting took place in the Emperor's presence, at once offered to submit a supplementary statement that would give a more precise definition of Bakufu intentions. Shimazu showed no such inhibitions. He insisted that Yokohama must not be closed; and he continued the argument next day in the Bakufu council at Nijō Castle, to which he was now admitted by authority of Matsudaira Keiei. The quarrel ended that afternoon in a most undignified scene at Prince Asahiko's residence. Keiki, who by most accounts is described as being drunk at the time,[2] poured upon Date and Shimazu a torrent of abuse and announced his intention of sending to the Court

[1] Document 53, pp. 266–7.
[2] Hara Tadanari's account of these events (Document 54, pp. 270–2) attributes to Keiki motives which one must suspect as being Hara's own and omits all mention of the fact that he was drunk, but its general picture of what happened is confirmed by other evidence: see especially *Date Muneki Zaikyō Nikki* (Nihon Shiseki Kyōkai series, Tōkyō, 1916), pp. 337–42. It also affords an interesting example of the complexity of Kyōto politics.

a letter of the kind that he had promised the previous day, reasserting the Bakufu's determination to close the port of Yokohama. This he did on 26 March 1864.[1]

In so far as this incident relates directly to foreign affairs, it serves to show that the Bakufu still chose to pay lip-service to the idea of expulsion—in its new and modified form of closing Yokohama—rather than to risk an attempt to convince the Court of the need for fundamental change, as advocated by Shimazu. In part this sprang from a belief that the passage of time would change the views of Kyōto as it had already changed those of Edo. In part it was due to a desire to preserve the Bakufu's prerogatives. It was this that most seriously handicapped the efforts to work out a national policy towards the West. The Bakufu was no more willing to transfer its power to Satsuma than it was to Chōshū and the *jōi* party, yet without Satsuma support it could not hope to overcome Imperial opposition. Keiki preferred to put his trust in the possibility of successful negotiations with the Treaty Powers.

After the quarrel with Shimazu, therefore, which again broke up the *kōbu-gattai* coalition and caused the great lords to resign their dignities at Court and retire to their fiefs, Keiki and the Rōjū turned their attention to the problem of discussions with the foreign envoys. Pending the return of Ikeda from France the question of Yokohama could be left in abeyance, but foreign demands for the punishment of Chōshū could not much longer be ignored. These had taken on a new insistence after Rutherford Alcock returned to his duties in Japan at the beginning of March. Alcock, having obtained copies of the letters exchanged between the Emperor and Shōgun, was convinced that only firm action on the part of the Western Powers could avert a general war. Moreover, the risk of disrupting trade was now far less of a deterrent to him than in the previous year, since recent Bakufu restrictions had in any case brought the trade of Yokohama virtually to a standstill.[2] He therefore urged the Treaty Powers to send a punitive expedition against Chōshū. This, he thought, would solve many problems, for it would convince the leaders of the *jōi* movement of the futility of attempting expulsion and so reduce pressure on the Bakufu. It was the same argument he had used to justify the attack on Satsuma the year before, but it was not much to the taste of his government, which did not want to find itself involved in another war as costly as that which had recently taken place in China. Nor was the proposal welcomed by the new French representative in Japan, Léon Roches. Russell's instructions from London, however, arrived too late to affect the issue, while Roches was eventually persuaded to join in a four-Power protest to the Bakufu without

---

[1] Document 55, pp. 272–3.
[2] See Ishii, *Bakumatsu no gaikō*, pp. 110–12. The new restrictive policy consisted of a fresh attempt to enforce the monopolies decreed in May 1860: see above, pp. 50–51.

actually committing himself to any subsequent action. Thus on 30 May 1863, under Alcock's leadership, the ministers of France, Britain, Holland, and America forwarded letters to the Bakufu demanding early action to reopen the Shimonoseki Straits and to punish Chōshū for its attacks on foreign ships.

The Bakufu reply to this demand was delayed for several weeks pending return of the Shōgun from Kyōto. After the withdrawal of the great lords Keiki had had some difficulty in resisting renewed demands for expulsion from the *jōi* party, but at the cost of repeating and re-emphasizing the promise to close Yokohama he had succeeded in obtaining an Imperial decree ratifying the Shōgun's powers as head of the administration.[1] This committed him to the attempt, despite opposition from the Edo officials. On 30 June, therefore, the foreign representatives were informed that domestic unrest necessitated a postponement of any action against Chōshū and that only the closing of Yokohama was likely to pacify the unrest sufficiently to make further progress possible. It was a reply they were quite unwilling to accept. Roches now abandoned his objections to the Chōshū expedition, partly because he saw that the Bakufu could take no action for itself and partly for fear that if France held aloof she would be unable to share in any benefits accruing from the negotiations which would follow, and on 22 July 1864 the four ministers sent a joint ultimatum to Edo threatening to use force against Chōshū unless the Bakufu gave evidence of so doing within twenty days. The request for the closing of Yokohama was rejected out of hand. Indeed, the statement added, the course of events might leave the Treaty Powers no choice but to withdraw the concessions granted in the London Protocol and insist on full execution of the 1858 treaties.

By the middle of August there was no longer any hope of compromise and the joint fleet was ready to sail. Before it could do so, however, Ikeda Nagaaki and his colleagues returned unexpectedly from Paris with news of the agreement they had signed.[2] Not only had they failed to secure French consent to the closing of Yokohama, but they had also returned much too quickly to give the Bakufu the breathing-space it had expected. These facts alone would probably have ensured their punishment. As it was, they had made a number of concessions which were highly embarrassing in view of what had happened in Japan since their departure. Finding the French government adamant on the subject of Yokohama—and even ready to insist that in recompense for injuries suffered by the foreign ships, the trade there and at the other two ports should be made free of duty—

[1] *Ishin-shi*, iii. 709–11. See also Murdoch, *History of Japan* (3 vols., London, 1903–26), iii. 738–9. Murdoch's account of this period generally, though somewhat highly coloured, contains much useful detail.

[2] The text of the convention is given as Document 56, pp. 273–4, and Ikeda's report as Document 57, pp. 274–82.

Ikeda had at last agreed that the Bakufu and Chōshū would pay cash indemnities for the damage to French ships at Shimonoseki and that action would be taken to reopen the straits, if necessary by force and with French naval assistance. These stipulations, quite outside the scope of his instructions though they were, he justified as the first step towards a complete reorientation of Bakufu policy.[1] As a suggestion it was not well timed. He and his colleagues were promptly relieved of their posts and their actions were formally disavowed.

Events now moved swiftly. Finding the Bakufu unwilling to accept the terms laid down in Paris, a refusal explained on the grounds that such 'disgrace' would precipitate civil war and so cause a final rupture with the West, the four ministers proceeded with the plan to bombard Shimonoseki. By 5 September the combined fleet, consisting in all of seventeen ships, was in the straits. Both the Bakufu and Chōshū sought desperately to avert hostilities by last-minute negotiations, but they had left their attempt too late and in the week that followed the attack was carried out. The batteries were silenced by gunfire, then captured and destroyed by a landing force of over 2,000 men. On 14 September Chōshū capitulated.

There remained the question of negotiations. By the armistice agreement, concluded by the naval commanders at Shimonoseki, the straits had been opened and facilities promised for the use of foreign ships passing through, while Chōshū had undertaken not to repair or rebuild the dismantled batteries. In Yokohama, soon after, in an interview with the *gaikoku-bugyō* Takemoto Masao, the four ministers explained the terms to be demanded of the Bakufu.[2] Since it was clear that Chōshū had acted under orders from Kyōto and Edo, they said, copies of these orders having been obtained from Chōshū during the armistice discussions, the Bakufu must be held responsible for the compensation required and for the costs of the expedition. Details were worked out in conversations with the Rōjū and embodied in a convention signed on 22 October 1864.[3] It provided for an indemnity of three million dollars, to be paid by the Bakufu as compensation for the attacks on shipping, ransom for the city of Shimonoseki, and costs of the punitive expedition. This was, of course, out of all proportion to the damage that had been suffered. It was also more than the Bakufu could reasonably be expected to raise when it was already in desperate financial straits. The fact was fully appreciated by the Western representatives. Their real motive was not so much to obtain the money

---

[1] In addition to his formal report on the mission, Ikeda also submitted on his return a series of memorials advocating among other points the conclusion of new treaties with countries in Asia and Europe, the dispatch of both resident ministers and students abroad, and the raising of restrictions that prevented Japanese from going overseas to trade and travel. The texts are given in *Bakumatsu Ishin Gaikō Shiryō Shūsei* (6 vols., Tōkyō, 1942–4), vi. 141–50, and *Zoku saimukiji* (Nihon Shiseki Kyōkai series, 6 vols., Tōkyō, 1921–2), iii. 199–217.

[2] See Document 58, pp. 282–8. [3] Document 59, pp. 288–9.

as to use it as a lever through which they could exact commercial advantages, for which reason the convention laid it down that the Powers would be willing to consider waiving the whole of the indemnity if the Bakufu offered to open Shimonoseki or some other equivalent port to foreign trade.

The Shimonoseki indemnity convention spelled total failure for the Bakufu's attempt to negotiate the closing of Yokohama. Far from reducing the outlets for foreign trade, it now faced the necessity of increasing them or else of paying an enormous indemnity. More ominous still, the foreigners had threatened to revoke the London Protocol, which would entail the immediate opening of Hyōgo, Ōsaka, and Edo, and to seek ratification of the treaties by direct negotiation with the Imperial Court and the *tozama* lords. Within Japan the position was no better. Satsuma and Chōshū had defied both the ultimatums of the West and the authority of the Bakufu. Both had suffered defeat, but it was at the hands of the foreigners and did nothing to restore the Bakufu's prestige. Meanwhile Edo had thrown away the one feasible chance of working out a practicable foreign policy by its refusal to sacrifice some part of its prerogatives in an alliance with Shimazu Hisamitsu. It is true that this might not have long postponed its fall, but rejection of it meant that at the end of 1864 there was already developing an anti-Bakufu alliance that would for the first time include the great *daimyō* as well as Court, *rōnin*, and lesser samurai.

6. '*A stick to beat the Bakufu*': foreign affairs in 1865–7

The last three years of Tokugawa rule witnessed important changes in the attitudes of the Western Powers and also in that of the domestic opposition within Japan. The two had been, and continued to be, related. Western policy since about 1860, under British leadership, had been based on a belief that the Bakufu was not only the legitimate and treaty-making government but also the authority in Japan most favourable to the development of foreign intercourse. The opposition, by the same token, was branded as at once rebellious and anti-foreign. Both international law and reasons of self-interest therefore led the Powers to support the Shōgun against his opponents, even to the point of offering him military assistance (provision for which, for example, had been embodied in the abortive Paris agreement of 1864), and when that was refused of taking action against Satsuma and Chōshū in such a way as might be expected to strengthen the Bakufu's position as well as serve the ends of trade. The very necessity for these steps, however, began to raise doubts about the assumptions on which they had been based. The fact that the Powers themselves had to conduct operations against the Shōgun's defiant vassals called in question the Bakufu's right to be regarded as a government *de facto*; while increasing knowledge of Japanese politics brought a realization that there was a powerful faction in Japan which denied Edo's right to govern *de jure*. It was a circumstance that resulted in a re-examination of the principles of Western policy and a growing divergence between the policies of France and Britain.

France, in the person of Léon Roches, the new minister resident in Edo, continued to take the stand that the Shōgun governed as of right. It followed that he was entitled to all the support the foreigners could give, both morally and materially, and that the Powers should moderate their demands upon Japan in order to avoid increasing the difficulties with which his government was already faced. It was not a new argument, though it was now carried farther than it had been before. What was new, rather, was the specific objective it was designed to attain. France, as Roches well knew, could not compete in the Japan trade on equal terms with Britain. If she were to compete at all, she must find means of counteracting the disparity of economic power between the two. This, he thought, it might be possible to accomplish. By establishing close relations with the Bakufu officials and offering them the help and friendship of France in the struggle with their enemies at home, he could secure for himself and for his country a position of considerable influence at Edo. It would then be possible to exploit this advantage in terms of trade. The strengthening of the Bakufu in military equipment and techniques, an obvious need if it were to exert its authority against the great fiefs, would involve considerable purchases abroad. These would probably be made in France, if France had shown herself a friend. Moreover, the continuing practice of government monopoly in Japan made the Bakufu itself a potentially valuable customer in other ways, one whose sales and purchases could be directly affected by political decisions.

The first step in the new direction was taken early in 1865.[1] Roches had by that time been in Japan less than a year, but through his interpreter, Mermet de Cachon, he had already secured the co-operation of a number of the Tokugawa officials and in February they formally requested French help in building a naval dockyard at Yokosuka. France was to provide the necessary engineers, machinery, and instructors, while in return she was to receive large deliveries of silk exported by the Bakufu on its own account. The pattern was rapidly extended in the years that followed. A French school was established at Yokohama, to teach history, geography, and mathematics in addition to language; large quantities of weapons, including artillery, were supplied for the campaign against Chōshū; naval instruction was begun aboard a Japanese warship in Edo Bay (though this was soon terminated because of British resentment); and a military

---

[1] A detailed account of Roches's policy and actions is given in Ōtsuka, 'Fukkoku kōshi Leon Roches no seisaku kōdō ni tsuite', *Shigaku Zasshi*, xlvi (1935), pp. 809–50, 982–1001. See also Ishii, *Bakumatsu no gaikō*, pp. 156–60, 165–7.

mission was eventually sent from France to advise on the modernization and training of the Shōgun's army. The arrangements that were to make possible the financing of all this were completed in September 1866 with the creation of a new company, under official sponsorship, to conduct the whole of Franco-Japanese trade. Thus by 1867, as a consequence of the policy pursued by Roches, French commercial transactions in Japan had for the first time reached really sizeable proportions.

Against the methods which had been used to achieve this success Britain protested vigorously both in Edo and in Paris. Her objections, however, did not arise solely from differences over economic theory or even from the potential threat to her trade. In the hands of her new representative, Harry Parkes, who succeeded Alcock in 1865, the whole of British policy towards Japan was taking a course directly contrary to that evolved by Roches. This was first made evident in the year of his arrival by the dispute over Imperial ratification of the treaties.

The foreign envoys had for some time suspected that the shadowy figure of the Emperor in Kyōto was something more than a 'spiritual ruler' without temporal authority. In 1863, for example, the American minister had reported his opinion that the Emperor was both practically and theoretically the real sovereign of Japan, from which it followed that the treaties were valid only for the Shōgun's own domains and would not be binding on the great lords until the Court confirmed them. His government tried, without success, to engage the other Treaty Powers in common action to obtain such confirmation. None the less, his reading of the facts received strong support from the events of 1863–4—not least from the arguments the Bakufu advanced to explain its inability to enforce the treaties—and the idea was revived after the Shimonoseki bombardment by Rutherford Alcock, who used the threat of appeal to Kyōto as a means of forcing Bakufu compliance with the demands then made.[1] On this occasion drastic action did not prove necessary, but in 1865 the question came up again and Imperial ratification was this time made an important object of British policy. In April the Bakufu informed the foreign representatives that it had decided to pay the Shimonoseki indemnity, being quite unable to open another port as had been proposed by way of alternative in the convention of October 1864,[2] but asked that the second and subsequent instalments might be postponed for a year in view of the difficulty being encountered in raising money. This request the four ministers decided to refer to their respective governments. In reporting

[1] See Document 58, at pp. 285–6. Alcock's earlier statements on the subject had been even more clear-cut: see Document 36, pp. 213–5.

[2] Document 59, pp. 288–9. On the indemnity payments themselves see Watanabe, 'Shimonoseki shōkin no shiharai ni tsuite', *Shien*, iv (1930), pp. 1–17. The best account of the incident as a whole, including the subsequent negotiations at Hyōgo and Ōsaka, is given in Ōtsuka, *Bakumatsu no gaikō*, pp. 85–93.

the matter to London, however, Winchester, who had become British chargé d'affaires pending the arrival of Parkes to take up his appointment, proposed a rather different basis of discussion. It was his belief that the Bakufu could only pay the indemnity by putting new burdens on the trade. Since this was obviously undesirable, he thought it would be best to accept payment of the first instalment and then to offer to waive all claim to the remainder in return for the following concessions: (1) the opening of Hyōgo on 1 January 1866, (2) imperial ratification of the treaties, (3) a general reduction of import duties. The plan was in full accord with the motives that had caused the foreign representatives to set their indemnity demands at so high a figure and was accepted by Lord Russell. In July he incorporated it in his instructions to Parkes, with the result that the Emperor's status now came formally into question in diplomatic negotiations with the Bakufu.

Russell's instructions reached Parkes in October 1865. He at once began to discuss them with his colleagues, and despite French objections the proposal was put to the Japanese government later in the month.[1] At the same time it was decided to transfer the scene of negotiations to Ōsaka, since the Shōgun and most of his council were there and it was argued that the presence of an allied squadron would give them valuable moral support in their attempt to concert measures for punitive action against Chōshū. In reality, whatever the motives that inspired it, the move destroyed one of the few tactical advantages the Bakufu had so far possessed in its handling of foreign affairs. As long as discussions with the Court took place in Kyōto and those with the Powers took place in Edo, the Bakufu, as the sole connecting link between the two, had been able with relative impunity to make simultaneous and contradictory promises concerning expulsion and foreign trade. This became very much more difficult with the appearance of Western diplomats less than thirty miles from the Imperial capital, in a city thronged with samurai from the great *tozama* fiefs.[2] Not only were secret agreements virtually impossible in such circumstances, but also the officials could no longer argue the difficulty of communications as a reason for delay. Robbed thus of its familiar methods of avoiding—or at least postponing—crisis, it is not very surprising that at one point in the negotiations the Bakufu was gripped by panic and confusion.

On 7 November Ogasawara Nagamichi, now restored to office, met the French and British interpreters at Ōsaka and received a copy of the letter in which the ministers set out their demands. If no reply were forth-

---

[1] Document 60, pp. 293–6.

[2] Ōsaka, as a great commercial and financial centre, handled most of the dealings in rice, including disposal of the rice revenues of the fiefs. Hence most large fiefs kept permanent establishments there, which in this period were as much engaged in politics as in commerce.

coming within seven days, he was told, they would proceed to Kyōto and negotiate directly with the Court. Four days later the Rōjū Abe Masatō took charge of the discussions and had an interview with the British, Dutch, and American representatives aboard the British flagship,[1] at which he agreed in principle to tariff revision and to the need for Imperial ratification of the treaties, but emphasized the difficulty of opening Hyōgo in view of the immediate opposition such a step would arouse in the country at large. His arguments had no effect on Parkes, however, and on 13 November the Bakufu council, meeting at Ōsaka in the presence of the Shōgun, decided that it had no option but to accept the foreign terms. Yet the decision was reversed again within a matter of hours. At dawn on the 14th Hitotsubashi Keiki arrived from Kyōto and at once demanded that a fresh council be summoned to hear his views. To act in this matter without consulting the Imperial Court, he said, would destroy the measure of co-operation between Court and Bakufu that had been so painfully achieved in recent months and would put an end to all hope of controlling the great lords. He gained his point, and it was decided to ask the ministers for more time in which to seek the approval of Kyōto. Later in the day, despite some biting comments from Parkes on the subject of Bakufu negligence and lack of spirit, the request was granted and 24 November was set as the new date for a reply.

Everything now turned on the attitude of Kyōto. When he returned there on 15 November Keiki found the city full of rumours about what had been taking place in Ōsaka. Some believed that the foreign fleet had come with Bakufu connivance, others that the Rōjū intended to open Hyōgo without attempting to obtain the Court's approval. The task of persuading the Emperor's advisers that Imperial ratification of the treaties had become an unavoidable necessity, not easy at best, was made more difficult still by the mounting excitement. It was also complicated by the Satsuma assertion that no decision should be taken without consulting the great lords.[2] Satsuma influence with the Court was unimpaired and nothing had been done to improve the fief's relations with the Bakufu since the quarrel over expulsion eighteen months before,[3] while the men who now represented Shimazu, notably Ōkubo Toshimichi, had little sympathy with the *kōbu-gattai* policy followed in the past. They opposed the Bakufu at every opportunity. Kyōto's reaction to the situation, therefore, was not compliance with Keiki's request but an unprecedented act of interference in Bakufu administration. On 17 November orders were issued calling for the dismissal and punishment of Abe Masatō and

---

[1] Throughout these negotiations Roches held aloof from his colleagues and attempted to act as mediator between Britain and Japan.

[2] See Document 61, pp. 296–7.

[3] See above, pp. 64–66.

Matsumae Takahiro, the two Rōjū who were popularly regarded as responsible for the decision to open Hyōgo.

This caused consternation in Ōsaka. Voices were again raised in the council urging the Shōgun's resignation as the only escape from the dilemma (meaning, perhaps, that the threat of resignation might convince even the Court of the need to accept foreign demands)[1] and a letter was sent to Kyōto announcing his wish to lay down office. It was accompanied by a memorandum arguing the case for opening Hyōgo and granting Imperial sanction for the treaties.[2] The impact of this on the senior *kuge* was considerable, while a strongly worded note from Parkes,[3] written when he heard news of the dismissal of the two Rōjū, helped to stimulate the Bakufu into fresh efforts to overcome the opposition. Even so, the Palace conference in Kyōto on 21 November was unable to reach a decision. That night a plan was made to send Ōhara Shigenori to the foreign envoys at Hyōgo as a direct emissary of the Court, accompanied by a Satsuma escort,[4] but this attempt to exclude the Bakufu altogether from the negotiations was bitterly resisted by its representatives. The debate continued all next day. Hitotsubashi Keiki and Ogasawara Nagamichi, however, together with the *Kyōto-shugoshoku* and the *Kyōto-shoshidai*, made it clear in the end that they would accept nothing less than a ratification of the treaties.[5] Their stubbornness was rewarded. Late that night, despite continued protests from the fiefs and lesser *kuge*, the Imperial decree was issued.[6]

The victory was not complete, for the decree specifically withheld approval for the opening of Hyōgo, and it seemed at first that Parkes would not be satisfied with less than full acceptance of his terms. It was Roches, in fact, who worked out a basis of compromise. In consultation with the Rōjū Honjō Munehide he drafted an announcement that the British minister was eventually persuaded to accept,[7] stating briefly that the Emperor had given his sanction to the treaties and that negotiations

---

[1] The evidence on this point is inconclusive. There were undoubtedly some who regarded the termination of Tokugawa rule as inevitable. However, the proposal actually made was that Iemochi be succeeded by Keiki, which was by no means the same thing. It was a familiar device in Japanese politics to reinforce one's proposals by an offer to resign—as familiar as that of registering dissent by pleading ill health—and Roches later claimed that this was the Bakufu intention here, formed in accordance with his own secret recommendations. The wording of the Shōgun's letter if anything tends to confirm this. On the other hand, his immediate attempt to depart for Edo does not.

[2] Document 62, pp. 297-9.   [3] Document 63, pp. 299-300.

[4] See Ōkubo Toshimichi's account, Document 65, pp. 301-3.

[5] See Document 64, p. 301. The letter is so short that it was obviously intended as a declaration of solidarity rather than an attempt at persuasion.

[6] Document 66, p. 304.

[7] Document 67, pp. 304-5. The text of the Imperial decree enclosed with this letter omitted the reference to Hyōgo and to treaty revision which had been part of the original—the implications of which differed notably from the promises now made to Parkes!

for the reduction of the tariff would shortly be undertaken in Edo, but that Hyōgo could not be opened until the date fixed by the London Protocol. Meanwhile, in default of opening the port, the Bakufu was to continue its payments of the Shimonoseki indemnity. Subsequent Bakufu attempts to withdraw these promises were firmly resisted both by France and Britain, and the negotiations ended in June 1866 with the conclusion of new and extremely favourable arrangements for the removal of restrictions on trade and the reduction of tariffs. To Parkes it was a most satisfactory result of the pressure he had brought to bear.

In the sense in which we have so far described it, the change in British policy consisted only in a greater willingness to apply coercive measures in its disputes with the Bakufu. This, however, was but the reflection of something more far-reaching. It was not merely that Parkes had doubts about the Shōgun's claim to sovereignty, but that there was a growing friendship between Britain and the western fiefs which persuaded him that their victory in the domestic struggle would not necessarily entail the closing of the ports. The fact was to play an important part in the events of 1866–7.

The operations against Kagoshima and Shimonoseki had for the first time brought Western diplomats into direct contact with the representatives of Satsuma and Chōshū. On both occasions there had been lengthy negotiations, which not only enabled the opposition to put its case to the foreigners in terms very different from those used by the Bakufu, but also led to the formation of ties of friendship and respect between some of the men concerned.[1] The smooth development of these relations was made easier by the impact of military defeat upon the advocates of expulsion. Even the most fanatical in the two fiefs were now convinced that the military strength of the West, especially the naval power of Britain, was such as could only be challenged by a Japan equipped with the most modern weapons and techniques. The result was a marked change of attitude. In September 1865 Ōkubo Toshimichi of Satsuma was able to write to two of his colleagues: 'the eyes of the so-called irresponsible-extremist group have for the most part been opened and their views changed, so that they recognise the impossibility of expulsion and recommend extensive opening of the country'.[2] There was, moreover, a sudden

[1] E. M. Satow, for example, who was one of the British legation interpreters, wrote of his experiences in Chōshū immediately after the Shimonoseki bombardment: 'Having beaten the Chôshiû people, we had come to like and respect them, while a feeling of dislike began to arise in our minds for the Tycoon's people on account of their weakness and double-dealing, and from this time onwards I sympathized more and more with the *daimiô* party, from whom the Tycoon's government had always tried to keep us apart.' Satow, *A Diplomat in Japan* (London, 1921), p. 129.

[2] Ōkubo's letter of 23 September 1865 to Ishigaki Einosuke and Ueno Ryōtarō, in *Ōkubo Toshimichi Monjo* (Nihon Shiseki Kyōkai series, 10 vols., Tōkyō, 1927–9), i, at p. 298.

eagerness for British trade.[1] Both Satsuma and Chōshū, in defiance of all
Bakufu orders to the contrary, began to import large quantities of weapons
through the British firm of Thomas Glover at Nagasaki, while a brisk
smuggling trade sprang up with foreign ships passing through the Shimonoseki Straits. Satsuma even sent envoys to Europe to arrange for imports
of machinery; and these men, in interviews at the Foreign Office in London
during 1865, sought with some success to persuade the British government
that the opposition of the great lords on questions of foreign policy was
not to an extension of trade as such but to its monopoly by Edo. Similar
arguments greeted Parkes on his arrival in Japan.

These facts, as Parkes saw them, tended to the conclusion that it was
an oversimplification, if not a complete inaccuracy, to describe the anti-
Bakufu movement as anti-foreign. Its leaders, at least, seemed to favour
trade and intercourse with the West. This being so, he thought, the whole
case for supporting the Bakufu against them fell to the ground. Its reputation as the sole defender of foreign privileges was undeserved; its right to
be regarded as a legitimate government was open to question; and its
ineffectiveness had been conclusively demonstrated by the events of
1863–4. On every count, therefore, it was best for Britain to avoid active
interference on the Bakufu's behalf. It would even be wise to cultivate the
friendship of those who seemed likely before long to be the new rulers of
Japan. Indeed, his obvious sympathy with the western fiefs aroused the
suspicion that he was actively conspiring with them,[2] a suspicion that was
given colour by the actions of members of his staff. His interpreter,
Ernest Satow, wrote an article recommending that the Shōgun should
become but one among a confederation of great lords governing the
country in the Emperor's name, which was translated into Japanese and
widely circulated as a pamphlet under the title *Eikoku Sakuron*.[3] It was
generally—though wrongly—taken to represent official British policy.
A similar impression was given by the visits made by Parkes and Satow
to Kyūshū and Shikoku in 1866–7, in the course of which they had long
political discussions with most of the anti-Bakufu leaders.

Despite the value to them of Britain's 'benevolent neutrality', Satsuma
and Chōshū did not relax their opposition to the opening of Hyōgo. In
Kyōto, as one would expect, they justified their stand by an appeal to
time-honoured prejudices against admitting foreigners to any city in the
neighbourhoood of the Imperial capital. To Britain they explained it as

---

[1] See Ishii, *Bakumatsu no gaikō*, pp. 149–53.

[2] The French consul in Nagasaki, for example, reported in June 1866 that the Satsuma-
Chōshū dealings with Thomas Glover, carried on apparently with the connivance of the British
fleet, strongly suggested the existence of an agreement between Satsuma and Britain to overthrow
the Bakufu: see Ōtsuka, 'Fukkoku kōshi Leon Roches', pp. 833–4.

[3] Satow, *A Diplomat in Japan*, pp. 159–60. Satow asserts that the pamphlet was written without
Parkes's knowledge.

a determination to resist any extension of foreign trade from which they would themselves be excluded by Bakufu monopoly. In so far as this implied a wish to share actively in the control of foreign affairs, it came somewhere close to the truth, for the real basis of their actions lay in the new objectives they had set themselves at home. Both fiefs had now rejected their former leadership.[1] Partly this was due to Satsuma disgust at the failure of the *kōbu-gattai* policy, especially the failure to secure any real concessions from the Bakufu in the spring of 1864. Partly it was due to the death of many of the Chōshū extremists in a series of clashes that took place in Kyōto during August of the same year. It was also connected with the success of foreign attacks on Kagoshima and Shimonoseki. The men who now came to the fore—Saigō Takamori and Ōkubo Toshimichi of Satsuma, Kido Kōin and Takasugi Shinsaku of Chōshū—were convinced already that Japan must be modernized if she were to take her proper place in the world and that the existence of the Bakufu was the chief obstacle to the accomplishment of their plans. It was not long before they began to draw together, despite the background of rivalry and hatred which had hitherto divided their respective fiefs. The process was closely linked with the development of Bakufu policy towards Chōshū.

Edo, as Hitotsubashi Keiki had anticipated,[2] had suffered a serious loss of prestige by leaving the Treaty Powers to take independent action against its chief opponents; and the Bakufu quickly became convinced, in the late summer of 1864, that only the public submission and punishment of Chōshū would serve to reassert its authority. On 23 August, therefore, just before the allied fleet left to bombard Shimonoseki, Chōshū was declared a rebel and forces were assembled for a punitive expedition. The prospect was alarming to most of the great lords as well as to the *sonnō-jōi* party. Bakufu success would put an end for a time to any hope of forcing it to share its power, so it was with some relief that they learned in December that Satsuma, in the person of Saigō Takamori, had negotiated a compromise agreement. The terms of settlement, however, were never carried out by either side. In May 1865 the Bakufu announced preparations for a second expedition, to be commanded by the Shōgun in person, and gave every evidence of a determination to force the issue. This brought Chōshū and Satsuma into definite alliance. Their first arrangement, made in September 1865, concerned only the supply of weapons, which Satsuma was to import through Glover at Nagasaki and deliver to Chōshū in return for rice; but in March 1866, after discussions at Ōsaka between Kido Kōin and Saigō Takamori, this was supplemented by a

---

[1] On this subject see Norman, *Japan's Emergence as a Modern State*, pp. 44–45, and the references there given. Also Murdoch, *History of Japan*, iii. 740–55.

[2] See his letter to the Rōjū, *c.* 10 August 1863, in Shibusawa, *Tokugawa Keiki Kō Den* (8 vols., Tōkyō, 1918), v. 562–5.

G

secret agreement defining their political objectives. Their aim was now to be the complete overthrow of Tokugawa rule. It was a final recognition by Satsuma that the *kōbu-gattai* policy had failed.

Thus in July 1866, when the Bakufu at last opened its campaign against Chōshū, it faced the veiled opposition of Satsuma—as well as some obstructive tactics by Harry Parkes.[1] The Chōshū forces, moreover, newly organized on Western lines, were more than a match for any Edo could assemble. In the event the death of the Shōgun Iemochi in September brought hostilities to an end before any military decision could be reached, but at the time the Bakufu troops were everywhere in retreat.

Hitotsubashi Keiki, succeeding Iemochi as Shōgun in the autumn of 1866, found a situation radically different from that which had obtained two years before. Essentially this was because the opposition had acquired a coherence and a solid core of power which had always previously been lacking. In place of scattered and uncoordinated unrest, manifesting itself on the one hand in the activities of *sonnō-jōi* adherents in Kyōto and on the other in the efforts of the *kōbu-gattai* lords to secure a share in the responsibilities of government, there was now a political movement relatively united in its leadership, however diverse it remained in its origins and motives. By their alliance, and by their adoption of the restoration of Imperial rule as an ultimate objective, Satsuma and Chōshū had been able to combine two hitherto conflicting elements: samurai discontent and the military resources of the great fiefs. The authority this gave them also made possible a divorce between the slogans 'honour the Emperor' and 'expel the barbarian'. That the closing of the ports had no part in their plans they were to prove when they came to power in 1868, while the statement of their intentions made to Parkes and Satow had been sufficiently convincing to gain them the sympathetic interest of Great Britain. Yet in 1866 the effective leaders of the two fiefs deemed it neither necessary nor politically advantageous to announce openly their change of heart within Japan. An opposition, unlike the government, could afford to act irresponsibly. What was more, anti-foreign feeling was still strong enough to make it a valuable weapon in the struggle against the Bakufu, both as a means of ensuring unity among the opposition factions and as a device to embarrass Edo in its relations with the foreigners. The fiefs intended to use it to the full. Specifically, it was to give them bargaining power in the attempt to gain pardon for Chōshū.

[1] For example, when Roches suggested to Ogasawara Nagamichi that the most effective route for an invasion of Chōshū would be across the straits from Kyūshū to Shimonoseki, thus cutting the supply route from Nagasaki, Parkes objected on the grounds that this would cause a disruption of foreign trade. The activities of the British and French envoys during this campaign are described in Ishii, *Bakumatsu no gaikō*, pp. 163–4, and Ōtsuka, 'Fukkoku kōshi Leon Roches', pp. 834–5.

This became evident in the negotiations that took place during the spring of 1867. Early in March Léon Roches had a series of interviews with Keiki and the Rōjū Itakura Katsukiyo at Ōsaka, during which he expounded a detailed plan for the re-establishment of Bakufu authority.[1] This could only be accomplished, he said, by means of a thoroughgoing reform of Japan's administration and economy. Edo must resume complete control of policy, consulting the great lords in reaching its decisions but carrying them out through an officialdom newly organized on Western lines, and must strengthen its military forces to the point where they could overcome any resistance likely to be encountered within the country. To pay for this taxes should be imposed on the *chōnin*, cash payments levied from the *daimyō* instead of military service, and steps taken to develop mining and industry. Foreign trade must also be encouraged. In addition it was necessary to convince the Treaty Powers, especially Britain, that the Bakufu was both able and willing to carry out the agreements it had signed. Hyōgo must undoubtedly be opened, as well as another port in place of Niigata, while an offer to open Kagoshima and Shimonoseki would not only give evidence of Bakufu sincerity but would also test that of Satsuma and Chōshū. With these concessions made, Roches thought, it would be possible to refuse the opening of Edo and Ōsaka on grounds of national unrest.

These proposals were altogether too sweeping to be acceptable to the Shōgun. In a sense, too, they were unreal, for the Bakufu no longer had the means of enforcing them even had it wished to do so. The need to conciliate the foreign representatives was obvious, however, and this began to be reflected in the greater friendliness shown by officials whose duty it was to carry on discussions with them. In April, moreover, they were invited to have formal audience with the new Shōgun at Ōsaka. In preparation for this, Keiki decided to seek Imperial permission for the opening of Hyōgo. On the 9th he submitted his request to the Court, in terms which made it clear that the Bakufu had abandoned all thought of expulsion, whether immediate or ultimate, and had decided that Japan must make a fresh start in her dealings with the West.[2] Kyōto, as it often had before, insisted that no decision could be taken without consulting the great lords.[3] Keiki had actually begun to do so a month earlier, but the impatience of Harry Parkes had prompted him to act before replies could be received and the same reason brought a speedy renewal of his request in rather stronger form.[4] The Court's response was to call for the written views of the fiefs and to summon the great lords to Kyōto, informing the

---

[1] On this plan and the steps taken to carry it out see especially Honjō, 'Leon Roches to Bakumatsu no shosei kaikaku', in that author's *Bakumatsu no shin-seisaku* (Tōkyō, 1935), pp. 178–214. See also Ōtsuka, 'Fukkoku kōshi Leon Roches', pp. 844–5.

[2] See Document 68, pp. 308–10. [3] Document 69, p. 310.

[4] Document 70, pp. 310–11.

Bakufu meanwhile that in no circumstances was the port to be opened until further instructions had been issued.[1]

Behind the answers of the Court there lay the work of Ōkubo Toshimichi of Satsuma. To Ōkubo the Hyōgo question was primarily of interest for the opportunity it offered of striking a blow against the Bakufu. His colleague, Komatsu, at an interview with Ernest Satow in February, had already tried to concert a plan for the coordination of British diplomacy with the actions of the fiefs;[2] and although Parkes had not taken the course which had then been proposed, namely of demanding treaties with the Emperor to replace those with the Shōgun, his insistence on the opening of Hyōgo provided just as good an occasion for manœuvre.[3] Satsuma's first object was to secure the pardon of Chōshū. This would enable Chōshū troops once again to enter Kyōto and would therefore set the stage for an anti-Bakufu *coup d'état*. As a means to this end it was desirable to have all the great lords present in the capital, for most were opposed to the Bakufu's uncompromising attitude in its dispute with the rebels.[4] Their presence in Kyōto, what was more, would enable Satsuma to complete its plans by effecting a reconciliation between the leading *kuge* of the *sonnō* party, notably Iwakura Tomomi, and those *kōbu-gattai* lords who still inclined to the support of Edo. Once the two groups had been brought together—and in this Shimazu Hisamitsu was to play his part, since his influence was strong with both—the Court could assume direct responsibility for decisions and order the Shōgun to take his place among the ranks of the other feudal lords. This was but part of the plan, however. The opening of Hyōgo, inevitable though it was, could be blamed on the Shōgun's incompetence and made the pretext for reducing his estates. Thus Keiki would be deprived of his preponderance of personal wealth and power, which might otherwise enable him to continue dominating the council even after he had been dismissed from office.[5]

By the beginning of June 1867 Shimazu Hisamitsu, Date Muneki,

---

[1] Document 71, p. 311.   [2] Satow, *A Diplomat in Japan*, pp. 189–90.

[3] Satow was not unaware of this, as he shows in his account of an interview with Saigō Takamori at about this time: 'I hinted to Saigô that the chance of a revolution was not to be lost. If Hiôgo were once opened, then good-bye to the chances of the *daimiôs.*' Ibid., p. 200.

[4] Hence Satsuma pressure to delay the decision about Hyōgo until the great lords had assembled. See Document 72, pp. 311–12. All the *kōbu-gattai* lords were by this time anxious to see a reconciliation between the Bakufu and Chōshū, though where Date and Shimazu, prompted by Ōkubo, saw this as a move in the campaign to destroy the Tokugawa power, Matsudaira Keiei and Yamanouchi Toyoshige still seem to have thought largely in terms of the need to unite the country and confined their political ambitions to a desire to secure a share of responsibility within the existing framework. It was this difference that made it necessary for Ōkubo to proceed with caution.

[5] Ōkubo's outline of this plan to Shimazu Hisamitsu (Document 73, pp. 312–13) is expressed with such brevity as to leave many of the implications vague—perhaps deliberately so, in view of Shimazu's earlier policies. The intention of reducing the Tokugawa territories was in any case made known only to a select few, for fear that knowledge of it might cause men like Yamanouchi Toyoshige and Matsudaira Keiei to withhold their support.

Yamanouchi Toyoshige, and Matsudaira Keiei, the four *daimyō* whose decisions were most likely to determine Ōkubo's success or failure, were gathered in the capital. It did not take them long to reach agreement on the immediate problems that were the ostensible reason for their meeting. Hyōgo must be opened, they decided, and the punishment of Chōshū must be limited to the enforced retirement of the head of the fief. These were terms which the Shōgun was on the whole willing to accept. The real point at issue, in fact, proved to be the question of timing, for it was on this that Ōkubo and his colleagues centred their attention. If Keiki were able to open Hyōgo at once, as he proposed, then he might so strengthen his position with foreign help as to make impossible for some time to come any attempt to overthrow the Bakufu. On the other hand, if the Chōshū decision were to be announced first and that concerning Hyōgo later, Chōshū would again be able to take an active part in politics at the Court and the scales would be tipped in favour of the opposition. Prompted by Ōkubo, therefore, Date and Shimazu insisted that the urgent need was to still national unrest, that is, to pardon Chōshū. They received lukewarm support from the other lords. Keiki himself denied their argument entirely, urging that the foreign problem held the greater danger for Japan. The resulting deadlock, not unlike that which had arisen between advocates of *jōi* and *kaikoku* ten years earlier, was broken at last by a compromise proposal from Matsudaira Keiei. On 23 June, at his suggestion, it was agreed that the two decisions should be taken simultaneously in fact but that the Chōshū announcement should be made first in form.

Such a compromise, of course, was in no way acceptable to Ōkubo Toshimichi, whose entire object had been to delay the Hyōgo decision until everything was ready for a *coup d'état*. He rapidly persuaded Date and Shimazu to withdraw their consent. Matsudaira Keiei, with some reluctance, followed suit. Yamanouchi, although by this time he had ceased active participation in the discussions on grounds of ill health, was ready to conform with the decisions of the majority. On the morning of 25 June, therefore, two days after agreement had first been reached with Keiki, the four lords wrote jointly to inform him that they were no longer willing to support his application to the Palace.[1]

Keiki does not seem to have taken this letter as a complete rejection of the earlier arrangements. Certainly its wording was vague in the extreme. At all events, he went ahead with his plans to get Imperial sanction and raised the matter at Court the same day, thereby initiating an acrimonious discussion which lasted until the following evening.[2] Shimazu boycotted

---

[1] The text of their letter is printed in *Zoku Saimukiji*, vi. 284–5. On the dispute generally see *Ishin-shi*, iv. 634–42.

[2] Extracts from the diaries of Prince Asahiko and the *gisō* Saga Sanenaru, who took an important part in these discussions, are given as Documents 74 and 75, pp. 314–19.

the proceedings altogether. Yamanouchi continued to plead ill health, but Date Muneki and Matsudaira Keiei, who answered the summons to attend, now denied that the fiefs were willing to approve the immediate opening of Hyōgo and pressed for a decision on the subject of Chōshū alone. They were strongly supported by the *gisō* and some of the lesser *kuge*. Keiki, however, had taken the precaution of securing in advance the co-operation of most of the senior Court officials, whose action finally brought the dispute to an end. On 26 June, prompted by the Kampaku's obvious indecision, a group led by Prince Asahiko and Takatsukasa Sukehiro threatened to resign from office and withdraw from Court unless the Bakufu's request were granted. This forced Nijō Nariaki's hand. That evening, despite continued opposition from Satsuma and the *gisō*, he issued an Imperial decree announcing that Hyōgo was to be opened and that Chōshū was to receive lenient treatment on the lines already agreed between the Shōgun and the *daimyō*.[1]

Edo's victory, if such it was, had been achieved only at the cost of alienating all the *kōbu-gattai* lords. On 28 June they put their protests formally on record in a joint memorial to the Court which in effect accused the Shōgun of having misrepresented their views on the subject of Hyōgo,[2] while the intrigues of Ōkubo and the other opposition leaders quickly renewed and strengthened the anti-Bakufu alliance. Within six months Keiki's position had been made so untenable that he was forced to resign. It was not till this was done that Satsuma and Chōshū revealed the full extent of their ambitions, but it was then too late for anything to keep them from success. Only the briefest of campaigns was needed to effect the total abolition of Tokugawa rule.

It is clear that in all the events of early summer the desirability or necessity of opening Hyōgo had never really been at issue. Some of the lesser *kuge* (and no doubt many of the *rōnin* and lesser samurai as well, though they played no direct part in the discussions) opposed this new concession to the West as a matter of conviction,[3] but the men who mattered most—the Shōgun, the great lords, and senior Court officials, Ōkubo himself—differed hardly at all in their willingness to accede to foreign demands for the opening of the port. What really divided them was the struggle for power within Japan. The anti-Bakufu forces had seen and seized the opportunity to make use of foreign pressure as a weapon in their own attacks upon the government. They had made foreign policy 'a stick to beat the Bakufu'. The coming of the West, which had helped to bring the conflict to a head, had also helped in shaping its solution.

[1] The text is given as Document 76, p. 319.
[2] Document 77, pp. 319–20.
[3] The tone of Saga Sanenaru's diary, for example, suggests that he must be included in their number: see Document 74, pp. 314–15.

7. Conclusions

An attempt to analyse and explain Japanese foreign policy in the years 1853 to 1868 must take account of the influence and ideas of many groups within society. The Bakufu, indeed, though ostensibly the government of the country and therefore responsible for the shaping of policy, was rarely able to act freely either in defining its objectives or in determining the methods by which they were to be attained. In part this was due to differences of attitude towards the outside world. In part it arose from the struggle for power within Japan, to which the discussion of foreign affairs was often made subservient. Yet the resulting conflicts should not blind us to the existence of certain fundamental similarities in the reactions of Japanese generally to the coming of the West, at all events among those who were politically active.

Conspicuous in this connexion is the prevalence of anti-foreign feeling. Among the samurai, especially, national traditions and habits of thought, reinforced by economic distress and a marked sense of insecurity, produced an emotional response vehement enough to be called xenophobia. It was an attitude repeated in varying degree throughout society. It pervaded all the writings of the period, whether pamphlets or official memoranda, and coloured the views even of those who urged the opening of the ports. When linked with sporadic outbursts of violence, moreover, it became a factor not lightly to be ignored in the formulation of policy. Yet influential though this was, it was not a decisive factor in the minds of the men who were the leaders of Japan, either before or after 1868. To them, hatred of the foreigner was subordinate to the needs of national safety. This is not to imply that the two were incompatible. It was simply that the more rational and sophisticated, to whom the encroachment of the Western Powers constituted a threat to the very existence of Japan as an independent State, were ready to suppress their feelings of distaste at least to the extent that would make it possible to adopt Western weapons and techniques for use in Japan's defence. By this estimate, the motive for westernization was itself anti-Western.

The leaders, in fact, of whatever party, had more in common than would appear from a superficial reading of the arguments they used. Because they were divided for and against the signing of the treaties, because it was questions like the opening of Hyōgo and the closing of Yokohama that aroused the greatest passion and formed the subject of continuing debate, it has been too readily assumed that the issue was joined between those who wanted to open the ports and those who wanted to retain the policy of seclusion. Seclusion undoubtedly had its appeal to the ill-informed and prejudiced majority. So, too, did the cry for expulsion of the foreigners. But it does not therefore follow that the two were necessarily the same. Again and again, in practice, one finds that expulsion was regarded as a prelude not to permanent closing of the ports but to the negotiation of new and equal treaties with the West. *Jōi* leaders, just as much as their opponents, looked forward to the day when Japan could assert her independence; and they recognized that this would only be achieved if she learned what the West could teach. The essential difference was their insistence that failure to control the degree and timing of foreign intercourse would bring dangers even greater than those attendant on refusal of the West's demands.

The policies of *jōi* and *kaikoku*, then, were not unlike each other in their aims and motives. That is not true, of course, of the specific steps their advocates wished the Bakufu to take. Still less is it true of the political movements with which they came in time to be associated. Indeed, the whole nature of their relationship is complicated, often concealed altogether, by the fact that disputes over foreign policy became part of the struggle between the Bakufu and its enemies at home.

Before 1853 it is only in the most general way that one can trace a connexion between political alignment on the one hand and ideas concerning foreign policy on the other. Relatively few men were committed on either subject. Of them, so far as valid distinctions can be made, *jōi* views tended to predominate among those who sought radical reform in politics. The demand for opening of the ports, by contrast, was heard most often from the ranks of Bakufu officialdom, though it was also a challenge to authority in the sense that it denied the doctrines of seclusion. At this time, moreover, both *jōi* and *kaikoku* represented attempts to influence policy from within. Neither involved a wish to overthrow the government. Gradually, however, out of an inability to resist the pressure of foreign demands, the Bakufu had to assume responsibility for opening Japan to trade, and by so doing brought together the elements of anti-Bakufu and anti-Western feeling. In and after 1858, therefore, the *jōi* party, as well as a number of *kaikoku* thinkers who rejected the manner and implications of Bakufu submission to the West, came into alliance with groups whose primary interests were political. In the process the slogans 'open the country' and 'expel the barbarian' took on a new significance. The one came to mean support for Bakufu policies and, by extension, for the Bakufu itself. The other became a symbol of opposition, embracing everything from blind resentment at a changing world to an almost fanatical belief in the necessity of change.

Thus there was much that was artificial about the discussions concerning foreign policy in the last ten years of Tokugawa rule. The pattern of ideas that had been built up around the words *jōi* and *kaikoku* was necessarily distorted by forcing it into a political framework with which it only loosely corresponded. So, too, was the distribution of those ideas in Japanese society. The result was to set a gulf, wider even than before, between what men said and what they meant. Of the Bakufu this is obvious enough. Publicly it avowed a policy of expulsion; privately it admitted it to be impossible; and to the foreigners it promised better facilities for trade. Yet the opposition was almost equally contradictory. The rank-and-file, for the most part, accepted the policy of expulsion at its face value. Many of the leaders, however, had never done so; and after 1863 events convinced them more and more that observance of the treaties was both desirable and necessary. They did not say so openly, for they could afford neither to alienate their followers nor to relinquish a weapon of considerable value in their attacks upon the government. Nevertheless, by 1868, when the fall of the Tokugawa brought them power and responsibility, their views were almost indistinguishable from those which in the Bakufu they castigated as spineless and dishonouring.

From this it is clear that the new policies towards the West initiated by the Meiji leaders after 1868 represented not a change of heart but an avowal of ideas that had already taken shape. In this sense there was no volte-face that needs explaining. What had really changed, in fact, was the government's ability to put its decisions into practice. The opposition that had stopped the Bakufu from doing so had been organized by the men who were now responsible for policy; and political victory had removed their motive for honouring the ideas of expulsion. The anti-foreign movement, in other words, had lost its most powerful adherents. Yet oppositon to the opening of the country did not thereby vanish altogether. Indeed, the attitudes and emotions inherited from the Bakumatsu period had an important influence on Japanese foreign policy for nearly eighty years thereafter. The demand for revision of the treaties, for example, which grew steadily in intensity after 1868, had many of the characteristics of the earlier movement for expulsion of the foreigners. Similarly, there continued to be a close connexion between foreign policy and domestic politics. As late as the twentieth century, those who wished to attack the government still found they could do so most successfully by charging it with weakness and subservience in its conduct of foreign affairs. It was an accusation that invariably aroused popular excitement, however little it accorded with the facts. Nor, in a wider perspective, is it surprising that fear and hatred of the West, harnessed as they were to the attainment of national equality and prestige, should have turned at last to an urge for conquest and expanding empire.

SELECT DOCUMENTS

The Perry Convention, 1853–4

On 8 July 1853 Commodore M. C. Perry brought his squadron of four ships into Uraga Bay with the object of negotiating a treaty with Japan. He carried a letter from the United States President (Document 1), which stated that America sought only peaceful relations with Japan: humane treatment for shipwrecked seamen, facilities for coaling and supplying ships in Japanese harbours, and, if possible, some arrangements for trade. However, Perry's own letter (Document 2), which was to accompany that of the President, implied that refusal of his request might bring Japan into some danger; the squadron then present was small, but more ships were expected and would accompany him when he returned for an answer in the spring of 1854.

In recent years the Japanese government had become more and more aware that the countries of the West wished to bring to an end Japan's two hundred years of seclusion. Specifically it had already been warned by the Dutch of the coming of an American expedition. It had not, however, used the interval to determine its policy with any clarity. The immediate problem posed by Perry's arrival was solved on 14 July by ordering the two Uraga *bugyō* to accept the letters in a ceremony at Kurihama and to promise that a reply would be made in the following year. But this gave only a respite. There remained the question of what to do when Perry returned.

The Tokugawa Bakufu was aware that its power in Japan was precarious, its finances in disorder, and its defences in no condition to protect the country against attack by American warships, however few. Moreover, it had no man of outstanding ability and determination among its higher officials able and willing to take a decision and force it upon the country. Apparently hoping that the step would enable him to discover a policy capable at once of satisfying the Americans and forestalling domestic criticism, Abe Masahiro, then head of the Rōjū, decided to sound out feudal opinion in the country at large. He circulated translations of the American letters not only to Bakufu officials and cadet houses of the Tokuwaga family but also to *daimyō* throughout Japan, instructing all to give their views on the action that should be taken. The unprecedented step was an open confession of Bakufu weakness.

The replies to Abe's request revealed fundamental differences of opinion. Tokugawa Nariaki, former head of the senior Tokugawa branch house of Mito and probably the most influential figure in Japan, strongly opposed concession on the grounds that it would only have the effect of giving the foreigners a foothold in Japan and by so doing would endanger the country's independence. Immediate war, he argued, however uncertain of success, was better than immediate capitulation (Document 3). Nariaki was supported in this by a small but powerful group which included another important relative of the Tokugawa, Matsudaira Keiei (Document 6). An equally small group maintained that since war could end only in defeat, the sensible policy would be to engage for a time in trade and use the profits thereof to build up military forces, thus eventually making possible a new expulsion of the foreigners. The chief advocate of this course was Ii Naosuke, most powerful of the *fudai daimyō* (Document 7). The majority, which included such lords as Shimazu Nariakira of the great Satsuma fief (Document 5), wanted neither war nor trade. They counselled the Bakufu to avoid hostilities while refusing the American demands—a recommendation that in many cases sprang rather from political caution than from conviction—but made no specific suggestions as to how this very desirable end could be achieved. The latter task, indeed, was attempted only by a very few, among them some Bakufu officials whose memorandum (Document 4) revealed more suspicion of Western cunning than respect for Western shrewdness.

These replies did nothing to solve Abe's problem. It was clear that to accept the policy of Nariaki would be to provoke hostilities which Japan had little hope of winning and might cost the Bakufu the support of Naosuke in domestic affairs. To adopt that of Naosuke, on the other hand, would arouse widespread resentment in Japan and might push Nariaki into open hostility. Domestic and foreign problems, in fact, were inseparable. In this dilemma Abe was incapable of decisive action. His policy was as negative as that of the majority of the *daimyō*, who had shown themselves opposed both to war and to trade. He sought to avoid war by making limited concessions to the foreigners and at the same time to minimize criticism at home by avoiding the ultimate concession, that of trade.

When Perry returned, in February 1854, Abe could temporize no longer. The American squadron now consisted of eight ships and the commodore was polite but insistent. Officials were appointed to negotiate with him; and though there is no extant copy of any instructions given to them, the first paragraph of their subsequent report (Document 9) makes it clear that they were under orders to avoid any action that might provoke hostilities. In the ensuing discussions they did their best to restrict the concessions made—and with some success. The convention signed on 31 March 1854 (Document 8) contained no specific approval of trade, though Article VII could be interpreted as making some kind of provision for it. It did, however, open the ports of Shimoda and Hakodate to American ships for the supply of coal and stores, and as such it represents the first step in the opening of Japan.

DOCUMENT 1. Millard Fillmore, President of the United States of America, to His Imperial Majesty the Emperor of Japan, 13 November 1852.[1]

GREAT AND GOOD FRIEND: I send you this public letter by Commodore Matthew C. Perry, an officer of the highest rank in the navy of the United States, and commander of the squadron now visiting your imperial majesty's dominions.

I have directed Commodore Perry to assure your imperial majesty that I entertain the kindest feelings toward your majesty's person and government, and that I have no other object in sending him to Japan but to propose to your imperial majesty that the United States and Japan should live in friendship and have commercial intercourse with each other.

The Constitution and laws of the United States forbid all interference with the religious or political concerns of other nations. I have particularly charged Commodore Perry to abstain from every act which could possibly disturb the tranquility of your imperial majesty's dominions.

The United States of America reach from ocean to ocean, and our Territory of Oregon and State of California lie directly opposite to the dominions of your imperial majesty. Our steamships can go from California to Japan in eighteen days.

Our great State of California produces about sixty millions of dollars in gold every year, besides silver, quicksilver, precious stones, and many other valuable articles. Japan is also a rich and fertile country, and produces many very valuable articles. Your imperial majesty's subjects are skilled in many of the arts. I am desirous that our two countries should trade with each other, for the benefit both of Japan and the United States.

We know that the ancient laws of your imperial majesty's government do not allow of foreign trade, except with the Chinese and the Dutch; but as the state of the world changes and new governments are formed, it seems to be wise, from time to time, to make new laws. There was a time

[1] The text of this letter was first published in F. L. Hawks, *Narrative of the Expedition of an American Squadron to the China Seas and Japan* (U.S. House of Repres. 33 Congress 2 Sess., Exec. Doct. 97; 3 vols., Washington, 1856), i. 256–7. The Japanese translations are to be found in *Dai Nihon Komonjo: Bakumatsu Gaikoku Kankei Monjo* (Tōkyō, 1911–; in progress), i. 242–6 (prepared from the Chinese text presented by Perry) and i. 247–51 (prepared from the Dutch text presented by Perry): the latter follows the English more closely, but together they give an adequate rendering of the original except for the one sentence noted below.

when the ancient laws of your imperial majesty's government were first made.[1]

About the same time America, which is sometimes called the New World, was first discovered and settled by the Europeans. For a long time there were but a few people, and they were poor. They have now become quite numerous; their commerce is very extensive; and they think that if your imperial majesty were so far to change the ancient laws as to allow a free trade between the two countries it would be extremely beneficial to both.

If your imperial majesty is not satisfied that it would be safe altogether to abrogate the ancient laws which forbid foreign trade, they might be suspended for five or ten years, so as to try the experiment. If it does not prove as beneficial as was hoped, the ancient laws can be restored. The United States often limit their treaties with foreign States to a few years, and then renew them or not, as they please.

I have directed Commodore Perry to mention another thing to your imperial majesty. Many of our ships pass every year from California to China; and great numbers of our people pursue the whale fishery near the shores of Japan. It sometimes happens, in stormy weather, that one of our ships is wrecked on your imperial majesty's shores. In all such cases we ask, and expect, that our unfortunate people should be treated with kindness, and that their property should be protected, till we can send a vessel and bring them away. We are very much in earnest in this.

Commodore Perry is also directed by me to represent to your imperial majesty that we understand there is a great abundance of coal and provisions in the Empire of Japan. Our steamships, in crossing the great ocean, burn a great deal of coal, and it is not convenient to bring it all the way from America. We wish that our steamships and other vessels should be allowed to stop in Japan and supply themselves with coal, provisions, and water. They will pay for them in money, or anything else your imperial majesty's subjects may prefer; and we request your imperial majesty to appoint a convenient port, in the southern part of the Empire, where our vessels may stop for this purpose. We are very desirous of this.

These are the only objects for which I have sent Commodore Perry, with a powerful squadron, to pay a visit to your imperial majesty's renowned city of Yedo: friendship, commerce, a supply of coal and provisions, and protection for our shipwrecked people.

We have directed Commodore Perry to beg your imperial majesty's acceptance of a few presents. They are of no great value in themselves; but some of them may serve as specimens of the articles manufactured in

[1] Neither of the Japanese translations (see previous note) catches the sense of this sentence, both reducing it to a flat statement that the laws were made very long ago.

the United States, and they are intended as tokens of our sincere and respectful friendship.

May the Almighty have your imperial majesty in His great and holy keeping!

DOCUMENT 2. Commodore M. C. Perry to His Imperial Majesty the Emperor of Japan, 7 July 1853.[1]

The undersigned, commander-in-chief of all the naval forces of the United States of America stationed in the East India, China and Japan seas, has been sent by his government to this country, on a friendly mission, with ample powers to negotiate with the government of Japan, touching certain matters which have been fully set forth in the letter of the President of the United States, copies of which, together with copies of the letter of credence of the undersigned, in the English, Dutch, and Chinese languages, are herewith transmitted.

The original of the President's letter, and of the letter of credence, prepared in a manner suited to the exalted station of your imperial majesty, will be presented by the undersigned in person, when it may please your majesty to appoint a day for his reception.

The undersigned has been commanded to state that the President entertains the most friendly feelings toward Japan, but has been surprised and grieved to learn that when any of the people of the United States go, of their own accord, or are thrown by the perils of the sea, within the dominions of your imperial majesty, they are treated as if they were your worst enemies.

The undersigned refers to the cases of the American ships Morrison, Lagoda, and Lawrence.

With the Americans, as indeed with all Christian people, it is considered a sacred duty to receive with kindness, and to succor and protect all, of whatever nation, who may be cast upon their shores, and such has been the course of the Americans with respect to all Japanese subjects who have fallen under their protection.

The government of the United States desires to obtain from that of Japan some positive assurance that persons who may hereafter be shipwrecked on the coast of Japan, or driven by stress of weather into her ports, shall be treated with humanity.

The undersigned is commanded to explain to the Japanese that the United States are connected with no government in Europe, and that

---

[1] The text of this letter was first published in F. L. Hawks, *Narrative of the Expedition*, i. 258–9. The Japanese translations are to be found in *Bakumatsu Gaikoku Kankei Monjo*, i. 258–60 (from Perry's Chinese version) and i. 261–4 (from Perry's Dutch version): the former contains a few errors, but these are not material and do not appear in the translation from the Dutch.

their laws do not interfere with the religion of their own citizens, much less with that of other nations.

That they inhabit a great country which lies directly between Japan and Europe, and which was discovered by the nations of Europe about the same time that Japan herself was first visited by Europeans; that the portion of the American continent lying nearest to Europe was first settled by emigrants from that part of the world; that its population has rapidly spread through the country, until it has reached the shores of the Pacific ocean; that we now have large cities, from which, with the aid of steam-vessels, we can reach Japan in eighteen or twenty days; that our commerce with all this region of the globe is rapidly increasing, and the Japan seas will soon be covered with our vessels.

Therefore, as the United States and Japan are becoming every day nearer and nearer to each other, the President desires to live in peace and friendship with your imperial majesty, but no friendship can long exist, unless Japan ceases to act toward Americans as if they were her enemies.

However wise this policy may originally have been, it is unwise and impracticable now that the intercourse between the two countries is so much more easy and rapid than it formerly was.

The undersigned holds out all these arguments in the hope that the Japanese government will see the necessity of averting unfriendly collision between the two nations, by responding favourably to the propositions of amity, which are now made in all sincerity.

Many of the large ships-of-war destined to visit Japan have not yet arrived in these seas, though they are hourly expected; and the under-signed, as an evidence of his friendly intentions, has brought but four of the smaller ones, designing, should it become necessary, to return to Yedo in the ensuing spring with a much larger force.

But it is expected that the government of your imperial majesty will render such return unnecessary, by acceding at once to the very reasonable and pacific overtures contained in the President's letter, and which will be further explained by the undersigned on the first fitting occasion.

With the most profound respect for your imperial majesty, and enter-taining a sincere hope that you may long live to enjoy health and happi-ness, the undersigned subscribes himself,

M. C. PERRY

DOCUMENT 3. Tokugawa Nariaki to Bakufu, 14 August 1853[1]

Observations on coast defence

It is my belief that the first and most urgent of our tasks is for the Bakufu

[1] The text is printed in *Bakumatsu Gaikoku Kankei Monjo*, i. 509-22. Only the first half of this

to make its choice between peace and war, and having determined its policy to pursue it unwaveringly thereafter. When we consider the respective advantages and disadvantages of war and peace, we find that if we put our trust in war the whole country's morale will be increased and even if we sustain an initial defeat we will in the end expel the foreigner; while if we put our trust in peace, even though things may seem tranquil for a time, the morale of the country will be greatly lowered and we will come in the end to complete collapse. This has been amply demonstrated in the history of China and is a fact that men of intelligence, both past and present, have always known. It is therefore unnecessary for me to speak of this in detail. However, I propose to give here in outline the ten reasons why in my view we must never choose the policy of peace.

1. Although our country's territory is not extensive, foreigners both fear and respect us. That, after all, is because our resoluteness and military prowess have been clearly demonstrated to the world outside by such events as the conquest of Korea by the Empress Jingō in very ancient times; by the repulse of the Mongols in the Kōan period [1278–88] during the middle ages; and in the recent past by the invasion of Korea in the Bunroku period [1592–6] and the suppression of Christianity in the Keichō [1596–1615] and Kanei [1624–44] periods. Despite this, the Americans who arrived recently, though fully aware of the Bakufu's prohibition, entered Uraga displaying a white flag as a symbol of peace and insisted on presenting their written requests. Moreover they entered Edo Bay, fired heavy guns in salute and even went so far as to conduct surveys without permission. They were arrogant and discourteous, their actions an outrage. Indeed, this was the greatest disgrace we have suffered since the dawn of our history. The saying is that if the enemy dictates terms in one's own capital one's country is disgraced. The foreigners having thus ignored our prohibition and penetrated our waters even to the vicinity of the capital, threatening us and making demands upon us, should it happen not only that the Bakufu fails to expel them but also that it concludes an agreement in accordance with their requests, then I fear it would be impossible to maintain our national prestige [*kokutai*]. That is the first reason why we must never choose the policy of peace.

2. The prohibition of Christianity is the first rule of the Tokugawa house. Public notices concerning it are posted everywhere, even to the remotest corner of every province. It is said that even so, during the Bunsei period [1818–30], men have been executed for propagating this religion secretly in Ōsaka. The Bakufu can never ignore or overlook the evils of Christianity. Yet if the Americans are allowed to come again this

long memorandum deals with the justification of Nariaki's proposed policy, however, the remainder outlining the specifically military steps to be taken. Hence only the first half is given here, the translation ending at *Bakumatsu Gaikoku Kankei Monjo*, i. 515, line 8.

religion will inevitably raise its head once more, however strict the prohibition; and this, I fear, is something we could never justify to the spirits of our ancestors. That is the second reason why we must never choose the policy of peace.

3. To exchange our valuable articles like gold, silver, copper, and iron for useless foreign goods like woollens and satin is to incur great loss while acquiring not the smallest benefit. The best course of all would be for the Bakufu to put a stop to the trade with Holland. By contrast, to open such valueless trade with others besides the Dutch would, I believe, inflict the greatest possible harm on our country. That is the third reason why we must never choose the policy of peace.

4. For some years Russia, England, and others have sought trade with us, but the Bakufu has not permitted it. Should permission be granted to the Americans, on what grounds would it be possible to refuse if Russia and the others [again] request it? That is the fourth reason why we must never choose the policy of peace.

5. It is widely stated that [apart from trade] the foreigners have no other evil designs and that if only the Bakufu will permit trade there will be no further difficulty. However, it is their practice first to seek a foothold by means of trade and then to go on to propagate Christianity and make other unreasonable demands. Thus we would be repeating the blunders of others, seen remotely in the Christianity incidents of the Kanei period [1624–44] and before [in Japan] and more recently in the Opium War in China. That is the fifth reason why we must never choose the policy of peace.

6. Though the Rangakusha group may argue secretly that world conditions are much changed from what they were, Japan alone clinging to ideas of seclusion in isolation amidst the seas, that this is a constant source of danger to us and that our best course would therefore be to communicate with foreign countries and open an extensive trade; yet, to my mind, if the people of Japan stand firmly united, if we complete our military preparations and return to the state of society that existed before the middle ages,[1] then we will even be able to go out against[2] foreign countries and spread abroad our fame and prestige. But if we open trade at the demand of the foreigners, for no better reason than that, our habits today being those of peace and indolence, men have shown fear merely at the coming of a handful of foreign warships, then it would truly be a vain

---

[1] i.e. before the feudal period; hence, presumably, direct Imperial rule. One might logically expect Nariaki to mean here the period before luxury and idleness had weakened the military class (say, for example, before the Genroku period), but I have no knowledge that the term *chūko* (*naka-mukashi*) can be used in this sense.

[2] The term used is *oshi-wataru*. It implies that Japan should take the initiative in foreign affairs and adopt an active rather than a passive policy, but does not, I think, necessarily suggest actual armed attack on other countries.

illusion to think of evolving any long-range plan for going out against foreign countries. That is the sixth reason why we must never choose the policy of peace.

7. The Bakufu entrusted the defence of the Uraga district to the Hikone and Wakamatsu fiefs, and I hear that the Aizu retainers [from Wakamatsu] have already gone there, travelling night and day for some 170 miles or more despite the heat. I also hear that in addition to this the *daimyō* ordered to defend Edo Bay are sending troops at once. All this is admirable. But if we ignore the fact that the foreigners went so far as to enter Edo Bay and carry out surveys without permission, if we do not take action to expel them, this will be to allow the men of all provinces to exhaust themselves in activity that is but vain and wasted effort, and in the end our people will be brought to a state of complete collapse. That is the seventh reason why we must never choose the policy of peace.

8. When Kuroda and Nabeshima[1] were made responsible for the coast defence of Nagasaki it was not intended that this be directed solely against the Dutch and Chinese. It was a measure directed against all foreigners. But by agreeing to receive written requests from the foreigners at Uraga— and still more were the Bakufu to conclude an agreement there in accordance with those requests—would we not, as it were, be allowing the foreigners to enter by the back door, thus rendering futile the guard-duties entrusted to those two families and arousing their resentment? That is the eighth reason why we must never choose the policy of peace.

9. I hear that all, even though they be commoners, who have witnessed the recent actions of the foreigners, think them abominable; and if the Bakufu does not expel these insolent foreigners root and branch there may be some who will complain in secret, asking to what purpose have been all the preparations of gun-emplacements. It is inevitable that men should think in this way when they have seen how arrogantly the foreigners acted at Uraga. That, I believe, is because even the humblest are conscious of the debt they owe their country, and it is indeed a promising sign. Since even ignorant commoners are talking in this way, I fear that if the Bakufu does not decide to carry out expulsion, if its handling of the matter shows nothing but excess of leniency and appeasement of the foreigners, then the lower orders may fail to understand its ideas and hence opposition might arise from evil men who had lost their respect for Bakufu authority. It might even be that Bakufu control of the great lords would itself be endangered. That is the ninth reason why we must never choose the policy of peace.

10. There are those who say that since the expulsion of foreigners is the ancient law of the Shōgun's ancestors, reissued and reaffirmed in the

---

[1] The *tozama daimyō* of Fukuoka and Saga respectively.

Bunsei period,[1] the Bakufu has in fact always been firmly resolved to fight, but that even so one must recognize that peace has now lasted so long our armaments are inadequate, and one cannot therefore tell what harm might be done if we too recklessly arouse the anger of the foreigners. In that event, they say, the Bakufu would be forced to conclude a peace settlement and so its prestige would suffer still further damage. Hence [it is argued], the Bakufu should show itself compliant at this time and should placate the foreigners, meanwhile exerting all its efforts in military preparations, so that when these preparations have been completed it can more strictly enforce the ancient laws. This argument sounds reasonable enough. However, to my mind the people here [in Edo] are temporizing and half-hearted; and even though the Shōgun exhort them day and night he cannot make them resolute. Now there is not the slightest chance that the feudal lords will complete military preparations, however many years may pass, unless they are set an example in military matters by the Bakufu. There have already been clashes in Ezo [Hokkaidō] during the Kansei [1789–1801] and Bunka [1804–18] periods,[2] but despite the Bakufu's efforts to effect military preparations they have not yet been completed. Again, relaxation of the expulsion laws was ordered in 1842, with the apparent object of first placating the foreigners and then using the respite to complete military preparations, but here, too, I do not think the various lords have made any particular progress in rearming in the twelve years that have since elapsed. On the arrival of the foreign ships recently, all fell into a panic. Some take matters very seriously while foreign ships are actually at anchor here, but once the ships leave and orders are given for them to revert to normal, they all relax once more into idleness and immediately disperse the military equipment which they had hurriedly assembled. It is just as if, regardless of a fire burning beneath the floor of one's house, one neglected all fire-fighting precautions. Indeed, it shows a shameful spirit. I therefore believe that if there be any sign of the Bakufu pursuing the policy of peace, morale will never rise though preparations be pressed forward daily; and the gun-batteries and other preparations made will accordingly be so much ornament, never put to effective use. But if the Bakufu, now and henceforward, shows itself resolute for expulsion, the immediate effect will be to increase ten-fold the morale of the country and to bring about the completion of military preparations without even the necessity for issuing orders. Hesitant as I am to say so, only by so doing will the Shōgun be able to fulfil his 'barbarian-expelling' duty[3] and unite the men of every province in carrying out their

---

[1] A reference to the severe expulsion decree of 1825, a translation of which is given in J. Murdoch, *History of Japan*, iii. 528.

[2] i.e. with the Russians, as a result of Russian raids on the Kuriles and surveys round Hokkaidō. See Murdoch, *History of Japan*, iii. 516–17 and 522–3.

[3] i.e. his duty as *Sei-i-tai-shōgun*, his full title as Shōgun, literally 'Barbarian-expelling Generalis-

proper military functions. That is the tenth reason why we must never choose the policy of peace, and it is by far the most urgent and important of them all.

I have tried to explain above in general terms the relative advantages and disadvantages of the war and peace policies. However, this [policy I recommend] is something that it is easy to understand but difficult to carry out. In these feeble days men tend to cling to peace; they are not fond of defending their country by war. They slander those of us who are determined to fight, calling us lovers of war, men who enjoy conflict. If matters become desperate they might, in their enormous folly, try to overthrow those of us who are determined to fight, offering excuses to the enemy and concluding a peace agreement with him. They would thus in the end bring total destruction upon us. In view of our country's tradition of military courage, however, it is probable that once the Bakufu has taken a firm decision we shall find no such cowards among us. But good advice is as hard to accept as good medicine is unpleasing to the palate. A temporizing and time-serving policy is the one easiest for men to adopt. It is therefore my belief that in this question of coast defence it is of the first importance that the Bakufu pay due heed [to these matters] and that having once reached a decision it should never waver from it thereafter....[1]

DOCUMENT 4. Jisha-bugyō, machi-bugyō and kanjō-bugyō to Rōjū; memorandum concerning the American letters, submitted to Abe Masahiro on 26 August 1853.[2]

... Of these matters [raised by the Americans], the question of kind treatment for castaways was settled by the Bakufu orders of 1842.[3] Hence

simo' (though when the title was first created, the term 'barbarian' applied specifically to the Ainu peoples of northern Japan).

[1] In the remaining pages of this memorandum, in which he deals with the specifically military steps to be taken, Nariaki recommends encouragement of training with sword and spear (for armed with them, no soldier will fear warship or cannon); the purchase of ships and cannon with the proceeds of the Dutch trade, using the Dutch as agents; the granting of permission to *daimyō* to build modern ships and guns; and the construction of defence works along the coast.

[2] From the superscription it would seem that this document was submitted jointly by the *jisha-bugyō* (of whom there were 3) and *machi-bugyō* (of whom there were 2), but by only one of the four *kanjō-bugyō*, namely Honda Yasuhide, Kaga-no-kami. The fact that Kawaji Toshiaki was at that time one of the *kanjō-bugyō* and does not appear to have been associated with the policy here recommended may be of significance in view of the part he later played in foreign affairs.
  The text of the document is printed in *Bakumatsu Gaikoku Kankei Monjo*, i. 603-12. It begins, however, with summaries of the Bakufu and American letters, and this section is not translated here. The translation therefore starts from *Bakumatsu Gaikoku Kankei Monjo*, i. 606, line 2.

[3] By the revised expulsion laws of 1842 officials were ordered to supply foreign ships with essential stores before requesting them to depart and to use force only if they then refused to go. A translation of the decree appears in Murdoch, *History of Japan*, iii. 530.

demanding it now may well be a subterfuge by which the Americans hope to find justification and pretext for such action as will force compliance with their [other] demands, a plan by which they may obtain a foothold. We must certainly tell them that the Bakufu has already made a pronouncement on this subject. For the rest, it is quite impossible for the Bakufu to agree to appoint a port at which they may be supplied with coal, food, and so on—to say nothing of such questions as friendship and trade. Previous to this there have already been requests for trade from various Western peoples, but on each occasion the Bakufu has cited our national laws as grounds for withholding its consent. That being the case, if the Bakufu approves trade on this occasion we do not see how there could be any grounds for refusal when other countries made the same request. For the Bakufu none the less to bow to the wishes of Western countries and grant permission for trade would be to take the first step towards destruction of our national strength; it would lead eventually to a policy of humbling ourselves before the might of the foreigners and so impair our national prestige. Moreover, what the foreigners describe as their desire to purchase supplies of coal, food, and so on is but, by another name, the exchange of commodities. It is a trick by which they hope to open trade and is therefore equally inadmissible. Again, mere friendship being a thing that brings no profit, it certainly seems unlikely that the foreigners would press their demands for that alone. Yet it may be that they have some long-range plan in mind which might lead them, on the grounds of the proximity of our two countries, to press for an agreement that embodies no more than this. But we have no present need for concluding new friendship agreements with neighbouring countries, more particularly as to do so would be in conflict with our national prohibition [against foreign intercourse]. That it is inadmissible is beyond dispute.

Thus, as we have seen, it is impossible for the Bakufu to accept any single one of the American requests. However, if we return a blunt refusal this will surely displease and disappoint them. It may make them present all manner of demands and even undertake acts of violence. The wording of our refusal, therefore, must at all costs be peaceable. It would be best for the Bakufu simply to explain that it must adhere to the national laws, but saying so in such a friendly manner as will not make us seem to be acting in bad faith, behaving generally in such a way as to convince them that in present circumstances they have no option but to sail home. However, these foreigners have claimed to be different from those who came before and have said that when they come again next spring they will bring several great warships with them. Moreover when they arrived, a short time ago, and the Bakufu, knowing that its military preparations were inadequate, acted peacefully and agreed to accept their letters, they even went so far as to enter Edo Bay and carry out surveys here and there. It does not seem likely, therefore, that they will make no difficulty, that they will return home empty-handed after a mere routine explanation from us. Indeed we are greatly concerned that, despising us, they may continue to press their demands. All foreign countries have been covertly eyeing our land for many years. And though one may belittle the importance of the proposal concerning 'an important matter' made by the Dutch king some years ago,[1] if one considers it closely one sees that it was no mere passing whim. More particularly, if one studies the letter in which the new Dutch Kapitan at Nagasaki, acting on the orders of the Governor-General in Batavia, last year forwarded a report from his king on this matter, one finds that it differs only in detail from the demands now brought by the American ships and omits none of the stipulations. Putting these facts together it seems clear that there is a connexion. Next year is that in which the Dutch Kapitan is to have his regular audience with the Shōgun. We very much suspect, therefore, that in fact both [Dutch and Americans] are in collusion in a cunning plot to betray us, that they will proceed in accordance with an agreed plan that they have prepared in advance, by which the American ships will time the date of their return next spring to coincide with the coming of the new Dutch Kapitan to Edo: if the nature of our negotiating makes it desirable they will then take military action and so throw the capital into confusion, whereupon the Kapitan, making use of the opportunity and of the fact that he is supposedly experienced in the ways of foreign countries, will intervene to settle the dispute and so ensure that the foreigners succeed in gaining their ends. Might not this be so? At all events, it will be impossible to handle matters effectively unless the Bakufu now acts so as to intensify defence preparations and devise means by which we may obtain victory even if the foreigners adopt illegal and violent methods, should matters reach a major crisis in which peace and war are brought to issue.

We understand that the foreigners surveyed various places in Edo Bay when they sailed through there recently, even the straits between Awa and Sagami provinces[2] which we regard as the most important of our strategic areas. Should it happen that they conceive ill-will towards us and sail at once to the capital, bombarding it with heavy guns and destroying the city's dwellings by fire, there would be great confusion in the city and it would naturally be impossible for the feudal lords to carry out defence measures. Again, should they, in order to get control of the straits at Uraga, seize the Izu Islands and establish a base there, equipping it with guns and ships of every size, they could interrupt our coastal

---

[1] This refers to the Dutch suggestion, made in 1844, that Japan should abandon the seclusion policy. See D. C. Greene, 'Correspondence between William II of Holland and the Shogun of Japan, A.D. 1844', *Trans. Asiatic Soc. Japan*, xxxiv (1907), pp. 99–132.

[2] i.e. the entrance to Edo Bay.

shipping and exhaust the rice and other commodities in Edo. The situation would then, indeed, be most critical, and we are therefore anxious that the Bakufu should decide what practical steps to take by sending men now to inspect the coastal areas and report their ideas on the subject after seeing the actual places; and that it should act with all speed, for the time being setting all else aside.

None the less, however much the Bakufu exerts itself to strengthen our land defences, the foreigners will be able to anchor wherever they choose and will come and go freely in our coastal waters. Each time they do so the defending forces, from the *daimyō* down, will exhaust themselves in ceaseless activity; and it is possible that this may bring about national collapse, arousing the people's resentment at last [against the Bakufu] and giving rise to some unlooked-for disaster in domestic affairs. Thus it will be impossible to regard the Bakufu's preparations as adequate or complete unless it builds powerful warships and gives orders for training in their use, thus setting up sea-borne defences to meet and overcome the foreign ships at sea when they come. It is therefore our hope that the Bakufu will now issue immediate orders that all those responsible for land defence are to undertake also the construction of warships and that both land and sea training is to be carried out, thus ensuring that morale is raised and military preparations completed. Once this is done our strength will be ample to meet whatever violence the foreigners may use and the Bakufu can negotiate a settlement without fear of difficulties arising.

No matter how earnestly the Bakufu exerts itself to complete these military preparations, however, it is doubtful whether success can be achieved in the space of one or two years. In the meanwhile, and as a temporary expedient, it would be wise for the Bakufu to plan its actions in such a manner that hostilities do not break out. Accordingly, having given full and careful thought to the reply the Bakufu should make, we believe it essential in present circumstances that our action provide the foreigners with no pretext for raising objections, and hence consider the most suitable reply to be as follows:

'It is not unreasonable of America to have sought trade and friendship with us on the grounds that our two countries are neighbours, and in some circumstances we would be willing to agree as long as this were restricted to America. However . . .[1] it is the ancient rule of our country that trade is limited to the Dutch and Chinese. Already, before this, various Western countries have requested trade, and each time we have refused on the grounds that our national laws prohibit it. Yet if these countries learn that we have now permitted America to trade, they will certainly make this a pretext for renewing their requests. In that event

[1] The next ten characters in the original document are illegible.

we would have no grounds for refusal. Not only that, but also, of course, there is the fact that we have no products that we can exchange. This must be clearly understood. As to coal, our national production has always been inadequate. As to food, our land is very fertile, but our population equally is large and there is no surplus to meet foreign requirements.

'On such occasions as ships have suffered damage in our waters, as long as it was beyond doubt that this was a case of shipwreck, we have shown the crews every kindness, have taken action to ensure the safety of their goods and have sent them back to their own country in Dutch ships. Such having been our action on previous occasions, it must be clearly understood that there is no need to raise this matter again. And apart from the question of kind treatment for castaways, the other requests are all matters which it is impossible to arrange. You must therefore understand that, conditions being what they are in Japan, you can do no other than depart at once, never to return again hereafter.'

It might happen, however, that the foreigners will not accept this answer and become vehement on the subject. If so, it would not be possible for the Bakufu to have peace and yet insist on refusing the things which they so earnestly request. We think it would then be best to inform them that it might be possible in certain circumstances for the Bakufu to permit trade if it were strictly confined to the Americans, but that it is difficult for us to tell exactly whether other Western countries would then seek trade with us; that we therefore want the Americans to conduct discussions with the other countries and, if there are no objections from them to our permitting trade only with America, to notify the Dutch of that fact so that we may be informed through Nagasaki; and that we would then be willing to discuss the agreement they have just proposed. If we were to do this, they would have no pretext for further discussion. The negotiations would thus be made to last for some years; and while they were going on the Bakufu should take action to complete its preparations both by land and sea. What we have proposed above, about America conducting negotiations with other Western countries and carrying on discussions to ensure that there will be no demands for trade from those other countries, is something they would find it quite impossible to accomplish. In effect, therefore, it is a method by which the Bakufu may postpone the question for the time being. However, since there is no telling what kind of tricks they may use to deceive us simply for the sake of opening trade, the Bakufu should first give instructions to the Dutch that they are to inform us when these discussions have been completed. If we should be informed [by the Americans] through Holland that all the negotiations in this matter have been completed, we may then inquire more fully of the Dutch. Once they have told us that this is fact and not error we may, on the basis of this report, permit the Americans to trade, though setting a limit of a specific term of years to the agreement. If the other foreigners then renew their demands, we can make that the pretext for immediately banning trade. Alternatively, it may be possible to ban it on the grounds that the Bakufu, on consideration, finds that trade brings no advantage. Whatever we do will be but a stratagem to last till the Bakufu can complete its military preparations. Hence even if the Bakufu agrees to permit trade for a time, this will only be a policy devised as a temporary expedient for the purpose of continuing the tradition [of seclusion] that we have maintained for so many generations; and we therefore think that such action can be taken without self-reproach.

DOCUMENT 5. Shimazu Nariakira to Bakufu, 2 September 1853.[1]

In accordance with Bakufu instructions, I have perused the Japanese translations of two letters recently presented by the American ships; and having been instructed that I must report my views without reserve on the problem of whether or no trade is to be permitted, this being a matter of the greatest national consquence, I comply herewith.

We were given prior notice of the American request by the Dutch and it was often rumoured by the foreigners then resident in Ryūkyū. It is no mere passing whim. For their part, too, they came and pressed their request despite full knowledge of the Shōgun's prohibition [of foreign intercourse]. Thus even if we decide to return a reply in accordance with our national laws it is unlikely that they will readily accept it. On the other hand, I do not believe we have any chance of victory if we try to expel them, for our defences are inadequate. Even if we succeeded in expelling them at the start, we know that they have ships that can traverse the seas at will and in particular that they have of recent days based many ships on China and the uninhabited islands,[2] with the result that they can at any time interrupt our sea communications. I therefore believe that what the Bakufu does on the present occasion will indeed prove to be of the greatest consequence.

If the Bakufu grants the requests on this occasion its prestige will be dimmed and it will have broken faith with the King of Holland. Then again, I believe, if foreign countries get the idea that the Bakufu will grant their requests under threat of war, this will cause us great and constant

---

[1] The text is printed in *Bakumatsu Gaikoku Kankei Monjo*, i. 636–8.

[2] This could possibly be read as 'the Bonin Islands', though these were usually known in Japan as the Ogasawara Islands.

difficulties for the future. I believe, then, that it might be inadvisable for the Bakufu to grant these present requests. However, if the Bakufu gives a blunt refusal when they come back next year, the foreigners might open hostilities. It is my belief, therefore, that the Bakufu should act so as to gain as much time as possible, explaining [to the Americans] that circumstances leave it no choice but to order them to return home, and should use the interval [so gained] to order completion of our coast defences. I think the Bakufu policy should be to seek to obtain some three years' grace, which should be ample. If we succeed in this, it is certain that by the time three years have passed all the provinces will have completed their preparations. When we have completed our military preparations, I believe, there will be ample means to obtain victory if the Bakufu orders expulsion, for Japan's military spirit has always been heroic.

As to the places at which preparations are to be made, I should wish that Uraga be given priority and that detailed instructions concerning other important places be issued after discussion. It is said that Japan's military valour is already held in respect by foreign countries and I therefore doubt whether the foreigners will act in an insulting manner once the Bakufu has made rigorous military preparations. Once we have constructed ample warships, even if the foreigners try to interrupt our sea communications the Bakufu will be able to take the necessary action; hence I think it might be best for the Bakufu to order expulsion as soon as this has been done [and not before].

Then again, once the preparation of coast defences has been ordered it would seem essential, if they are to be carried to completion, to appoint someone to exercise overall supervision and command. Since morale is of first importance in this connexion I would recommend the appointment, as commander, of a member of one of the Tokugawa branch houses. While it is an act of the greatest temerity on my part to enter upon a discussion of whom the Shōgun should appoint to this task, yet in terms of age and in terms of popular esteem, as well as in his detailed knowledge of foreign affairs, I do not believe there can be any man more suitable than the former Mito Chūnagon [Tokugawa Nariaki]. I therefore respectfully submit my request that the Bakufu may entrust him with the duties of coast defence.

This present problem is of the greatest importance to our country. And I believe that it will be impossible for us to find means of achieving victory unless the Bakufu directs its action in the light of the necessity to 'know one's enemy and know oneself'. Hence I think orders should be issued only after the fullest discussion. Certainly were the Bakufu to give immediate approval to the present [American] request I should have the greatest fears for the future of our country.

What I have written above is indeed temerity on my part, but it is a statement of my views made without reserve and without thought of consequences.

Forwarded with respect.

(*Note.* I think it would be even more dangerous for the Bakufu to give permission for the establishment of coaling stations and the other matters.)

DOCUMENT 6. Matsudaira Keiei to Bakufu, 9 September 1853.[1]

The Bakufu having sent me Japanese translations of the two letters presented by the American ships which came recently to Uraga and instructed me to consider carefully the question of whether or no we should permit trade, taking into account all the advantages and disadvantages of so doing as well as the possible future repercussions, and then to report my views in full, I accordingly submit below a statement of my views.

The President's letter, in contravention of the strict [seclusion] system we have maintained for over two hundred years, makes a number of impossible requests. What is more, there are passages in the letter presented by Perry, such as those in which he threatens the use of force to attain the objects of his mission and refers to our national laws as an unenlightened form of government, which are truly outrageous and show the utmost contempt for our country. They are such as to arouse extreme anger, and make it absolutely essential, I believe, for us to demonstrate our martial vigour to the whole world by completely destroying his ships. However, careful study of the present situation reveals that we are in fact helpless and cannot handle matters in that way. I believe that we have never been presented with a more difficult situation, that this is a national crisis more serious than any we have faced since the dawn of our history. For the Bakufu to grant the foreign request in its present form would, it is needless to say, disgrace our martial repute. Moreover, if other countries heard reports of it and all made similar requests, we would, by using up our limited resources in trade to satisfy the insatiable greed of the foreigners, bring daily nearer the collapse of our country. One might think, then, that we should pursue a policy of expediency, namely to grant their request while setting a three- to five-year limit [on the agreement], thus for a time warding off their insistence and leaving ourselves free to withdraw permission once our defences are completed, which would enable us to hold up our heads once again. This would [at first sight] seem the most appropriate action at this time. On the other hand, the Bakufu made no special preparations by way of strengthening our defences, despite the fact that ever since last year there had been frequent reports

---

[1] The text is printed in *Bakumatsu Gaikoku Kankei Monjo*, ii. 52–58.

that the foreigners would come this summer, and even had to make up its mind about accepting the letters as a last-minute decision; and while this, too, was described as a policy of expediency, men of perception feel it to have been most reprehensible. Thus should the Bakufu decide, again in the name of expediency, to conclude treaties of friendship with foreigners, it would give the appearance of having fallen into the foreigners' toils simply from fear of their military might. Should this happen, I believe, our superb national morale would decline; and when we reached the end of the term of years [set for the agreement], there would not be the slightest hope of being quickly able to raise that morale again.

There is a possibility that the foreigners would readily depart if the Bakufu were to grant their requests. But they have completed a survey of Edo Bay and have learned that there is nothing they need fear in our defences, especially at the Uraga entrance. This naturally increases their greed, and it is possible that when they come again they may resort to all kinds of violent action without even waiting for the Bakufu reply. Again, realizing that our defence preparations are being steadily effected, they may, even though the Bakufu grants their requests, decide to open hostilities while those preparations are still incomplete, indulging in such acts of violence as the English did at Chusan[1] and making such outrageous demands as for the right to swagger about in our capital or to open trading establishments. If they did this it is clear that even though the Bakufu issued orders for their lenient treatment, conflicts would occur and would lead to the opening of hostilities, for the Yamato spirit, which excels that of all other countries, is inherent in our people and they could not endure such things with patience. Then again, for the Bakufu to grant trade to all countries, even for a limited term of years, would be to humble itself before all countries. It would be the height of disgrace. And when the time came to withdraw permission, I believe, we would find ourselves the object of simultaneous attack by many powerful enemies. This would make it all the more impossible to conduct a successful defence. When it was realized that military weakness forced us to endure such disgrace, I very much fear that it would not only be in foreign countries that men might question the competence of our rulers, even the *daimyō* and lesser lords throughout the country. It might even be that Bakufu control of Japan would become ineffective, as happened at the end of the Ashikaga period.[2]

All this being so, I believe that the Bakufu's policy must be to refuse its consent for any of these concessions. However, I also believe that if the Bakufu does not grant the foreign demands war will break out and that

---

[1] The reference is to the British occupation of Chusan during the Opium War in China.

[2] In the fifteenth and sixteenth centuries the authority of the Ashikaga Bakufu broke down in a period of intermittent civil war. The Ashikaga themselves were eventually overthrown and replaced by the Tokugawa.

the Bakufu cannot therefore refuse unless it is resolved to fight no matter how many warships are sent against us. Accordingly it is my belief that the greatest and most urgent task of the moment is for the Bakufu to notify the lords of all ranks in all provinces that the American requests are unacceptable and will be refused and that they are therefore to make preparations in anticipation of an outbreak of war when the Americans return next spring; for the Bakufu itself to undertake studies of defence technique and to unite opinion throughout the country; and for the early appointment of a supreme commander entrusted with complete authority in military affairs. . . .[1]

By returning an answer that it is impossible to grant the [American] requests, except for that seeking kind treatment for castaways, the Bakufu would be rebuking the foreigners for their faults without arousing their anger, would be deferring to prestige without humbling itself. This would be both a just and proper policy, as well as a firm one. By acting in this way the Bakufu would gradually break down their attitude of contempt and tacitly forestall their greedy designs. And only thus, I believe, can the military valour of our land be restored to its former glory and our unexampled fair name and our permanent independence be fully maintained. If, on the other hand, we should lap ourselves in the luxury of peace to which we have for so long been accustomed, content with idleness and taking no decision either for peace or for war; if the foreign ships should come again while we wasted time in indecision and the foreigners should come to realize our lack of preparedness as we resorted to a policy of makeshifts; and if they should then set aflame our capital with their shells and cut down our troops with their small-shot, then it is evident to me that almost nothing could prevent the total collapse of our country. The dead would pile mountain-high and the streets would be filled with the sound of weeping. The confusion would be immense. When that time came, even if the Bakufu ordered the feudal lords to undertake defence, as it did recently, no general plan of defence would exist and all would have to do what they could individually. Complete victory would be impossible. However many troops were summoned from the provinces, the brave soldiers would fall in vain under the fire of foreign guns. All this would be inescapable. And not only would it call forth all our pity and regret, but also it would lead to national collapse. In the end peace negotiations would be undertaken and our country might even become a colony, a very slave, of the foreigners. At the very thought I cannot contain my wrath and indignation. The prospect so disturbs me that I can neither eat nor sleep. And since it is my belief that the safety and even the existence of our country are now at stake, I feel that the most urgent of

[1] The next passage (*Bakumatsu Gaikoku Kankei Monjo*, ii, p. 55, line 6, to p. 57, line 3), which discusses details of the actual military preparations to be made, is here omitted.

all the urgent tasks of the present time is for the Bakufu to forbid all foolish talk of peace, to issue an immediate announcement that it is from this moment going to make plans for war, and to appoint a supreme commander. If a single day is wasted, then our defences are thereby one day delayed. I therefore ask with respect that the Bakufu may make its decision firmly and at once. . . .[1]

DOCUMENT 7. Ii Naosuke to Bakufu, 1 October 1853.[2]

Before the year 1635 there were nine government-licensed trading vessels belonging to Nagasaki, Sakai, Kyōto, &c., but with the prohibition of Christianity in the time of the Shōgun Iemitsu the Bakufu put an end to the voyages of these nine ships and laid down laws closing the country. Commerce was entirely limited to the Dutch and Chinese, no others being allowed to participate in it. Careful consideration of conditions as they are today, however, leads me to believe that despite the constant differences and debates into which men of patriotism and foresight have been led in recent years by their perception of the danger of foreign aggression, it is impossible in the crisis we now face to ensure the safety and tranquillity of our country merely by an insistence on the seclusion laws as we did in former times. Moreover, time is essential if we are to complete our coast defences. Since 1609, when warships of over 500 *koku* were forbidden,[3] we have had no warships capable of opposing foreign attack on our coasts with heavy guns. Thus I am much afraid that were the foreigners now to seize as bases such outlying islands as Hachijō-jima and Ōshima, it would be impossible for us to remain inactive, though without warships we should have no effective means of driving them off. There is a saying that when one is besieged in a castle, to raise the drawbridge is to imprison oneself and make it impossible to hold out indefinitely; and again, that when opposing forces face each other across a river, victory is obtained by that which crosses the river and attacks. It seems clear throughout history that he who takes action is in a position to advance, while he who remains inactive must retreat. Even though the Shōgun's ancestors set up seclusion laws, they left the Dutch and the Chinese to act as a bridge [to the outside world]. Might this bridge not now be of advantage to us in handling foreign affairs, providing us with the means whereby we may

---

[1] The translation ends at *Bakumatsu Gaikoku Kankei Monjo*, ii, p. 58, line 5. The remaining sentences reiterate the statement already made and make the usual formal disclaimer of any intention of disrespect. An enclosure (*Bakumatsu Gaikoku Kankei Monjo*, ii. 59–71) goes into further detail on the question of the specifically military steps to be taken.

[2] The text is printed in *Bakumatsu Gaikoku Kankei Monjo*, ii. 255–9. There is an earlier translation of this document in Gubbins, *The Progress of Japan, 1853–1871* (Oxford, 1911), pp. 285–8.

[3] The decree of 1609 in fact only prohibited the construction of such ships by the *daimyō*. The *koku* (5 bushels approx.) was the usual unit of measure for designating the size of a Japanese ship in this period.

for a time avert the outbreak of hostilities and then, after some time has elapsed, gain a complete victory?

I understand that the coal for which the Americans have expressed a desire is to be found in quantity in Kyūshū. We should first tell them, as a matter of expediency, that we also have need of coal, but that should their need of it arise urgently and unexpectedly during a voyage, they may ask for coal at Nagasaki and if we have any to spare we will provide it. Nor will we grudge them wood and water. As for foodstuffs, the supply varies from province to province, but we can agree to provide food for the shipwrecked and unfortunate. Again, we can tell them, of recent years we have treated kindly those wrecked on our coasts and have sent them all home. There is no need for further discussion of this subject, and all requests concerning it should be made through the Dutch. Then, too, there is the question of trade. Although there is a national prohibition of it, conditions are not the same as they were. The exchange of goods is a universal practice. This we should explain to the spirits of our ancestors. And we should then tell the foreigners that we mean in future to send trading vessels to the Dutch company's factory at Batavia to engage in trade; that we will allocate some of our trading goods to America, some to Russia, and so on, using the Dutch to trade for us as our agents; but that there will be a delay of one or two years because we must [first] construct new ships for these voyages. By replying in this way we will take the Americans by surprise in offering to treat them generally in the same way as the Dutch.

We must revive the licensed trading vessels that existed before the Kanei period [1624-44], ordering the rich merchants of such places as Ōsaka, Hyōgo, and Sakai to take shares in the enterprise. We must construct new steamships, especially powerful warships, and these we will load with goods not needed in Japan. For a time we will have to employ Dutchmen as masters and mariners, but we will put on board with them Japanese of ability and integrity who must study the use of large guns, the handling of ships, and the rules of navigation. Openly these will be called merchant vessels, but they will in fact have the secret purpose of training a navy. As we increase the number of ships and our mastery of technique, Japanese will be able to sail the oceans freely and gain direct knowledge of conditions abroad without relying on the secret reports of the Dutch. Thus we will eventually complete the organization of a navy. Moreover, we must shake off the panic and apprehensions that have beset us and abandon our habits of luxury and wasteful spending. Our defences thus strengthened, and all being arranged at home, we can act so as to make our courage and prestige resound beyond the seas. By so doing, we will not in the future be imprisoning ourselves; indeed, we will be able, I believe, so to accomplish matters at home and abroad as to achieve national security. Forestalling the foreigners in this way, I believe, is the best method of ensuring that the Bakufu will at some future time find opportunity to reimpose its ban and forbid foreigners to come to Japan, as was done in the Kanei period. Moreover, it would make possible the strictest prohibition of Christianity. And since I understand that the Americans and Russians themselves have only recently become skilled in navigation, I do not see how the people of our country, who are clever and quick-witted, should prove inferior to Westerners if we begin training at once.

The national situation being what it is, if the Bakufu protects our coasts peacefully without bringing upon us permanent foreign difficulties, then even if that entails complete or partial change in the laws of our ancestors I do not believe such action could really be regarded as contrary to the wishes of those ancestors. However, I think it is essential to win the support of the country for Bakufu policy on this occasion, so the Bakufu should first notify the [Imperial] Court and then arrange to send Imperial messengers to the Ise, Iwashimizu, and Kashima shrines and a Tokugawa messenger to Nikkō,[1] announcing there its resolve to secure tranquillity at home and security for the country. Trust in the will of the gods, after all, is the ancient custom of our land; and I believe, moreover, that by so doing the Bakufu may be able to unite national opinion.

It is now no easy matter, by means of orders concerning the defence of the capital and the nearby coast, to ensure that all will be fully prepared for any sudden emergency, so not a moment must be wasted. However many iron walls we construct, they will certainly not be as effective as unity of mind if the unforeseen happens. The urgent task of the moment, therefore, is for the Bakufu to resolve on relieving the nation's anxieties and issue the appropriate orders.

I am conscious of my temerity in putting forward views that conflict with the existing [seclusion] laws, but I have so reported in accordance with your orders that I was to do so fully and without reserve.

DOCUMENT 8. Convention between the United States of America and Japan, signed at Kanagawa, 31 March 1854. Ratifications were exchanged at Shimoda, 21 February 1855.[2]

The United States of America and the Empire of Japan, desiring to establish firm, lasting, and sincere friendship between the two nations,

[1] i.e. to report to the Imperial and Tokugawa ancestors. The Ise shrine is that dedicated to the sun-goddess Amaterasu, founder of the Imperial line. Iwashimizu and Kashima are also important Shintō shrines (in Kyōto and Hitachi respectively), dedicated to former emperors. At Nikkō were the Tokugawa family mausolea, enshrining Tokugawa Ieyasu, first Shōgun of that house.

[2] The English text was signed by Commodore Perry. *Bakumatsu Gaikoku Kankei Monjo*, v. 449–60, gives the Chinese (*kambun*) text, the Japanese translation thereof, and the Japanese translation

have resolved to fix, in a manner clear and positive, by means of a treaty or general convention of peace and amity, the rules which shall in future be mutually observed in the intercourse of their respective countries; for which most desirable object the President of the United States has conferred full powers on his commissioner, Matthew Calbraith Perry, special ambassador of the United States to Japan; and the August Sovereign of Japan has given similar full powers to his commissioners, Hayashi, Daigaku-no-kami, Ido, prince of Tsus-Sima, Izawa, prince of Mima-saki, and Udono, member of the Board of Revenue.[1] And the said commissioners, after having exchanged their said full powers and duly considered the premises, have agreed to the following Articles:

ARTICLE I

There shall be a perfect, permanent, and universal peace, and a sincere and cordial amity, between the United States of America on the one part, and the empire of Japan on the other part, and between their people respectively, without exception of persons or places.

ARTICLE II

The port of Simoda [Shimoda], in the principality of Idzu, and the port of Hakodade [Hakodate], in the principality of Matsmai [Matsumae], are granted by the Japanese as ports for the reception of American ships, where they can be supplied with wood, water, provisions, and coal, and other articles their necessities may require, as far as the Japanese have them. The time for opening the first named port is immediately on signing this treaty; the last named port is to be opened immediately after the same day in the ensuing Japanese year.

Note: A tariff of prices shall be given by the Japanese officers of the things which they can furnish, payment for which shall be made in gold and silver coin.

ARTICLE III

Whenever ships of the United States are thrown or wrecked on the coast of Japan, the Japanese vessels will assist them, and carry their crews to Simoda and Hakodade, and hand them over to their countrymen, appointed to receive them; whatever articles the shipwrecked men may have preserved shall likewise be restored, and the expenses incurred in the rescue and support of Americans and Japanese who may thus be thrown upon the shores of either nation are not to be refunded.

of the Dutch text. The second of these was signed by the Japanese negotiators, namely the Confucian scholar Hayashi Noboru, Daigaku-no-kami; the *machi-bugyō* Ido Satohiro, Tsushima-no-kami; the *Uraga-bugyō* Izawa Masayoshi, Mimasaka-no-kami; and the *metsuke* Udono Chōei, Mimbu-shōyū. There are some discrepancies between the English and Japanese texts, and where these are differences of substance they are indicated in the footnotes that follow.

[1] See previous note.

ARTICLE IV

Those shipwrecked persons and other citizens of the United States shall be as free as in other countries, and not subjected to confinement, but shall be amenable to just laws.

ARTICLE V

Shipwrecked men and other citizens of the United States, temporarily living at Simoda and Hakodade, shall not be subject to such restrictions and confinement as the Dutch and Chinese are at Nagasaki; but shall be free at Simoda to go where they please within the limits of seven Japanese miles (or *ri*) from a small island in the harbor of Simoda, marked on the accompanying chart, hereto appended; and shall in like manner be free to go where they please at Hakodade, within limits to be defined after the visit of the United States squadron to that place.[1]

ARTICLE VI

If there be any other sort of goods wanted, or any business which shall require to be arranged, there shall be careful deliberation between the parties in order to settle such matters.

ARTICLE VII

It is agreed that ships of the United States resorting to the ports open to them shall be permitted to exchange gold and silver coin and articles of goods for other articles of goods, under such regulations as shall be temporarily[2] established by the Japanese government for that purpose. It is stipulated, however, that the ships of the United States shall be permitted to carry away whatever articles they are unwilling to exchange.[3]

ARTICLE VIII

Wood, water, provisions, coal, and goods required, shall only be procured through the agency of Japanese officers appointed for that purpose, and in no other manner.[4]

ARTICLE IX

It is agreed that if, at any future day, the government of Japan shall grant to any other nation or nations privileges and advantages which are not herein granted to the United States and the citizens thereof, that these same privileges and advantages shall be granted likewise to the United States and to the citizens thereof without any consultation or delay.

[1] In the Japanese texts, 'and at Hakodate the limits shall be decided later'.
[2] There is no mention of 'temporarily' in the Japanese texts.
[3] In the Japanese texts, 'whatever articles the Japanese do not desire'.
[4] The Chinese text and Japanese translation thereof read 'and shall not be procured privately'; the Japanese translation from the Dutch reads 'and shall not be procured from any other person'.

ARTICLE X

Ships of the United States shall be permitted to resort to no other ports in Japan but Simoda and Hakodade, unless in distress or forced by stress of weather.

ARTICLE XI

There shall be appointed by the government of the United States, consuls or agents to reside in Simoda, at any time after the expiration of eighteen months from the date of the signing of this treaty; provided that either of the two governments deem such arrangement necessary.[1]

ARTICLE XII

The present convention, having been concluded and duly signed, shall be obligatory, and faithfully observed by the United States of America and Japan, and by the citizens and subjects of each respective power; and it is to be ratified and approved by the President of the United States, by and with the advice and consent of the Senate thereof, and by the August Sovereign of Japan, and the ratifications shall be exchanged within eighteen months from the date of the signature thereof, or sooner if practicable.

In faith whereof, we, respective plenipotentiaries of the United States of America and the Empire of Japan aforesaid, have signed and sealed these presents.

Done at Kanagawa, this thirty-first day of March, in the year of our Lord Jesus Christ one thousand eight hundred and fifty-four, and of Kayei the seventh year, third month, and third day.[2]

DOCUMENT 9. America ōsetsu-gakari to Rōjū, 2 April 1854.[3]

Report on negotiations with the American envoy Perry and the conclusion of a treaty with him

The American envoy Perry, having last year presented to the Bakufu a

---

[1] The Japanese subsequently argued that the appointment of a consul to Shimoda required the consent of both governments. It is true that the Chinese text and the Japanese translation thereof both read 'An American official shall be sent to Shimoda if circumstances seem to both governments to make this necessary . . .' and this presumably represents Hayashi's intentions. But the other Japanese translation (that made from the Dutch text) reads 'With respect to a consul or agent resident at Shimoda, the American government shall send such a person if there comes a time when either one of the two governments wishes to establish such an office. . . .' All three texts add that this shall in any case be not less than 18 months after the signing of the treaty.

[2] The Chinese text and translation of it give the date only in Japanese style (Kaei 7.iii.3). The translation from the Dutch gives also '31 March 1854', but avoids (probably deliberately) anything that might suggest the Christian connotations of such a date.

[3] The text is printed in *Bakumatsu Gaikoku Kankei Monjo*, v. 478–85. The document is signed by the four plenipotentiaries who had conducted the negotiations with Perry, namely Hayashi

letter from his country's President and believing that since the Bakufu accepted delivery of this letter it would grant the requests made therein, recently requested the Bakufu to give him a written reply expressing its consent. Were the Bakufu not to agree, he said, he would have failed to accomplish his mission; and even at the cost of unavoidable war he could not return to his own country without succeeding in these requests. He had accordingly arranged to bring several warships with him, and still more were being sent from his home country. This being so, the Bakufu ordered us to undertake discussions and negotiations on this matter, giving us secret instructions, however, that we were to handle the matter peaceably. In accordance with these instructions we have conducted negotiations and concluded a treaty.

When the negotiations began, the foreigners brought with them a draft of the treaty they sought and urged that we conform fully to their wishes [as expressed in it]. In the course of the discussions we succeeded in modifying this and reducing it to what is shown in the enclosure.[1]

We informed Perry that the Bakufu had last year asked the Dutch Kapitan [at Deshima] to inform him that the question of a written reply must be postponed, since a new reign was starting and the great pressure of business in domestic affairs made an immediate answer impossible;[2] but that since he had come none the less, officials had been sent to conduct negotiations and he would receive a reply from the persons so sent after discussions had been held. Thus the matter was settled without giving him any written reply from the Bakufu. Moreover, the agreement was concluded in the names of the four envoys, without any official document from the Rōjū.

Perry stated repeatedly that when American castaways landed in Japan the Bakufu had hitherto treated them as enemies, immediately imprisoning them in confined quarters. This was to treat them like criminals, he said, and was assuredly an inhuman policy. In his country human life was highly valued. It was therefore his desire that the Bakufu should in future treat castaways in the same way as they were treated in other countries, no distinction being made between foreigners and ourselves. We accordingly informed him that human life was, of course, highly valued in our country too, and that castaways not only of his country but also of all other countries invariably received kind treatment. However, we said, when these castaways without our consent took matters into their own hands it

Noboru, Daigaku-no-kami; Ido Satohiro, Tsushima-no-kami; Izawa Masayoshi, Mimasaka-no-kami; and Udono Chōei, Mimbu-shōyū.

[1] i.e. the Japanese text of the Perry convention (*Bakumatsu Gaikoku Kankei Monjo*, v. 449-60). See Document 8 above.

[2] The Shōgun Ieyoshi died on 27 July 1853, just after Perry's first visit to Japan, and the Bakufu had tried to use this as an excuse for postponing negotiations.

was not possible to treat them in this way. We would not hereafter treat them as prisoners if they were peaceable, but we would certainly have to punish any who broke our country's laws.

With respect to the request that we provide food, wood, water, and other supplies needed by ships, we informed them that we would agree to this because such things were vital to human life. We would, moreover, provide coal, which with the development of navigation in recent years has become an article of daily use in his country; but since this was an article not much used in Japan, we said, it could be supplied only to the extent that it was available at any specific place. We also stated it as the Bakufu's intention to provide such things as food, wood, water, and coal free of charge for a period of three to five years, but Perry said that they never accepted goods from other countries without payment and that he must therefore request that they be allowed to offer something in return. We replied that they were quite free to offer something by way of acknowledgement.

The foreigners stated that our work would really be incomplete unless we decided upon the ports at which the Bakufu was to provide food, wood, water, and so on. They asked that we should open Ryūkyū [Loochoo], Hakodate, and three other ports, and also that one of these ports should be Uraga. We informed them that Ryūkyū was a distant frontier outpost about which we could give no answer; nor could a decision be taken at once about Hakodate, because it was in the territory of one of the feudal lords. Still less could permission be granted for Uraga, we told them, as it was a place much frequented by Japanese vessels. Perry then asked that Kanagawa-Yokohama be made one of the ports and suggested various places that he would like opened. We accordingly had no choice [in the end] but to open Shimoda in Izu and Hakodate in Matsumae and designate them as places at which food, wood, water, and so on would be provided.

We proposed an agreement by which the Bakufu would provide food, wood, water, coal, and so on at Nagasaki, but the foreigners stated that Nagasaki was not suitable for their country and they probably would not go there at first. They asked that these facilities be provided at the two ports of Shimoda and Hakodate. However, they said, only fishing-vessels would go in numbers to Hakodate, so coal would not be needed there. At that place only food, wood, water, and other supplies necessary to ships would be required.

The foreigners urged that if food, wood, water, and so on were to be supplied at Shimoda, then they would want to be able to move about freely in the vicinity of Shimoda harbour. We replied that it was our intention to prescribe bounds in the immediate vicinity of the harbour within which they could move about. However, they insisted that they must be free to act as they chose in this, without being restricted in any way, and claimed that they wished first to make a chart of Shimoda harbour and then to be allowed to walk for pleasure within a distance of one day's travel [from that place], which is a distance of seven *ri*. (This is not seven Japanese *ri*.)[1] We advanced various arguments to show that this was impossible, saying that it was in any case our intention to set wide bounds within which they could move about, but they were most insistent that if we did so they would [consider themselves free to] land at will elsewhere on the coast and even go to Edo itself. They would by no means accept our suggestion; and we realized on careful consideration that if we left the matter like this they would certainly land hereafter at a number of [other] places and that this trivial detail might well lead to the outbreak of hostilities. To grant this foreign request would assuredly be no light matter; yet if we proved stubborn in discussing it they might, after all, land and walk about wherever they chose, not only at Shimoda but at a number of other places as well, and we would be helpless [to prevent it]. Hence rather than leave the foreigners to land and act violently [elsewhere] and so provoke hostilities, we decided it would be better to allow them to move about in the vicinity of the one port of Shimoda. However, we reached agreement with them that having once decided on the two ports of Shimoda and Hakodate, no ships would ever enter any other port, except for the special case of vessels in distress.

They also requested similar arrangements for walking at Hakodate, but we told them that a reply to this would be made after further investigation, since Hakodate was not only distant but was also part of the territories of one of the feudal lords.

The envoy Perry frequently expressed a desire to go to Edo, but by citing our national laws as the reason we eventually succeeded in making him accept our refusal of this. Then he said he wanted to survey Edo Bay, urging that the sea was common to all countries and could not be divided into 'ours' and 'theirs'; moreover, he said, he had no evil purpose, his sole object being to make a survey. However, we insisted on refusing this, on the grounds that to let him enter Edo Bay would cause disturbance in the capital, while our national laws forbade the entrance of foreign ships into Edo Bay. When we pointed out that having granted most of his requests we must really insist on his observing our national laws in this one matter, he was forced to agree.[2]

With regard to the question of trade, Perry presented a paper drawn up in accordance with the regulations governing trade between his

---

[1] The meaning of this parenthetic note is not clear, since the treaty specifies 'seven Japanese miles (or *ri*)'. Possibly the negotiators (or the interpreters) were confused by the expression 'Japanese miles'. A distance of 7 *ri* is approximately 17 English miles.

[2] None the less, Perry did in fact survey part of Edo Bay on this occasion.

country and China and proposed that we begin negotiations on that basis. We refused this, however, pointing out that in Japan we had little experience of trade and could not lightly permit it; that the main theme of his present request was kind treatment for the citizens of his country and we had, after full consideration, given an undertaking to provide wood, water, and so on; that trade was conducted entirely with a view to profit on both sides, having no relevance to considerations of humanity, and that we were therefore unable to discuss this question at the present time. There was accordingly no further discussion of this matter in the subsequent negotiations.

He asked us to open Shimoda harbour at once, so we informed him that it would be impossible to do so until the third month of next year [17 April–15 May 1855]. He then said that if the text of the treaty did not state that at least one port would be opened at once, the United States President would certainly consider that he had failed in his mission; and, moreover, that this would only be a paper provision, for he was sure no ships would actually go there before the third month of next year, though since wood and water would be wanted at all places where ships might go, it might happen that ships would ask for wood and water there before that time. We said we would agree only on this understanding and asked him to state his acceptance thereof in writing. And though he was reluctant to send us such a letter, he was eventually persuaded to do so.

In these negotiations with the foreigners, our country sent no written reply to their letter and the business was concluded by us whom you sent for that purpose, without any official letter from the Rōjū. By this, our national prestige was maintained.

The envoy Perry was persuaded to abandon his idea of going to Edo and of circumnavigating Edo Bay and surveying there. By this, respect for our national laws was preserved.

As evidence that he would have no future designs on Japan, the envoy presented a flag to [Hayashi] Daigaku-no-kami and cannon to [Ido] Tsushima-no-kami and [Izawa] Mimasaka-no-kami. He said that should Japan hereafter suffer foreign attack we could use these in repelling it and that the United States would come to our aid with similar weapons. By this, our national prestige was maintained.

It is the custom of all countries that when a treaty is concluded the representatives of both countries meet and affix their seals in each other's presence. Thinking greater respect due to our country, we refused to seal the treaty jointly [with Perry] and arranged that each party should use a separate copy of the text, ourselves employing one to which we had previously affixed our seals. He said that if this was the custom of our country he must necessarily conform to it, but added in a letter he sent us on the following day that when he returned home this might be thought improper in an envoy. By this, our national prestige was maintained.

We regret to report that after texts of the treaty had been exchanged he sent us a letter stating that while he accepted the admonitions we had issued on the basis of our national laws, it might not be possible in the future for those laws to continue indefinitely in their present form.[1]

The text of the treaty was agreed as in the enclosure herewith, but there were also a number of other matters which he wished to add. Had we discussed them at this time, we believe he would have turned to the questions of the immediate establishment of consulates and the dispatch of officials to Japan. But when the time comes that we have to accept the dispatch of officials to Japan, the treaty will have to be further expanded.

It was our object in these negotiations to win him away from any previous idea he had of opening hostilities and to temper our admonitions with leniency, thus completing the whole affair in peace: and at the same time we sought to handle the discussions in such a way as to bring no disgrace upon our country.

Submitted with respect.

[1] The reference is to Perry's letter of 1 April 1854, in which he stated that he had accepted the present restrictions in the belief that changes in world conditions would bring about changes in Japan as well and that the opening of other ports would come once Japan understood the new conditions. The Japanese translation of this letter is printed in *Bakumatsu Gaikoku Kankei Monjo*, v. 475–6.

The Dutch Supplementary Treaty of 1857

FOR more than two years after the Perry convention there was no important change in Bakufu foreign policy. Agreements similar to that concluded with America were made with Britain and Russia and a number of concessions were made to the Dutch, but this was no more than a recognition of the inevitable. Abe Masahiro continued to work closely with Tokugawa Nariaki in defence and domestic affairs, though without accepting his advice in all respects. Opposition to this policy was increasing, however. The group of feudal lords led by Ii Naosuke and Hotta Masayoshi, together with a number of the Bakufu officials themselves, were becoming insistent that the Bakufu must compromise with the foreigners if it was to survive. And when the choice was forced on him in the autumn of 1855, Abe Masahiro abandoned his tacit alliance with Nariaki. In November Hotta was appointed to the Rōjū. He soon succeeded Abe as titular head of the council and thereafter, though not immediately, his influence on policy increased as that of Abe gradually declined. It was not until the end of 1856, however, that this caused major changes.

Meanwhile pressure was being brought upon the Bakufu from outside. In September 1856 Townsend Harris arrived at Shimoda and took up residence as American Consul-General there. He at once began pressing for some relaxation of the restrictions on foreigners, at the same time warning the Bakufu that Sir John Bowring, British Superintendent of Trade with China, would soon be coming to negotiate a commercial treaty with Japan. A similar report was made by the Dutch at Deshima. The Bakufu's problem was made suddenly more acute by news that hostilities had again broken out between Britain and China. Neither Harris nor the Dutch minister, Donker Curtius, failed to point out that refusal to grant concessions or to observe treaties might involve Japan in difficulties as great as those of China. Indeed, said Curtius, Japan would be wise not to provoke such great Powers as Britain, France, Russia, and the United States, but to change her national customs with the needs of the time. Her opportunity for so doing, or at least to show her willingness so to do, lay in making a new trade agreement with Holland such as he had already proposed during 1856.

The Nagasaki *bugyō*'s letter reporting the outbreak of the new Anglo-Chinese war and his conversations with Curtius arrived in Edo early in

March 1857. The reaction to it was immediate. On 19 March the Rōjū ordered officials to report their views on future policy, and a new note of urgency was apparent in the wording of the instructions (Document 10). Shortly after, Hotta addressed a memorandum to the *Gaikoku bōeki torishirabe-gakari*, the ten officials whom he had appointed in the previous November to make a study of the problems of foreign trade. This memorandum (Document 11) made it clear that the Bakufu had already decided to permit trade and now sought advice concerning two main problems: the first, whether it would be better to reach agreement first with the Dutch and Americans or to wait for the arrival of the British envoy; the second, to what extent government control of trade was to be retained.

The replies to this memorandum revealed that there were still differences among the officials. Many were reluctant to commit themselves at all, but the *ōmetsuke* and *metsuke* strongly favoured a minimum of government interference in trade and urged that the policy, once decided, should be made public in Japan before negotiations began (Document 12). The *kanjō-bugyō*, on the other hand, argued that as trade was to be granted not because it was desirable but because it was inevitable, Bakufu policy must always be to make the minimum of concession that was consistent with safety (Document 13). It was perhaps in an attempt to reconcile these differences that in May 1857 the *kanjō-bugyō* Mizuno Tadanori (now temporarily appointed also as Nagasaki *bugyō*) and the *metsuke* Iwase Tadanari were sent to Nagasaki to study the subject further in discussions with Donker Curtius.

In Nagasaki Donker Curtius, apparently with Iwase's support, succeeded in persuading Mizuno of the necessity for granting extensive trade privileges (Document 14). The investigation soon became a discussion of specific terms for a commercial agreement with Holland and by the end of August a draft had been agreed. This Mizuno sent to Edo for consideration by the Rōjū, emphasizing that if the British envoy reached Nagasaki before the Bakufu's instructions he would at once sign the agreement with Curtius and negotiate with Britain on the same basis (Document 15). The report was accompanied by a private letter to the other *kanjō-bugyō* in the capital, asking for their support of these proposals. In fact, however, it was the Russian envoy, not the British, who was first to arrive. On 21 September Admiral Poutiatine arrived at Nagasaki and sought an interview with the *bugyō*. Mizuno at once informed Edo that if Poutiatine demanded a commercial treaty he would adopt the same course as he had already proposed for handling negotiations with Britain (Document 16), but it proved that on this occasion Poutiatine was in a hurry to get to China and had no time for discussions. He returned unexpectedly, however, on 11 October, and demanded a treaty granting trade privileges to Russia. Still without instructions from the Bakufu, Mizuno, Iwase, and the other Nagasaki *bugyō*, Arao Narimasa, decided to act on their own responsibility. Their reasons were again explained by Mizuno in a letter to his colleagues in Edo (Document 17). On 16 October 1857 they signed the supplementary treaty with Holland (Document 18), which extended to the whole of Dutch trade the system previously limited to the 'private' trade at Deshima; that is, it retained government supervision of trade but allowed it to be conducted directly with private merchants and without limitations as to its total volume. Eight days later a similar agreement was made with Poutiatine.

The Bakufu, although it had not yet sent orders to Nagasaki, had already decided to accept the main points of Mizuno's draft, and this despite objections from the other *kanjō-bugyō* (directed especially against the proposal to remove restrictions on the number of ships and the volume of trade). Since the agreements as signed differed little from the draft, therefore, the action of Mizuno and Iwase was not repudiated. The two treaties were accepted and came to be regarded as models for the concessions that the Bakufu would be prepared to make in due course to France, Britain, and the United States.

DOCUMENT 10. Rōjū to all members of the Hyōjōsho, the Kaibō-gakari, and the Nagasaki, Shimoda, and Hakodate bugyō, 19 March 1857.[1]

The Dutch Kapitan has made a statement concerning an attack made by the English on Canton. We have given careful consideration to this and it seems that the matters raised by the Dutch, though not immediate, are becoming more and more urgent. It is not insisted that we should reach an agreement that would accomplish all the foreign demands, but it is a fact that our present manner of dealing with foreigners is generally recognized, even among our own people, to be unsuited to existing conditions. Thus if we continue adding to the anger of the foreigners it is even possible that Japan might suffer the fate of Canton. Against this the Bakufu must be on its guard.

The Shōgun has already revised the ancestral laws which have been in force since the Kan-ei period [1624–44] and has concluded friendship agreements. This done, it seems necessary that we should also revise our policy to accord with that which was observed before the Kan-ei period. Any attempt on our part to cling to tradition, making difficulties over the

---

[1] The text is printed in *Bakumatsu Gaikoku Kankei Monjo*, xv. 566–8. Members of the Hyōjōsho included most senior officials of the rank of *kanjō-bugyō* and above. The *kaibō-gakari* were those officials charged with a special responsibility for defence and foreign affairs.

merest trifles and so eventually provoking the foreigners to anger, would be impolitic in the extreme. Should there once be the sound of a single cannon-shot, then it will already be too late to turn back. The position is such, therefore, that we must adopt a realistic policy, handling affairs in the same way at each of the three ports of Nagasaki, Shimoda, and Hakodate and so acting with respect to all questions of protocol in negotiations and the exchange of documents [treaties] as to convince the foreigners of our sincerity.

Urgent problems are already pressing upon us one after another—the published [newspaper] reports about English intentions, the demands of the American consul, and now the demands of the Dutch. It is evident that the policy we have pursued so far cannot long be maintained. Therefore while we are still in safety we must make a long-term plan, devising means whereby the laws so far in force may soon be revised and the Bakufu's actions may thereafter be guided. With these objects in mind, you are accordingly to give full and careful consideration to the question of future Bakufu policy and after investigation are to submit an early report.

DOCUMENT 11. Draft memorandum by Hotta Masayoshi, on the points to be discussed by the officials responsible for the study of foreign trade, 1857, 3rd month (26 March/23 April).[1]

I. *Dealing with foreigners*

It seems that the American consul [Townsend Harris] is inclined to regard the Shimoda *bugyō* as of little consequence. How can it be possible, then, for the discussions between them to be brought to a successful conclusion? Is it not more likely that in the course of further negotiations Harris will become more and more incensed and make all kinds of unreasonable demands, until we are in the end forced to accept terms many times worse than those now under discussion? Indeed, he has never been satisfied with the present arrangements for discussions. Is it not possible, therefore, that he may report home accordingly and that as his dissatisfaction mounts we may be drawn into considerable difficulties?

Since the consul [Harris] has recently sent us yet another letter, we might send him a friendly and carefully-reasoned letter in reply, thus taking steps to complete the negotiations by an exchange of correspondence. Alternatively, we might send one of the original *ōsetsu-gakari*[2] to him as a special envoy. What do you think of this?

It having been decided that we shall open trade, do you consider it

---

[1] The text is printed in *Bakumatsu Gaikoku Kankei Monjo*, xv. 682–7.
[2] i.e. one of the officials appointed to negotiate with Perry in 1854.

desirable that we, for our own part, should initiate discussions with the American consul, the Dutch Kapitan, and the others? And if by our so doing their resentment is evaporated, ought we to discuss other matters as well and reach agreement with them?

There is also the fact that the Dutch Kapitan has been making proposals [for a treaty]. So far the Bakufu has not taken up any single one of them. Since we have decided that we must open trade at some future time, do you think it advisable that we should leave this question as it stands, holding no discussions at all with him?

Both Russia and America have asked that we substitute some other port for Shimoda; and if they continue to urge this strongly hereafter, it seems likely that we will find ourselves in a position where we have no choice but to open some other port. Do you know of any port that would be suitable [to propose] in such an eventuality?

Hitherto it has been our general practice to reject all foreign requests, both the important and the unimportant; then, when they have been repeated and become demands, we have been forced to grant them. On the present occasion, too, our first action was to refuse even the slightest request as being impossible. Thus we have [now] to tell them that we have repeatedly refused all requests, but since they will not listen to us [we must grant them].[1] This seems to be our accustomed procedure. It is due to the fact that the situation here is difficult and we have no choice but to act in this way, but the Dutch have already told us that such action is harmful to our national prestige, and it is certainly not wise to give the impression that our actions are being forced on us by foreigners. Moreover, if other countries are made aware that this is our practice, they will simply seek means of enforcing their demands by threat. If that happens, will it not be detrimental to our interests both at home and abroad? Would it not better serve our interests, in the long run, that instead of leaving the problem until it is too late we should from the beginning make up our minds what it is that we are unable to refuse?

II. *Plans for trade*

With regard to the opening of trade, for the Bakufu to open trade when the English come and demand it, might seem proper for purposes of discussion and negotiation, but it might be thought that this, too, would be for Japan to have her action forced on her by others and thus be harmful to her prestige. Would it not therefore be better for the Bakufu first to make a public announcement, though only within Japan, that such is its intention? The Dutch have urged trade plans upon us with every argument at their disposal. The American consul has told us that there is a

---

[1] Literally 'since they will not listen to us, etc., etc.' The ending is omitted, but by implication it is the formula usually employed on such occasions.

matter of the utmost importance which he wishes to report at once.[1] In the past year we have been repeatedly informed that the Englishman Bowring will come to Japan and published [newspaper] reports from that country have been forwarded to us. I do not know how true it may be, but I suspect that this is because all countries have agreed that they will first try the effect of threats against us, using America and Holland to influence us by this means, and that if this fails the English will use a show of force to intimidate us. If this is the truth of the situation, it would not seem to be a wise plan to wait for the arrival of the English. While this is no more than a suspicion, I am anxious that you should give it consideration. Then again, if we refuse the requests of America and Holland and complete an agreement at the request of the English, will this not give the first two countries grounds for questioning Japan's good faith and making yet more presumptuous demands?

If the English come and request trade, of course, our action must depend on circumstances; but if it seems that to refuse will do no great harm, should we even so return a refusal as the first step? Alternatively, should our plan be to effect an immediate settlement? The Bakufu having decided that, whatever the course we pursue, trade must be opened, it is my wish that you shall without a moment's delay complete an investigation of the main questions involved, such as how trade is to be handled, what goods are to be used in it, and at which ports it is to be conducted. Were the Bakufu to grant foreign requests while these questions were still not completely decided, there is no telling what disadvantages we might suffer from the resulting confusion. Moreover, if we on our side have neither plan nor purpose, we will find ourselves in the end unable to do anything but accept foreign proposals as they stand. This would put our national strength in lasting jeopardy. Is it not necessary, then, that we prepare an overall plan?

In connexion with the opening of trade, it would seem necessary to investigate the volume of our national production. However, this certainly cannot be achieved all at once. Generally speaking, if we use our products in large quantity, production will automatically increase, as has been largely shown by the production of saltpetre in recent years. Should we not give this some attention?

The products of the territories of the feudal lords will also be considerable. I want you also to give consideration to the circulation of these goods and to the fact that once the Bakufu opens trade, discontent will be caused unless the lords, too, receive similar benefit to alleviate the poverty

---

[1] At this time Harris had not disclosed to the Bakufu that he had instructions to negotiate a commercial treaty, confining himself to the statement that he wished to visit Edo, where he would communicate 'a matter of the utmost importance'. This last phrase, therefore, is frequently found in the Japanese reports and memoranda of the summer of 1857.

they have felt for many years. In general, would it be better for us to have government trade in Japan? Or would it be better to prescribe regulations for mixed government and private trade such as has existed at Nagasaki hitherto? Such questions as the regulations governing shipping dues and customs duties, and whether or not we are to establish trading factories, are all vital matters for which it will not be easy to plan; but were we to do nothing about them at all, we should soon be forced to face them and they would cause us constant difficulty hereafter. This would be greatly to neglect our duty. It is a matter that must certainly be given our attention. It is therefore my wish that there shall be full discussion of these questions and that a decision shall then be reached in advance [of negotiations] as to what goods are to be reserved for government monopoly.

DOCUMENT 12. Kaibō-gakari ōmetsuke and metsuke to Rōjū, 1857, 4th month (24 April/22 May).[1]

Having received Bakufu orders that we were to undertake investigation of plans for trade with foreign countries, we have given much thought and discussion to this matter. It is clearly shown by the communication sent some years ago by the Governor-General in Batavia and by the letter in which the Dutch Kapitan at Nagasaki recently reported some important matters, as well as by the texts of the treaties concluded with America and Russia, that unless the Bakufu changes the regulations under which Dutch and Chinese have conducted trade at Nagasaki since the reform of the Shōtoku period [1711–16], it will find it completely impossible hereafter to put trade on a permanent footing. By doing no more than cling to our ancient methods, while engaging in fruitless debate of impracticable plans, we give the impression of trying to impose restrictions on the foreigners. There may be those who mistakenly believe that in present circumstances this is in some degree the seemly thing to do; but when the time comes, with the arrival of the foreigners, to conduct actual negotiations with them, all will fall to ruin. Not only that, but we shall find in the end that all we have done has been to consume valuable time to no good purpose. This could never be in the interests of our country. It is therefore essential that from this time forth the Bakufu determine its policy in accordance with the needs of the time.

Turning our attention more closely to specific points, there is the question of the places at which trade is to be opened. Were Nagasaki to be the only place, it does not seem in the least likely that the foreigners

---

[1] The text is printed in *Bakumatsu Gaikoku Kankei Monjo*, xv. 819–24. The memorandum is signed by the *ōmetsuke* Toki Yorimune and Izawa Masayoshi and the *metsuke* Iwase Tadanari and Tsuda Masamichi.

would agree: they would press for Ōsaka as well, and that is in the immediate neighbourhood of Kyōto. (It appears that the foreigners are generally aware that the aforesaid Ōsaka is one of our most important centres and a thriving commercial city.) The Bakufu should, however, select instead of Ōsaka a place which would satisfy the foreigners, which would be to our advantage and which would, of course, be under Bakufu control. It should establish there a new guardhouse to regulate the entry and departure of both Japanese and foreign ships and set up a large trade centre in accordance with Bakufu decisions. (It would be best to lay down in the text of the treaty the rate of shipping dues and customs duties for foreign ships, and to establish suitable regulations for taxing our own ships by value of cargo in conformity with the practice regarding shipping charges in force at the Oki-no-kuchi port office at Hakodate.) Trade goods from the different provinces and useful products of the area could be loaded there after examination, a suitable tax being imposed. (This would be set at so much per package of a given article: generally speaking, it would seem best to impose a rate of about 20 per cent.)[1] Similarly, foreign cargoes could be landed there, their value assessed in the presence of the officials and a suitable duty levied from the foreigners also. (Like the previous points, this would also be laid down in the text of the treaty.) As for our own people, all owners of cargo should be allowed to come to the trade centre. Arrangements should be made to prevent disputes over the settlement of accounts, and the officials should in no way interfere in the purchase and exchange of goods. Thus the merchants of the different provinces would all bring such goods as are to the liking of the foreigners and the volume of our exports would naturally increase. And as it did so, from taxes alone the Bakufu would derive enormous profit. This is the universal rule throughout the world, and the Bakufu has therefore not the slightest need to worry about the expansion of our production— though it would be well to enact regulations imposing the strictest ban on trade in such things as gold, silver, copper, iron, and weapons. Moreover, if the Bakufu were to announce widely throughout Japan that the products not only of Bakufu territories but also of the territories of feudal lords might be sent if desired to the above trade centre, accompanied by an official letter from the head of the fief or the Bakufu steward, and that once the regular shipping dues had been levied at the port office and customs dues had similarly been paid at the trade centre, the officials there would arrange for them to be traded with the foreigners, then by these means the country and the government would both profit. The government would not be competing for profits with the common people

---

[1] The term *ni-bun*, here translated 20 per cent., literally means 'two parts' and could be used to signify either 2 per cent. or 20 per cent. It seems certain, however, that 20 per cent. is intended in this context.

and would benefit accordingly, while the system would not differ from that now generally in force throughout the world, so that the foreigners for their part would also gladly accept it.

Now as the Bakufu has been appointing officials to study plans for trade and the increase of national production, it is everywhere widely rumoured that it will make public its plans in this connexion. If it continues indefinitely without making even the first step in that direction, it will give the impression that somehow or other its whole political policy is directed to concealing as far as possible the action it is taking in foreign affairs. Thus not only the fiefs but also the people in general will be made suspicious, which might hereafter cause us no little disadvantage. This is particularly so as there have already been reports that the English are coming to Japan. There is also the confidential report made recently by the Shimoda *bugyō* concerning what he had learned from the [American] consul resident at that port regarding three matters on which the consul had been instructed by his country's president, and there are the statements made by the [Dutch] Kapitan concerning the English attack on Canton. Reference to these shows it to be inevitable that at no distant date the foreigners will assuredly come and insist on trade and the other privileges they have long desired. If the Bakufu announces its plans for trade only when that occasion arises, it will be said that these plans have been forced upon it by the foreigners. It will thus have been in vain that the decision was taken to plan in anticipation of events, and general feeling in the country may thereby be made much worse. This thought greatly troubles us.

It is very true, as you stated in your recent instructions to us, that once the ancestral laws have been revised it will be essential for the Bakufu immediately to adopt a flexible policy appropriate to that change. The fact is that our people now desire the opening of trade. What is more, we believe, at a time like this when there is hesitation and doubt, for the Bakufu to issue an announcement that it will soon open trade would be a means whereby it could bring the whole country under control and also lay the foundations of national wealth and military strength. As regards other details, it is not possible to commit to paper particulars of such matters as the amount of taxes and duties and the handling of trade until negotiations have been held and they are settled by treaty, but we have discussed this question in relation to the general principles on which trade should be based and the state of world conditions at large. We append a proposed draft of a public announcement to be made by the Bakufu on this subject.[1] Submitted with respect.

[1] The enclosed draft announcement says simply that trade is to be granted to all friendly countries and that further announcements will be made concerning details.

DOCUMENT 13. Kaibō-gakari kanjō-bugyō to Rōjū, 1857, 4th month (24 April/22 May).[1]

As you have already informed us, it is inevitable that the Bakufu should sooner or later open trade with the foreigners. There are, however, various ways in which this might be effected. There are many questions, of course, that cannot be decided until after negotiations, among them such matters as that of prices. The merchants of Nagasaki are expert in this and it would therefore be best to make use of them. The responsible officials, too, must be consulted on such questions. But as regards fundamental principles, it would seem necessary that the Bakufu should issue a definite statement. It seems hardly proper for us to propose arrangements for so important a matter, but having been charged by you with responsibility for such matters and having been privy to the government's secret plans regarding coast defence, we have given the subject much thought. At first sight, trade seems to be of the utmost importance as profiting the government, while it is also, of course, to be regarded as a source of national wealth and military strength. Thus it would seem the utmost folly not to adopt a policy which brings profit to the government. This seems a strong argument. Yet if one considers the matter from the point of view of fundamentals, on the other hand, must one not agree that the only sound and far-sighted policy for the Bakufu to adopt would be to aim in all things at fully preserving the laws established by generations of Shōgun for the good of all ages, at maintaining permanent peace and thereby saving the whole people from plunging into misery? Our country is unparalleled in the world in that it has both fertile soil and habits of simplicity. In this we differ from the foreigners, who love luxury though their lands are poor and barren. What is particularly important is the very grave danger of the propagation of Christianity, for if we become intimate with foreigners we shall come inevitably to be tainted by that creed. It was for this reason that the seclusion system was originally established, and if the Americans had not entered our waters there would certainly have been no talk of the desirability of trade with foreigners. This, we believe, is the true substance of our people's attitude. This being so, it is incumbent on the Bakufu to manifest its military strength by killing the men and destroying the ships of these cunning foreigners. Yet the change in world conditions and the vicissitudes of the time give us no choice but to announce a policy of peace and friendship towards foreigners. Thus we must never forget that our alternative to bringing war and unspeakable calamity on our country, which has known almost three hundred

---

[1] The text is printed in *Bakumatsu Gaikoku Kankei Monjo*, xv. 824–7. The memorandum is endorsed: 'Confidential report made by Matsudaira [Chikanao] Kawachi-no-kami, Kawaji [Toshiaki] Saemon-no-jō, and Mizuno [Tadanori] Chikugo-no-kami.'

years of peace and tranquillity, is trade. We must conform to the wishes of the cunning foreigners and act in accordance with treaty. We must take care not to give them pretext [for the use of force]. And while the Bakufu is acting in this way, it is best that its ideas and its inner thoughts be rooted in the former system. If, on the contrary, we were to look favourably upon this trade which foreigners from distant and barren lands make their daily task, if we were to devote ourselves only to the scramble for profit, then we would in the end have to show the foreigners true friendship and follow their ways. In that event, what would become of government in our country? The Bakufu, we believe, has a more far-sighted policy.

It has also been argued that, quite apart from our original national customs, we have already adopted Chinese customs in Japan and have changed from the province and district system[1] to the feudal system. Even in such important matters as this the government has had to effect changes in accordance with the times. Thus, it is said, the Bakufu's vacillation over policy in face of the foreign problem of recent times is quite un-justifiable. This, too, seems a reasonable point of view. Yet, to make a parallel between the national system and the construction of a house, for example, to change the superficial structure of the house according to the tastes of the moment will do no great harm to the building, but to change the framework or replace the pillars and foundation-stones is to introduce weaknesses and cause complete collapse. Similarly, to change the system which is the framework, pillars, and foundation-stone of our country would inevitably bring about unforeseen weakness. What is more, there is no doubt that great revolutions have always sprung from the mind of a ruler who possessed originality of thought and who therefore had no great difficulty in bringing men to accept his actions. Such a man, of course, can act freely even when the unexpected happens. The Bakufu's ad-ministrative policy, however, is to preserve tranquillity and issue orders only after full consultation, thus uniting high and low in preserving with care the system handed down by generations of Shōgun. This is much the same thing as if it were acting as a caretaker. Thus, it seems, if the Bakufu holds to the former system without taking any special action, the situation may be difficult but collapse can be postponed; if it adopts a new policy and fails, collapse may well follow at once. To give a familiar example, when one's lord or father is ill and one has a choice between an unusual, untried medicine and a medicine that has been used before, even though there is some chance that the unusual one would be effective, as his vassal or his child one can do no other than continue with the medicine that has been used before. This is the distinction between [on the one hand] safety and security and [on the other] constructive action.

---

[1] The *gun-ken seido*, that is, the administrative system introduced in the seventh century on the Chinese model, by which Imperial nominees were appointed to govern provinces and districts.

It is desirable, therefore, that the Bakufu should open trade, as we recommended this winter. However, it must regard as the reason for so doing not the profit it might make but rather the fact that such action is inevitable. Its general plan should be first to open trade at Nagasaki, taking care that it attract no particular attention, and to provide necessities at Shimoda and Hakodate. It should then observe the results, meanwhile coming to a decision about whether to expand or reduce the privilege. This seems the best course, for by so doing men will not be alarmed and all will be accomplished peacefully. If, on the other hand, we act in such a way as to reveal a desire to acquire profits, we very much fear that it might quickly happen that we should soon go too far and find it difficult not to become barbarians ourselves. Of course, men of resolution will call our views the height of indecision and vacillation, but it seems to us better that the Bakufu's essential aim should be to do only that which it is forced into doing, rather than that it should fix its eyes only on profit, thereby destroying our national laws and bringing unforeseen calamity upon us.

The immediate question of trade that faces us at this moment is not of the first importance, but it will in the future become the fundamental factor in peace and war and the one that determines the fate of our country. It therefore seems best that the Bakufu should decide the outlines of its policy after the matter has been given careful thought.

We report this as our opinion for your secret perusal.

DOCUMENT 14. Mizuno Tadanori, Arao Narimasa, and Iwase Tadanari to Rōjū, Nagasaki, *circa* 20–28 August 1857.[1]

We have perused the letter submitted by the Shimoda *bugyō* which you forwarded to us on 22 July. It states that the consul [Townsend Harris] is convinced that he can hand over the American President's letter to no other person than the Shōgun and that it would most certainly be contrary to his country's orders not to present it to him in person. Our negotiators have failed to dissuade him from this. Moreover, the consul says that once this question is disposed of he may have 'a most important matter' to communicate. Being of the opinion that the consul meant by this that he will seek private discussions concerning trade and also the opening of another port, the *bugyō* has recommended that the question be postponed temporarily until [Mizuno] Chikugo-no-kami and [Iwase] Iga-no-kami return to Edo. Then, he says, the Bakufu can quickly reach a decision concerning trade and the opening of another port, whereupon he will inquire concerning this 'important matter' at Shimoda and conclude a

[1] The text is printed in *Bakumatsu Gaikoku Kankei Monjo*, xvi. 722–5.

treaty there. By so doing it might be possible to find means to persuade the consul to hand over the letter there. If he then still refuses to hand it over, the *bugyō* wishes the Bakufu to send an official letter [to Shimoda] in the names of the Rōjū.[1] He appends a draft of such a letter.

We have accordingly given attention to this matter. To do no more than carry out the investigations which you have already ordered would be to consider only our own point of view, not to ascertain and study that of the other side, so that even if the question were postponed until Chikugo and Iga return to Edo it seems doubtful whether the Bakufu could thereby at once make the decision to permit foreign trade. Yet for the Bakufu to discuss the question after our return and then renew its investigations would consume much time. Meanwhile' the American consul would be urging his demands more and more arbitrarily. What is more, as the consul himself has said, it might well happen that the English and other foreigners would come and press demands of their own; and for the Bakufu to grant them would be a major blunder and might bring us into all kinds of difficulties. Quite apart from the question of opening another port, difficulties would certainly arise if the Bakufu opened trade without laying down permanent regulations to control it and it would then be impossible for the decision to be reversed.

On the basis of the instructions you gave us recently, we have compared and studied the various trade and customs arrangements of all countries. Moreover, we have had our subordinates inquire of the Dutch Kapitan concerning points which were in doubt, and the general principles to be followed are now clear. However, it is not possible to open trade on a liberal scale without first giving close attention to such matters as the development of production and the institution of regulations for the control of trade. Fortunately, it seems there would be no difficulty about conducting trade on the lines of the 'private trade' which the Dutch have hitherto been permitted in addition to their 'Company trade'.[2] The Kapitan has said that other countries would also agree to this method and that it would therefore be best for the Bakufu to institute this 'private trade' system until we become experienced [in trading methods]. It is our belief that we should in the first place pursue our investigations with the object of converting all the present Dutch trade to this 'private trade' system. Thus although we feel we must refuse to conclude supplementary

---

[1] i.e. authority for the Shimoda *bugyō* to receive the President's letter in the government's name.

[2] When Dutch cargoes arrived at Nagasaki the officials were provided with lists and samples. The bulk of the goods, those shipped on the Company's account, were usually priced by the officials and purchased by the Bakufu's agents. This was the system known as *hompō* or 'Company trade'. Any remaining Company goods, together with those brought in by members of the Dutch factory on private account, were then thrown open to competitive bidding by individual Japanese merchants. This was the system known as *waki-ni* or 'private trade'.

regulations to the Dutch treaty, as ordered by you in reply to [Arao] Iwami-no-kami's inquiry,[1] yet there are among the provisions of the [draft] document some that we should use. We believe that those privileges already granted to Russia, England, and America should similarly be granted to Holland. We therefore suggest that we should study and compare the decisions reached in the treaties and supplementary regulations with those three countries, effect suitable revision of the methods for the control of trade, and then conclude a supplementary agreement [with Holland] with the object of converting the present system to 'private trade'. And if the Shimoda *bugyō* discusses this with the American consul, making him a proposal to the same effect, this will be concrete evidence [of our goodwill] and it is probable that he will agree to accept the general terms of such a precedent.

The question of how to receive the [American President's] letter is more of a problem. Certainly it is impossible to decide it here and now. If we were to settle the Dutch matter at once, therefore, and make that our general criterion, there might in some cases be difficulties of detail but the general prospects would be good and there would probably be no major difficulties. In carrying out this plan, however, it would be inconvenient to have just the one open port at Nagasaki. We might purchase from foreigners at Nagasaki the goods desired by American whaling vessels or by the Russian territories and send them to Hakodate [for sale]; or we might purchase them there and supply them severally [to the foreigners]. This would be both profitable to us and of great convenience to those two countries. It would also eventually provide the Bakufu with means of effecting the withdrawal of the merchants.[2] But should conditions in Hakodate be left as they now stand, this would be but to stand idly by watching the trade of merchants sent from America. Russia would send merchants in the same way, or would open trading posts in the Kurile Islands, making those places prosperous and thus threatening Bakufu control of Ezo [Hokkaidō]. It therefore seems that difficulties must arise unless the Bakufu opens trade at Hakodate on the same 'private trade' basis as is now proposed for Nagasaki.

We therefore propose that we should open negotiations with the Dutch Kapitan with the object of making arrangements for trade at both these ports; and that, having conducted exhaustive discussions to determine how to preserve Japan from future inconveniences, we should fix upon such regulations as are indicated above. In this way, whenever the English

---

[1] Curtius had for some months been pressing for a supplementary treaty. The reference here is to the proposed draft which he had already sent to the Bakufu and which the Rōjū had earlier ordered the Nagasaki *bugyō* to reject.

[2] The argument seems to be that by itself supplying the stores required by foreigners at Hakodate, the Bakufu would be able to prevent foreign merchants from establishing themselves there for that purpose—as had been unsuccessfully attempted by American traders in 1855.

and other ships come to press their demands we can meet their expectations in general terms by use of this system, with which we will by then already be familiar; and we believe that this course would be to the Bakufu's advantage not only in providing it with experience here at Nagasaki but also, more immediately, in providing means of settlement at Shimoda. We therefore wish to ask that you will in all haste send us instructions announcing your decision on this matter.

We submit our request after full discussion of the question.

DOCUMENT 15. Mizuno Tadanori, Arao Narimasa, and Iwase Tadanari to Rōjū, Nagasaki, 29 August 1857.[1]

A short time ago we received from you [a copy of] the report submitted by the Shimoda *bugyō*, saying that in his opinion the 'most important matter' which the [American] consul wished to raise was probably a request for trade and the opening of another port and that the question should therefore be postponed until [Mizuno] Chikugo-no-kami and [Iwase] Iga-no-kami returned to Edo. Despite this report from the Shimoda *bugyō* it seemed to us, in view of the way the negotiations had been proceeding, that there was considerable doubt whether the consul would accept this. We accordingly came to the conclusion that it might be better for the Bakufu to grant trade to the Dutch in the first instance, at the two ports of Nagasaki and Hakodate and using the system of 'private trade',[2] and then to extend it to the English, Americans, and others. This we reported to you by the last mail. We have now received from you a further report of the Shimoda *bugyō*, which has crossed our own letter to you, and to this we have given careful consideration. It seems to us that for the opening of trade to depend on the course of future negotiations between the consul and the Shimoda *bugyō* would be inconsistent with our own investigations here. It would probably cause difficulties, and we are not in any position to afford such delay. Under pressure from the Dutch to reach a decision at once we have completed a study of the provisions which it is intended shall be included in the supplementary treaty to be concluded with them and which we enclose herewith.[3] To act on this would both prevent future abuses and also obviate difficulties at home. It would cause inconvenience neither to the Nagasaki Treasury[4] nor to

---

[1] The text is printed in *Bakumatsu Gaikoku Kankei Monjo*, xvi. 726–9.

[2] See above, Document 14, p. 140, note 2.

[3] See *Bakumatsu Gaikoku Kankei Monjo*, xvi. 729–44, a draft agreement in 39 articles which differs in various details from the text as eventually signed (Document 18), but chiefly in that it includes a stipulation for the prohibition of Christianity which was subsequently omitted (see Document 17).

[4] The Nagasaki Treasury (*Nagasaki Kaisho*) was the office of those local officials, subordinate to the Nagasaki *bugyō*, whose duties were concerned largely with trade. It was here that the sales of Dutch goods were held and discussions with the Dutch usually conducted.

local officials. What is more, we believe, whenever the English envoy may come we can on these terms reach settlement with him.

On the last occasion when we concluded a treaty with Holland[1] the Dutch put forward a proposed draft and this was then hastily translated and agreed. For this reason, it later transpired that the text contained some stipulations of which we had not been fully apprised and which were inconvenient to us. On this occasion, therefore, we have ourselves gone through the wording and meaning of every article and have checked the Dutch version by having it retranslated into Japanese by different inter- preters. To ensure that not the slightest difference of opinion shall arise hereafter, we have held full and repeated discussions of the various pro- visions. For example, to refuse to use gold and silver coins in making payments would be contrary to the purpose of trade. In order to obviate this difficulty, however, we have arranged not to make payment by means of Japanese gold and silver. When we cannot provide goods in exchange [for imports], we will pay by means of Western gold and silver; when our goods are not sufficient, the foreigners will ask for Western gold and silver in part exchange and we will make up the required sum by this means. In such ways as this we have discussed and studied every single article to the utmost of our ability. However, to describe in full all that we discussed would make this report tediously long. We have, therefore, appended a note [to the enclosed draft] about the list of prohibited goods, in that this article might seem to conflict with what we proposed in a recent report on the subject, but we have omitted such explanations for the other items.

We have in all things taken the greatest care to avoid future abuses and have examined every word and phrase with close attention. We have ensured that no objection will be made even if ships return home empty, on such occasions as we cannot provide return cargoes or when these are insufficient, and that we will be able to limit exports to suit our own convenience. Hence we will not be inconvenienced even if a large number of ships should arrive before our production has developed. We therefore ask that the Bakufu may send us instructions which are in full accord with what we now propose. Since the discussions are not yet over, it is still possible that the Kapitan will make some proposals concerning provisions which are not to his liking, but his views in general have been ascertained [and embodied in the text]; and if such orders are sent, we will try every means to bring him to compliance. It is our intention, moreover, that there shall no longer be any question of discussing the supplementary treaty proposed by the Kapitan last year. We mean to make him conform fully to the provisions of the enclosed text.

[1] The treaty of 30 January 1856. For an English translation of the text see *British and Foreign State Papers*, xlvii (1856–7), pp. 1091–4.

Our investigations have been pursued in haste, so there are still some provisions that are unsatisfactory, but in present conditions there is no possibility of better. Dutch merchant ships are still arriving here, and by their account the war between England and China is apparently reaching its climax. However, the English territories in India are in a state of revolt and peace will probably be made soon. In that event, it is said, the war-ships that have been sent there, together with the steamships which were dispatched for the purpose of assisting them, being already in a state of readiness, will all be assembled and sent to Japan. The American consul, too, has made similar statements; and although foreign reports of this kind cannot be trusted, such messages have become frequent. Now the supplementary treaty is not yet settled. At the same time, though we cannot tell how soon it will be, the English are sure to come. If they should come while we are still awaiting your instructions, it is our intention to engage them in detailed discussions and so detain them until the Bakufu has its orders ready. If, however, it proves that they will not consent to this, if they insist that they will go to Edo and demand an answer directly from the Bakufu unless we at once conduct definitive negotiations with them, then we think it best that we should settle the matter here, first reaching agreement with the Kapitan on the terms stated in the enclosure to this report and exchanging signatures of the text with him, and then immediately entering into negotiations with the English on the same basis. It would be much the best course for a decision to be reached before then, on the lines we have here proposed; and since settlement at Shimoda must also be held up meanwhile, we are anxious that the Bakufu should send us instructions in all haste.

We enclose herewith the draft of a supplementary treaty and ask for instructions concerning this matter. Submitted with respect.

Document 16. Mizuno Tadanori, Arao Narimasa, and Iwase Tadanari to Rōjū, Nagasaki, 22 September 1857.[1]

As we have reported separately, a Russian ship arrived here yesterday, 21 September. Poutiatine, who was sent to Japan a few years ago as his country's envoy, is on board and has requested an interview with the *bugyō*. This being so, we will have an interview with him and then, having made inquiries concerning the nature of his negotiations, will submit a further report.

We cannot tell what sort of questions he is going to raise, but should he ask that Japan open trade with his country, we can reply that inquiries are in progress concerning the conclusion of a commercial agreement with

[1] The text is printed in *Bakumatsu Gaikoku Kankei Monjo*, xvii. 274–6.

Holland; and since your instructions regarding our previous report will in any case arrive here soon, we will seek to postpone any such negotiations [with Russia] until that time, so far as it may be possible to do so. There is this point, however. When Poutiatine came to Japan some years ago, Tsutsui [Masanori] Hizen-no-kami and Kawaji [Toshiaki] Saemon-no-jō handed him a letter promising that should Japan ever decide to permit trade with foreign countries, Russia would be granted it before the other Powers. Thus if it is decided to conclude a commercial agreement with Holland and yet no discussions of any kind are held with the Russians, this might provide Poutiatine with a pretext for causing still more trouble to the Bakufu. There is no escaping the fact that once trade was arranged with Holland the Bakufu would have had to notify Russia, even if the Russian ship had not come, so it is in some degree fortunate that they have come now. Even if Poutiatine does not bring up the question of trade, we should, by broaching the subject ourselves, be keeping our word in accordance with the promise previously made to him, which would be both proper and advisable. And though we realize that we must never open discussion of the subject ourselves while still not in receipt of your instructions, yet if by the nature of Poutiatine's demands we are left no choice but to discuss it, then we shall handle the negotiations in the manner that seems best calculated to serve the Bakufu's future interests. Before leaving Edo, two of us, [Mizuno] Chikugo-no-kami and [Iwase] Iga-no-kami, were able to inform ourselves as to the kind of instructions issued for the negotiations that have taken place previously when the ships of the English and other envoys were here. We shall therefore negotiate with the object of ensuring that Japan grants Russia only those concessions that the Bakufu is willing to make to Holland.

To act thus will demonstrate how the Bakufu always keeps its word. And it is not only that the edge of foreign attacks on us will thereby be blunted. If an agreement is concluded with Russia as well as with Holland and the pattern of trade is thus established by two models [rather than one], then even if the English, French, and others come subsequently and conduct separate discussions, it is not easy to see how they could with propriety find occasion for the use of force. It is therefore our belief that if the situation proves to be such as makes it necessary, we must act in accordance with what has been said above. If [on the other hand] Poutiatine's discussions are concerned with some different matter, we will consider them in the light of the decisions reached regarding the Americans at Shimoda and Hakodate and, having consulted together how best to serve the Bakufu's interests, we will act accordingly.

This we submit with respect.

DOCUMENT 17. Mizuno Tadanori to Kawaji Toshiaki and Toki Tomoaki, Nagasaki, 14 October 1857.[1]

The Russian ship returned on 11 October with Poutiatine on board. For details of our discussions with him, I beg to refer you to my official report[2] and the conference minutes [sent therewith].

I had hoped by this time to have received the Bakufu's special instructions concerning the question of trade, on which I have been forwarding constant reports. My difficulty is this. At the time of his first arrival, Poutiatine promised another visit for about the end of this month, but it was his intention then to send one of his officers to us, not to come himself. As he said at our discussions on that occasion, he had received orders from his country's monarch to go to China and it would therefore be impossible for him to negotiate concerning trade [with Japan]. He now says that while in Canton he reported home that he would deal with this matter and demands that we shall at once conclude an agreement with him, ordering matters in the same way as when the Bakufu sent [Kawaji] Saemon-no-jō to him on the previous occasion.[3] What is more, it is nearly time for the departure of the [Dutch] ships and we expect to come to terms with the Kapitan almost at once. As we have said in our official report, we have been sending our subordinates to the Kapitan and have now reached a settlement with him in general terms, and there is no telling what he might say if we change the date[4] and so give him grounds for claiming that we have broken the agreement. This being so, it will be quite impossible to achieve a satisfactory solution if we suspend the negotiations yet again on the grounds that we are seeking instructions [from Edo]. We all discussed the problem, therefore, and on the same day sent our subordinates to Deshima to settle the final details, even though the Bakufu's orders had not arrived. Tomorrow I shall send the text to the Kapitan. Today I am sending a preliminary draft to Poutiatine. If these are accepted, I intend at once to exchange texts [of the agreement] and notes of acceptance.

I am, however, much concerned about whether the agreement will prove entirely acceptable in its present form. For the Kapitan's part, we have generally succeeded in satisfying him by saying that we have asked for instructions. Moreover, as our reports will have shown, we brought

---

[1] The text is printed in *Bakumatsu Gaikoku Kankei Monjo*, xvii. 382–6. Kawaji and Toki were both *kanjō-bugyō*, as also was Mizuno.

[2] Nagasaki *bugyō* to Rōjū, 14 October 1857, in *Bakumatsu Gaikoku Kankei Monjo*, xvii. 378–81.

[3] i.e. on the occasion of the negotiation of the Russian treaty at Shimoda at the beginning of 1855.

[4] i.e. the date by which a definite decision was promised. No specific date was mentioned in any of Mizuno's reports.

him to general agreement with our proposed revisions of the articles, as
the result of a number of further conferences after the communication
forwarded recently. Even in the matter of the article prohibiting Christianity[1] we at last succeeded, though with considerable difficulty and by
exerting all our efforts, in overcoming his objections. It seems that
Poutiatine, however, on learning of this from the Kapitan, became extremely angry and implied that for the Kapitan to accept such a stipulation was tantamount to a neglect of duty. He urged the Kapitan, therefore, to reject it; and although our subordinates all sought to dissuade him,
he told them that while it might be included as applying only to the Dutch,
Russia would certainly reject it, as also would England and France; that
to include this article would in fact hold up agreement on the others, thus
disrupting the negotiations. We have all, therefore, given attention to this
matter. The stipulation concerning religion was discussed at length the
year before last at Shimoda when [Iwase] Iga-no-kami and I were sent
there to join [Kawaji] Saemon-no-jō, but no solution could be found and
it was for that reason that we had to break off discussions. We went into
it in detail, but no solution of any kind could be found. If Poutiatine
recalls this when making his demands, it is altogether unlikely that a
settlement can be reached. This is especially so, as in what he said to the
Kapitan he insisted that if Japan wishes to impose such a strict prohibition,
she may act at will in relation to her own people, but this is no reason for
including in treaties with other countries a prohibition applying [only] to
her own. It is said that the Kapitan seemed much troubled at this. And
since it would be regrettable if this did in fact hold up or prevent agreement on the other articles, we intend to omit this article when we send the
draft to Poutiatine. In the circumstances it would equally be a waste of
time to include it in the Dutch agreement, so we have decided to omit it
from this as well. It would in fact be wrong to include this article in
regulations for trade. It should properly be included in a regular treaty
opening the ports. However, being most reluctant that it should be left
out of any agreement with England, we all agreed, when we last discussed
the matter, that we would first try the effect of persuasion on the Kapitan.
But although, as I have told you before, we have explained to him in full
the dangers of complete national collapse, we are driven to the conclusion
that short of using force we cannot avoid doing as he has asked.

With respect to other points, we have decided as follows. Of those
specific issues on the essential substance of which the Kapitan has throughout shown himself adamant, we shall omit and include respectively those
provisions which are to our disadvantage and those in which we can make

---

[1] The Japanese negotiators had sought to include in the treaty an article prohibiting the
practice of the Christian religion in Japan. There was no such provision, of course, in the draft
originally proposed by Curtius.

no impression on him. We shall extract those provisions which should properly find their place in a full treaty and deal with them by separate letter. This will be made a supplement to the former formal treaty. The question of government ratification will be handled on this occasion in the same way as before. Articles which do not relate to the question of trade with Holland only will also be dealt with by separate letter, and this document will be sent in our names alone. Thus all things will be managed in such a way as will preserve Bakufu dignity, cause no difficulties when applied to other countries, and avoid inconvenience for the future.

Nevertheless, as we have said in our official report, it is an act of the greatest temerity on our part to decide a matter of such immense importance on our own responsibility and before receiving the Bakufu's instructions. Yet nothing could be worse than to cause the Bakufu further difficulties and we have therefore all resolved to take this step even though it cost us our lives. If, however, what we have done should prove contrary in substance to present government policy, even the sacrifice of our lives would not justify us. Since this step is our responsibility alone you can, when next you send us orders, send us where you will, regardless of our personal fate, whether it be to Poutiatine or to the Russian monarch, to explain this and to withdraw the agreement. And yet I fear that once matters have been mismanaged, though only here in this distant province, all else would be of no avail.

Since we have formed our resolution on these lines and are acting upon it, we ask that if our action seems wrong and contrary to the present ideas of the Bakufu, you may accord us the severest treatment, that we may serve as a warning to others. We do not ask for any leniency. There is but this. Although we said, in the reports sent by previous mail concerning the [expected] arrival of the English and the attitude of Poutiatine, that we would take no decisive action before receiving Bakufu orders, the fact that to this day we have still received no orders might mean that the views of the Bakufu do not greatly differ from our own in substance. Moreover, before I was sent here, [Kawaji] Saemon-no-jō allowed me to see a report from which I understood that he has no immediate objections [to such a course]. And recently I had word from [Toki] Tamba-no-kami to the same effect. It is these indications alone that encourage me to hope that we may have a chance of escaping punishment.

I will report further on these matters hereafter, when the [Dutch] agreement has been handed over and it has been possible to discuss in more detail with Poutiatine the nature of his demands, but I send now for your information this preliminary report giving the main outlines of what has happened so far. Please be so good as to convey my respects to Bitchū-no-kami, Yamato-no-kami, Etchū-no-kami, and Tajima-no-kami.[1] For-

---

[1] The first two were Rōjū, the others Wakadoshiyori: Hotta Masayoshi, Bitchū-no-kami;

give the total lack of arrangement in this letter, but I have written it in haste during the discussions.

DOCUMENT 18. Additional articles to the Dutch Treaty of 1856, signed at Nagasaki, 16 October 1857.[1]

Additional articles agreed upon between the Netherlands and the Japanese Plenipotentiaries: Master Jan Hendrik Donker Curtius, Netherlands Commissioner in Japan; and Midsoeno Tsikoegono Kami, Financial Governor and Governor of Nagasaki,[2] Alao Iwamino Kami, Governor of Nagasaki,[3] Iwase Igano Kami, Imperial Superintendent.[4]

In order to form part of the Treaty concluded between the Netherlands and Japan, at Nagasaki, on the 30th January, 1856.

I. Trading shall be allowed from henceforth in the ports of Nagasaki and Hakodate.

Trading at Hakodate shall begin 10 months from the date hereof.

II. Tonnage dues calculated at Sp. m. 0·5 (5 maas), or f. 0·80 (80 cents) Netherlands currency per ton, shall be paid within two days after arriving.

For ships of less than 150 tons burden Sp. m. 0·1 (1 maas) or f. 0·16 (16 cents) Netherlands currency is to be paid per ton.

Ships of war pay no tonnage dues, but they pay pilot dues, and the hire of towing vessels.

In case the tonnage dues have been once paid at Nagasaki, and the ships depart from thence direct for Hakodate, the tonnage dues are not to be paid a second time. For this effect a receipt shall be given at Nagasaki on the manifest for the tonnage dues paid, and *vice versa*, in like manner on departing from Nagasaki for Hakodate. After having visited a foreign port a manifest must again be produced, and tonnage dues paid whenever new articles are brought.

In case vessels are hired for unloading, loading or towing, coolies are to be employed who are registered as such. No coolies shall be employed who are not provided with a certificate of registration.

III. Merchant ships which do not trade but remain longer than twice 24 hours in a port pay tonnage dues.

Kuze Hirochika, Yamato-no-kami; Honda Tadanori, Etchū-no-kami; Endō Tsunenori, Tajima-no-kami.

[1] This English translation (from the Dutch text) is taken from *British and Foreign State Papers*, xlvii (1856–7), 1094–1100. The Japanese text is to be found in *Bakumatsu Gaikoku Kankei Monjo*, xvii. 396–422. Where the two differ in meaning (as distinct from wording or arrangement), this is indicated in footnotes.

[2] *Kanjō-bugyō/Nagasaki bugyō* Mizuno Tadanori, Chikugo-no-kami.

[3] *Nagasaki bugyō* Arao Narimasa, Iwami-no-kami.

[4] *Metsuke* Iwase Tadanari, Iga-no-kami.

Merchant ships which run in for repairs, from distress, &c., without trading or transhipping, pay no tonnage dues. In case the cargo disembarked before the repairs should be sold, tonnage dues must be paid.

IV. Within 48 hours after the arrival of a merchant-ship at Nagasaki the name of the ship and of its commander[1] shall be sent in by the highest Netherlands officer at Deshima, accompanied by the manifest and the burden of the ship in tons, on pain of punishment for the commander, as provided in Article XXII. At Hakodate the same shall be done by the commander within 24 hours. At Nagasaki the unloading can take place at once during the day;[2] but at Hakodate the unloading must be after the manifest is presented, and in presence of Japanese officers appointed for the purpose. If a place for the examination of imported or exported goods should be provided also at Nagasaki, negotiations shall take place thereon, and the necessary regulations shall be established.

V. The number of merchant ships is unlimited. There is no limitation of the trade to a certain sum of money. In case goods brought in are not bought by the Japanese,[3] or that there is deficiency of goods for return, then they remain unsold. In case the goods brought in are bought, but there is a deficiency of goods for return, then payment shall be made in foreign gold and silver coin, whenever there is any in the Treasury, more or less in quantity.

VI. A duty of 35 per cent. shall be levied on the produce of all merchandize sold at public sale, or by private contract; but this levy is not applicable in regard to goods which are disposed of to the Treasury. Duties upon importation, transit, and exportation shall be fixed by negotiation from time to time. Until then, the present levy continues.

VII. After inspection of the goods for sale, the sales take place at the Treasury, which receives and takes care of the purchase money unless goods are received in payment by the sellers. If the buyers who have purchased at the public sales fail to pay the purchase money, it shall be made good by the Treasury. But if the purchase money of goods sold privately, be not paid, it is not made good by the Treasury. The Netherlands merchants shall be at liberty to have such public sales held as often as they think fit, without limitation of the number of merchants who are admitted thereto.

VIII. Whenever any goods are brought for sale, but remain unsold, and these are kept at Deshima, to be again offered for sale, the proceedings

---

[1] Japanese text: 'its commander and supercargo'.

[2] Japanese text: 'during the day at the water-gate of Deshima'.

[3] Japanese text: 'are not to the liking of the Japanese'. In this and subsequent Articles, references to 'the Treasury' are to the Nagasaki Kaisho (see Document 15, p. 142, note 4).

shall be always according to the foregoing Article. The goods may also be sold privately.

But all articles bought privately by the Japanese must be paid for in hard cash at the Treasury. Direct returns must not be given for them by the Japanese buyers. In case a list of goods privately sold to the Japanese be presented through the highest Netherlands officer at Deshima, to the Treasury with a statement of the purchase money, then the goods shall be delivered to the buyers, upon production of a proof of payment at the Treasury.

IX. Not only the appointed purveyors, but all merchants may come to Deshima to treat concerning the buying and selling of goods. At Hakodate a place (commercial house or bazaar) shall be appointed for the purpose.

X. In case the Japanese merchants have bought goods privately, and these have been delivered by the Netherlands merchant before the purchase money has been paid at the Treasury, and thereupon difficulties arise; if the goods should have disappeared or the buyers have fled, or also, if agreements for commission cause difficulties, the matter shall be inquired into as far as possible; but the Treasury shall not be answerable for the damage. After the delivery and reception of goods, complaint can no longer be made respecting the quality, the weight, and the measure of the goods bought or sold.

XI. If a Netherlander buy goods of a Japanese he shall pay for them in notes which are to be issued by the Treasury. These notes shall be immediately paid by the Treasury to the Japanese holders in Japanese coin. All the expenses of Deshima, the hire of towing vessels, &c., shall be paid for with money kept by the Treasury.

XII. The Netherlanders may also pay in foreign gold and silver coin. In case the Japanese should wish to receive foreign gold and silver coin, they shall arrange thereupon with the Netherlanders. All foreign gold and silver coin must, however, be taken only to the Treasury.

The silver Spanish dollar, or pillar dollar, is reckoned at the value of f. 2·50 (2 guldens 50 cents). The silver Mexican dollar at the value of f. 2·55 (2 guldens 55 cents).[1]

XIII. Munitions of war in general may be delivered to the Japanese Government,[2] but not to the merchants.

---

[1] In the Japanese text this reference to the value of the dollar is omitted. Instead, there is a statement that 1 gulden is to be taken as equivalent to 6·25 *momme* of silver.

[2] The terms 'Government' and 'Japanese Government' are somewhat loosely used in this English translation. In Articles XVI, XVII, XVIII, and XXXIV they are represented in Japanese by terms which mean or imply the central government of Japan. Here, and also in Articles XIX, XXIII, XXV, XXX, and XXXV, they refer to the *bugyōsho*, the local office of the Nagasaki (or Hakodate) *bugyō*.

If amongst goods brought to Japan for the first time, articles should be found, which the merchants are forbidden to deliver in Japan, the matter shall be officially arranged.

XIV. The introduction of opium into Japan is forbidden.

XV. Gold and silver must not be bought by the Netherlanders, but this does not apply to gilt articles, nor to manufactured gold and silver. Japanese coin must not be exported. If there should be any other articles, the exportation of which cannot be allowed, official communications and decisions shall take place thereon in each case.

XVI. Rice, barley, wheat, 'daitz',[1] 'schoods',[2] coals, 'mino' paper, 'han-shi' paper, books, maps, brasswork, shall only be delivered by the Treasury. But this restriction has no application to articles bought for personal use of the purveyors or in the town. Books and maps which have been printed, or written, or sold without the permission of the Japanese Government, must not be exported.

XVII. Copper, sabres and appurtenances, 'Jamato nisiki' (a certain silk stuff),[3] armour, fire-arms, bows with appurtenances, harness and other warlike apparatus, must not be delivered by the Japanese merchants. But upon a contract for the delivery of goods to the Japanese Government, it may be agreed to make them serve in part payment. If there should be other forbidden articles, they shall be treated in the same way, according to official arrangement.

XVIII. All the goods sold by the Japanese are to be delivered at prices agreed upon in each case, and not at fixed prices.

On the failure of the harvest, the Japanese Government shall have the power of forbidding, for a time, the exportation of any provisions. The exportation of wax and paper may also be temporarily forbidden upon occasion of any disaster.

XIX. During the stay of the merchant-ships at Hakodate, all ships' papers shall be delivered into the keeping of the Government there. At Nagasaki they are to be given into the keeping of the highest Netherlands officer at Deshima. In both ports Japanese guard-ships shall be placed near the merchant vessels, to prevent smuggling. The number of these vessels may be increased or diminished, according to circumstances. The Netherlanders pay nothing for these.

XX. As the boats for loading and unloading are hired privately, the goods

---

[1] *Daizu*, the soya bean.   [2] *Shōzu*, the red bean.
[3] *Yamato nishiki*, a rich silk brocade.

which may be lost thereby are not to be made good by the Treasury. But the matter shall be inquired into, as far as possible, on the Japanese side.

XXI. If on the arrival of a merchant-ship a false manifest should be delivered, the highest Netherlands officer shall inquire into the matter, and impose a penalty on the commander to the amount of 500 silver dollars for the Treasury.

XXII. If on the arrival at Hakodate no manifest is delivered within 24 hours, the commander shall pay to the Treasury a penalty of 50 silver dollars for every day's neglect; but in no case shall this penalty amount to more than 200 silver dollars. If unloading take place at Hakodate before the manifest has been delivered, the goods unloaded shall be declared forfeited, and the commander shall pay a penalty of 500 silver dollars to the Treasury.

XXIII. Nothing belonging to the cargo shall be transferred from one ship to another lying in the port, whether the ships be native or foreign, without the previous permission of the Government and in the presence of the appointed Japanese officers. Cargo transferred from ship to ship without this permission shall be declared forfeited to the Treasury.

XXIV. If smuggling should be carried on in the open ports, the Japanese smugglers shall be punished according to the Japanese law. The Netherlands smugglers shall be subject to the forfeiture of the goods smuggled in or out when legally seized. If smuggling should be carried on along the Japanese coasts, the boat and the cargo shall be declared forfeited. The highest Netherlands officer residing in Japan shall, after examination, make no difficulty in regard to these matters.

XXV. No Japanese may stay on board a Netherlands ship without the knowledge of the Government. If a Japanese goes on board a Netherlands ship of his own accord, or without consent, he shall be taken up and delivered to the Japanese officers.

XXVI. The highest Netherlands officer at Deshima shall not allow any Netherlands merchant-ship to depart before all accounts are settled. At Hakodate, the goods bought there by the Netherlanders must not all be loaded before they have been entirely paid for, or goods have been delivered for them.

XXVII. Goods smuggled in or out through the land-gate of Deshima (not agreeing with the permit) shall, when legally seized, be declared forfeited.

XXVIII. Goods for private use, given by a Netherlander to a Japanese, can only be taken out at the gate, on a permit granted by the highest Netherlands officer at Deshima.

XXIX. On the arrival of ships of any nation which has already entered into a Treaty with Japan, there shall be free personal intercourse between the Netherlanders and the persons coming on board such ships, both in the ships and at Deshima. Due care shall be taken herein, that it may appear to the officer on guard, upon examination, to what nation the ships belong.

XXX. The Netherlanders shall not, unless invited to do so, enter batteries, Government buildings, houses or other places having a door. Temples, tea and resting houses, &c.,[1] are excepted. The prohibition of this Article is not applicable when the highest Netherlands officer residing in Japan wishes to visit the Government respecting matters of business.

XXXI. For payments in resting or tea houses and in temples, and for what is bought in the shops for private use, and for carriage hire, payment shall be made in notes to be issued by the Treasury.

XXXII. The boundaries for the excursions of the Netherlanders at Nagasaki are shown upon the accompanying map. At Hakodate the boundary is fixed at five Japanese miles. If a Netherlander has exceeded these bounds without the consent of the Government,[2] upon receiving notice from those present, he shall go back. If he does not attend to such a notice, he shall, without respect of person, be taken up and delivered to the highest Netherlands officer.

XXXIII. The Netherlanders are at liberty to practise their own or the Christian religion[3] within their buildings and at the burying-places appointed for them.

XXXIV. Letters from the Netherlands Government to that of Japan shall be delivered by the highest Netherlands officer to the Governor of Nagasaki, or in his absence to the highest Japanese officer present there, in order that they may be sent on.

Vice versa letters from the Japanese Government to that of the Netherlands shall be delivered by the Governor of Nagasaki to the highest Netherlands officer at Deshima in order to be sent on. Autograph letters from His Majesty the King of the Netherlands to His Majesty the Emperor of Japan, or from His Majesty the Emperor of Japan to His Majesty the King of the Netherlands[4] shall be transmitted in the same way.

---

[1] The Japanese text excepts only *jisha*, 'shrines and temples'.

[2] Japanese text: 'has exceeded these bounds in error'.

[3] The Japanese text does not use the word 'Christian'; hence it here reads 'the religion of their own country'.

[4] The Japanese text makes no mention of autograph letters from the Emperor of Japan to the King of the Netherlands.

XXXV. In case Netherlanders should wish to learn the Japanese language or other Japanese sciences and arts, then, at the request of the highest Netherlands officer at Deshima, teachers shall be chosen and sent by the Japanese Government to give instructions therein at Deshima in the day time.

XXXVI. In case disputes or disagreements should arise between the foreigners who arrive, they shall be settled without the interference of the Japanese Government.[1]

XXXVII. If such should be the case between Netherlanders and Japanese, or if fighting, wounding, robbery, incendiarism, should take place between them, the matters shall be examined into, and if possible settled by officers on both sides. And such occurrences shall not of themselves interfere with the mutual friendship of the two States.

XXXVIII. All matters on the part of the Netherlands shall, in the absence of the highest Netherlands officer at Deshima, be managed by the Netherlands officer immediately next to him in rank.

XXXIX. All rights that are or shall be granted to other foreign nations shall at the same time be immediately extended to the Netherlands. As for the rest, the local regulations shall be observed.

XL. The stipulations of the Treaty which are not altered hereby, and all other stipulations not annulled hereby, remain as at present. At Hakodate, things shall be managed as nearly as possible in the manner provided in these Articles.

If any alteration or explanation should appear to be necessary in regard to some stipulations or subjects, they shall be settled by negotiation.

The foregoing Articles shall be looked upon as forming part of the above-mentioned Treaty between the Netherlands and Japan of the 30th January, 1856, and they shall have the same force as if they had been inserted word for word therein.

These Additional Articles shall be submitted for the ratification of His Majesty the King of the Netherlands and of His Majesty the Emperor of Japan, and the ratifications drawn up according to the provisions of Article XXVIII of the Treaty, shall be exchanged at Nagasaki within one year from the date hereof.[2]

---

[1] The Japanese text could more closely be rendered 'Japanese shall take no part in them'.

[2] In addition to the text proper, a number of letters were also handed to Curtius in the name of the Japanese negotiators. These chiefly provided that (i) wives and children of Dutch traders might reside in the open ports; (ii) negotiations should continue concerning the export of Japanese coins; (iii) the Nagasaki Treasury would continue to trade in some goods as long as financial requirements made it necessary; (iv) with the exception of Portugal, other countries would be permitted to trade in like manner at the two open ports; (v) a further communication would be made concerning Shimoda; (vi) the practice of *fumi-e*, the trampling on Christian images, would be abolished, but the introduction of Christian worship and the import of Christian and other foreign books, prints, and images would not be allowed.

The American Commercial Treaty of 1858

THAT the Dutch and Russian agreements of 1857 did not in fact become the basis of Japan's relations with other Powers was due largely to the work of Townsend Harris, American Consul-General at Shimoda. Throughout the summer of 1857 he had been insisting in his discussions with the Shimoda *bugyō* that the letter he brought from the U.S. President could be handed over only at an audience with the Shōgun in Edo. At the same time, he said, he would communicate to the Bakufu officials a matter of the greatest importance to Japan and would make available to them such information as he had regarding British intentions towards Japan. The Bakufu officials, concluding that this was but preliminary to a demand for a commercial treaty, were divided on the question of permitting Harris's visit to Edo very much as they were over the negotiations with Holland (see Section II). Harris's arguments, however, supported as they were by the Shimoda *bugyō* Inoue Kiyonao and the *kaibō-gakari ōmetsuke* and *metsuke*, gradually prevailed. In August the idea of the visit was agreed in principle. By the end of the following month, after the arrival of an American warship had made it possible for Harris to proceed direct to Edo by sea, even without Bakufu consent, the date itself was settled.

On 30 November 1857 Townsend Harris arrived at Edo and a week later had an audience with the Shōgun, at which he handed over the President's letter. On 12 December he had an interview with Hotta Masayoshi at the latter's residence. He now made a long statement on the subject of Japan's foreign relations, emphasizing not only that it would be much to Japan's advantage to open trade but also that a refusal to do so would incur the hostility of Britain and France, who might easily resort to force to gain their ends as they had in China. He was able to quote letters from Sir John Bowring to support this contention and according to contemporary Japanese accounts he made a deep impression on his audience.

On 16 December copies of the Japanese minutes of Harris's statement (Document 19) were circulated to *daimyō* and officials with a request for their views thereon. At about the same time, Hotta drew up a detailed statement of his own views for the information of other Bakufu officials (Document 20), making it clear that he favoured the immediate conclusion of a treaty with the United States, to be followed by a policy of friendship with the West through which Japan could adopt Western techniques and so strengthen herself to the point where she need fear no foreign threat. Not even his colleagues were unanimous in their support, however. Still less so were the other *daimyō*, though many had changed their attitudes since 1853. Tokugawa Nariaki, although he recognized the impossibility of revoking the treaties already made, was adamant that the foreigners must not be allowed to increase their foothold in Japan (Document 21). Mizuno Tadanori, on his return from Nagasaki, urged the Rōjū to open only ports that were distant from Edo and to insist that all foreigners, including the diplomatic representatives, reside therein (Document 22). Iwase Tadanari, as was to be expected, supported the American request for the opening of Yokohama (Document 23). The *tamari-no-ma-zume daimyō*, under the leadership of Ii Naosuke, replied jointly in terms which suggested that they were not in fact in full agreement with each other. As first choice they proposed an attempt to postpone the whole problem, but said that if this proved impossible Harris's recommendations must be accepted (Document 24). Matsudaira Keiei, who in 1853 had supported Nariaki (see Document 6), now recognized the inevitability of concluding treaties, though he took the opportunity of urging domestic reform as well (Document 25). Indeed one might say that the previous four years had made most Japanese in responsible positions not 'less anti-foreign' but 'more realistic'.

While these discussions were continuing, Hotta had appointed the Shimoda *bugyō* Inoue Kiyonao and the *metsuke* Iwase Tadanari to conduct negotiations with Harris in Edo. By 25 February they had agreed to a draft treaty which conformed in all important respects to Harris's proposals (Document 28), though only after they had failed in their attempts to limit trade to three ports and fix the place of residence of the diplomatic representatives at Shinagawa rather than Edo. It was not yet possible for the treaty to be signed, however. There was still widespread opposition to the making of such concessions and Hotta was reluctant to force a trial of strength with his opponents. He had already sent envoys to Kyōto to inform the Imperial Court of the negotiations that were in progress, and he now decided to go there himself to seek Imperial approval of the agreed treaty, in the hope that this would silence criticism. He left Edo on 6 March 1858, having arranged with Harris that the treaty would be signed when his mission was completed.

At Kyōto, Hotta met with unexpected opposition. The Emperor Kōmei himself resolutely opposed the extension of Japan's foreign relations and was ardently supported in this by most of the important nobles. Indeed, only the *kampaku* Kujō Naotada (who was in communication with Ii Naosuke) and the former *kampaku* Takatsukasa Masamichi wanted to approve the Bakufu request. It seemed for a time that these two, by virtue of their authority and prestige, would be able to override opposition from the rest of the Court and send a moderate reply, one which would indicate Imperial displeasure yet leave the actual decision to the Bakufu. At the last moment, however, a storm of protest from the general body of Court nobles forced them to reword the Imperial reply. On 3 May 1858 Hotta was summoned to the Palace to receive Imperial orders that the Bakufu was to reconsider its policy—in effect, a rejection of the draft treaty (Document 26). On 1 June, having completely failed in his mission, he arrived back in Edo.

Meanwhile the political situation had been complicated by another problem. The Shōgun Iesada was in poor health and without male issue, which meant that an heir had to be nominated from one of the Tokugawa branch houses. Next in line of succession, by blood, was Tokugawa Yoshitomi of Kii (later the Shōgun Iemochi), whose claim was strongly supported by Ii Naosuke, largely because of the rival claimant's connexion with Nariaki. Yoshitomi was still a minor, and a rival party, led by Matsudaira Keiei and a number of powerful *tozama daimyō*, maintained that only an adult, of proved ability and popularity, could rule Japan in such a time of crisis. For this reason they supported Hitotsubashi Keiki (later Tokugawa Keiki and the last of the Tokugawa shōgun), a son of Nariaki who had been adopted into the Hitotsubashi, another Tokugawa cadet family. This latter group was influential at the Imperial Court, and Hotta's experiences there in the spring inclined him to the belief that only by nominating Keiki could the Bakufu obtain sufficient support for its foreign policy. Ii Naosuke did not agree. Hotta's absence and his failure in Kyōto had weakened his position in Edo and on 4 June 1858, with the assistance of the Rōjū Matsudaira Tadakata, Naosuke was appointed Tairō. He thus superseded Hotta as head of the Bakufu administration.

It was, therefore, Ii Naosuke who had to decide whether to sign the American treaty. This problem was soon forced upon him as a matter of urgency, for on 27 July Townsend Harris arrived at Kanagawa with news of the Anglo-French victory in China. To Inoue and Iwase, who were sent to meet him, he explained that a joint Anglo-French expedition was about to visit Japan and he urged them to sign the American treaty at once. There would be little hope, he said, of persuading the new envoys to accept as their model an unsigned draft. If they did not sign, therefore, the Japanese would be forced to begin negotiations afresh, this time in much less favourable circumstances.

It was this argument that Inoue and Iwase repeated to a hastily summoned council in Edo on 29 July. Ii Naosuke himself had long favoured the opening of trade, but he was still anxious to obtain Imperial consent before signing the treaty. He received little support in this, however, and in the end, though with reluctance, instructed the negotiators to sign the treaty if no other course seemed possible (Document 27). The treaty was signed the same day (Document 28).

The next step was to obtain Imperial consent. But Naosuke's first action was to strengthen his own position in the crisis caused by the simultaneous occurrence of the foreign and succession problems. He ordered the punishment or dismissal of his chief critics and rivals, including Hotta Masayoshi and Matsudaira Tadakata, and appointed to office his own nominees, men of submissive will but little ability. It was one of these, Manabe Akikatsu, that he finally sent to seek Imperial approval of the treaty in Kyōto.

Manabe's task was not made any easier by the nomination of Tokugawa Yoshitomi as the Shōgun's heir, and it was not until 29 November that he was first allowed to present his case at Court. The Emperor's views, he found then, had in no way changed since Hotta's visit in the spring. He was completely opposed to any increase of foreign privileges, such as was effected by the American treaty. Against this Manabe's strongest argument, which he now reiterated (Document 29), was that the Bakufu had signed the treaty not out of choice but out of necessity, from fear of immediate and catastrophic war. This argument at length took effect, but it was not until several more exchanges that the Imperial sanction was obtained. Even then it was in a grudging and unsatisfactory form (Document 30). Although this fact was not explicit in the document, the Bakufu had been forced to make a number of concessions. Manabe had promised in effect that the Bakufu would try to prevent the opening of Hyōgo and Ōsaka, despite the provisions of the treaty; that the Court would be more frequently consulted on foreign affairs for the future; and that the Bakufu would seek to return to a policy of seclusion as soon as circumstances made this possible. These promises, though it is doubtful whether they were seriously intended, were to prove a constant source of embarrassment to the Bakufu in future years.

DOCUMENT 19. Statement made by Townsend Harris at his interview with Hotta Masayoshi, 12 December 1857.[1]

The ambassador said:

'The matters concerning which I am now about to speak are of the

[1] The translation given here was made after the Meiji Restoration by an American interpreter in Japan, from a manuscript in the possession of the Hotta family, and was published in U.S. Congress, *Foreign Relations 1879* (Series 1902), pp. 627–31. A Japanese text of the minutes of this interview (from a different manuscript) is published in *Bakumatsu Gaikoku Kankei Monjo*, xviii. 104–25. It seems that the translation was based not on the full Japanese text prepared for the officials but on a slightly shorter version circulated to the *daimyō*. With one or two exceptions, which are shown below in footnotes, the differences between the translation and the full text are not material, since they lie in the occasional use of simpler phrasing and the omission of Hotta's

utmost importance, and are so regarded by the President; and as everything springs from good-will and is done with kind consideration for His Majesty, the Taikun, I beg you to hear with attention.

'As I will only repeat what is said in the letter to the Taikun, please regard what I say as coming directly from the President.

'All that I say today shall be very plain and simple. There shall be no concealment of the least particular. By following this course I shall carry out the wishes of the President, who desires the negotiations to be carried out with the utmost frankness.

'As the treaty made with the United States was the first treaty entered into by your country with other countries, therefore the President regards Japan with peculiar friendliness.

'The United States have no possessions in the east and do not desire to have any, as other countries do. To acquire such possessions is prohibited by the Government of the United States. Heretofore many countries have asked to be admitted into the Union, but their requests have not been granted.[1] Three years ago the Sandwich Islands asked to be admitted into the Union, but admission was refused.

'It is the uniform custom of the United States, while frequently making treaties with other countries, not to annex any country merely by force of arms. Many changes have taken place in the West within the last fifty years. Since the invention of steamships distant countries have become like those that are near at hand. Since the invention of the electric telegraph especially, rapid communication may be had between the most distant parts. By means of this instrument a reply may be had in an hour to a message sent from Yedo to Washington. By means of steam one can go from California to Japan in eighteen days. Commerce has become very extensive since the invention of steam, and the countries of the West have in consequence become rich. The nations of the West hope that by means of steam communication all the world will become as one family. Any nation that refuses to hold intercourse with other nations must expect to be excluded from this family. No nation has the right to refuse to hold intercourse with others.

'Two things are desired in order that intercourse may be had: First, that a minister or agent be allowed to reside at the capital. Second, that commerce between different countries be freely allowed. Not only America but also all other countries desire the above-mentioned two things; and to grant them would be for the benefit of all, and not for the benefit of the United States only. Misfortunes are now threatening Japan in consequence of the state of things in England and other European states.

---

few questions. This is, in any case, very much more detailed than Harris's own account of the interview (see Harris, *Complete Journal*, pp. 485–6).

[1] Japanese text: 'but places which are distant and far removed from us have been refused.'

England is not satisfied with the treaty made with Japan by Admiral James Stirling. The English Government hopes to hold the same kind of intercourse with Japan as she holds with other nations, and is ready to make war with Japan, as I will now show. England greatly fears that Russia will disturb her East India possessions. Quite lately England and France united to fight against Russia because the latter was disposed to annex other countries. England does not want Russia to hold Saghalien and the Amoor. England fears that Russia will take possession of Man-churia and China. Should Russia take possession of Manchuria and China, she may then attack the possessions of England in the East Indies, and thus the war between England and Russia break out again. Should Russia do as above indicated, it will become very difficult for England to defend herself, and in order to be in a position to defend herself success-fully, she desires to take possession of Saghalien, Yezo, and Hakodate. Should England take possession of these places, she will send a large fleet to each place and cut off communication between Petropauloski, the port of Kamchatka, and Saghalien. England would rather have possession of Yezo than of Manchuria.

'Japan and China are isolated and without intercourse with other countries; hence the President directed me to attend to or watch the state of affairs in China also.

'Eighteen years ago a war broke out between England and China, which might have been avoided by an agent residing in the capital of China. The above unfortunate war broke out because the Government of China committed the management of affairs to the governor of Canton instead of managing them directly. The governor of Canton acted deceit-fully and made false reports to the government, and, besides, treated the English haughtily, thereby provoking the war.

'By that war China lost a million people. By the same war China lost many ports.[1] The city of Nankin, too, fell into the hands of the English.

'China paid to England £5,000,000 for peace as an indemnity. The loss of millions of men and millions of money, as mentioned above, is only a tenth part of the whole loss incurred by China. By this war China was greatly weakened, and her cities and fortifications were destroyed. Thus China, though formerly very strong, has become weak as she was when conquered by the Tartars. Everything there is in disorder, and another war will break out there before long.

'The two nations England and France are now engaged in war with China, and what will be the result as respects China no one can conjecture. The indications are at present that China will yield to the demands of England and France, or, if not, the whole nation will be subjected to said

---

[1] Japanese text: 'all Chinese ports without exception fell into the hands of the English.

two countries.[1] In any case, the action of China can only result in rendering England stronger. France wants to have possession of Corea, and England wants Formosa. If the present war ceases, China must pay all the costs of the war.

'The above facts are mentioned that you may be on your guard and take proper care. I am quite certain that the war would not have broken out had an agent been admitted to reside in Pekin. The Governments of England and France asked the United States to unite in the war against China, but the President refused. The United States was also provoked by the Chinese; but, not being anxious for war, the government refused to unite with England and France. Some time ago the Chinese fired on the American man-of-war Portsmouth, and when an explanation was asked of the Chinese Government no answer was given, whereupon Commodore Armstrong opened fire on and destroyed four ports;[2] but when, in consequence of the attack, the vice-governor of Canton made explanations, the hostilities were stopped. In this America did not act in concert with England. All nations unite in denouncing the unjust conduct of China. Opium has been the cause of the troubles in China. Thirty years ago opium was used only at one place, near Canton, in China, but now it is used in many parts by millions of people, who spend vast sums to obtain it. I have heard that two years ago, China imported opium to the amount of $25,000,000. Opium is the one great enemy of China.[3] If it is used it weakens the body and injures it like the most deadly poison; it makes the rich poor and the wise foolish; it unmans all that use it, and by reason of the misery it brings robbers and acts of violence increase. About one thousand criminals are executed annually for crimes committed while under the influence of opium; but notwithstanding this punishment crimes are on the increase. The uncle of the reigning Emperor of China died from the effects of opium. The opium used in China comes from India, which is subject to England.

'Though opium is, as I have said, a very bad thing for China, England will not prohibit it, because the trade is profitable. Hence the word 'opium' is not used in the treaty between the two countries.

'China has prohibited the importation of opium; but the English bring it in armed vessels and smuggle it in. The Chinese officials are aware of this practice, but they have no power to put a stop to it, and hence let it be carried on in the ports without opposition. It appears that the English think the Japanese, too, are fond of opium, and they want to bring it here also. If a man use opium once he cannot stop it, and it becomes a life-

---

[1] Japanese text: 'or, if not, the whole country will become the territory of those two countries.'
[2] Presumably a misprint; the Japanese text reads: 'destroyed four *forts* at the entrance to Canton.'
[3] Japanese text: 'And this [expense] is not the only harm it does to China.'

long habit to use opium; hence the English want to introduce it into Japan.

'The President of the United States thinks that for the Japanese opium is more dangerous than war. The expense of a war could be paid in time; but the expense of opium, when once the habit is formed, will only increase with time.

'The President wishes the Japanese to be very prudent about the introduction of opium, and if a treaty is made, he wishes that opium may be strictly prohibited. If American merchants should bring opium to Japan, the Japanese authorities may burn it or do what they please with it. Besides, a fine may be required if landed and introduced among the people of Japan.

'The President assures you that if you have intercourse with other countries, and allow agents to reside in the capital, the country will be quite safe. I must congratulate your country that no war has taken place for hundreds of years; but peace, when continued too long, may be injurious, as thereby the military power may become weak and inefficient.

'The President regards the Japanese as a brave people; but courage, though useful in time of war, is subordinate to knowledge of arts; hence, courage without such knowledge is not to be highly esteemed. In time of war steamships and improved arms are the most important things. If war should break out between England and Japan, the latter would suffer much more than the former. The damage that might be done to Japan on the coast alone is very great.

'The Japanese are very fortunate, because they have had no experience of war and only know about it from history. The President hopes that hereafter also you will only know about it from history, and have no actual experience of its evils.

'If Japan had been near to either England or France, war would have broken out long ago. The great distance between the countries is the reason why peace has been preserved thus long. In case of war, a treaty would have to be made at the end of the war. The President wants to make a treaty without any war, and with mutual goodwill and respect.

'A famous foreign general has said that an ordinary peace is better than an extraordinary victory.

'The President is of opinion that if Japan makes a treaty with the United States, all other foreign countries will make the same kind of a treaty, and Japan will be safe thereafter.

'The President wants to make a treaty that will be honorable to Japan, without war, in a peaceable manner, after deliberate consultation. If Japan should make a treaty with the ambassador of the United States, who has come unattended by military force, her honor will not be impaired. There will be a great difference between a treaty made with a single individual, unattended, and one made with a person who should bring fifty men-of-war to these shores. We were sent to this country by the President, who desires to promote the welfare of Japan, and are quite different from the ambassadors of other countries. We do not wish to open your ports to foreign trade all at once. It will be quite satisfactory if you open them gradually, as the circumstances may require; but the President assures you that this will not be the case if you make a treaty with England first.

'If you make a treaty first with the United States and settle the matter of the opium trade, England cannot change this, though she should desire to do so.

'When the ambassadors of other foreign countries come to Japan to make treaties, they can be told that such and such a treaty has been made with the ambassador of the United States, and they will rest satisfied with this. . . .[1]

'On my way to Japan I met the English governor of Hong-Kong, John Bowring, who told me that he was about to be appointed an ambassador to go to Japan, and I have received four letters from him since my arrival in Japan. Our conversation was of course private, but in his letters he discusses Japanese Government matters. He says he intends to bring with him a larger fleet than the Japanese have ever seen, and anchor at Yedo, where the discussions will be carried on. He says also that Yedo is the only place to hold consultation with the Japanese; that his object is, first, to get permission for a minister or agent of England to reside in Yedo, and, secondly, to get permission to carry on free trade at several places in Japan. If these two things are not granted war will be declared at once. The sending this ambassador he says is delayed by the war in China. He said he would be in Yedo in the third month, but he has been detained by the war. France will also send an ambassador at the same time with England. I understood from the first that he would come with many ships. In his last letter I learn that he will come with more than fifty steamers. I think he will come to Japan as soon as the Chinese war, which detains him, ends.

'The best-informed people think the Chinese war cannot last long; hence the English ambassador may be expected before long. I hope therefore that you will arrange all matters before he comes. In my opinion it will be necessary in any case to make a commercial treaty.

'If I write in my name to the agents of England and France residing in

---

[1] In view of the length of this document, a section is here omitted (*Foreign Relations 1879*, p. 629, line 65 to p. 630, line 57; *Bakumatsu Gaikoku Kankei Monjo*, xviii, p. 118, line 2 to p. 122, line 11). This section includes a number of briefer statements—discounting the danger from Christianity in present conditions; urging the value of customs duties as a source of revenue, and of treaties as a safeguard against aggression (in that Siam, having treaties, escaped attack, while the Indian States, having none, were conquered piecemeal by Britain).

Asia and inform them that Japan is ready to make a commercial treaty with their countries, the number of steamers will be reduced from fifty to two or three.

'I have today told you what is the opinion of the President and the intention of the English Government. Today will be the happiest day of my life if what I have said is attended to so as to secure the welfare of Japan. I hope you will consider what I have advanced and communicated to your associates in office. What I have told you are unadorned facts acknowledged in all the world.'

DOCUMENT 20. Hotta Masayoshi's memorandum on foreign policy, undated [probably late December 1857].[1]

As I informed you some days ago,[2] the American envoy recently made certain requests; and after consideration of the circumstances the Shōgun has come to the conclusion that he must make major changes in our long-standing laws. In view of the fact, however, that in a matter of such importance to the State it will naturally be impossible to devise appropriate regulations unless national opinion is united, there being some in Japan who feel disagreement and dissatisfaction in this matter, he has accordingly given instructions that we are to discuss the question in full and then act as may seem best in all the circumstances. Those who have views on the subject, therefore, are to report them without reserve. I shall first inform you in detail of my own views. If there are still points which are not clear, I will discuss them with you as often as may be necessary. I ccmmunicate this to you after careful consideration.

There are at this time two views about the way in which the foreigners should be treated. According to the first, the peace our country has enjoyed for almost three hundred years has accustomed both high and low to indolence; what is more, our national strength has declined, our military preparations are inadequate, and we are in no position to eject the foreigners by means of war. Even if we were to open hostilities resolutely and without fear of the consequences, we have neither the warships nor the cannon adequate to match the foreigners if large numbers of their warships infest our coasts and begin to burn and plunder. The feudal lords and all their followers would be exhausted in ceaseless activity; resentment would grow among the whole people; and once our strength

---

[1] The text is printed in *Bakumatsu Gaikoku Kankei Monjo*, xviii. 492–6. This is the second and revised version of the memorandum. The first version (*Bakumatsu Gaikoku Kankei Monjo*, xviii. 485–92) differs in phrasing and expression, but not in essential argument.

[2] Rōjū to Bakufu officials, 14 December 1857 (*Bakumatsu Gaikoku Kankei Monjo*, xviii. 130–1), enclosing Harris's statement of 12 December (Document 19).

was exhausted we would have to sue for peace. We would then have no choice but to pay an indemnity, to cede coastal territories, and to consent to all the hundred other demands that they would make. Our country, which has been independent since the very dawn of its history, would on that account suffer disgrace a hundred times worse than any it could incur by its present policy. We are in imminent danger of suffering the same fate as China and have, indeed, no choice as to our policy. We must, say those who hold this view, ward off for a time the insistence of the foreigners. For the time being our duty lies in acting in accordance with their wishes in trade and other matters, postponing conflict year by year and meanwhile completing our military preparations so that the foreigners cannot use us with contempt. Now this view, when all is said, offers no more than that we should complete our military preparations and so ensure that the foreigners do not use us with contempt. Such a plan has no prospects of success, for in the meantime all kinds of incidents would arise and year by year we would lose ground. There is no knowing what the end of it would be.

There is another view held by some. They say that ever since the expulsion decree was rescinded in 1842[1] foreigners have vied with each other in voyages to Japan and more particularly since the Americans entered Edo Bay they have become extremely active here. Year by year they press upon us and there seems no limit to it. What is more, they say, that we should be intimidated by a handful of foreigners, reviving ceremonies that have been forbidden for hundreds of years, bowing our knees to men no better than beasts and suffering their insults, is infuriating to the point of madness. That the ancient system of our State should now be sacrificed must at all costs be prevented. No matter how many thousands of warships the foreigners may send, by putting forth the whole strength of a united people it will not be impossible for us to effect our defence. Such an argument shows great resolution. But after all, even if everything was accomplished in accordance with its expectations we could still do no more than hold our own for a time in our own waters. The war would be ceaseless, unending. We would have no means of alleviating the [resulting] economic distress at home, nor does it seem that we could ever ease the burdens on our people.

Neither of these views is apt to the present state of affairs. Nor do they hold out any prospect of ultimate success. One inclines to procrastination, one relies on violence, and both alike would lead us astray in national affairs. Of recent times a change has come over world conditions in general. All countries are alike in concluding treaties by which they make friendly alliances, open trade, exchange their products, and help each

---

[1] i.e. ever since the Bakufu rescinded the order that foreign ships were to be driven off the Japanese coast by force.

other in difficulties. Should it happen that one of them breaks or repudiates an agreement, others form an alliance and open hostilities. When the war ends they resume friendly relations. Hence not to enter into friendly relations entails war and not to wage war entails entering into friendly relations; there is no other way, and there is not a single country which avoids both friendly relations and war, which spurns diplomacy and yet enjoys peace and maintains its independence. By behaving now as though the foreigners were our enemies, unreasonably rejecting offers of friendship and alliance, we are clearly making ourselves a hindrance to all countries; and it is certain that all the countries, which are now divided among themselves, will on that account unite their forces and one after another send warships to demand explanations and open hostilities. After incurring the enmity of all countries in the world, we could not long hold out in this remote and isolated island of the East. Such a policy would not only be to fold our arms and humble our spirit. It would be to inflict destitution on the innocent people of our country, and would leave us virtually no prospect of restoring our national strength.

Hence, although one can limit the essential tasks facing us at this time to two, namely to foster national strength and to raise morale, yet military power always springs from national wealth, and means of enriching the country are principally to be found in trade and commerce. I am therefore convinced that our policy should be to stake everything on the present opportunity, to conclude friendly alliances, to send ships to foreign countries everywhere and conduct trade, to copy the foreigners where they are at their best and so repair our own shortcomings, to foster our national strength and complete our armaments, and so gradually subject the foreigners to our influence until in the end all the countries of the world know the blessings of perfect tranquillity and our hegemony is acknowledged throughout the globe. If, on the other hand, ignoring the realities of the situation, we argue about trifles and show hatred for the foreigners, we will without reason make enemies of countries which from the beginning have been part of the same world as ourselves and which might all, by proper action, be made to serve and assist us. That would be unwise in terms both of divine law and human sense. It would be a failure to understand conditions and might put us in some danger of going astray in national affairs. From the dawn of its history our country has always preserved one Imperial line unbroken, has observed the proper distinction between ruler and subject, between high and low, and has held an enlightened moral code. And although ours is a small country, its land is fertile, its population much denser than that of other countries, and it cherishes a spirit of resoluteness and valour. Once we have laid the foundations of national wealth and strength, therefore, it will be by no means impossible for us to accomplish thereafter the great task of uniting all the world. We must fix our eyes on that objective. And because the policy we adopt towards foreigners today will be the foundation on which we will later build and extend our national strength, it is my wish that you tax your ingenuity to the utmost in your discussions of this matter, devoting yourselves wholeheartedly to this task in order that our country might reap the maximum advantage for the future.

DOCUMENT 21. Tokugawa Nariaki to Rōjū, 30 December 1857.[1]

I acknowledge receipt of your recent communication stating the purport of the statements made by the American minister and ordering myself and my son to submit at once our views thereon, and I report herewith without loss of time. I do not know what ideas you had in mind when you sought my views, but I am greatly worried lest you may possibly, with some idea of gaining a temporary respite, decide to permit such things as the establishment of consulates[2] in Edo. At this time the government seems much concerned by what is but a statement from the American envoy. Yet if, hereafter, the English, French, Russians, and others should also come and seek to establish consulates in Edo, and if on each occasion they negotiate directly with the Rōjū, then you will find yourselves in still greater difficulties. What is more, if the matter be not settled by direct negotiations with the Rōjū, it is quite clear that they will demand direct negotiation with the Shōgun himself. And however great the Shōgun's ability, it is quite impossible that he should be able to deal properly with questions concerning finance and everyday life when the problem is such as the Rōjū themselves cannot solve. I therefore think that for the Bakufu in any way to consider permitting the establishment of consulates in Edo would be contrary to the interests of our country.

The fact is, it is undesirable that the foreigners should be admitted to any port at all, though nothing can be done for the time being about the three ports now open, since this matter is already settled. Even the foreigners are fellow humans, and superficially, at least, they urge that it is in Japan's own interest that they seek friendship with us. It may be impossible, therefore, for the Bakufu to refuse outright. That being so, and although the suggestion is not at all to my liking, since my position is such that the Bakufu could without difficulty inform the Americans that I am a person closely connected with the government, having but recently

---

[1] The text is printed in *Bakumatsu Gaikoku Kankei Monjo*, xviii. 360–8. In view of its length, and the fact that the last section largely repeats Nariaki's previous arguments (see Document 3), only the first part of the document is translated.

[2] The term *shōkan* used here generally means a trading factory of the seventeenth-century type, but it seems sometimes to have meant 'consulate', the distinction not always being clearly understood in Japan at this period.

withdrawn from public life, there could be no greater expression of our friendship than for the Shōgun to send me, one of his close relatives, to America. For myself, rather than spend my declining years as I am, unable to repay the favours my house has been shown for more than two hundred years, I would wish that the Bakufu should firmly announce to the foreigners that I am to be sent to America on Japan's behalf and that this gesture is being made instead of granting them permission to establish consulates here.

If it is decided to send me to America in accordance with this request, I ask that you should announce that whoever wishes to do so may go with me; that you should not only allow *rōnin* to accompany me, but also the younger sons of farmers and townspeople, three or four hundred in all; that you should pardon even those who have been exiled or sentenced to death for relatively slight offences, and attach them to me; and that you should let me act as middleman for the goods in which Americans want to trade. By so doing, I do not think harm would come to Japan even if it should happen that we all, myself included, were to suffer death there. Mito would suffer no harm, for the present head of the fief would still be in Japan. Nor would it inflict serious hurt on the farmers, townspeople, and others, for you would be granting me only the younger sons, always unwanted, and hence the existence of the families would not be endangered whatever happened.

For the last twenty years I have been expecting some such situation as this. Many times since 1834 I have, for that reason, asked the Bakufu to grant me general supervision over the whole of the Matsumae and Ezo territories. (Had matters been accomplished as I asked at that time, I believe I could have prevented the Russians from establishing posts in those territories.[1] I remember that we learnt of them for the first time in the negotiations with the Russians, without any previous report from Matsumae. It is because of such things that the situation has become what it now is, to our very great distress.) However, not only did the Bakufu refuse, but in 1844, suspicious of the motives that prompted my request, it decreed the strictest punishment for me. Even if the Americans would agree to my going to America, therefore, I cannot be sure what decision the Bakufu will reach in the matter. If the Bakufu does decide upon it, I believe, its best course would be to demonstrate its friendliness by dispatching our own people to all countries, sending me to América and others elsewhere if other foreigners make similar demands. It would place Japan in extreme danger if the government were to allow foreigners to enter Edo. . . .[2]

[1] Presumably Nariaki here refers to the Kurile Islands, then part of the Ezo territories. Matsumae was the fief in southern Hokkaidō in which the port of Hakodate was situated.
[2] This translation ends at *Bakumatsu Gaikoku Kankei Monjo*, xviii. 363, line 8. In the rest of the

DOCUMENT 22. Mizuno Tadanori to Rōjū, 2 January 1858.[1]

After the American consul came to Edo recently, the members of the Hyōjōsho and my official colleagues were ordered to discuss the statements he had made and have submitted a joint report to you. I myself recently returned from Nagasaki and saw the relevant papers; and having views of my own on the subject, I discussed them with my colleagues and informed you of them a short time ago. I have now received instructions that I am to submit a further written report on this and have therefore again given the matter consideration, [reaching the following conclusions].

The President's letter asked only that the Bakufu grant permission for trade on a liberal scale, but the consul has added a request for the admittance of 'agents' to Edo. This, he said, is because among Western countries which have treaty relations with each other, it is customary to accord this right of residence in the capital, though there are cases in which it is exercised by only one of the two parties concerned. If the Bakufu permits trade, the ships of all Western countries will be able to come at will to the open ports, while warships and the vessels of envoys will also come. It therefore seems likely to him that there will be occasions when matters cannot be handled by the usual 'consul' alone. It seems to me, therefore, to be impossible for the Bakufu to refuse outright the establishment of such officials here, but it is most undesirable that they should be established in Edo. As I have several times said in oral reports since my return to the capital, if the Bakufu were to grant this it might be possible to settle in accordance with our own desires such questions as that of foreigners walking for exercise, by following the precedents established at Nagasaki, Hakodate, and Shimoda, but it would be impossible for us to maintain effective control either in regard to secret [smuggling] trade or in other matters, since people of all ranks and all provinces are gathered together there. There is no telling what difficulties might arise in the course of time. There is a particular danger that the people's loyalty might be subverted by the introduction of Christianity, which has hitherto been strictly prohibited. (In this connexion see various passages in the recent book *Tsūkō Ichiran*. Study of the converts to this sect in Nagasaki, as I have also reported recently, shows that they all, fathers, sons, and brothers, find no satisfaction in a quiet and natural death, regarding it as the essence of their religion to go to their death by the sword, head-down in a pit, with

document Nariaki repeats some of his former arguments (see Document 3). He makes a lengthy plea that the Bakufu finance him to build warships and guns, by which alone he can see any chance of countering foreign attack, and reiterates his demand that foreign posts be not permitted in Edo; urges that trade could have no value for Japan and is but a means whereby foreigners could rob the country and that the Shōgun's duty, as his title indicates, is to expel the barbarians.

[1] The text is printed in *Bakumatsu Gaikoku Kankei Monjo*, xviii. 384–92.

iron nails driven through hands and feet. From such a root can grow even murder of one's rightful lord. Then again, as is brought out in parts of *Tsūkō Ichiran*, about the beginning of the Tokugawa period, when the vain beliefs of that sect were being spread about Ōsaka and elsewhere, the Christians made a point of giving large sums of money and other things not only to the poor but even to the very beggars, thus seeking to attract men's loyalty to themselves. Even today, in Nagasaki and elsewhere, there are occasional instances of such activities; and when the [American] consul was on his way to Edo a short time ago, there were similar cases, when he caught sight of beggars and gave them silver. These, I think, are matters to which the Bakufu should pay attention.) If Christianity be introduced and difficulties arise which cannot be ignored, the Bakufu will seem in imminent danger of collapse, whereupon those who have always been turbulent and discontented may seize this opportunity to stir up disaffection. I can conceive no greater danger to the State.

The best course would be for the foreigners to reside in outlying ports like Nagasaki and Hakodate, but even if they go elsewhere, it is my hope that the Bakufu will designate places some distance removed from Edo and permit trade to be carried on there. If this is done, matters can readily be handled even if difficulties arise. Harris sought direct negotiations with the government. Were he to reside in Edo the Bakufu would face all kinds of difficulties. He might eventually, for all we know, enter into negotiations with the *daimyō* and all sorts of other people. Such a thought causes me great anxiety. By Harris's account, if the agent is permitted to reside in the capital he will be able to handle matters even if we become involved in disputes with the other countries, which might be to Japan's advantage. Yet in the case of the Anglo-Russian and Indian wars, at least, it seems that among Western countries war is not always averted even when the residence of agents is permitted. Peace and war depend on the actions of the two parties concerned, and would not appear to have any connexion with the presence or absence of the resident agent of any third party. More particularly, we gather that those who follow Harris will be chiefly concerned with questions concerning the ships that come from their own country to the open ports. Thus if one of them is separated from those ports by being resident in the capital, he will be too far away to understand what is happening there. There would be delays in questions which should be settled quickly and the result might be, in fact, to cause still more difficulties. That being so, would it not be in the best interests both of Japan and of America that the agent should, like the consuls, reside in the open ports? (With respect to this sudden request for residence in the capital, consideration of the records of the negotiations leads me to think that their secret misgivings and their suggestions concerning Yokohama and Edo began only after they had discovered a number of disadvantages about Shimoda. Hence it is my opinion that they will eventually agree [to Bakufu counter-proposals] if we fully explain our objects.)

If the Bakufu decides to open trade at Edo, the residence of agents there is inevitable. Moreover, ships of all Western countries would come there and large numbers of foreigners would be everywhere, walking about unescorted and at will, which might vastly increase the possible sources of dispute, more even than the mere residence of agents. I think, therefore, it goes without saying that the Bakufu cannot grant this. It would seem that the permanent interests of the country would best be served by permitting both the opening of trade and the establishment of agents only in places some distance removed from Edo. However, Bakufu refusal must apply to Ōsaka as much as to Edo, for that city is close to the Imperial capital and is, moreover, a place where people of all provinces are to be found. Fortunately, on my way back from Nagasaki recently I made a tour of inspection of the coasts of Kii, Ise, and Shima provinces[1] and found that there are two or three good ports there, not as good as Nagasaki but far more suitable than Shimoda or Uraga. It might therefore be well for the Bakufu to decide on one of these. If circumstances make it necessary, it might even be wise to suggest the port of Toba in Shima province or that of Uraga in Sagami. Toba, of course, is close to the [Ise] shrine territories, but these places would provide some means of settling the discussions. Then again, I understand that it is the opinion of those who have conducted the negotiations so far that the foreigners are resolved on having either Edo or Ōsaka and hence that the Bakufu may not be able to deny them both these places. But by the Bakufu's instructions, both Edo and Ōsaka are at present used only by ships engaged in coastal freight and transportation for internal trade; they are not ports at which foreign ships could call. Generally speaking, the reason the foreigners seek to change Shimoda for another port is that the American consul arrived there immediately after a Russian ship met with misadventure in a tidal-wave,[2] and saw that the dwellings had been largely destroyed by the waves. It is apparently on this account that he emphasizes the need for a port free from dangers of wind and sea, seeking such a port at which trade goods are available in quantity. Nagasaki and Uraga are the only really good ports free from dangers of wind and sea, but as I said above my recent tour of inspection showed that there are good ports in Kii, Ise, and Shima provinces. Of course, they are at present only used as anchorages by coasting vessels under certain wind conditions and are therefore not as busy as the two ports above; but if the Bakufu decided to make them into centres for foreign trade, it would be possible to collect trade goods there

---

[1] The provinces of the Ise peninsula, south of Nagoya.
[2] The wreck of Poutiatine's flagship, the frigate *Diana*, at the beginning of 1855.

in sufficient quantity. That done, the merchants would follow and trade would prosper. In former times, when foreign ships used to come to Karatsu[1] and when the port office was first set up at Shimoda, both Nagasaki and Uraga seem to have been mere outlying harbours, their position being similar to that of the ports of Kii, Ise, and Shima today. Hence I do not think we need to worry about the present number of people and houses there.

If the Bakufu should open Edo, even though there are some stocks of such stores as rice and corn there we could not supply them to the foreigners at the risk of creating a shortage for ourselves. If it comes to the point, then, we must either let them find this out for themselves, it seems, or refuse their request on the grounds that such supplies are not available. These facts will inevitably give rise to future difficulties.

Of course, it has been suggested that if the open ports are very distant from Edo the agents will not be content to reside in them and will assuredly insist on [the right of residence in] Edo. If they are allowed to reside in Edo, there will be grave danger of the kind of future difficulties I have described above; and therefore, rather than permit trade in outlying ports and allow the agents to establish themselves in Edo, it seems to me the better plan would be for the Bakufu to secure a lasting settlement by making the agents reside in the open ports even if that means the ports have to be close to Edo. Kanagawa and Yokohama, however, are on the shore of a shallow bay and can hardly be termed ports. When the American ships anchored there some years ago, they only dropped anchor for a time off-shore; these are not places where many foreign ships could anchor with protection from sea and wind. Thus even if the foreigners accepted this port initially, they would soon urge the same sort of objections to it as to Shimoda and would quickly come to demand Edo itself. Hence to decide on this place would be the same thing as deciding here and now to open Edo and would, I believe, be to give ourselves needless trouble and expense for a mere ephemeral benefit.

There certainly seems no reason why the residence of agents should apply only to the capital, especially as I do not believe that major disputes will be occurring all the time or every year. If, therefore, the Bakufu once again carefully discusses with the foreigners their object in seeking to substitute another port [for Shimoda] and in seeking residence for agents, and if it explains the facts as I have stated them above, advancing its case both truthfully and logically, then there is every reason to suppose that they will agree not only to our designating places distant from Edo as open ports but also to the agents taking up residence in those ports. If they do not agree, if they advance arguments to support their request and

---

[1] A port on the north coast of Kyūshū, which before the sixteenth century was a centre for trade with China.

leave us absolutely no alternative, then in that event the Bakufu can agree to designate ports close to, but outside, Edo. To do so should not provoke any critics to say that the Bakufu is dominated by the foreigners. Whatever may be said, the closer to Edo the places designated for trade and the residence of agents, the greater and the sooner the subsequent difficulties will be. What is more, this is a matter of the greatest importance, in which the safety of the State is at issue, so that even if it proves impossible at first to persuade the consul [Harris] to our point of view, during the negotiations now being conducted with him, this would be but a temporary setback and should not in fact furnish cause for any loss of reputation by the Bakufu, since his requests have been made clearly and reasonably. The Bakufu need not feel undue concern on this account. In case of need, matters can be carefully explained to the *daimyō* on the above lines, when I think they will probably recognize that the Bakufu could have taken no other course. . . .[1]

DOCUMENT 23. Iwase Tadanari to Rōjū, *circa* 4 January 1858.[2]

I have given careful thought to the statements made by the American envoy who came recently to Edo, to the orders issued by the Bakufu from time to time, and to the present situation in regard to the various foreign countries. While I believe that the advice given to the Bakufu [by Harris] has not always been free from an element of threat, I also believe that in so far as the situation is a difficult one which cannot be left as it now is, the most logical course is for the Bakufu to take action without concerning itself unduly about whether or no the foreigners are uttering threats; and that the only appropriate policy is for the Bakufu to act in accordance with the facts of the situation so as best to serve the permanent interests of our country and at the same time ensure the concurrence of foreign countries. (Ever since the arrival of the Dutch envoy's ship, the advice given by foreign countries has again and again been dismissed as mere threat, while subsequent events have shown all their statements to be fact, much to our present regret. Hence I feel that if we indiscriminately classify their advice as threats on this occasion, too, and therefore take no steps to safeguard the future interests of our country, we should but be securing ourselves a temporary respite and would, indeed, be acting to our own embarrassment.) Thus were the Bakufu to enter into negotiations with the intention of barring foreigners from the vicinity of Edo and opening trade

---

[1] Since this is a lengthy document, the translation ends at *Bakumatsu Gaikoku Kankei Monjo*, xviii, p. 390, line 8. The rest adds little to the essential argument. It argues that the prosperity of Edo would not be adversely affected by the choice of other ports and that, if necessary, it would be better to open Uraga than Yokohama.

[2] The text is printed in *Bakumatsu Gaikoku Kankei Monjo*, xviii. 396–9.

at places in such provinces as Kii and Shima,[1] this would not only be contrary to the interests of the country as a whole, but would also give us no prospect of obtaining the foreigners' consent. Even in the event of their agreeing, the farther the ports are from Edo the more strongly they will insist on establishing 'ministers' in the capital, and once a treaty is concluded the Bakufu will be hard put to it to find excuses for preventing this. That being so, the result would be no more than a temporary transfer of the trading ports to places somewhat removed from Edo. Hence it is absolutely essential that the Bakufu should now firmly resolve on permitting the establishment of ministers in Edo. (The Japanese coastline extends only between the 33rd and the 41st or 42nd parallel, and in the eyes of foreigners one cannot talk of 'near' and 'distant' in such a case. While we speak of keeping them as far as possible from Edo, their ships are at anchor in our harbours. That is to call a thing 'distant' because the eyes do not see it, when you have drawn a curtain between yourself and it and so made it invisible; raise the curtain and you are surprised to find it near at hand. Distance from and nearness to the capital can be spoken of only within Japan itself. In case of emergency, all provinces would be in equal danger, without distinction between 'far' and 'near'. The fact is that we are accustomed to peace and our danger is invisible to us, so that we neglect our military preparations. And when unexpected crises occur, we will at once suffer damage, with no distinction between 'far' and 'near'. I therefore believe that it is in fact against the national interest to talk of distance from and nearness to the capital when deciding to open ports to trade.)

Should the foreigners subsequently insist that it is inconvenient for trade centres to be established in out-of-the-way places and that they therefore want the Bakufu to open Ōsaka or some place in the vicinity of Edo, then here again we could find no pretext at all for refusing them. Thus in both problems [the residence of ministers and the opening of ports] our efforts would end in failure and it would then be impossible to retract.

It is therefore my belief, as I reported to you recently, that as a first step, with the idea in mind of opening the port of Yokohama in Musashi province, the Bakufu should reply to the American envoy in the following terms:

As the envoy is already aware, the Bakufu has taken various steps looking toward the opening of trade: it first intends to set up regulations which will be in general accordance with the precedent established in the Russian and other agreements. Since difficulties will be caused not only in Japan but also in our relations with foreigners unless the vicinity of Edo is designated as one of the places [to be opened], the Bakufu intends to open some place near Edo which is suitable for anchoring

[1] See Mizuno Tadanori's report, Document 22, above.

large vessels. On the arrival of the minister it will designate some suitable place in that vicinity as his place of residence. The competent officials will enter into discussion with the envoy concerning details of the treaty and other matters, and we therefore ask that these discussions be carried on with the utmost frankness.

As the next step. I believe, the Bakufu should ensure that all our negotiators, from [Toki Yorimune] Tamba-no-kami down, put forth their best efforts in discussion and after full consultation reach a decision that will best serve the permanent interests of the country, including the opening of Yokohama, the establishment of trading centres, and also the conclusion of commercial regulations and a treaty.

It appears from what has been said during the negotiations that from the beginning the fundamental aim of all foreign countries has been the opening of a port in the vicinity of Edo. However, in the belief that conditions within Japan make it quite impossible for the Bakufu to accede to this, it seems that in the first place they insist only on the residence of ministers there. If, therefore, the Bakufu were to take the foreigners completely by surprise by stating categorically that it intends agreeing to the major step of opening Yokohama and admitting foreigners of all countries to our ports, then it is probable that the question of the residence of ministers would be but a trifling problem and that a settlement could be reached without undue difficulty. It is not, after all, simply that the foreigners would glady agree to the opening of Yokohama. There is also the point that while ostensibly keeping the foreigners away from the Imperial Palace, the shrine territories, and the private fiefs and demonstrating its sense of responsibility by undertaking a task of such importance to the whole country, the Bakufu would in fact be reasserting its authority in overall supervision of national affairs, would be carrying out a policy that would be to our lasting advantage, and would be laying the foundations of national wealth and strength. This is not some minor question in which we can split hairs about the accuracy or otherwise of foreign statements. I therefore think it proper that the Bakufu should reach a decision at once, without giving itself undue concern over a number of trifling arguments about detail.

Submitted with respect.

DOCUMENT 24. Daimyō of the Tamari-no-ma to Rōjū, 10 January 1858.[1]

Having received from you a document containing the recent statemen made by the American envoy and having been instructed that after perus-

[1] The text is printed in *Bakumatsu Gaikoku Kankei Monjo*, xviii. 439–43. The *daimyō* whose rank entitled them to enter the palace chamber known as the *Tamari-no-ma* were the most powerful of

ing it carefully we were all to report our views thereon, we have given this document our close and careful attention. He makes a number of requests, but it is our opinion that the chief of them is the desire to open trade and to establish in the capital a 'minister' who will handle any business arising between our two countries. Our view is that if the Bakufu grants these points, then no matter what sort of agreement is made now, the boundless greed of the foreigners will certainly bring more and greater demands hereafter. Nor will the matter end with America alone. The Bakufu will have to grant privileges on the same footing to other foreigners as well, and all sorts of difficulties will arise therefrom. In that case, even if the Bakufu refuses to grant any additional requests, it is doubtful whether the foreigners will accept its decision. It follows that if they press their demands, the situation will inevitably deteriorate to the point where hostilities will break out, which is, after all, the reason why the Bakufu has always granted foreign requests hitherto. The ideal course would be for the Bakufu to return a courteous refusal to any further requests on the ground that circumstances compel it to do so. We fear, however, that such action is impracticable. We accordingly suggest that the Bakufu might now, as a first step, send a reply such as might obtain their understanding, first expressing its satisfaction at the great friendship shown by the President and then continuing in the following terms:

The Bakufu accepts the statement made by the American envoy to the effect that friendly countries dispatch ministers to reside in each other's capital cities; and after first concluding a commercial treaty with America, it will be most desirous of sending an envoy from Japan as a proper response to the present mission. Moreover, once matters arising from the present requests have been brought to a successful conclusion, Japan will also dispatch officials to serve in America. Only thus will it be possible to achieve the end stated by the American envoy, namely, that each dispatch ministers to the other's capital. The Bakufu is therefore fully resolved that it will act in this way. However, as the envoy is aware, this would be the first time such action had been taken by Japan. Hence, were it decided too quickly, there are many in Japan who would be dissatisfied. It is necessary that the Bakufu should gradually reason with and persuade such persons. Moreover, this is not a matter that can be handled without careful study. Were ministers now to be dispatched only to this country, public feeling would be aroused and this would not in fact bring about those friendly relations which you so warmly recommend. We therefore propose that the

the *fudai daimyō* and a number of the *Kamon* (Matsudaira families related to the Tokugawa). This letter is signed by the *fudai daimyō* Ii Naosuke, Matsudaira Sadamichi (of Kuwana), Matsudaira Noriyasu (of Nishio), Sakai Tadateru, and Makino Tadamasa; and the *kamon* Matsudaira Yoritane (of Takamatsu), his heir Yoritoshi, and Matsudaira Tadanori (heir to the Oshi fief).

question be postponed until such time as officials can be dispatched from here to America and from America to this country simultaneously. The Bakufu trusts you will recognize that in the circumstances no other course is open to us.

Then again, with respect to the question of England, we suggest that the Bakufu seeks American understanding by making a statement in the following terms:

> The Bakufu is most grateful for the trouble taken on our behalf in this matter and asks that America may inform England in courteous terms that in the circumstances we have already stated, even if the English were to come to Japan at this time it would be impossible for us to return an immediate reply and they would thus achieve nothing by coming: we ask that they give this their earnest consideration; and it would be to show exceptional consideration for Japan were the English to postpone their visit for a time and come hereafter when we inform them that our deliberations and investigations have been completed.

Since the facts of the [foreign] problem are not at all clear, we think the Bakufu should use the interval to investigate carefully. The position being what it is, we are most anxious that you should select a few groups of suitable officials and send them to foreign countries. That is why we submit the above proposal.

Of course, while we do not think major difficulties would arise by seeking foreign understanding of our ideas as proposed above, such a plan may in fact be impracticable, in that we do not know what course the negotiations may have taken so far. Should the envoy refuse [such a reply], the facts of the position would be inescapable. It would be most distasteful and on all counts regrettable to do so, we believe, but it would seem advisable that the Bakufu should in that event accede completely to the requests, moderating them by limiting the operation of the agreement to a given number of years and minimizing its stipulations as far as possible.

Even if it should happen, as the envoy has stated, that when the China war ends England should send many warships here to make demands upon us, it would still seem necessary that we should return a refusal similar to that given to America. It might well be that they would in that case open immediate hostilities. Then, we believe, America, Russia, England, and other friendly countries would without exception unite their forces and engage in war with us, one after another sending their warships against our ports and harbours, to east and west, to north and south. If they did so, we would have to carry out defence measures at all these places. The expense would be considerable. Moreover, they would probably interrupt our shipment of rice from the provinces, in which case our food supplies [in Edo] would soon be exhausted. This is a question which gives us much concern. If, in that eventuality, our defences proved ineffective and we had no choice but to agree to their demands, we fear our country would indeed suffer great disgrace. This fact, too, we submit for your consideration. Furthermore, we believe it would be best that the Bakufu designate some place other than Edo as that to which ministers may be sent. And again, though this is not a matter on which we were required to report, we believe it desirable that the Bakufu should henceforth take steps to strengthen our defences.

Submitted with respect.

DOCUMENT 25. Matsudaira Keiei to Rōjū, 10 January 1858.[1]

Having received from the Bakufu Japanese translations of the American envoy's statement and the minutes of a meeting with him, together with instructions that we were to submit our views thereon, my colleagues and I have discussed this matter. There being some differences of opinion among us, we are all reporting our views separately.

To men of discernment, I believe, it is quite clear that present conditions make national seclusion impossible.

It is most desirable that we should begin the practice of navigation and visit other countries in search of trade. The Bakufu, therefore, should not refuse those who come and present their demands reasonably and should reply similarly concerning the question of 'ministers'.

A wealthy country is the basis of military strength. It is therefore my desire that we should henceforward establish a commercial system and begin the study of trade. We should engage in the exchange of products and thus take advantage of our country's geographical advantages to make her the richest country in the world.

Since commerce depends on the circulation of money, however, there is a danger that such a plan may in fact give rise to luxury and weakness within Japan.

Again, in these critical times, the fact that there are dangerous tendencies in public feeling at home and that our customs differ from those of the foreigners might cause a serious crisis at any moment. Nor do I believe that the mere presence or absence of a minister could determine whether or no we should suffer the same fate as overtook China in the Opium War.

The thing most to be feared is not the influx of other countries, but the rivalry between England and Russia. The fact that these two Powers cannot coexist has been made abundantly clear by the envoy's statement. That one of these two might sometime seek privileges that would inevitably endanger the State is the thought that fills me with the greatest concern.

[1] The text is printed in *Bakumatsu Gaikoku Kankei Monjo*, xviii. 444–7.

In dominating men or being dominated by them, the issue turns simply on the question of who has the initiative. I believe that in present conditions this is our chief problem.

That being so, rather than sitting idly awaiting the coming attack of the foreign countries, we should construct innumerable warships, annex neighbouring small territories, and foster commerce. By so doing we will in fact accomplish deeds far excelling those of European countries, will in the end make glorious for ever our country's honoured name and shatter the selfish designs of the brutish foreigners. This alone is my cherished wish.

In this connexion, the Bakufu will never be able to achieve success by means of the traditional policy it has so far pursued in domestic affairs. The essential and first action to be taken, as I have recommended before, is to nominate a man of genuine ability as successor to the Shōgun. Then the services of capable men must be enlisted from the entire country; peacetime extravagance must be cut down and the military system revised; the evil practices by which the *daimyō* and lesser lords have been impoverished must be discontinued; preparations must be made both on land and sea, not only in the main islands but also in Ezo; the daily livelihood of the whole people must be fostered; and schools for the various arts and crafts must be established.

These are important and weighty matters, but the time has come when radical reforms must be carried out. Moreover, the American requests have been stated clearly and reasonably. The Bakufu should therefore inform the envoy that it intends to put these recommendations into effect and should question him closely concerning conditions abroad. After carefully considering what he says, we should seek the views of the Emperor and zealously put this policy into operation. By so doing, I believe, we shall find that here and now we have the opportunity of revolutionizing our fortunes. I cannot explain in so short a letter how this is to be carried out in detail, but if you should be so good as to ask me to do so, I will then speak frankly and without reserve. I sincerely desire that you will give close attention to the various ideas I have advanced.

Submitted with respect.

DOCUMENT 26. Imperial Court to Hotta Masayoshi, 3 May 1858.[1]

The American affair is a great sorrow to our divine land and a matter truly vital to the safety of the State. The Emperor keenly feels his responsi-

[1] The text is printed in *Bakumatsu Gaikoku Kankei Monjo*, xix. 636–7. Hotta is here acting as the official representative of the Bakufu.

bility in this to his Imperial Ancestors, most of all those enshrined at Ise. He greatly fears that to revolutionize the sound laws handed down from the time of Ieyasu would disturb the ideas of our people and make it impossible to preserve lasting tranquillity. The treaty opening the port of Shimoda some years ago was serious enough, but it is the Emperor's belief that the provisional treaty now proposed would make impossible the preservation of national honour. Furthermore, the Court officials have reported after consultation that the present stipulations would cause immeasurable future difficulties and, more especially, would endanger the national prestige [*kokutai*].

It is the Imperial command that the Bakufu shall again call the *sanke* and other *daimyō* into consultation and report further to the Court thereafter.

DOCUMENT 27. Journal of Utsuki Roku-no-jō, 29 July 1858.[1]

Today the negotiators Inoue [Kiyonao] Shinano-no-kami and Iwase [Tadanari] Higo-no-kami returned from Kanagawa. By what they said, they had been informed [by Townsend Harris] that he had heard many English and French warships were expected shortly to reach Japan. Those two countries, he said, had gained complete victory in China and would use their success as a means of putting pressure on Japan: this would make it extremely difficult for us in negotiations with them, but if the Bakufu were to complete the exchange of signatures on the draft treaty [with America], he would make every effort so to handle matters as to prevent trouble for Japan. As a result of this report, all officials were called into conference, including all three ranks of *bugyō*.[2] All said with one accord that it would be advisable for the Bakufu to consent to this at once, for to do so after the arrival of many warships would impair our national prestige. They were accordingly told [by the Tairō Ii Naosuke] that it would be impossible to sign the treaty until the Emperor's sanction had been obtained, whatever the difficulties that this might cause, but only the *wakadoshiyori* Honda [Tadanori] Etchū-no-kami agreed that this was the proper course. The others present urged that if negotiations were left till after the arrival of many warships, the matter would certainly not end with the present draft treaty alone. Indeed, they said, the matter was a vital one. What the Imperial Court had ordered was that the Bakufu act so as not to bring harm upon the body politic. The Bakufu could explain

---

[1] Utsuki Roku-no-jō, a *samurai* of the Hikone fief, was Ii Naosuke's secretary. The Japanese text of this entry in his journal has been published on a number of occasions; for example, in Kobayashi Shōjirō, *Bakumatsu-shi* (*Nihon jidai-shi*, vol. xi), pp. 424-6 in the 1907 edition and pp. 388-90 in the 1927 edition, and most recently in *Ii Tairō no kenkyū*, No. 1 (March 1950), pp. 37-39.

[2] i.e. the *jisha-bugyō*, *machi-bugyō*, and *kanjō-bugyō*.

fully to the Court that by clinging now to the ancient system our country's hardships would have been increased tenfold and that circumstances made this step inevitable. Once let hostilities begin and it would be impossible to defend either the coast or the Court itself. Hence, they maintained, there was nothing else for it but to sign the treaty.

Saying that he would give the matter further thought, the Tairō withdrew to his office and held a further consultation there.[1] Hotta Bitchū-no-kami and Matsudaira Iga-no-kami had always intended at heart to grant the treaty. The rest held that as no other course offered, it would be best to seek as much delay as possible. Inoue and Iwase were then summoned and instructed that they were to make every possible effort to obtain a postponement until Imperial sanction had been obtained. Inoue said that they would certainly respect these instructions, but asked whether their orders were to sign the treaty if that proved unavoidable. He was therefore told that in such an event there would be no help for it, but that every possible effort was to be made to avoid this. Iwase then said that they could never succeed if they started with such an attitude, so they must negotiate with a firm resolution to obtain a postponement at all costs. This statement being approved, the two men departed.

All this the Tairō told me on his return to his residence. Going to him once more, I told him that even though he were to obtain the Shōgun's authority to do so, to announce the signature of the treaty without waiting for the Emperor's instructions would be to put himself completely at the mercy of the Hitotsubashi party. They would accuse him of opposing the Imperial will, which would be most serious for his house and would bring severe punishment upon him personally. I therefore urged him to send messengers at once to Kanagawa and stop the signing of the treaty. He replied that he could no longer stop it by act of his own, for the Shōgun had been consulted and the orders issued. Again I pressed my arguments upon him, asking how it was that he who had always shown respect for the Imperial Court could ever have given such orders without awaiting instructions from Kyōto. He said that I was right up to a point, but the matter was urgent and there was no time to wait for Imperial sanction. Again, he said, reflection showed that the position of the foreigners was quite different from that of former times. They were skilled in navigation and distance was no obstacle to them. They had developed trade and commerce; and their weapons and military organization, moreover, had all been tested in actual warfare. They had both wealth and military power. If we rejected this treaty and hostilities broke out, even though we might be fortunate enough to obtain an initial success, complete victory was unlikely when all beyond the sea were our enemies. There could be no greater national disgrace than to suffer defeat and so be forced to con-

---

[1] Apparently with the Rōjū only.

cede territory and pay an indemnity. Which, he asked, would be worse—
to reject the treaty now and bring lasting disgrace on our country, or to
avoid national disgrace by not waiting for Imperial sanction? Our coast
defences, he said, are at present inadequate. For the time being we can
only select those foreign demands which cause us no harm and grant them.
Moreover, what the Imperial Court has said is that the Bakufu must act
so as not to bring harm upon the State. In any case, State policy is the
responsibility of the Bakufu, which in an emergency must take such administrative action as seems expedient. None the less, he said, he was
resolved willingly to take upon himself alone full responsibility for the
failure to obtain Imperial sanction. With this he ordered me to say no
more.

DOCUMENT 28. Treaty between the United States and Japan,
signed on 29 July 1858.[1]

The President of the United States of America and His Majesty the Ty-
Coon of Japan, desiring to establish on firm and lasting foundations the
relations of peace and friendship now happily existing between the two
countries, and to secure the best interest of their respective citizens and
subjects by encouraging, facilitating, and regulating their industry and
trade, have resolved to conclude a Treaty of Amity and Commerce for this
purpose, and have, therefore, named as their Plenipotentiaries, that is to
say: the President of the United States, his Excellency Townsend Harris,
Consul General of the United States of America for the Empire of Japan;
and His Majesty the Ty-Coon of Japan, their Excellencies Ino-oo-ye,
Prince of Sinano [Inoue Kiyonao, Shinano-no-kami], and Iwasay, Prince
of Hego [Iwase Tadanari, Higo-no-kami]; who, after having communicated to each other their respective full powers, and found them to be in
good and due form, have agreed upon and concluded the following Articles:

ARTICLE I

There shall henceforth be perpetual peace and friendship between the
United States of America and His Majesty the Ty-Coon of Japan and his
successors.

The President of the United States may appoint a Diplomatic Agent to
reside at the city of Yedo, and Consuls or Consular Agents to reside at any

---

[1] The English text is taken from *British and Foreign State Papers*, xlviii (1857–8), 596–602.
The Japanese text has been printed in *Bakumatsu Gaikoku Kankei Monjo*, xx. 474–84. The wording
of the two texts does not exactly correspond—for example, in the Japanese text references to
Japan and Japanese are always given before those to America and Americans, while some sentences appear in a different order—but only the few points at which they differ in meaning are
shown here in footnotes.

or all of the ports in Japan which are opened for American commerce by this Treaty. The Diplomatic Agent and Consul General of the United States shall have the right to travel freely in any part of the Empire of Japan from the time they enter on the discharge of their official duties.

The Government of Japan may appoint a Diplomatic Agent to reside at Washington, and Consuls or Consular Agents for any or all of the ports of the United States. The Diplomatic Agent and Consul General of Japan may travel freely in any part of the United States from the time they arrive in the country.

ARTICLE II

The President of the United States, at the request of the Japanese Government, will act as a friendly mediator in such matters of difference as may arise between the Government of Japan and any European Power.

The ships-of-war of the United States shall render friendly aid and assistance to such Japanese vessels as they may meet on the high seas, so far as it can be done without a breach of neutrality; and all American Consuls residing at ports visited by Japanese vessels shall also give them such friendly aid as may be permitted by the laws of the respective countries in which they reside.

ARTICLE III

In addition to the ports of Simoda [Shimoda] and Hakodade [Hakodate], the following ports and towns shall be opened on the dates respectively appended to them, that is to say: Kanagawa, on the 4th of July, 1859; Nagasaki, on the 4th of July, 1859; Nee-e-gata [Niigata], on the 1st of January, 1860; Hiogo [Hyōgo], on the 1st of January, 1863.

If Nee-e-gata is found to be unsuitable as a harbor,[1] another port on the west coast of Nipon shall be selected by the two Governments in lieu thereof. Six months after the opening of Kanagawa, the port of Simoda shall be closed as a place of residence and trade for American citizens. In all the foregoing ports and towns American citizens may permanently reside; they shall have the right to lease ground, and purchase the buildings thereon, and may erect dwellings and warehouses. But no fortification or place of military strength shall be erected under pretence of building dwellings or warehouses; and, to see that this Article is observed, the Japanese authorities shall have the right to inspect, from time to time, any buildings which are being erected, altered, or repaired. The place which the Americans shall occupy for their buildings, and the harbor regulations, shall be arranged by the American Consul and the authorities of each place, and, if they cannot agree, the matter shall be referred to and settled by the American Diplomatic Agent and the Japanese Government.

---

[1] In the Japanese text: 'If Niigata cannot be opened'.

No wall, fence, or gate shall be erected by the Japanese around the place of residence of the Americans, or anything done which may prevent a free egress and ingress to the same.

From the 1st of January, 1862, Americans shall be allowed to reside in the city of Yedo; and from the 1st of January, 1863, in the city of Osaca [Ōsaka], for the purposes of trade only.[1] In each of these two cities a suitable place within which they may hire houses, and the distance they may go, shall be arranged by the American Diplomatic Agent and the Government of Japan. Americans may freely buy from Japanese and sell to them any articles that either may have for sale, without the intervention of any Japanese officers in such purchase or sale, or in making or receiving payment for the same; and all classes of Japanese may purchase, sell, keep, or use any articles sold to them by the Americans.

The Japanese Government will cause this clause to be made public in every part of the Empire as soon as the ratifications of this Treaty shall be exchanged.

Munitions of war shall only be sold to the Japanese Government and foreigners.

No rice or wheat shall be exported from Japan as cargo, but all Americans resident in Japan, and ships, for their crews and passengers, shall be furnished with sufficient supplies of the same. The Japanese Government will sell, from time to time at public auction, any surplus quantity of copper that may be produced. Americans residing in Japan shall have the right to employ Japanese as servants or in any other capacity.

ARTICLE IV

Duties shall be paid to the Government of Japan on all goods landed in the country, and on all articles of Japanese production that are exported as cargo, according to the tariff hereunto appended.[2]

If the Japanese Custom House officers are dissatisfied with the value placed on any goods by the owner, they may place a value thereon, and offer to take the goods at that valuation. If the owner refuses to accept the offer, he shall pay duty on such valuation. If the offer be accepted by the owner, the purchase-money shall be paid to him without delay, and without any abatement or discount.

[1] In the Japanese text: 'while carrying on trade only.' This would seem to be a relic of the earlier differences of the plenipotentiaries on this subject, when the Japanese wanted foreigners to *live* in Kanagawa and only *visit* Edo to trade. See *Complete Journal of Townsend Harris*, entries for 30 January and 1 and 2 February 1858.

[2] In the trade regulations, duties were laid down as follows: *Exports*, 5 per cent. (except gold and silver coin and bar copper). *Imports*: *class I*, free of duty (gold and silver; clothing, books, and furniture for use of foreign residents, not for sale); *class II*, 5 per cent. (gear for ships and whaling gear, house timber, various foodstuffs, animals, coal, zinc, lead, tin, raw silk); *class III*, 35 per cent. (all intoxicating liquors); *class IV*, 20 per cent. (all other goods). These duties were subject to revision at Japanese request five years after the opening of Kanagawa.

Supplies for the use of the United States navy may be landed at Kanagawa, Hakodade, and Nagasaki, and stored in warehouses, in the custody of an officer of the American Government, without the payment of any duty. But, if any such supplies are sold in Japan, the purchaser shall pay the proper duty to the Japanese authorities.

The importation of opium is prohibited; and, any American vessel coming to Japan for the purposes of trade having more than three catties (four pounds avoirdupois) weight of opium on board, such surplus quantity shall be seized and destroyed by the Japanese authorities. All goods imported into Japan, and which have paid the duty fixed by this Treaty, may be transported by the Japanese into any part of the empire without the payment of any tax, excise, or transit duty whatever.

No higher duties shall be paid by Americans on goods imported into Japan than are fixed by this Treaty, nor shall any higher duties be paid by Americans than are levied on the same description of goods if imported in Japanese vessels, or the vessels of any other nation.

ARTICLE V

All foreign coin shall be current in Japan and pass for its corresponding weight of Japanese coin of the same description. Americans and Japanese may freely use foreign or Japanese coin in making payments to each other.

As some time will elapse before the Japanese will be acquainted with the value of foreign coin, the Japanese Government will, for the period of one year after the opening of each harbor, furnish the Americans with Japanese coin in exchange for theirs, equal weights being given and no discount taken for re-coinage. Coins of all description (with the exception of Japanese copper coin) may be exported from Japan, and foreign gold and silver uncoined.

ARTICLE VI

Americans committing offences against Japanese shall be tried in American Consular courts, and, when guilty, shall be punished according to American law. Japanese committing offences against Americans shall be tried by the Japanese authorities and punished according to Japanese law. The Consular courts shall be open to Japanese creditors, to enable them to recover their just claims against American citizens; and the Japanese courts shall in like manner be open to American citizens for the recovery of their just claims against Japanese.

All claims for forfeitures or penalties for violations of this Treaty, or of the Articles regulating trade which are appended hereunto, shall be sued for in the Consular courts, and all recoveries shall be delivered to the Japanese authorities.

Neither the American or Japanese Governments are to be held responsible for the payment of any debts contracted by their respective citizens or subjects.

ARTICLE VII

In the opened harbors of Japan, Americans shall be free to go where they please, within the following limits:

At Kanagawa, the River Logo [Rokugo] (which empties into the Bay of Yedo between Kawasaki and Sinagawa), and 10 ri in any other direction.

At Hakodade, 10 ri in any direction.

At Hiogo, 10 ri in any direction, that of Kioto [Kyōto] excepted, which city shall not be approached nearer than 10 ri. The crews of vessels resorting to Hiogo shall not cross the River Enagawa, which empties into the Bay between Hiogo and Osaca. The distance shall be measured inland from Goyoso [Goyōsho], or town hall of each of the foregoing harbors, the ri being equal to 4,275 yards American measure.

At Nagasaki, Americans may go into any part of the Imperial domain in its vicinity. The boundaries of Nee-e-gata, or the place that may be substituted for it, shall be settled by the American Diplomatic Agent and the Government of Japan. Americans who have been convicted of felony, or twice convicted of misdemeanors, shall not go more than one Japanese ri inland from the places of their respective residences, and all persons so convicted shall lose their right of permanent residence in Japan, and the Japanese authorities may require them to leave the country.

A reasonable time shall be allowed to all such persons to settle their affairs, and the American Consular authority shall, after an examination into the circumstances of each case, determine the time to be allowed, but such time shall not in any case exceed one year, to be calculated from the time the person shall be free to attend to his affairs.

ARTICLE VIII

Americans in Japan shall be allowed the free exercise of their religion, and for this purpose shall have the right to erect suitable places of worship. No injury shall be done to such buildings, nor any insult be offered to the religious worship of the Americans. American citizens shall not injure any Japanese temple or *mia* [*miya*], or offer any insult or injury to Japanese religious ceremonies, or to the objects of their worship.

The Americans and Japanese shall not do anything that may be calculated to excite religious animosity. The Government of Japan has already abolished the practice of trampling on religious emblems.[1]

ARTICLE IX

When requested by the American Consul, the Japanese authorities will

[1] The Japanese text inserts 'at Nagasaki'.

cause the arrest of all deserters and fugitives from justice, receive in jail all persons held as prisoners by the Consul, and give to the Consul such assistance as may be required to enable him to enforce the observance of the laws by the Americans who are on land, and to maintain order among the shipping. For all such service, and for the support of prisoners kept in confinement, the Consul shall in all cases pay a just compensation.

ARTICLE X

The Japanese Government may purchase or construct in the United States ships-of-war, steamers, merchant ships, whale ships, cannon, munitions of war, and arms of all kinds, and any other things it may require. It shall have the right to engage in the United States scientific, naval and military men, artisans of all kinds, and mariners to enter into its service. All purchases made for the Government of Japan may be exported from the United States, and all persons engaged for its service may freely depart from the United States: provided that no articles that are contraband of war shall be exported, nor any persons engaged to act in a naval or military capacity, while Japan shall be at war with any Power in amity with the United States.

ARTICLE XI

The Articles for the regulation of trade, which are appended to this Treaty, shall be considered as forming a part of the same, and shall be equally binding on both the Contracting Parties to this Treaty, and on their citizens and subjects.[1]

ARTICLE XII

Such of the provisions of the ‚Treaty made by Commodore Perry, and signed at Kanagawa, on the 31st of March, 1854, as conflict with the provisions of this Treaty are hereby revoked; and, as all the provisions of a Convention executed by the Consul General of the United States and the Governors of Simoda, on the 17th of June, 1857, are incorporated in this Treaty, that Convention is also revoked.

The person charged with the diplomatic relations of the United States in Japan, in conjunction with such person or persons as may be appointed for that purpose by the Japanese Government, shall have power to make such rules and regulations as may be required to carry into full and complete effect the provisions of this Treaty, and the provisions of the Articles regulating trade appended thereunto.

---

[1] The trade regulations [*British and Foreign State Papers*, xlviii (1857–8), pp. 602–6; *Bakumatsu Gaikoku Kankei Monjo*, xx. 485–93] govern such matters as declaration of cargo, loading and unloading, customs, smuggling, &c. Unlike the Dutch agreement of 1857 (Document 18), it provides that no tonnage dues be paid, while the regulations are generally less rigid and the penalties much less severe than those accepted by the Dutch.

ARTICLE XIII

After the 4th of July, 1872, upon the desire of either the American or Japanese Governments, and one year's notice given by either party, this Treaty, and such portions of the Treaty of Kanagawa as remain unrevoked by this Treaty, together with the regulations of trade hereunto annexed, or those that may be hereafter introduced, shall be subject to revision by Commissioners appointed on both sides for this purpose, who will be empowered to decide on, and insert therein, such amendments as experience shall prove to be desirable.

ARTICLE XIV

This Treaty shall go into effect on the 4th of July, 1859, on or before which day the ratifications of the same shall be exchanged at the City of Washington; but if, from any unforeseen cause, the ratifications cannot be exchanged by that time, the Treaty shall still go into effect at the date above mentioned.

The act of ratification on the part of the United States shall be verified by the signature of the President of the United States, countersigned by the Secretary of State, and sealed with the seal of the United States.

The act of ratification on the part of Japan shall be verified by the name and seal of His Majesty the Ty-Coon, and by the seals and signatures of such of his high officers as he may direct.

This Treaty is executed in quadruplicate, each copy being written in the English, Japanese, and Dutch languages, all the versions having the same meaning and intention, but the Dutch version shall be considered as being the original.

In witness whereof, the above-named Plenipotentiaries have hereunto set their hands and seals, at the City of Yedo, this 29th day of July, in the year of Our Lord 1858, and of the Independence of the United States of America the eighty-third, corresponding to the Japanese era, the 19th day of the sixth month of the 5th year of Ansei, *Mma*.[1]

DOCUMENT 29. Manabe Akikatsu to Kampaku (Kujō Naotada), 21 December 1858.[2]

I have the honour to acknowledge receipt of the Imperial instructions sent to me through Sakai [Tadayoshi], Wakasa-no-kami. It was stated

---

[1] *Uma*, year of the horse.

[2] The text is printed in *Bakumatsu Gaikoku Kankei Monjo*, xxi. 722–8. There are two extant texts of this letter, one in the Kujō family records and one in those of the Ii family. This translation follows generally the Kujō text, but where the Ii text is substantially different this fact is shown by insertions and footnotes.

therein that the Emperor had taken into consideration the detailed statement on foreign affairs which I made recently on coming to Kyōto, but
while he recognized that the Bakufu had acted as it did by force of circumstance, his views on the subject had not in any way changed since last
spring;[1] and were he to permit our people to mix with the foreigners and
to allow trade and trading posts, though it be but for a single day, to say
nothing of five or six years, this would be to contradict the announcement
he made in July last when he sent lords to Ise as his envoys and would
cause him the deepest concern. In addition to this, though the position
had many times been notified to the Bakufu, I was also sent in strictest
confidence a copy of the Emperor's letter on this subject,[2] in order that
the Bakufu might be given early and confidential notice of the need to give
this close attention and devote further thought to finding some way of
fulfilling the Emperor's wishes.

I have already fully explained that, facing as we were difficulties both
at home and abroad, the Bakufu had no choice but to sign the treaties.
Perhaps the Court does not fully appreciate this fact. I am told the
Emperor has in no way changed his views since last spring and cannot see
his way to approving the treaties. Yet the question of how to deal with
foreign countries is a crucial one. In the Bakufu, too, there would be much
less concern if our action conformed to Imperial commands; and the
Shōgun seeks to act in whatever way will serve to carry out the Emperor's
wishes, for no matter what the circumstances an Imperial pronouncement
is something commanding respect. But there are other considerations, too.
With the arrival of the English and French we were faced with a choice
between war and peace, and the Shōgun therefore took action in accordance with his hereditary responsibilities. Even so, he is deeply concerned
and feels it a matter of the utmost regret that the treaties were signed
without reference to the Court. I have already reported to you his statements in this connexion.

As I have said above, not to have signed the treaties would have provoked war. Moreover, to repudiate the treaties after both sides have
signed them is equally impossible. You might think that negotiations for
cancelling the treaties would be possible on the grounds that they are
termed 'provisional' treaties,[3] but the expression 'provisional' does not
here have the meaning of 'temporary'. As long as a treaty does not bear
the monarch's name and seal it is described as 'provisional', but although

---

[1] i.e. when Hotta Masayoshi went to Kyōto to seek Imperial approval for the treaty.

[2] *Bakumatsu Gaikoku Kankei Monjo*, xxi. 702–4, Emperor Kōmei to Kujō Naotada, 13 December
1858, stating his complete opposition to more extended foreign relations, for however short a
time, and saying that if foreigners cannot be excluded altogether, then they must be subject to
the same restrictions as had been imposed on Dutch and Chinese hitherto.

[3] The term *kari-jōyaku* ('provisional treaty') in its technical sense was, of course, new to the
Japanese. The discussion here turns on the meaning of *kari*, literally 'temporary'.

it is not yet formally concluded, it is valid from the date of the original agreement.

More generally, the treaties have been negotiated, agreed, and signed as a result of the Shōgun's decision to adopt a policy of friendship [and all countries believe that the Bakufu possessed the necessary political authority for such action].[1] Repudiation of the treaties would never be accepted now, no matter what arguments we advanced. As the Emperor's orders now stand, I fear, they are tantamount to ordering repudiation of the treaties and the opening of hostilities. If we disown the treaties we shall be dishonoured, while the reputation of the foreigners will be untouched. All countries would join in branding us faithless and unjust and would send their warships against us. If that happened, our position would indeed be critical. Our preparations in terms of ships and guns are still incomplete. If we plunge thus recklessly into war, not only will we have no prospect of victory, but the domestic tranquillity we have known for nearly three hundred years would change to disorder. [To revive today all the calamities that have occurred in the centuries since the Ōnin period would be serious indeed.][2] Where lies the advantage or the wisdom in opening hostilities thus recklessly?

Even if the Court issued orders that the foreign envoys were to be summoned to Kyōto, the Bakufu would not be able to carry out such orders, for it would not be in the country's interests to do so.[3] This is not a question of America alone. Provisional treaties have also been concluded with Russia, England, France, and Holland. Thus whatever the orders of the Court may be, to rescind the treaties at this time would be to invite both foreign and domestic dangers at once. To insist on abrogating them would be nothing less than to resolve on war. Yet, as I have already said, our military equipment, in terms of warships and cannon, is still incomplete. The *daimyō* are equally ill equipped with such weapons. [High and low are alike impoverished.][4] It matters little how courageously our people bear themselves in war. Our opponents have had many years' experience of actual warfare[5] and are amply provided with warships and guns. The five above countries for certain, and probably other countries in alliance with them, would send hundreds of ships against our coast on every side, burning and laying waste. We should be fighting alone. With all countries ranged against us we should not, as things are, have even the

---

[1] The clause given in square brackets appears only in the Ii text.

[2] This sentence appears only in the Ii text. The Ōnin period (1467–8) began a period of almost constant civil war which did not end until the Tokugawa pacification of Japan at the beginning of the seventeenth century.

[3] The Ii text says simply—and more intelligibly—'The Bakufu can do nothing that is against the country's interests'.

[4] This sentence appears only in the Ii text.

[5] In the Ii text: 'many years of naval experience'.

means of defending ourselves. Our outlying islands, such as Oki, Sado, Iki, Tsushima, and the seven islands of the Izu group, would be seized by the foreigners; and we might even be unable to protect the Imperial Palace. How great, then, would be the hardships we should inflict on our people! This would truly be the height of inhumanity, a cause of indescribable suffering.

When finally the war ended and we began to discuss peace terms, we should be forced to bow to their wishes and complete treaties entirely dictated by them, leasing them territory and granting them the right to live among Japanese.[1] In that, we should suffer the same tragic fate as China. Although a large country, China was defeated in war by England and had to conclude a new and revised treaty with her. This treaty, as I have reported separately, followed English ideas. It opened several ports, granted English officials equality of status, authorized English subjects to travel freely throughout the country and if they wished to live among the Chinese outside the treaty-port settlements, and provided that the term 'barbarian' was not to be used in official documents. It certainly contained no such regulations as are to be found in the provisional treaties we have just concluded. Thus there can be no question that if we should ever find ourselves in the same position as China, we should suffer such disgrace as could never be wiped out.

It is a matter of the utmost regret to us that we cannot now act in accordance with the Imperial will, [but knowing as we do that it would not be in the country's interest to do so, to provoke war none the less and make it impossible for men to dwell in tranquillity at home, as in the time of the disorders that followed the Ōnin period, would be contrary to the purposes for which generations of Shōgun have been entrusted with the responsibilities of government. The Shōgun would be much troubled by it, despite the respect which generations of his predecessors have felt for the Imperial Ancestors.][2] In the interests of the country as a whole, the Bakufu must respectfully but unremittingly remonstrate against any present opening of hostilities. Were the Emperor to announce that he recognizes that in the circumstances the Bakufu had no choice but to act as it did and that it must so act for the future as to fulfil the Imperial will, then, since those in Edo, too, have always been of this same mind, the Shōgun could act so as to unite Court and Bakufu and thereafter, in the course of time, effect the withdrawal of the foreigners. But it would be most unfortunate were the Imperial instructions to state that the treaty could never be justified to the Imperial Ancestors, most of all those en-

---

[1] The term used is *zakkyo*, literally 'mixed residence', i.e. the right to live among the Japanese rather than in specially designated and segregated foreign settlements like that of the Dutch at Deshima.

[2] The passage shown in square brackets is omitted from the Ii text.

shrined at Ise, and was contrary to the announcement made in July last when the Emperor sent lords to Ise as his envoys. For some time now the Shōgun has been anxious to act only after making a detailed report on the situation to the Emperor. It is, after all, his wish to show proper respect for the Imperial Court. He is convinced that the Emperor's completely unexpected attitude was due to lack of detailed information concerning foreign affairs. As such, it is most proper and reasonable. There are those, however, who put about exaggerated reports of the foreigners' attitude, calling them haughty, arrogant, and so on. It is generally said, too, that the Emperor's ideas may gradually have been contaminated by these base and idle rumours. [However, full investigation shows that there are some most important persons among those guilty of this great crime; and since we should indeed be jeopardizing the very existence of our country were we now to bring about foreign and domestic conflict simultaneously, the Shōgun is generally willing to overlook what they have done on the assumption that it sprang from misunderstanding. But should it happen that despite what I have been saying it is still not recognized that Bakufu policy is in the true interests of the country, should there still be rebellious talk, then the Shōgun may have to distinguish between right and wrong. In that event, it will indeed become impossible to effect the objects of domestic tranquillity and Court-Bakufu unity which the Emperor regards so highly.][1] And since it would be much to be regretted were the Imperial mind to be further disturbed in this way, we shall investigate carefully and make everything clear to the Court. Investigations are already in progress both in Kyōto and in Edo, and after the strictest and most searching examination a further report will be submitted on this question.

The question now before us is truly one on which the peace of our country turns. The decision [concerning the treaty] was taken by the Bakufu in accordance with its proper responsibilities; but in that it was signed without reference to the Court, the Shōgun Iesada instructed me to submit detailed explanations to you. I respectfully ask that you will again convey these statements to the Emperor.

DOCUMENT 30. Imperial Court to Manabe Akikatsu, 2 February 1859.[2]

The treaty providing for friendship and trade with foreigners and other matters is a blemish on our Empire and a stain on our divine land. This question caused the Emperor's predecessor great anxiety and he issued instructions concerning it. The present Emperor greatly fears that were

---

[1] The passage shown in square brackets is omitted from the Ii text.
[2] The text is printed in *Bakumatsu Gaikoku Kankei Monjo*, xxi. 934–5. Manabe is here acting as official representative of the Bakufu.

such things to start in his reign, he would find it truly impossible to justify himself to his Imperial Ancestors, most of all those enshrined at Ise. He has thought much on this and his anxiety concerning it is constant, as you have often been informed since last spring. However, since the recent arrival in the capital of Manabe [Akikatsu] Shimōsa-no-kami and Sakai [Tadayoshi] Wakasa-no-kami, several reports have been submitted to the effect that the Shōgun himself, as well as the Tairō, Rōjū, and other officials, all are in agreement with the Emperor in thinking that we must assuredly keep aloof from foreigners and revert to the sound rule of seclusion as formerly laid down in our national laws. The Emperor was much eased in his mind to learn this.

Accordingly, we must at all events secure greater unity between Court and Bakufu and so adopt the sound policy of reverting [to seclusion] as described above. The Emperor fully understands that in the circumstances the Bakufu could have done no other than it did; and he will therefore exercise forbearance on this occasion. The Bakufu is enjoined to pay special attention to the coastal areas near Kyōto and the Ise shrines, as was stated the other day, for this is a matter touching the respect due to the sacred Imperial Regalia by which our country is preserved.

The Kazunomiya Marriage and the London Protocol, 1860–2

THE methods adopted by Ii Naosuke to force acceptance of the American treaty and the adoption of Tokugawa Yoshitomi as the Shōgun's heir (he became Shōgun under the name of Iemochi before the end of 1858) achieved their end at the cost of still further alienating the Imperial Court and the Hitotsubashi party. His arbitrariness was resented even among Bakufu officials. When, therefore, he was assassinated on 24 March 1860 outside the Sakurada-mon in Edo by a band of Mito samurai, the control of Bakufu policy quickly passed to less assertive but more generally acceptable men.

The new Council was dominated by the Rōjū Andō Nobumasa and Kuze Hirochika. The problems they faced were the same: at home, an opposition increasingly centred on the Imperial Court and expressed in criticism of the treaties; abroad, foreign 'aggression' newly provoked by personal attacks on foreign merchants and officials. In this dilemma Andō and Kuze found it impossible to pursue a consistent policy. On the one hand they sought to patch up differences with the Hitotsubashi and Mito groups and to secure agreement with the Court. On the other, they tried to persuade the foreign Powers to abandon or postpone some of the rights granted by treaty, meanwhile making such concessions to them as seemed unavoidable.

This policy was expressed in the negotiations for the Kazunomiya marriage. In May 1860, after a number of private discussions going back as far as Manabe's mission to Kyōto in 1858, the Bakufu formally proposed a marriage between the Shōgun and the Emperor's sister, Princess Kazunomiya—a means, it said, of demonstrating to the country the harmony existing between Edo and Kyōto and so achieving that national unity which alone would make possible an effective foreign policy. Despite an initial rebuff, the Bakufu persisted in this request. The Emperor Kōmei, therefore, sought the advice of Iwakura Tomomi, a Court noble who had come into prominence as one of the opponents of the treaties in 1858 and who was later to become one of the leaders of the Meiji Restoration. Iwakura believed that this Bakufu overture should be used to strengthen the Imperial authority with a view to the ultimate overthrow of the Tokugawa. The time was not yet ripe for direct action, he said, but by insisting that Imperial sanction for the marriage must be conditional on the expulsion of the foreigners, or at least on a Bakufu promise of such expulsion, the Emperor would be able to obtain effective (though not nominal) control over national policy (Document 31). This advice undoubtedly influenced the Emperor's decision. On 6 August he informed the Kampaku that the Bakufu must secure abrogation of the treaties before the marriage could be agreed. This the Rōjū could not accept. In a new memorandum they argued that while their ultimate aim, like that of the Emperor, was to effect the withdrawal of all foreigners from Japan, two preliminary steps were indispensable: first, national unity must be achieved, for which reason the marriage should take place as soon as possible; second, military preparations must be made, which meant that some years must pass before action could be taken (Document 32).

As a result of these exchanges the Bakufu finally secured Imperial sanction for the Kazunomiya marriage, but only by undertaking to effect the complete withdrawal of the foreigners within 'from seven or eight to ten years time'. Meanwhile, in the hope of quieting criticism within Japan, it had opened discussions with the foreign diplomats to secure postponement of the opening of the ports of Hyōgo and Niigata and the cities of Edo and Ōsaka (see Document 28, Article III). Despite Japanese arguments that the domestic situation made such a course inevitable, the envoys were reluctant. Townsend Harris, however, suggested that if Japan concluded a treaty with Prussia, whose envoy had recently arrived to seek a trade agreement, but omitted the stipulation providing for the opening of these four places, then her case would be greatly strengthened. In December 1860 the Kyōto-shoshidai was informed that this suggestion was to be adopted (Document 33). His report to the Kampaku (Document 34), despite its reassurance that no change of ultimate objective was involved, caused fresh misgivings in Kyōto; and these were only overcome by a new promise that such temporary deviations were but part of the strategy, that they in no way affected the decision to expel foreigners after the necessary military preparations had been made.

This made it the more important that some concession be obtained from the Treaty Powers. In March 1861 the Bakufu announced that it proposed to send a mission to Europe, the object being to negotiate directly with the governments concerned for the postponement of the opening of any further ports. In May it formally stated its reasons for making this request, mainly in terms of the unrest existing in Japan (Document 35). The chief problem was to secure British and French concurrence. This had to wait upon a reply from the two governments. Lord Russell's reply, the most important, was dated 23 November 1861 and was not entirely unfavourable, though it insisted that settlement of British claims arising out of an attack on the Edo legation must precede any negotiations and that 'equivalents' must be obtained for the privileges relinquished. Rutherford Alcock, the British minister in Japan, was more suspicious of Japanese policy and less willing to make concessions (Document 36). However, discussion with his French, American, and Dutch colleagues convinced him that no support would be forthcoming for a joint *démarche* and the Rōjū succeeded in persuading him of the reality of their difficulties. In March 1862 he agreed to support the Japanese request that the opening of further ports be delayed for five years.

Meanwhile the Japanese envoy, Takeuchi Yasunori, had left for Europe. At the end of April, after brief and abortive discussions with the French government in Paris, he reached London, only to find that Russell refused to open negotiations until Alcock's views were known. Alcock, however, was already on his way home, accompanied by the Japanese senior interpreter, Moriyama, who brought fresh instructions for Takeuchi. With their arrival in England the situation changed. It took only a few days to reach agreement on the new basis worked out with the Rōjū before Alcock left Japan, and on 6 June 1862 the London Protocol was signed (Document 37). The British government agreed to waive its rights concerning Hyōgo, Edo, and Ōsaka for a time, these places, together with another instead of Niigata, to be opened on 1 January 1868; while in return the Japanese signatories promised the removal of all existing restrictions on trade (a reaffirmation of rights granted in the original treaties), further consideration of the question of opening Tsushima Island, and a few small concessions in the matter of customs duties and similar problems. Similar agreements were concluded with Russia, Holland, and France later in the year.

As the *gaikoku-bugyō* later observed (Document 38), the concessions made by Japan—with the possible exception of that concerning Tsushima, which was in any case still open to negotiation—were inconvenient at worst and seemed a small price to pay for the advantages gained. At first sight, indeed, Bakufu policy had been remarkably successful. By emphasizing the foreign danger it had secured the Court's consent to the Kazunomiya marriage. By emphasizing the danger of civil war in Japan it had persuaded the foreigners to waive some of their treaty rights, if only temporarily, and thereby strengthened its position *vis-à-vis* domestic critics. Unfortunately, however, none of the essential causes of danger had been removed. To the Court the Bakufu had promised the eventual expulsion of foreigners; to the foreigners it had promised the progressive removal of restrictions on trade. In the next two years this contradiction was to cause a conflict sharper than any that had occurred before.

DOCUMENT 31. Iwakura Tomomi to the Emperor Kōmei: memorandum on the Kazunomiya Marriage, undated. Written between 21 July and 6 August 1860.[1]

Having been honoured by an Imperial request for my views regarding the Bakufu's confidential proposal for a marriage between the Shōgun and Princess Kazunomiya,[2] I herewith submit them with the utmost respect.

Manabe [Akikatsu], Shimōsa-no-kami, came to Kyōto the year before last and reported that provisional treaties had been concluded with the foreigners. He said at that time that the decision to do so had been taken by the former Rōjū, Hotta [Masayoshi], Bitchū-no-kami, on his own responsibility. However [he added], should we hasten at once into negotiations to rescind the treaties, we would acquire a reputation for bad faith, the foreigners would become incensed, and there was no telling what disorders might follow, particularly as military preparations for the country as a whole had still not been completed. Moreover, he said, there were some [in Japan] who opposed and plotted against the Bakufu. If, therefore, we suddenly got ourselves into difficulties in foreign affairs, this would inevitably open the way to rebellion at home, bringing about complete national collapse and so rendering us helpless. For these reasons the Bakufu submitted that the Court, paying due attention to conditions at home and abroad, should postpone abrogation of the treaties.

The Court had no choice but to give its assent to Shimōsa-no-kami's request. So far, however, the Bakufu officials have neglected and postponed that which they should have done by way of completing our military preparations in order whole-heartedly to carry out chastisement [of the foreigners]. Thus the whole country is becoming more and more dissatisfied with them. It is my belief that the Bakufu officials, growing alarmed at this, have resolved to make use of the prestige of the Court to bolster the authority of the Bakufu and quell the people's unrest. They have urgently and confidentially proposed a marriage between the Shōgun and Princess Kazunomiya; and they now repeat that request.

I have given much thought to the present position of Japan. At home our people are disunited and hold a myriad different views. Abroad, it seems likely that the five enemy Powers, crowding in upon our ports, might open hostilities, interfere in our domestic politics, and seize by aggression such territory as they covet. Our situation, indeed, is critical and gives me much concern. To my mind the way of resolving these diffi-

---

[1] The text is printed in *Iwakura Kō Jikki*, i. 383–7, and *Iwakura Tomomi Kankei Monjo* (8 vols., Tōkyō, 1927–35), i. 141–5.

[2] Princess Kazunomiya was a younger sister of the Emperor Kōmei.

culties would be to order the Bakufu to return in private[1] to the Court the substance of political power. We could thereby unite the people in loyalty to the Court, and correct and reinforce our national policy by basing it on the views of the country at large. The hegemony of the Bakufu has now vanished. It no longer has the strength it had of old. Though he held the office of *Tairō*, Ii [Naosuke], Kamon-no-kami, could not even protect his own life and was cut down by *rōnin* in the street. This is conclusive evidence. Thus to rely on the Bakufu, which has so far fallen in authority, for protection against foreign and domestic dangers and the extension of Imperial prestige would be idle and ineffective. It would be, as the proverb says, 'to try to pull a star down from the sky by use of a long stick'. I believe, therefore, that the plan which would best serve the interests of the country would be to make the Bakufu return in private to the Court the substance of political power and thereby revise and correct our national policies by basing them on the views of the country at large.

However, to accomplish so great a task quickly has never been possible by words alone. It must necessarily entail the use of force. Yet it would not be proper to make this grounds for plunging the whole country into civil war. The Court must await its opportunity, moving slowly and in accordance with plan. It is true that the authority of the Bakufu is now in decline, but for over two hundred years, since the time of Ieyasu, it has bestowed peace on the country, and for this boon men are grateful. There are many *fudai daimyō* and lesser lords who have been specially favoured [by the Tokugawa], and should the Court attempt to punish the Bakufu by force of arms for its years of negligence, it is not impossible that these *fudai* and lesser lords who have long been favoured might take up arms even against the Court, out of reluctance to see their overlord brought to ruin. Nor is it impossible that there be some among the other lords who, thinking this to be the Court's private war, might stand aloof and determine their action only after weighing the strength of the two sides. What is more, it would be difficult to deny that there are those who might withdraw to their own territories to await an opportunity for action, those who might plot ultimately to seize power for themselves in place of the Bakufu. Moreover, *rōnin* and other men of violence might take advantage of the situation to seek temporary satisfaction [of their hatred of foreigners] by destroying the consulates[2] of the five Powers; the foreigners would then join forces, and with great outcry, on the pretext of protecting themselves against such violence, would occupy areas along our coastline and arbitrarily plant their national flags therein. If that should happen, domestic and foreign dangers would be upon us at the same time. The Court's

---

[1] 'in private': presumably, that is, without any public or avowed redefinition of Bakufu authority.

[2] *Shōkan*: 'consulate' or 'trading factory'. See Document 21, p. 168, note 2.

solemn attempt to resolve the problem of national policy would thus in fact bring us into the toils of the foreigners. That is a course no man of intelligence could adopt.

In my view our policy at this time must essentially be a willingness to concede in name what we retain in substance. It is even fortunate that the Bakufu has recently been making earnest proposals for the Shōgun's marriage to Princess Kazunomiya. The Court should send solemn orders to the Bakufu saying that its request will be granted as a mark of the Emperor's special favour, demonstrating to the country at large the accord between Bakufu and Court; that it is expected as a matter of course that the five treaties will be gradually rescinded; and that important affairs of State must [hereafter] be put into effect only after consultation with the Emperor. If this is done I think the Bakufu is sure to accept the instructions, for it could not oppose them and still retain the special protection of the Court. By planning it in this way that the Bakufu returns the substance of political authority in private to the Court, the Court will have succeeded in grasping the reality of power while the Bakufu retains but the appearance of it.

The Kazunomiya question is today of the utmost importance, and the problem of whether or not to permit her marriage to the Shōgun is a matter vital to the Imperial prestige. While I therefore hesitate to speak on so great a matter, it is my view that the Court should first issue orders to the Bakufu for the early abrogation of the five treaties. Then, when the Bakufu has reported its whole-hearted acceptance of these orders, the Emperor may explain to Princess Kazunomiya that he thinks this marriage is in the national interest and [finally], having obtained her assent, could inform the Bakufu that its request is granted.

DOCUMENT 32. Rōjū to Imperial Court: memorandum on the Kazunomiya Marriage, undated. Presented to the Court on 14 September 1860.[1]

With reference to the question of Princess Kazunomiya's marriage, we have perused with respect the copy of a further statement of the Emperor's views which was sent to us in confidence.[2] We think it altogether understandable that the Emperor should write as he does. However, this marriage is a matter of the utmost importance and we did not request it without full deliberation. The Shōgun himself has given it much thought and has given us various orders on the subject, and it would therefore give

[1] The text is printed in *Iwakura Kō Jikki*, i. 393–7.
[2] Emperor Kōmei to the Kampaku (Kujō Naotada), 6 Aug. 1860, a letter based in part on Iwakura's memorandum (Document 31 above) and forwarded by Kujō to the *Kyōto-shoshidai* Sakai Tadayoshi for the information of the Bakufu. See *Iwakura Kō Jikki*, i. 387–9.

us great gratification if we could carry out his ideas and accomplish this marriage with the Court's approval. Hence after much thought and discussion we wish, while recording our acceptance of the Court's orders, to forward the following observations.

It is a matter of the utmost gratification to us that the Emperor has not refused outright our request for this marriage and that he is pleased to think it would be a basis for the greatest possible accord between Court and Bakufu. The Emperor, however, as he has always said, fears it might arouse nation-wide disquiet to marry his sister into a place where foreigners are resident. Moreover he is most anxious that the foreigners be expelled and envoys have already been sent to report this at the three shrines;[1] should this be the reign to see the beginning of friendly relations with foreigners, the Emperor could never excuse himself in the eyes of his Imperial Father and the Imperial Ancestors at Ise. This gives him constant anxiety. And the thing which he would feel especially unforgivable would be to send in marriage to a place where foreigners are resident a daughter of his own Imperial Father. Were foreign affairs to be handled in the same manner as in the early Kaei period,[2] he has said, he would make no difficulties. He would explain matters fully to Princess Kazunomiya and would allow the marriage to take place at once. But as things stand he cannot bring himself to do so. We think that in this the Emperor's attitude is a very reasonable one, yet while we believe him to be fully informed as to the Bakufu's present policy regarding foreign affairs, in that we have often submitted reports before, we beg to append here a further detailed statement on the subject.

Ever since the Keichō period [1596–1614] it has become a more and more frequent occurrence for foreigners to come into our waters and enter our ports. In modern times, as we have often reported before, the foreigners pressed demands for trade. And since we could not arbitrarily use force against them we were finally driven by circumstance to permit trade. This, however, was no more than an unavoidable political expedient. In the Bakufu neither those who at that time bore responsibility for administration nor any other person, high or low, had any liking for trade. We have now no choice but to seek to gain time. We are gradually completing our military preparations, and our idea is that once this is done we will carry out expulsion in accordance with the Emperor's commands. However, in the last two years there have been some divergent policies and a number of disputes among us, with the result that the people have been

---

[1] i.e. to report the Emperor's decision to the Imperial Ancestors at the shrines of Ise, Iwashimizu Hachiman, and Kamo.

[2] i.e. by a return to the seclusion policy. The Kaei period [1848–53] was that immediately before the arrival of Perry.

made uneasy. There have been such illegal actions as that taken by retainers of the Mito fief,[1] which must have been due, we think, to misunderstanding of the situation, a failure to recognize that complete accord exists between Court and Bakufu throughout the country. If our affairs are not in good order at home we shall be unable to strike successfully abroad. Should civil war break out before the foreigners' very eyes, we think it certain that Japan would suffer incalculable harm. The Shōgun therefore wishes to demonstrate to the country without delay the accord that exists between Court and Bakufu, thereby uniting the whole people, and earnestly and single-mindedly to pursue measures for defence against the foreigners. He will hereafter make ever more stringent preparations and will engage whole-heartedly in planning the expulsion of foreigners. He is convinced that the present marriage project would be of the utmost importance in attaining that end, and therefore respectfully submits that the Court, taking these facts fully into consideration, may make early arrangements for it.

We believe the Emperor to be right in thinking that to send an Imperial Princess in marriage to a place where foreigners are resident might disquiet the people. However, Edo is in fact distant about twenty miles from Yokohama, the place where foreigners reside. Between the two lies the river Rokugo, which can only be crossed by boat, and it is already strictly enjoined by treaty that foreigners can walk for pleasure in the direction of Edo only as far as this river. Thus foreigners have never been allowed to go freely to Edo, except for the special case of officials who must necessarily go there to conduct negotiations.

It would seem from the Emperor's instructions to us that he wishes the withdrawal of foreigners to be accomplished by immediate expulsion. Yet the Bakufu did not grant the five foreign Powers permission to trade merely out of a passing whim. As we have reported time and again, officials who had long been responsible for such matters gave the question careful thought; and the present agreements were reached in the end by steadily whittling down the foreigners' demands. The Court having taken no action two years ago and the treaties having thus been finally completed, it would be an act of treachery even towards foreigners were we to carry out expulsion now without just cause. It might lose us our good name and make it impossible to preserve our national reputation for good faith. It might well, indeed, be the occasion of our losing national prestige. Moreover, as we have said before, to get into difficulties with the foreigners before we have fully achieved harmony at home might create an opportunity for rebellion in Japan. The foreigners in turn would then seize their opportunity. Thus we would become involved in domestic and foreign difficulties at the same time, and would have no hope of

---

[1] This is presumably a reference to the assassination of Ii Naosuke on 24 March 1860.

settling matters. That being so, this is no time to open hostilities. Two years ago we begged the Court to postpone action on these grounds. Since then the Bakufu has given much thought to its plans; and although it has sought to postpone action it has not been in the least unmindful of its duty. It is now, in fact, engaged in the construction of ships and guns, which certainly cannot be called idleness. Policy must be determined only after the fullest discussion. Within seven or eight to ten years from now action will certainly be taken either to cancel the treaties by negotiation or to expel the foreigners by force. The Bakufu has made various calculations as to how this may be done, but until the time comes it will be impossible to decide which method is to be used. Certainly these plans must be kept a strict secret. Since we will be able to attain complete success only if we adjust our actions to immediate circumstances, we cannot exactly determine our course in advance, but the Court may rest assured that when the time comes the Shōgun's action will be such as to accomplish the Emperor's wishes and allay his anxiety. Although we have here stated in general terms the period within which we will take action, it is possible that before then the foreigners might open hostilities, might break the treaties, or might transgress our national laws. We are unanimously of the opinion that should this happen we must take action at once. To accomplish all this our first and most important task is to achieve the unification of the country. We therefore earnestly entreat the Court to give these matters full consideration and to grant early permission for the marriage to take place.

Since the reports about foreigners which have reached the Princess Kazunomiya have caused her to view them with dread, it is but natural that the Emperor's brotherly affection should make him unwilling to persuade her to this marriage before the expulsion of foreigners has been effected. As we reported earlier, however, we would take special pains about the care and protection of the Princess. Moreover, as we have pointed out above, the conclusion of this marriage would be of fundamental importance in enabling the Shōgun first to demonstrate to the country the accord existing between Court and Bakufu, thereby pacifying opinion at home; and then to sweep out the foreigners, thereby setting at rest the Emperor's long-standing anxiety and bringing complete peace to our land. Should the Emperor reject our present request, even though in a secret correspondence, the country would fall into yet greater doubt and unrest and decades of care might not suffice to repair the damage. And if it came to the point of waging war simultaneously against foreign and domestic enemies, however great his efforts the Shōgun's exertions could never provide him with means of setting the Emperor's mind at rest. This question, then, is vital to the peace and order of the country; and we most earnestly request that the Court may overlook our presumption and, having pondered this matter deeply, may persuade the Princess to this marriage. . . .[1]

DOCUMENT 33. Rōjū to Kyōto-shoshidai, 21 December 1860.[2]

In September of this year an envoy arrived from Prussia and asked that we conclude a treaty. The American minister, too, stated that the President had instructed him to seek Bakufu approval of the said envoy's request. Since this was strongly urged both by the envoy and by the minister, we advanced arguments to show that there were a number of difficulties which made it impossible for the Bakufu to consent. We did everything to persuade them of this, but they would not by any means agree. They objected variously that since the envoy had been entrusted with this duty and a warship had been sent out specially by his country, he could not possibly return home having accomplished nothing; and again, that since his country was in much the same position as America and England, it would cause us national dishonour if we refused to conclude a treaty with them. The envoy seemed prepared to stay indefinitely. We were told that even if we insisted on his departure now, another envoy would be dispatched at once. Moreover, as we explain below, there was also this to be considered, that we are proposing to postpone the opening of Hyōgo and a port on the west coast and the opening of trade at Edo and Ōsaka.[3] Circumstances therefore compel us to conduct discussions for the purpose of concluding a treaty [with Prussia], though we shall deal only with the three ports of Kanagawa, Nagasaki, and Hakodate. At an early date after the completion of negotiations we shall sign a provisional treaty. However, we will advance various arguments to show that we cannot allow this treaty to come into effect until later, when [the ratifications of] the treaty proper have been exchanged. We will report further when the provisional treaty has been signed, but meanwhile we send this initial report for your information.

As we recently informed you through Hayakawa Shōjirō,[4] the postponement of the opening of Hyōgo and a port on the west coast and of the opening of trade at Edo and Ōsaka is a matter which has been causing us much trouble and anxiety. The fact that these stipulations were in-

---

[1] A short final paragraph of recapitulation is here omitted.

[2] The text is printed in *Iwakura Kō Jikki*, i. 450–2. Although the memorandum was intended for the information of the Court, the addressee was the Kyōto-shoshidai, Sakai Tadayoshi. It was signed jointly by the Rōjū Honda Tadamoto, Andō Nobumasa, Naitō Nobuchika, and Kuze Hirochika.

[3] By the 1858 treaties Edo was to be opened on 1 January 1862, Hyōgo (Kōbe) and Ōsaka on 1 January 1863. Niigata, or another port on the west coast, was to have been opened on 1 January 1860, but this had already been deferred, Niigata being found unsuitable and no other port yet chosen.

[4] Hayakawa Hisatake, a minor Bakufu official who later rose to the rank of Kanagawa *bugyō*.

cluded in the treaties is now making the situation very difficult. Nothing can be done, moreover, unless all the Treaty Powers give their consent. In that we have for some time been explaining our reasons [for seeking postponement] and have exerted every effort in the discussions of this matter, we seem to have secured general recognition that our action is made unavoidable by circumstance. We have been told, however, that since these are stipulations laid down in treaties which have been ratified by the signatures and seals of the sovereigns of our respective countries, a definite answer cannot be given by the [resident] ministers alone, but must wait on the views of their governments. We thereupon went on to urge that communication be opened with foreign governments by letter to persuade them to let the resident ministers handle this matter, but it seems there is no possible reason why the stipulations should not hold good, being part of treaties which bear the signatures and seals of national sovereigns. If, however, we were now to conclude a treaty with Prussia which omitted the matter of the two ports, then this would provide grounds for communicating with foreign governments concerning postponement of the opening of Hyōgo and a port on the west coast and of the opening of trade at Edo and Ōsaka. It is the private opinion of the [American] minister that if we concluded a treaty with Prussia on the basis of [opening] three ports, foreigners would be made to realize that we cannot permit more than three ports, even to so great a country as Prussia; their governments would be made to take thought on this question; and there would be ample reason for proposing postponement in the matter of the two ports and the two cities. Now even though it means admitting two or three more countries to the three ports now open, this would be greatly to our advantage if it enabled us to conduct negotiations for postponement of the opening of Hyōgo and a port on the west coast and of the opening of trade at Edo and Ōsaka. We have all given thought to these considerations, therefore, and have decided as a matter of immediate policy that we will grant Prussia a treaty, as we have stated above, omitting the stipulation about the two ports and the two cities.

Though we cannot tell what reply the foreign governments will make concerning postponement, we are at all events making every effort to postpone the opening of the port [of Hyōgo] which was fixed for the year after next. If postponement is decided, we will communicate with you again. Moreover, once the present treaty is concluded we intend to notify all countries, through the American minister and others, that we will not thereafter entertain requests for treaties from any more countries. However, an envoy has recently been sent from Switzerland, while the English minister asked some time ago that we should conclude a treaty with Belgium, because of [the Belgian monarch's] kinship with the Queen of England. We have deferred decision on the requests of these two countries, which were made before that of Prussia, but there seems to be no pretext by which we could refuse them. Since the circumstances are compelling, therefore, we intend to grant their requests if they send envoys to ask again for a treaty, concluding treaties with these two countries alone and on the same lines as that with Prussia, applicable only to three ports. It is not at all to our liking to increase the number of treaties in this way, but once we announce that we will refuse all countries other than these, then there will be no further increase. What is more, if this enables us to conduct negotiations for postponement in the matter of the two ports and the two cities, this course will actually be to our advantage, as we have explained above. We therefore intend to act on the above lines. We will continue to report on this matter, but we now forward for your information this preliminary outline of the circumstances surrounding the negotiations.

DOCUMENT 34. Kyōto-shoshidai to Kampaku, *circa* 8 January 1861.[1]

I submit for your perusal the enclosed communication[2] sent to me by the Rōjū. It is generally true that reports were submitted by Manabe Shimōsa-no-kami[3] to ask that the Court withhold judgement for a time on the question of trade with the five foreign countries; and we had no intention thereafter either of increasing the number [of treaties] or of expanding [their provisions]. We have continued to exert every effort to secure postponement of the opening of Hyōgo and abrogation of the stipulation for the opening of trade at Ōsaka. This we have reported. Now, however, Prussia has made a friendly request [for a treaty] and the Bakufu is inclined to grant it, though only with respect to the three ports that have been opened hitherto, and it seems likely that this will arouse the Court's suspicions. I have therefore been confidentially informed of the circumstances that make this action unavoidable. These I set out below.

For the last three years there have been within Japan those who cherish evil designs. They have put about all kinds of false reports and almost caused a breach between Court and Bakufu, but thanks to the Emperor's enlightened perception the difficulties were soon resolved, with the result that the plotters have failed in all their designs and harmony reigns between Court and Bakufu. This is truly a circumstance calling for our gratitude. It seems, however, that in remote and outlying areas there are still some who do not yet fully comprehend this harmony, so that unity has

---

[1] The text is printed in *Iwakura Kō Jikki*, i. 447–50. The letter is dated only Manen 1, 11th month (12 December 1860–10 January 1861), but it was handed to the Kampaku, Kujō Naotada, on 8 January 1861. The Kyōto-shoshidai at this time was Sakai Tadayoshi, Wakasa-no-kami.

[2] Document 33.　　　　　　　　　　　　　　　　　　[3] See Section III, Document 29.

still not been achieved throughout the whole of the land. This the Emperor will have realized from the outbreak which took place outside the Sakuradamon this spring.[1] If we were to open hostilities against the foreigners before achieving unity at home, we should, as we have explained before, be bringing about both domestic and foreign difficulties at the same time. What means would we then have of settling internal unrest? Still less, indeed, could one foresee when recovery would be possible. This has caused the Shōgun great concern and the Rōjū have all discussed the matter fully. Since the spring of this year we have been seeking Imperial consent to a marriage between an Imperial Princess and the Shōgun, with the object of demonstrating to the Empire the complete harmony that exists between Court and Bakufu. Such a course would ensure the unity of the whole country and bring gratitude and peace of mind to all, even those stubborn and obstinate men in remote and outlying areas. Within a period of from seven or eight to ten years our cannon would be ready and our military preparations completed. That done, we would insist on the withdrawal of the foreigners. If they then opened hostilities, we would unite the whole strength of the Empire against them. With forces fully equipped and thoroughly trained we would expel all of them together and make resplendent throughout the world the military prestige of the Imperial Court. It was with this plan in mind that the Emperor was pleased to sanction the marriage in accordance with our request, a fact which has produced in all his subjects both gratitude and ease of mind.

Before the Imperial Princess could come to Edo, however, an envoy was sent from Prussia to make a friendly request for trade. Those entrusted with the negotiations firmly refused, advancing many and varied arguments, but he would by no means accept this. The American President, too, as our neighbour, earnestly entreated us to consent. He even went so far as to say that if we granted permission for this one country, there would be no further requests, that America would notify all countries of this. Moreover, if we refused we should certainly incur national dishonour. In their anger they would assuredly send warships and go to war with us at once. And it is clear that if we opened hostilities against Prussia now, not only America but also the other four Treaty Powers would all come to her assistance. If that happened, our original plan would truly be no more than foam upon the water. The whole land of Japan would at once become a scene of warfare. Our farmers would be in extreme distress, military operations would be unending, and never again would we be able to recover. This is beyond all question. And in that event there would be serious disturbances throughout the Empire and we should be in imminent danger of suffering the same fate as befell China.

Hence this was reported to the Shōgun and further consultations were

[1] i.e. the assassination of Ii Naosuke on 24 March 1860.

held. As a result of these consultations it was decided that the safest course would be, first, as a means of avoiding hostilities for a time, to grant Prussia [access to] three ports; then, as our controlling strategy and in accordance with the plan originally laid down, to wait for a period of from seven or eight to ten years until the whole country is united and military preparations are completed, when all the foreigners will be expelled together. For us to say that the position is truly such that we can do no other than grant the three ports as an initial step is reprehensible indeed, and must certainly be thought to conflict with and contradict our original statement that we would assuredly neither multiply nor expand the treaties. Yet as we are situated today, that is indeed the position. The objective, after all, is to prevent civil commotion in Japan and to expel all the foreigners together after the lapse of from seven or eight to ten years. All emergency measures that we take [meanwhile] come within the scope of that strategy. It is for this reason that, being myself fully informed on these matters, I have been instructed in confidence to submit a detailed report to you if you should be in any way suspicious. I accordingly submit this report in the utmost secrecy.

Should it happen that the Court issue an Imperial command that we effect the withdrawal of foreigners at once and without fail, then the Bakufu will have no pretext for delay and the whole country would at once become the crossroads of war. I therefore respectfully submit that the Court be pleased to give this matter the most careful consideration.

Document 35. Kuze Hirochika and Andō Nobumasa to Rutherford Alcock, 30 May 1861.[1]

We have hereby to communicate the following to your Excellency.

Since the conclusion of the Treaty between our Empire and Britain, the intercourse between both Empires has daily become more and more extended, by the arrival of the Envoy, by friendly correspondence, and by the exchange of the respective productions. A number of important matters has also from time to time been thereby set in order, and that which is written in the Treaty has mostly had the opportunity of being carried into effect.

Nearly three hundred years have now elapsed since our Empire discontinued its intercourse with foreign Powers.

Recently, however, in consequence of the urgent advice of the President of the United States of America and of the King of the Netherlands, this old-standing law was almost entirely altered, and it was agreed that foreign ships sailing near our coasts should be supplied with fuel, water,

[1] This is a contemporary official translation, published in *Parliamentary Papers 1862*, vol. lxiv, pp. 36–37. I have not seen the original Japanese text.

provisions, and necessaries, at the ports of Simoda [Shimoda] and Hako-dadi [Hakodate].

Again, after the arrival of the American Minister, Townsend Harris, as the circumstances of all countries were occasionally communicated to us, our Government having taken into consideration the existing posture of foreign affairs, concluded the Treaty of Amity which lately entered into operation, and established free trade in the same manner, first with Britain, subsequently with Russia, France, Holland, America, &c.

But it is found that in carrying this into effect the actual result differs considerably, in respect of the general circumstances, from what was anticipated, and no profit has yet been derived, but the lower classes of the people have already suffered loss thereby.

The price of things is daily increasing, in consequence of the large quantity of products which is exported to foreign countries, and which is seldom, in return, imported into our Empire. And while the lower classes of the people, in every case, when deprived of the means of gaining their livelihood, ascribe the cause to trade, they occasionally give expression to their ingratitude (discontent); yea, even the respectable and wealthy classes have mostly now no satisfaction in trade, so that there will soon be those who will declare their condemnation of the abrogation of the pre-vious existing prohibition, and who will desire the restitution of the former law.

As probably the form of government which excluded foreign nations, since it was established, its practice forming the usage, has been deeply rooted into the national spirit, and the intercourse with foreign Powers thus unknown, it would be very difficult to reconcile the national feeling to the altered form of government, even did the difficulty previously alluded to not exist.

Since, now, such a prejudice (loss) has already extended itself through-out the whole Empire, everyone is grieved on reading the stipulation that the ports of Hiogo [Hyōgo] and Ne-egata [Niigata] are to be opened, and that foreign trade will be carried on at Yeddo [Edo] and Osaka, as stated in Article III of the Treaty everywhere published, and regards with de-jected aspect the speedy approach of the appointed time in contemplating whether the loss and injury will be still further increased.

The popular spirit having already arrived at such a pitch, it is very diffi-cult, even for the power and authority of the Government, so to manage that each one should clearly understand the future advantage, and to cause them to endure for a time the present grief.

Also, to accustom themselves to what is at hand, and not to regard what is looming up in the distance, is the custom of the ignorant people. Should, therefore, violence be used to attain the object, it would be uncertain what mischief would result from such an act against the national spirit.

Meanwhile, as far as regards the port of Ne-egata, as it is not capable of being entered by ships of foreign nations on account of the sand-banks at its entrance, and the American Minister was also of opinion that it is wanting in the capabilities requisite for a permanent place of trade, another suitable port ought to have been selected and opened on the west coast, as it is stipulated. This has, however, hitherto been postponed, while the appointed time has already passed, because the selection could not be proceeded with in consequence of the adverse state of wind and tide during the time of the search.

To take meanwhile into consideration the arrangement suitable to the present circumstances, the time might be expected, should the opening of the two ports and the two cities be postponed, when the national spirit will be appeased and slowly led, trade from time to time become regularly established, the price of things stand on an even scale, the old custom in like measure altered, and every one shall wish for the flourishing state of the intercourse with foreign Powers. In such a case, how shall it be possible for any difficulty to exist in opening the above-mentioned two ports and two cities? To take a simile: as the seaman avoids the contrary wind and waits for a fair wind, so will not patiently to allow the time to pass and to wait for the (favourable) period to accomplish the object, be an arrangement of necessity?

As Tsoosimanokami [Andō Nobumasa, Tsushima-no-kami] communicated the circumstances to you at an interview last year, and discussed the above-mentioned postponement of the time, a letter from His Majesty the Tycoon to Her Majesty the Queen shall be sent with this. And it is desired to defer the opening of the two ports and the two cities for the space of seven years, and to agree that they shall be opened, according to our calculation, at the end of the year of the approaching Hinoto-oo, corresponding to the year 1868 according to your calculation.

While waiting for the arrival of the time, the arrangement of affairs will in general speedily produce a satisfactory issue, without occasioning trouble. Should, however, the matter of necessity be urged, however just it may be, the evil result could not be averted; for such is the nature of the case. And what one person advises another, is found unworthy (unsuitable by the person advised), but in everything which he himself originates he places importance, which is a common feeling among the people.

To follow thus for a short time the nature of the case and the popular feeling, not to force it in distress, but to enlighten it slowly, and to give everyone the opportunity of waiting of his own accord for the arrival of the time, it is just the above-mentioned advice. And certainly no other remedy will be found which will be so efficacious in the present conjuncture.

As, nevertheless, the postponement of the time stipulated in the Treaty is an unpleasant act, we have repeatedly, and in various ways, deliberated if no other remedy could be discovered; but the manner in which we must arrange the matter is only and simply according to the foregoing advice, which is not only for the interest of our Empire, but will also tend as a means adapted lastingly to secure our mutual friendship, and permanently to enjoy the benefit of trade. For that purpose a letter from His Majesty the Tycoon is sent to Her Majesty the Queen, and the before-mentioned postponement of the time is desired.

As you are aware we have also already communicated the foregoing circumstances to the Prussian Envoy, who was recently here, and with whom we concluded a Treaty, from which the Article concerning the two ports and two cities was omitted.[1] We therefore urgently desire your Excellency to take this into mature consideration; to ponder well over the necessity of the conjuncture, and the truth of our expressions, while reflecting on and comparing what was related to you by [Andō] Tsoosimano-kami at an interview last year with what your Excellency actually sees and learns; to give an exact account of it to Her Majesty the Queen; and so to arrange that our wish be complied with, to the continuance of our mutual friendship.

As, meanwhile, the foregoing has in the same manner been proposed to the Governments of the several Powers, it is desirable that it be taken into your consideration.

Proposed with respect and consideration, 21st day, 4th month, 1st year of Boon-kew [Bunkyū] (30th May, 1861).

DOCUMENT 36. Rutherford Alcock's confidential memorandum of 14 February 1862.[2]

The general spirit of my instructions precludes

1. Any *concessions* without *equivalents*.
2. I may neither *restrict* nor *abandon* the Trade with Japan; but on the contrary am bound to maintain and, if possible, enlarge it.
3. I am further bound to preserve undiminished the reputation of the British name.

These are the three fundamental conditions of any action on my part.

.   .   .   .   .

The position of Her Majesty's Government at this moment is in some respects peculiar as regards any negotiations with that of Japan.

[1] The Prussian treaty was signed on 24 January 1861.

[2] This memorandum, written at Yokohama on receipt of Russell's instructions concerning the Japanese request for postponement of the opening of the two ports and two cities, was circulated to the French and Dutch ministers in Japan for information and comment. It was forwarded to London as enclosure 4 in Alcock to Russell, No. 23, Confidential, 17 March 1862 [Foreign Office, *General Correspondence, Japan* (F.O. 46), vol. 21].

Simultaneous with an attack on H.M.'s Legation, and an attempt to massacre all its members[1] residing at Yedo on the faith of Treaties and protected by the inviolate character attaching to H.M.'s Envoy, a letter was addressed to the Queen by the Taikoon, proposing that Her Majesty should abandon or suspend for several years the right secured by Treaty, of frequenting two Ports and two Cities.

The juxtaposition of these two matters is embarrassing. A concession under these circumstances would have too much the air of an indemnity for past outrages, and impunity, if not encouragement, to future murderous assaults. Hence *concession* without *equivalent* has been rendered impossible to Her Majesty's Government.

Again, the British Government will not abandon any right which would necessarily involve the *restriction or curtailment* of Trade, Trade being the avowed object of the Treaty; and to Great Britain a more serious object than to any other Treaty Power.

Hence it seems well-nigh impossible to entertain any propositions to abandon Hiogo [Hyōgo] and O-osaca [Ōsaka]; and a suspension of our rights for five years has very much that effect.[2]

The reputation of the British name, moreover, cannot be upheld or preserved untarnished if Treaty rights in any direction are modified or foregone to the advantage of the Japanese, not only in the face of menace and outrage, without adequate satisfaction; but with no guarantee against any future violence of like kind.

It follows, therefore, that any negotiations affecting Treaty rights must be based upon redress and satisfaction for the attack on the Legation on the 5th of July, first in the capture and punishment of the assassins who escaped; secondly, an indemnity to Mr. Oliphant and Mr. Morrison for the injuries sustained by them; and thirdly, as a security from future attacks, a site for the Legation rendered defensible by walls, ditches, and stockades. The cost of maintaining a British guard to be permanently kept therein for the safety of the inmates, may even be a question to be considered. These granted and secured, any concession of rights already stipulated by Treaty may then be considered on a basis of equivalents.

We are asked to concede a right of residence and Trade to our mer-

[1] This refers to an attack on the British legation in Shinagawa (at Tōzenji) made by 14 former Mito samurai on 5 July 1861. Two members of the legation staff, Oliphant and Morrison, were wounded in this attack.

[2] This conclusion is Alcock's own and does not follow necessarily from Russell's instructions (*Parliamentary Papers 1862*, vol. lxiv, pp. 74–75, Russell to Alcock, 23 November 1861). Russell certainly stipulates that concessions be obtained—the opening of Tsushima, a defensible position for the British legation, indemnity for the attack and punishment of the offenders —but he says that the 'equivalent' for waiving British rights at Edo, Ōsaka, Hyōgo, and Niigata should *consist* of these four points. He makes no special reservations about Hyōgo and Ōsaka. Alcock is here basing his argument on the more general lines of policy which Russell laid down in the last paragraph of his instructions.

chants at two ports and two cities. As O-osaca and Hiogo, for reasons stated, can hardly be conceded by the British Government, there remains principally for consideration Yedo and Nee-egata [Niigata] as open to a less serious objection in a commercial point of view.

Her Majesty's Government is not unwilling to give full consideration and weight to the difficulties, causes of anxiety, and trouble which the Government of the Taikoon may actually experience in giving effect to the sudden and fundamental changes introduced by the Treaties. Her Majesty's Government neither desire to bring civil war nor political convulsion upon the country, and rather than this, might forego for a time the assertion of some of the privileges and rights secured by Treaty. But they must be well assured the dangers are real; and that this forebearance would not lead to abuse, but in a great degree, at least, answer the proposed end of securing peace, allaying discontent, and disarming opposition; in a word, promote a mutual good understanding and render life in Japan more secure.

With this in view, by far the most important concession would seem to be the relinquishment for a time of the right of residence in Yedo to merchants; that City being the focus of all hostility, and the great centre of attraction to the armed classes, which are least favourable to the existing relations with foreigners.

But assuming this were conceded, and with it the right to reside and trade at Nee-egata also, equivalents must be sought, for the reasons already stated. The Taikoon's Government have already offered Tsusima as an equivalent for Hiogo. It cannot be accepted in lieu of Hiogo, but it might for Nee-egata. And in return for the temporary relinquishment of Yedo for foreign merchants, the Port of *Tsauliang* (or Kamiyama) on the Corean Coast and a dependency of Tsusima, might be tried, as offering some prospects of indemnity to the merchants for any loss occasioned by non-access to Yedo. These two Ports might simply be stipulated for on trial, and pending the forced suspension of treaty rights in Yedo and Nee-egata.

In this manner mutual concession might possibly conciliate all interests, relieve the Japanese Government of some of its more pressing difficulties, and yet maintain without essential injury the rights and interests of the Foreign Merchant.

.   .   .   .   .

There are some general considerations on the actual state of our relations in Japan and the position of the Japanese Government which may be appealed to, in support of the above proposed arrangement.

The Treaties actually in force are in some degree delusive and invalid, by reason of *informality*. No Treaty can be valid, or legally take effect in Japan, (nor can change in any fundamental law), without the sanction of the Mikado.

Either this has not been obtained, or if it has, as the Ministers assert, it has not been publicly made known, and this they admit. To all the Daimios hostile to the Taikoon's Government, therefore,—and some of great power and influence are well known—the Treaties are but waste paper, and have no legal force. Either this assent should be obtained and promulgated, if the Treaty Powers would put their relations on a legal and stable footing, or these leading Daimios, 24 in number, should bind themselves by some public declaration or document to acknowledge and respect the Treaties without it, as valid and binding instruments.

Without one or other of these guarantees can be obtained, Treaties give no available rights out of the Taikoon's own immediate territories, and afford no security to life and property anywhere.

There is a fundamental law of Gongen-Sama [Tokugawa Ieyasu], prohibiting under pain of death the presence of a stranger on the Japanese Soil. This has never been publicly abrogated. The Ministers admit it; and until this is done, any Japanese killing a Foreigner is legally justified and not justiciable, for the Foreigner is outlawed.

All stability in foreign relations, all security to life, all protection to trade and free intercourse between Natives and Foreigners hinge upon these two fixed points of policy. Whatever Foreign Diplomacy may effect, leaving these untouched and unchanged, are but palliatives.

The true sources of evil will continue in full vigour, a perpetual menace, and a cause of danger.

Any concessions made in the direction indicated by the Japanese Government, while these pregnant evils are allowed to exist, may at best defer a rupture or collision. Be the concessions large or small, many or few, the result will still be the same. They may stave off the evil day of reckoning for a time, but can never suffice wholly to avert it, or to work a radical cure. Because that which threatens the very existence of the relations now established by Treaty, lies deep in the popular heart, and is founded on the faith that *one* only can give legal sanction to Treaties, or abrogate a time-honoured Law; and that is their Sovereign, the Mikado. Our rights, interests and security in Japan are all based therefore on a lie and a delusion. No valid Treaty exists, having the force of Law with Japanese.

Is it better to patch up the rents and flaws in the Treaties already made, with like stuff—temporize and palliate, only seeking to conduct our Trade and our relations on *sufferance* as we best may; and by concessions ever seeking to defer, if we cannot wholly prevent, catastrophes? Or would it be better and safer to strike at the root of the evil, endeavour to cast out the lie, and put in its place a truth?

The Mikado's ratification would do this, and its promulgation throughout the Empire would give to all existing Treaties legal effect. If the first course be deemed alone practicable, then concessions with equivalents (the best that can be found or obtained) seems to be the principle; if the second, determined action on the part of one or more Powers would be needful.

A second class of general considerations present themselves. Assuming all the Japanese now ask were granted, what are the prospects of gain to Foreigners? and what finally the results? Will trade be more freely developed at the three Ports, discontent allayed, hostilities appeased, or life and property rendered more secure?

The Japanese Government hope so, but will not undertake to guarantee or even promise it. We have to decide for ourselves in the face of this fact, whether such results are likely? It is probable we should be, at the end of five or seven years, very much where we are now. Only that, judging by all we know of the Japanese and our past experience in China, it would be more impossible or more certainly dangerous to insist then on our rights of trade and residence at the four places, than at present. Those who are opposed to the policy and hostile to the Foreigners would have had all the time required for preparation to resist. They would be further strengthened in their conviction of Power, by the apparent evidence of weakness in the Foreign Powers having shrunk from the assertion of those rights in the first instance. To concede and defer now, in any ample or unconditional manner as desired, is then in reality to abandon altogether; or to accept the almost certain contingency, at the end, of war.

As regards Nee-egata, and even the right of Trade at Yedo, that might not be much to give up in material interests; but in principle it cannot be so lightly esteemed. As regards O-osaca and Hiogo, it is the whole question of a large and an everincreasing commerce, or a small and artificially restricted Trade.

Concession, it would seem then, could only be justified as a measure of sound policy on one of three grounds: Either that Foreign powers want time; or, secondly, believe that its lapse and the tendency of Trade to soften asperities by developing interests, would be all in favour of a gradual but sensible amelioration; or, lastly, that neither the political nor commercial relations of Japan are worth the cost and trouble it would entail on any single Power, or several combined, to compel the satisfactory legalization of the Treaty and its execution.

A final question presents itself. Might not everything be gained *peaceably*, by firmness and determination in our dealing with the Government at this moment? That seems possible, probable even. The Russians have given some lessons in this direction, which should not be lost upon us. But it must be admitted also, that this course once entered upon, there is no retreat with honour, or indeed without serious discredit and peril. And that undoubtedly is a grave objection, since only a *Government* could decide upon such a policy, accepting the risk. No Diplomatic Agent is likely to feel himself in a position to take this responsibility upon himself, or venturing on such perilous ground without distinct and specific authority.

DOCUMENT 37. The London Protocol, 6 June 1862.[1]

It has been represented to Her Britannic Majesty's Minister in Japan by the Ministers of the Tycoon, and to Her Majesty's Government by the Envoys who have been sent to England by the Tycoon, that difficulties are experienced by the Tycoon and his Ministers in giving effect to their engagements with foreign Powers having Treaties with Japan, in consequence of the opposition offered by a party in Japan which is hostile to all intercourse with foreigners.

Her Majesty's Government having taken those representations into consideration, are prepared, on the conditions hereinafter specified, to consent to defer for a period of five years, to commence from the 1st of January, 1863, the fulfilment of those portions of the IIIrd Article of the Treaty between Great Britain and Japan of the 26th of August, 1858, which provide for the opening to British subjects of the port of Ne-egata [Niigata] or some other convenient port on the West Coast of Nipon on the 1st day of January, 1860, and of the port of Hiogo [Hyōgo] on the 1st day of January, 1863, and for the residence of British subjects in the city of Yeddo [Edo] from the 1st day of January, 1862, and in the city of Osaca [Ōsaka] from the 1st day of January, 1863.

Her Majesty's Government, in order to give to the Japanese Ministers the time those Ministers consider necessary to enable them to overcome the opposition now existing, are willing to make these large concessions of their rights under Treaty; but they expect that the Tycoon and his Ministers will in all other respects strictly execute at the ports of Nagasaki, Hakodadi [Hakodate], and Kanagawa, all the other stipulations of the Treaty; that they will publicly revoke the old law outlawing foreigners; and that they will specifically abolish and do away with:

1. All restrictions, whether as regards quantity or price, on the sale by Japanese to foreigners of all kinds of merchandise according to Article XIV of the Treaty of the 26th of August, 1858.
2. All restrictions on labour, and more particularly on the hire of carpenters, boatmen, boats, and coolies, teachers, and servants of whatever denomination.

[1] The text has been published in *Parliamentary Papers 1863*, vol. lxxiv, Cd. 88, and in *Hertslet's Commercial Treaties*, xii. 586–8. The protocol was signed by Earl Russell and by the three Japanese envoys, the *gaikoku-bugyō* Takeuchi Yasunori and Matsudaira Yasunao and the *metsuke* Kyōgoku Kōrō.

3. All restrictions whereby Daimios are prevented from sending their produce to market, and from selling the same directly by their own agents.
4. All restrictions resulting from attempts on the part of the Custom-house authorities and other officials to obtain fees.
5. All restriction limiting the classes of persons who shall be allowed to trade with foreigners at the ports of Nagasaki, Hakodadi, and Kanagawa.
6. All restrictions imposed on free intercourse of a social kind between foreigners and the people of Japan.

In default of the strict fulfilment by the Tycoon and his Ministers of these conditions, which, indeed, are no other than those which they are already bound by Treaty to fulfil, Her Majesty's Government will, at any time within the aforesaid period of five years, commencing from the 1st of January, 1863, be entitled to withdraw the concessions in regard to the ports and cities made by this Memorandum, and to call upon the Tycoon and his Ministers to carry out, without delay, the whole of the provisions of the Treaty of August 26, 1858, and specifically to open the aforesaid ports and cities for the trade and residence of British subjects.

The Envoys of the Tycoon accredited to Her Britannic Majesty announce their intention, on their return to Japan, to submit to the Tycoon and his Ministers the policy and expediency of opening to foreign commerce the port of Tsusima in Japan, as a measure by which the interests of Japan will be materially promoted; and they engage to suggest to the Tycoon and his Ministers to evince their goodwill to the nations of Europe, and their desire to extend commerce between Japan and Europe, by reducing the duties on wines and spirits imported into Japan, and by permitting glass-ware to be inserted in the list of articles on which an import duty of 5 per cent. is levied, and thereby remedying an omission inadvertently made on the conclusion of the Treaty; and they further engage to recommend to the Tycoon and his Ministers to make arrangements for the establishment at Yokohama and Nagasaki of warehouses in which goods coming from abroad may be deposited, under the control of Japanese officers, without payment of duties, until such time as the importers shall obtain purchasers for such goods, and be prepared to remove them on payment of the import duties.

Her Britannic Majesty's Principal Secretary of State for Foreign Affairs and the Envoys of the Tycoon have accordingly signed this Memorandum, which will be transmitted by the former to Her Majesty's Representative in Japan, and by the latter to the Tycoon and his Ministers, as an evidence of the arrangement made between them on this 6th day of June, 1862.

DOCUMENT 38. Gaikoku-bugyō to Bakufu, 9th month (23 October–21 November), 1862.[1]

The envoys who were sent to the various countries of Europe have completed negotiations at the capital city of England with the Foreign Secretary of that country, concerning postponement of the opening of the two ports and the two cities, and have signed and exchanged with him copies of a memorandum in which such postponement was agreed. It also embodied six provisions which the Bakufu is asked to carry out in return for this [concession], together with an undertaking by our envoys that on their return to Japan they would recommend to their government the opening of Tsushima Island to trade, the reduction of duties on wine and glassware, and the establishment of warehouses. We have perused this memorandum and given consideration to its provisions. It is stated that all six of the provisions are embodied in the treaties; and we find that the second appears in Article VIII of the treaty while the first, third, fourth, and fifth are contained in Article XIV thereof.[2] The sixth is a different matter, not being included explicitly in the treaty, but as its whole purpose is friendly and its tenor conforms with what is laid down in Article I of the American Treaty of Kanagawa, we see no need to propose any change in it. Thus the provisions which were agreed and signed are not such as to force us into difficulties. Ever since the Bakufu first decided to open trade relations with foreign countries, however, commodities have been growing scarce, national opinion has become restless, and we have had to face many difficulties both at home and abroad; and so there have been a number of incidents, at all the ports, which we have been forced to handle with discretion and to settle amicably in accordance with the dictates of expediency. This has most often been so in respect of trade, and the first, third, fourth, and fifth items of the present [English] demands all relate to this. Bakufu policy has not been entirely in accordance with treaty provisions and must, therefore, sooner or later be revised. With the signature of the present agreement the Bakufu must certainly effect some alteration. What is more, if the Bakufu does not uphold the authority of its servants when it sends them abroad as envoys and entrusts them with full powers, it must expect its own authority as a government to suffer. Again, we believe, if the Bakufu subsequently seeks to alter an agreement which its envoys have already concluded, this will not only bring to nothing the work of those envoys but might also, thereafter, when the Bakufu next sends envoys abroad to conduct negotiations of some kind, lead men every-

---

[1] The text is printed in *Kaikoku Kigen*, ii. 1544–8.
[2] These references, of course, are to the treaty negotiated by Lord Elgin on 26 August 1858, the text of which is to be found in *Parliamentary Papers 1859*, vol. xxxiii, pp. 387–94.

where to say that little reliance can be put upon them and thereby make it impossible for them to accomplish their mission. Thus even if we are caused some slight inconvenience by so doing, the Bakufu must carry out the provisions of this agreement. The provisions stated above are all points on which revision of Bakufu policy will be necessary and on which firm action must be taken in accordance with the agreement. The actual measures for putting them into effect, however, can only be decided in the light of practical knowledge. We therefore believe that the best course would be for the Bakufu to instruct the *bugyō* of the three open ports to state their views on the methods by which these six provisions be carried out and then issue orders for the revision of the policies by which these questions have been handled hitherto.

Apart from this, there is the question of opening, under the treaty stipulations, Niigata or some other port 'on the west coast of Nippon'.[1] Although negotiations for the postponement of this have now been completed, there seems to be no good reason why we should not open such a port eventually. The approaches to Niigata are shallow and the anchorage is poor. Since this will not meet the wishes of the foreigners, they are certain to ask for a different port. We think the best plan would be for us, for our own part and before the limit of the present postponement is reached, carefully to select a place which suits our own convenience, and then, when the time limit is up, to discuss this with the foreigners and reach a decision on it.

Then again, there is the question of opening the port of Tsushima. As was said when all the appropriate officials discussed the question in March of this year, Anglo-Russian rivalries cause both these countries to show an interest in the island. We are therefore much concerned about what might happen should a crisis occur. If we open Tsushima to all countries, and people of all countries take up residence there, we might expect that their mutual rivalries would in fact enable us to keep them under control and so derive some degree of future advantage for ourselves. On the other hand, the name 'Nippon' is usually taken by the countries of the West to signify [the island stretching from] Ōu to Chōshū, which would exclude Shikoku and Kyūshū. Thus even if the Bakufu opened Tsushima, the foreigners would probably object that this could not be a substitute [for Niigata], as it would not be in conformity with treaty stipulations.[2] In Japan we make no such distinction and this is only the foreigners' view, but they have always said that the question of Tsushima falls outside the scope of existing treaties. Thus even if the Bakufu opened Tsushima and

---

[1] When the treaties were drafted, foreign diplomats were under the impression that 'Nippon' (Japan) was the name of the main island (Honshū). The word 'Nippon' is here written in *katakana*, to point up the fact that although this is the actual wording of the treaty, its meaning to foreigners was more restricted geographically, i.e. 'the west coast of Honshū'..

[2] i.e. was not a port on 'the west coast of Nippon' (Honshū).

then began negotiations for the cancellation of the two stipulations which provide for the opening of Hyōgo[1] and the residence of foreigners in Ōsaka when they have business there, there would still not seem to be any prospect of the foreigners agreeing to this, for when treaty negotiations were originally conducted with the Americans the Bakufu repeatedly urged in discussion that it could not open these two places, but was forced to permit their opening in the end as an alternative to other concessions which it was impossible to grant, such as the opening of Kyōto and giving foreigners the right to travel in Japan. However, as we said above, Tsushima has an additional importance to foreign countries in their relations with each other.[2] There is, therefore, a basis for negotiation in this, especially as the question is one that falls outside the scope of existing treaties. Hence the Bakufu should at all events make one or two overtures on the subject; and if we find they do not succeed, we can still act in accordance with the treaties in regard to Hyōgo and Ōsaka and can open Tsushima, while refusing in exchange to open any other port on the west coast. If the Bakufu makes up its mind to such a policy in advance, we believe, one or other of these two courses will succeed. And by so doing, moreover, it will be possible for the Bakufu to choose a suitable time for subsequent negotiations, in the light of conditions at Kyōto. However, since the matter is an important one and these negotiations cannot be put off indefinitely, it would be best for the Bakufu to question the envoys closely on their views about this when they return to Japan, and then reach a final decision.

With regard to the reduction of duties on wines, glassware, &c., it would [at first sight] seem appropriate that this be postponed until the time when [all] customs duties are to be reviewed, since this will be but a few years hence. However, as a result of such incidents as the recent affair at Namamugi,[3] not only the English, but all the foreigners, show signs of doubting whether our government has any desire for permanent friendship. Certainly their newspapers and other accounts seem to reflect some such uneasiness. If, therefore, the Bakufu were to decide to lower the duties now, this would furnish them with evidence that our government does desire lasting friendship and does not seek to restrict trade. It would help to still the clamour of opinion. Moreover, if the volume of imports rose because of this, the Bakufu might not in fact be losing revenue [by the change]. We think it best, therefore, that the Bakufu should make no difficulties on the lines that a date has been fixed for a general review of customs duties, but should decide to reduce these duties at once.

[1] The text actually reads 'the closing of Hyōgo', but the passage only makes sense on the assumption that this was written in error.

[2] These references to foreign rivalries concerning Tsushima refer to the Anglo-Russian disputes over that island in the summer of 1861. See Norman, *Japan's Emergence as a Modern State*, p. 36, and above, introduction, p. 55, note 2.   [3] See Section V below.

We turn now to the question of warehouses. Some time ago, when the Dutch minister raised the question of implementing the Treaty of Nagasaki, all appropriate officials were summoned to discuss this and advise what kind of an answer the Bakufu should give. If the Bakufu should now decide after all to construct these warehouses, we will go into this matter in greater detail, in consultation with the representatives of foreign countries, and report further.

This we submit with respect.

SECTION V

Expulsion and the Namamugi Indemnity, 1862–3

THE diplomatic success represented by the London Protocol was not in time to keep Andō Nobumasa and Kuze Hirochika in power. By the end of June 1862 both had been replaced. It was not only that their policies were bitterly criticized by extremists who desired the overthrow of the Tokugawa and the immediate expulsion of foreigners from Japan. They were also opposed by the influential group whose names are associated with the policy of *kōbu-gattai* ('Court-Bakufu unity'). In the summer of 1862 this group, under the leadership of Shimazu Hisamitsu of Satsuma, persuaded the Court to send Ōhara Shigenori on a special mission to Edo. The chief object was to force the Bakufu to appoint supporters of the *kōbu-gattai* policy to the more important offices of state. In this Ōhara succeeded. At the beginning of August Hitotsubashi Keiki was appointed *Shōgun-kōkenshoku* (Guardian to the Shōgun), while Matsudaira Keiei, as *Seiji-sōsaishoku*, assumed all the functions and authority of a Tairō. Shortly after, Matsudaira Katamori was appointed *Kyōto-shugoshoku* and thus became the Shōgun's chief representative in Kyōto, superseding the *Kyōto-shoshidai* in this capacity.

These appointments, the last two being to newly created offices, ostensibly gave the *kōbu-gattai* party control of the Bakufu. However, the *fudai daimyō* did not welcome their supersession by relatives of the Shōgun, and did all they could to obstruct or circumvent the new administration. Moreover, the new officials themselves were soon in disagreement about foreign policy. Early in November Matsudaira Katamori submitted proposals for compromising existing Japanese differences over foreign affairs, urging that while the three ports of Yokohama, Nagasaki, and Hakodate should remain open to foreigners, all other concessions already made or promised should be revoked (Document 39). This caused an immediate dispute. Most Bakufu officials thought such a scheme impracticable, since the foreigners would never accept it. Hitotsubashi Keiki and Matsudaira Keiei, as the latter revealed in a long memorandum (Document 40), were in fundamental disagreement about the weight they were prepared to give to the Imperial Court's views on the subject. Keiki insisted that the Bakufu was morally bound to do what it thought best for the country, even if this meant refusing to carry out the Emperor's orders for expulsion; Keiei, on the other hand, maintained that if argument could not move the Emperor, then the Imperial command must be considered binding.

The dispute was resolved by renewed pressure from Kyōto. The influence of Satsuma there had now been replaced by that of Chōshū and Tosa, whose leaders urged the immediate expulsion of foreigners. Shimazu Hisamitsu retired to his fief, and the extremists dispatched a new Imperial envoy to Edo, this time to insist on Bakufu acceptance of an immediate expulsion policy. The result was that Matsudaira Keiei gained his point. By the end of the year it had been agreed that the Shōgun should visit Kyōto in the spring to concert effective measures for securing the withdrawal of foreigners.

Keiki, Keiei, and Matsudaira Katamori preceded the Shōgun to Kyōto. Their object was to reach agreement on policy before his arrival, that is, before the Shōgun's presence in a city dominated by turbulent samurai from Tosa and Chōshū should offer too important a hostage to fortune. They found, however, that the situation was already out of control and that the Court officials, often against their own wishes, were unable to resist the clamour for immediate expulsion. Late in March they were finally forced to fix an early date for the withdrawal of foreigners from Japan (Document 41). Certainly they meant no more by this than that they would seek to effect foreign withdrawal by negotiation. It is doubtful if even this was promised in good faith. But officials in Edo showed themselves unwilling to accept such a decision (Document 42). What is more, Shimazu Hisamitsu now returned to Kyōto and condemned his former colleagues for the compromises they had made, thereby splitting the *kōbu-gattai* party. Matsudaira Keiei, together with sympathizers at Court and among the feudal lords, at once withdrew from active participation in affairs, leaving Hitotsubashi Keiki to face the problem with the help only of the Rōjū.

In Edo, meanwhile, the Bakufu was facing a very real crisis in its relations with Britain. In September 1862 an Englishman named Richardson was killed at Namamugi on the Tōkaidō by Satsuma samurai of Shimazu Hisamitsu's escort. This came as the culmination of a long series of attacks on foreigners, and the British representative insisted on the punishment of the men involved. Satsuma refused to give them up, however, and the Bakufu was helpless to make it do so. In March 1863 the British chargé d'affaires received instructions on the subject from Lord Russell. Early in April he communicated them to the Bakufu in the form of an ultimatum (Document 43). Within twenty days the Bakufu must make formal apologies and pay an indemnity; Satsuma must punish the offenders and pay compensation to the attacked. And if such satisfaction was refused, it was made clear, Britain would proceed to exact it by force.

Officials in Edo saw no alternative but to agree to the British demands. Mizuno Tadanori, now in retirement, even suggested that such action might facilitate later attempts to restrict foreign privileges (Document 44).

In the emotional atmosphere of Kyōto, however, such a concession would seem to accord ill with the Bakufu's promise to effect the withdrawal of foreigners, an event now set for 25 June. Faced with this new and acute conflict between the facts of foreign relations and the pressures of domestic politics, the Rōjū played for time. In Kyōto there began a complicated series of intrigues and manœuvres. Ogasawara Nagamichi, who had been raised to the rank of Rōjū in the previous autumn and had since been closely associated with Hitotsubashi Keiki, now recommended that the expulsion agreement with the Court be repudiated or its execution postponed (Document 45). Keiki seems secretly to have shared these views. At all events he sent Ogasawara to Edo to take charge of the situation there, and followed himself, as the Shōgun's representative, after making a private agreement with the more moderate Court officials that the indemnity must be paid. No hint of this was allowed to appear in his official correspondence, however. His orders were still that the indemnity must not be paid. Moreover, on 12 June, just after leaving Kyōto, he instructed the Rōjū that 'expulsion negotiations' must be opened with the foreigners without fail on 25 June (Document 46).

In Edo, Ogasawara still tried formally to overcome the objections of other officials to Keiki's policy (Document 47). It was plain, however, that no negotiations could even be proposed to the British representative until the indemnity question was settled. Keiki had still not arrived—perhaps deliberately so, for it seems probable that he connived at all Ogasawara's actions, despite the disclaimer which he later made for the benefit of the Imperial Court (Document 48). In the circumstances, Ogasawara saw no alternative but to pay the indemnity, as an indispensable preliminary to negotiations for the closing of the ports (Document 49). The first instalment was therefore handed over at Yokohama on 24 June 1863.

Ogasawara claimed that while he took this decision on his own responsibility, all officials had previously urged its necessity (Document 49). The implication, that it was in effect a Bakufu decision, is borne out by the fact that he was only nominally punished for his actions. Indeed, Edo's 'refusal' to obey Keiki's orders gave the latter an opportunity to repudiate the whole expulsion policy (Document 48). It is likely that he had always intended to do so, once the Shōgun returned from Kyōto. But while Ogasawara had thus averted the immediate danger from Britain, the situation was no longer under the Bakufu's control. Satsuma refused to surrender Richardson's attackers, and in August a British squadron bombarded Kagoshima. Meanwhile, Chōshū had taken independent action against the foreigner. On 25 June 1863, the date set for 'expulsion', Chōshū guns opened fire on an American ship in the Straits of Shimonoseki. The Bakufu thereby faced a new challenge to its authority at home and a new crisis in its relations with foreign Powers.

DOCUMENT 39. Matsudaira Katamori to Bakufu, 8 November 1862.[1]

I am most conscious of the honour that the Shōgun has done me, unworthy as I am, in entrusting me with important matters of administration, and especially in appointing me as *Kyōto-shugoshoku*. I have never ceased to apply myself, therefore, that I might to some slight degree repay the favours conferred on me by my country. Yet I fear I have neither the knowledge nor the ability to fulfil such expectations. However, the fact being that I hold this office, I venture to risk displeasure by submitting my views without reserve.

The position today is that the foreigners become daily more overbearing, so greatly, indeed, that the Emperor is concerned and the people unsettled. Being much perturbed by this, I have instructed my retainers to sound [feudal] opinion generally, and have even sent to Kyōto to inquire into the state of affairs there; and I am told that the Emperor himself is firmly resolved on national seclusion and the expulsion of foreigners, with the result that in Kyōto itself and throughout the Kansai region, from the great lords to the very *rōnin*, there is now not a man who would argue in favour of opening the country. Thus the fact is that men hate the foreigner. Yet the Bakufu continues to treat foreigners with consideration. It is because of this circumstance, I believe, that men's ideas are in tumult and disturbances arise. After all, the Bakufu signed the treaties in 1858 without reference to the Court and has granted permission for the opening of ports in Settsu and Izumi,[2] while there is also the action it has taken in such matters as the residence of foreigners in Edo and the building of the [British] legation at Goten-yama.[3] All these actions were opposed to the Emperor's wishes. They have aroused his wrath and caused general discontent; and this, I conceive, is why there have been attacks on foreigners.

Then again, although Hotta [Masayoshi] Bitchū-no-kami, Manabe [Akikatsu] Shimōsa-no-kami, and others have been sent to Kyōto in recent years, it would seem that some misunderstanding still exists. The Bakufu, I fear, has now acquired a reputation for seeking to control Kyōto by trickery and intrigue. There is less and less public confidence in the Shōgun, who is forced into dependence on the *tozama* lords.[4] All this is due

[1] The text is printed in *Kyōto-shugoshoku shimatsu*, pp. 19–22. The document itself is dated only Bunkyū 2, 9th month (23 Oct.–21 Nov. 1862), but it was submitted to the Bakufu on 8 November.

[2] i.e. Hyōgo and Ōsaka.

[3] As a result of the attacks on foreigners, in particular that on its own legation in July 1861, the British government had insisted that the Bakufu build a new and defensible residence for the British minister. The site chosen was at Goten-yama in Edo.

[4] Katamori presumably means that the Bakufu is dependent, especially in Kyōto, on the support of such fiefs as Satsuma and Tosa.

to the incapacity of officials, not to any ill will on the part of the Shōgun himself, but in that it results in reports of a lack of harmony between Court and Bakufu I cannot but think it a truly grievous state of affairs. And if the Bakufu decides hereafter to complete the Goten-yama legation, to establish foreigners in permanent residence in Edo, and to open the various ports, then the Emperor's anger will know no bounds. The great fiefs will assuredly be stirred to action and discontent will become general throughout the Empire. It is impossible to tell what disasters might follow. I therefore believe it is vital that the Bakufu should at all costs act in conformity with the Imperial will, so handling matters as to calm men's minds, preserve the fabric of the State, and achieve harmony between ruler and ruled. I desire that the Bakufu, leaving arrangements at Naga-saki, Hakodate, and Yokohama to continue as they have been hitherto, should firmly withdraw its sanction for such matters as the Goten-yama legation, the opening of ports in Settsu and Izumi, foreign residence in Edo, and travel by foreigners. I think it desirable, moreover, that punish-ment be decreed for those officials who have mismanaged affairs hitherto; and that it be explained fully [to the foreigners] that they will be reim-bursed for the expenses they have incurred.

Now since the Emperor himself believes in national seclusion, it might seem that for us to say that nothing is to be done about the three ports men-tioned above would be to oppose the Imperial will. Nagasaki, however, has long been an open port, while the opening of Shimoda was recognized as unavoidable by the Emperor himself. Moreover, close consideration of world conditions shows that all countries overseas are daily progressing in their pursuit of trade and intercourse, and in the competition for privi-lege among themselves. If our Empire is alone in maintaining national seclusion and isolation, then we will have no means of understanding foreign conditions and adopting their ways where they are good. We could achieve fully neither attack nor defence. Already, it is clear, by the trade and intercourse we have permitted hitherto, we have built great ships and guns, and thus aided the completion of our naval and military establishment. Hence, while revising the treaty arrangements, we should leave matters at these three ports as they are. And if the Bakufu decides that the foreigners will be expelled at once should they break our regula-tions and behave in an insulting and disrespectful manner, then it will, I believe, be fulfilling the Emperor's wish for the expulsion of foreigners, thus easing the Emperor's anxiety and uniting the people.

Hitherto, despite the fact that foreign arrogance and disrespect mounted daily, the Bakufu has given men the impression that it was con-cerning itself not with preparations but solely with the rigid control of our own people. This, it is realized, was entirely due to the temporizing action of the officials, who from mortal fear have thus enlarged and strengthened foreign arrogance. It is therefore my wish that, no matter what detailed arguments be advanced to the contrary, the Bakufu now in truth resolve to bring matters to an issue. As to the negotiations [with the foreigners], if national policy first be clearly laid down and then suitable men be entrusted with full powers, it will be possible to pursue whatever course best accords with the changes and opportunities of the moment.

This, I believe, is our opportunity to achieve Court-Bakufu harmony. It is a moment of immense importance, in which the Empire might be said to stand at the dividing line between prosperity and impoverishment, between tranquillity and upheaval. The Shōgun having appointed me to the office of *Shugoshoku*, it follows that he must announce his intention of showing proper respect for the Imperial Court.[1] Hence it is especially necessary, I believe, that he should respect those views about the expulsion of foreigners which the Emperor feels so deeply. However, this question of opening or closing the country is a matter of the utmost consequence. I therefore think it desirable that before the Shōgun goes to Kyōto, next spring, the Bakufu should at once seek the views of all the feudal lords, both great and small, both *tozama* and *fudai*;[2] then, when the Shōgun has reported to the Court, a suitable decision can be reached. If this is not done, I believe, it will be impossible for me to carry out the duties imposed by my office of *Shugoshoku*, which is why I have devoted myself constantly to this question, reaching my decision only after seeking the views of all, even of my retainers. If the Shōgun does not approve my recommendations, I see no prospect of my being able successfully to bear the responsibilities of my great office. It is for this reason, though with the greatest reluctance, that I find myself with no alternative but to submit this report, despite the risk of your displeasure. I most earnestly request that the views I have submitted above may be given the most careful consideration, and that a firm decision may be reached on this matter.[3]

DOCUMENT 40. Matsudaira Keiei to Bakufu, 4 December 1862.[4]

In the autumn of this year, the Emperor's wishes in the matter having been made known, I was appointed *Seiji-sōsaishoku*. Since then, I have come after long and careful thought to the conclusion that there are many

[1] The term *Kyōto-shugoshoku* might be translated 'Defender of Kyōto', a title which implies more respect for the Emperor than *Kyōto-shoshidai* or 'Governor of Kyōto'.

[2] The contraction *naigai*, here rendered as '*tozama* and *fudai*', might mean merely 'in Edo and in the provinces', though this seems less likely in the context.

[3] In a long postscript, not translated here, Katamori emphasizes that the representatives who are to negotiate with the foreigners must be chosen 'regardless of personal status' (presumably meaning that the choice should not necessarily be restricted to the usual Bakufu officials); and that Bakufu intentions must be made public, so that it be clear to all that this time there is no intention of evading the issue.

[4] The text is printed in *Tokugawa Keiki Kō Den*, v. 317–26, and in *Zoku saimukiji*, i. 144–54.

respects in which Bakufu policy is confused and unsatisfactory. Most important is the question of clarifying the relationship between ruler and ruled. While the Shōgun's ancestors have handed down certain laws to guide us, the Bakufu, in its administration of the Empire, should at all times show proper respect for the wishes of the Emperor. As a servant of the Emperor, the Shōgun must in all things respect his will. When a question of great national importance is to be decided, an envoy should be sent, in all frankness, to learn the Emperor's wishes. Moreover, the Shōgun should go himself to Kyōto to seek the Emperor's advice. He should keep the feudal lords informed, both great and small, and should act in such a way as to unite the country and consolidate national opinion. Unless this is done, it will be impossible either to carry on the administration of Japan or to conduct our relations with other countries overseas. This, I believe, should be the national policy of the Bakufu at this time.

In this respect, Bakufu policy hitherto seems to have suffered from a lack of decision induced by two hundred years of peace. It is completely wrong, I believe, to follow those old and mistaken practices; to ignore the Court, to make light of the feudal lords, and to conduct affairs solely according to the ideas of the Bakufu. The Bakufu must therefore abandon this total self-sufficiency and act consistently with the ideas of the whole Empire. I explained all this in detail to the Rōjū on the day on which I was ordered to undertake the duties of *Seiji-sōsaishoku*; and since they said they were all of the same opinion, I replied that this being so, I would undertake this important office and make every possible effort to carry out its duties. Without further objection, I formally accepted the appointment.

After Lord Ōhara [Shigenori] returned to Kyōto, a number of consultations took place at the Imperial Court. Many *rōnin* of Satsuma, Chōshū, Tosa, and other fiefs were in the capital, and the confusion was such that the unrest seemed impossible to quell. Even the Emperor, I hear, appeared to be in doubt and anxiety, a circumstance which must truly be felt as cause for deep regret. It was therefore decided that the Shōgun should go at once to Kyōto to offer apologies to the Emperor for the many objectionable steps taken by the Bakufu hitherto, both in its handling of foreign affairs and in other matters. He would then earnestly implore the Emperor's advice in the formulation of a national policy. However, preparations for such an event as the Shōgun's journey to Kyōto could not be made all at once, so it was announced that Hitotsubashi Keiki would proceed immediately to the capital to act as his deputy in these matters.

This, I thought, gave us a real opportunity to settle the relations of Court and Bakufu. It was an occasion of the utmost importance, which would decide whether the Empire was to have internal peace or civil war, and I therefore gave the matter the most careful thought. It seemed to me that the fundamental reason why the Bakufu had handled matters hitherto in a hesitant and vacillating manner was because it had not abandoned its self-sufficiency, had not based its policy as it should on both Court and feudal opinion. Thus its actions could only be described as submission to the strong and oppression of the weak. Its foreign policy lacked resolution. It could neither show proper respect for the Emperor, which is the most important thing of all, nor clarify the relations between ruler and ruled. It no longer commanded the respect of the feudal lords, but it still held consistently to the old ways. Completely arbitrary in the domestic affairs of Japan, it could not rid itself of the self-centred idea that the Imperial Court was dependent on the existence of the Bakufu. The. result was to provoke unrest throughout Japan. This, I thought, was why men would not accept the Bakufu's rule. The time had come to sweep away the Bakufu's former indecision and show respect for the wishes of the Emperor. When Hitotsubashi Keiki went to Kyōto, we would have to seek the Emperor's pardon for the objectionable steps taken by the Bakufu hitherto. We must renounce the treaties concluded with foreign countries since 1853, seek the Emperor's views afresh, and consult with the nobles of the whole country, both great and small. The decision could then be made to renew friendly intercourse with foreign countries. By this course the Bakufu would give unmistakable evidence of its remorse for having opposed the Emperor's wishes since 1858. As to the foreign countries, we should explain these circumstances in detail to their resident ministers here and tell them that we intended to send plenipotentiaries to the governments of the five Treaty Powers. By opening negotiations in this way, national policy would be made to conform completely to the Emperor's will; the lords both great and small would be consulted and the whole country united. Policy would not have been determined by the Bakufu alone.

Believing these considerations to be of the first importance in national policy, I explained all this to Keiki and the Rōjū in the council-chamber. There was at that time a letter to the same effect from [Matsudaira Katamori] Higo-no-kami. It appeared, however, that some ministers held contrary views. They argued with Higo-no-kami, urging that we had no choice but to open the country in present circumstances, that although the attitude of Kyōto was in some ways a proper one, there was no possibility of foreign countries accepting it.

Subsequently, when Keiki came to Edo Castle, I asked him his opinion. He said that the question at this moment, after all, was not whether it was intended to open or close the country. The ideas that he intended first to submit to the Emperor and then to discuss with the Court officials, when he went to Kyōto, were not the same as those I had expressed. To his mind, the Bakufu had mishandled matters right from the start. It was not only [Ii Naosuke] Kamon-no-kami, Kuze [Hirochika], and Andō [Nobumasa] who were to blame. Going back to the beginning, to the summer of 1853, when the envoy Perry arrived, it all began with Abe [Masahiro] Ise-no-kami, who permitted friendly relations with the foreigners out of fear of their military might. The guilt, then, lay in the first place with Ise-no-kami. It was by no means confined to Kamon-no-kami, Kuze, and Andō. Since that time all sorts of schemes had been devised. In the first place, the Imperial Court had been scorned and slighted. More serious still, some had even sought to follow the example set in the Jōkyū and Genkō periods.[1] He definitely knew that decided views to this effect had been advanced, he said. His intention was to seek the Emperor's pardon, so far as that might be possible, for the past sins of the Bakufu, for this mishandling of affairs and these objectionable schemes. However, he said, when one considered the present state of the countries of the world, one found that they governed themselves in accordance with the principles of fidelity, justice, and natural law. They were not like primitive savages, leading a nomadic life. Moreover, Japan was an island, and quite unable to maintain her independence. More especially since the invention of the steamship, foreigners regarded travelling between countries much as we travelled to a neighbouring village. If, therefore, we trusted to being surrounded by sea, our natural defence in the past, and expelled the foreigners, there was no question but that they would return. And if all countries then entered into an alliance and agreed to make a joint attack on us, he said, we might win one or two battles, but would have not the least prospect of final victory. We would, obviously, suffer total defeat. There could certainly be no comparison with the Mongol invasions of the Kōan period [1278–87]. In the very nature of things, Japan no longer had the ability to maintain her independence. Since this was abundantly clear, even if the Emperor should now seek the expulsion of foreigners and gave orders that it be carried out, the Bakufu could not accept such orders. Therefore, Keiki said, whatever the personal consequences to himself thereafter, he must submit a clear statement of these facts to the Emperor and argue them in detail with the Court officials. He must expound them to all who were ignorant of them, especially to the men of Satsuma and Chōshū. He hoped that under the Shōgun's careful persuasion the Emperor would gradually abandon the idea of expulsion and turn to support the opening of the country; that the indecision shown so far might then be minimized and deceitful ways changed; and that Japan might thus in large measure be put in the ascendant and her military preparations brought steadily to completion.

---

[1] i.e. attempted to force the Emperor's abdication, as had been done in Jōkyū (1219–21) and Genkō (1331–3).

True respect for the Emperor most certainly did not lie in forcing Kyōto into a policy of opening the country, as had been tried hitherto. But, he believed, for the Bakufu to accept an expulsion policy simply because the Emperor wished it, knowing that it was not in the country's interests to do so, would be morally indefensible and would render nugatory both the office of Shōgun and his own appointment as *Kōkenshoku*. He had never wished to force through an arbitrary decision by the Bakufu, without showing proper respect for the Court. On this point he was certainly in agreement with me, he said. He would like me to give some thought to his own views. Such were the arguments Keiki advanced, and I told him that I thought them most just and reasonable.

It was subsequently decided that the Imperial envoys should be received at Edo,[1] so I again communicated with Keiki. I told him that the present visit of Imperial envoys would be of vital importance to the fate of the Tokugawa family, to the existence of the Bakufu and, indeed, to the fortunes of the Empire as a whole. In my view, this was a matter of unprecedented difficulty. Hence, I considered, we must at all costs conduct our discussions with them in the full intention of abandoning the arbitrary methods adopted by the Bakufu hitherto and of manifesting a sincere desire to show proper respect for the Imperial Court. Keiki could explain to the Imperial envoys, on the lines of the ideas which he had expressed so fully to me a little earlier, that although the Emperor desired the expulsion of foreigners, it was the Shōgun's duty to refuse to carry out such orders because he thought that they would not be in the country's interests. He could say that apart altogether from the fate of the Tokugawa house, a decision to carry out expulsion now would neither be for the good of the country nor, perhaps, in the long run, would it really relieve the Emperor's anxiety. The Shōgun, who had borne the responsibility of governing the country hitherto, could not accept the task of carrying out expulsion and closing the country if he gave thought to the interests of the Empire. But, I told him, however convincingly he explained all this to the envoys, it might be that they would not agree, that they would insist on the Bakufu carrying out the ·expulsion of foreigners now. If so, then the Shōgun's duty would be inescapable. He would have no alternative but to return to the Emperor those administrative rights which the Bakufu had held for the two hundred and more years since the time of Ieyasu. He would have to entrust the fate of the country to the will of the Emperor. Once the position of the Tokugawa house had become that of but one among the feudal lords, it would have to respect the Emperor's desire for the expulsion of foreigners and, in common with other lords, put this policy

[1] The reference is to the mission led by Sanjō Sanetomi, who was to demand Bakufu acceptance of immediate expulsion. The mission was announced in November 1862 and Sanjō eventually arrived in Edo on 18 December.

loyally into effect. If this were not done, I said, if, while still retaining the official responsibilities of the Bakufu, we should inflict injury on this land which has known more than two centuries of peace, and thereby plunge our people into misery, we should be acting contrary to the dictates of universal law. For this reason, I thought, the Shōgun must resolve not to accept the [present] Imperial orders. Moreover, in this matter of returning administrative rights to the Emperor, it would be unpardonable in us all, I believe, from the Shōgun himself down to the Rōjū and other officials, if we did it merely in name, as a means of evading responsibility. If Keiki was of the same opinion, I said, he should at once inform the Rōjū. Once the council was in agreement, the matter should be reported to the Shōgun, who would give his decision on it after due deliberation. Keiki agreed that this was a very reasonable course. He said he would give it careful thought and then discuss it with me again.

Subsequently I asked Keiki what he thought of the matters I had proposed to him on this occasion. He answered that the present visit of the Imperial envoys was indeed a difficult problem, as I had said. They would probably not be satisfied to have one or two meetings and then return to Kyōto. However, he would tell them that it was impossible to carry out expulsion, so the ports must necessarily remain open. Thereafter he intended to accompany them to the capital. He doubted whether this was the time to talk of returning the administration to the Emperor. Some of the officials had already said that if the Emperor's ideas were genuinely his own, then he would admit the logic of the argument when it was put to him forcibly, even though he were not completely satisfied. But after all, although these men were styled Imperial envoys, their mission sprang not from the ideas of the Emperor but from those of the *rōnin*, and especially from Satsuma and Chōshū. To surrender on their account the administrative rights which the Bakufu had held for two hundred years would be most improper. Keiki thus gave me the impression that there was not the slightest intention of renouncing the Bakufu system and respecting the wishes of the Emperor.

Subsequently [Matsudaira Katamóri] Higo-no-kami brought to the council-chamber a copy of the letter which the Tempōrin [Sanjō Sanetomi] was to carry,[1] sent to him secretly from the Court by one of his retainers. We discussed its contents in detail. One of the officials[2] said that in so important a matter it was a grave error on the part of Higo-no-kami's retainer to have accepted the letter from the Tempōrin; and it was also very thoughtless of Higo-no-kami, when his retainer sent it, to receive the letter and bring it to the council-chamber. For the Court to hand the letter over in secret to the *Shoshidai* or *Kinritsuki* would have been proper.

---

[1] i.e. the Court's instructions to the envoy concerning the demands to be made on the Bakufu.
[2] From other evidence this would appear to have been the Rōjū Itakura Katsukiyo.

But to give it to Higo-no-kami and, what is more, order him to act as intermediary, was a most irregular action on the part of the Court.[1] Moreover, he said, the Emperor had hitherto been accorded complete respect by the Bakufu, ever since the time of Ieyasu. He saw no reason for change now. This was spoken in a rude and angry manner, and it was with shame that I listened to it. Such talk is truly unendurable. So I sat there in silence, for I do not believe that the interests of the country can ever be advanced by arguments of this kind.

Ever since I was first appointed *Seiji-sōsaishoku*, it has been my belief that we will find it quite impossible either to govern Japan or to expel the foreigner unless, in our national policy, we show respect for the wishes of the Emperor and unite the whole country behind us. Yet as the Bakufu is at present situated, it clings to the arbitrary methods of the past and shows not the least inclination to respect the Emperor's wishes. Thus its whole idea is to leave the ports open as they are now, to try all means to force the Court to its policy, and to hold the feudal lords in subjection. It grants the demands of foreign countries just because it fears them. This inevitably and invariably makes its actions indecisive. The Imperial Court is well aware that the Bakufu is in abject terror of the foreigners, and that it is this feeling which makes its whole policy one of submission to their never-ending rapacity and causes the Shōgun to ignore the 'barbarian-subduing' duties of his office.[2] The Emperor, out of his indignation at this, out of his sincere desire to see the prestige of the Bakufu once more resplendent throughout the land, uses this question of expulsion as a means of correcting the Bakufu's faults. We should shed tears of gratitude for his benevolence. Having made careful inquiries concerning the Emperor's views, I am convinced that he bears not the least ill will towards the Tokugawa. All he does springs from kindness and compassion.

I understood that Keiki's intention, originally, was to express complete respect for the wishes of the Emperor, while explaining that it was in the interests of the country that the ports be open. Now, however, it seems from what he says that he is, after all, of the same opinion as the Rōjū about opening the country, and has put aside all idea of showing respect for the Court. He has, in fact, adopted the policy of vacillation, that of opening the country. I think he has not realized how ardently the Emperor desires the expulsion of foreigners. The ideas that Keiki expresses now, I believe, are irreconcilable with those he advanced a short time ago. The issue that faces us at this moment is not whether we are to

---

[1] The *Kinritsuki* were Bakufu officials stationed in Kyōto who were primarily responsible, under the *Kyōto-shoshidai*, for the maintenance of order and the supervision of those with whom the Court was in contact. The objection of the Rōjū, clearly, is to the use of the new *kamon* officials to by-pass the regular channels of communication between Court and Bakufu.

[2] *Sei-i-tai-shōgun*, literally 'Barbarian-subduing Generalissimo', was the full title of the Shōgun. It is the expression *sei-i* that is used here. Cf. Document 3, p. 106, note 3.

open or close the country, but simply whether we are to respect the Emperor's wishes. When the present Imperial envoys arrive, I believe, our only loyal course, in terms of the relationship between ruler and subject, is to seek pardon for past errors and show proper respect for the Emperor by at once accepting his commands. Moreover, it is my constant and unending plea that we should reconsider our attitude not only with respect to the questions raised by Higo-no-kami the other day, but also to all other matters in which the Bakufu has acted disloyally or presumptuously towards the Court; and that we should decide to show the fullest respect for the Emperor in the [coming] discussions. . . .[1]

Document 41. Hitotsubashi Keiki and others to the Imperial Court, 29 March 1863.[2]

It is agreed by the Bakufu that the withdrawal [of foreigners] will be effected without fail twenty days after the Shōgun's return to Edo; it being understood that the Imperial Court will issue instructions limiting the Shōgun's stay in Kyōto to ten days.

Document 42. Jisha-bugyō, machi-bugyō, and kanjō-bugyō to Bakufu, early April 1863.[3]

We have perused the letter sent by Okabe Suruga-no-kami[4] and his two colleagues in Kyōto. On the night of 29 March, it appears, the Imperial messenger *Tempōrin* Sanjō [Sanetomi] Chūnagon and seven other nobles called on Lord Hitotsubashi at his lodging and discussed urgently with him the question of fixing a date for the expulsion of foreigners. After exhaustive discussions, Lord Hitotsubashi and the three *daimyō* with him decided that expulsion should take place on the Shōgun's return to Edo, this decision to be announced publicly when the Shōgun goes to the capital. Lord Hitotsubashi and the others, having reached this decision, handed to the eight nobles a letter to this effect.[5]

[1] In a final passage, not translated here, Keiei submitted his resignation 'on grounds of ill health'. It was not accepted.

[2] The text is printed in *Zoku saimukiji*, i. 372. The document was in fact a joint undertaking handed to the Imperial messenger, Sanjō Sanetomi, by the three senior Bakufu officials, Hitotsubashi Keiki, Matsudaira Keiei, and Matsudaira Katamori, and the former *daimyō* of Tosa, Yamanouchi Toyoshige. Although not an official communication between Bakufu and Court, therefore, it was regarded as binding on the Bakufu.

[3] The text is printed in *Tokugawa Keiki Kō Den*, v. 461–3, and, with slight textual variations, in *Kaikoku Kigen*, iii. 2476–8. The memorandum was dated Bunkyū 3, 2nd month (19 March–17 April 1863), but internal evidence makes it clear that it could not have been written before the beginning of April.

[4] The *ōmetsuke* Okabe Nagatsune, with other officials, had accompanied Hitotsubashi Keiki to Kyōto.   [5] See Document 41 above.

No doubt Hitotsubashi and the other lords gave careful thought to the matter before deciding on this course. Yet while the Emperor's instructions were that he wished the Bakufu to decide on the expulsion of foreigners and at once to announce this decision to the *daimyō*, since he feared that it would be impossible to pacify national unrest and that there might even be a danger of civil war unless the whole Empire were at one in deciding on expulsion; even so, his orders were that the detailed execution of this plan was the responsibility of the Shōgun, who should reach a decision in consultation with all appropriate elements of opinion and then report to the Throne the date set for the withdrawal of the hated foreigner. Thus, since the execution of the plan is the responsibility of the Bakufu, the views of the *daimyō* should be sought before the Shōgun sets out for Kyōto, and the necessary announcement made while he is there. For an announcement to be forced upon us before the Shōgun's visit to Kyōto, as is stated in the above document, means that action is taken without ascertaining the views of the *daimyō*, without concerting means of unifying opinion, and without considering the plan which it is the Bakufu's duty to submit. Rashly to open hostilities, and thereby at once to inflict the extremes of hardship and poverty on a people which has known centuries of peace and good government, would be to fail in our duty. It must, we believe, at all costs be avoided. If the Bakufu does not announce the withdrawal of the foreigners, the situation will certainly be difficult. Yet our first and most important task, the defence of the Imperial capital, is not completed, while the building of emplacements at Ōsaka and elsewhere is still under investigation. Until this is done, however desperate might be our efforts, we will not have the means even of defence, let alone of victory. It is therefore impossible for the Shōgun, on the grounds of his 'barbarian-subduing' duties,[1] to accept an Imperial command which would entail immediate war. During his visit to Kyōto, no matter how long it may take to do so, he must repeatedly urge on the Court arguments to this effect.

This question has the gravest significance for Japan, especially as the Shōgun no longer wields the authority or military might that have been his since the time of Ieyasu. To accept the Imperial command would not serve the interests of the Empire as a whole. There seems nothing else for it, therefore, but for the Bakufu to take a firm stand. If it should happen that evil men band themselves together and try to influence the Bakufu by threats, we hope that use will be made of the opportunity offered by the Shōgun's visit to Kyōto to take the most stringent measures to destroy them. By so doing, we believe, the Shōgun will be showing a provident care not only for the fate and fortunes of the Tokugawa house, but also for the permanent interests of the whole people of the Empire. He would ensure that

[1] The term *sei-i* is used. See Document 3, p. 106, note 3, and Document 40, p. 233, note 2.

we do not acquire a reputation for recklessness and injustice among the countries of the world, that Japan may suffer not a single blemish.

These matters are at once vital and difficult of solution. On them the safety and very existence of the State depend. We have, therefore, even at the risk of incurring displeasure, expressed our innermost convictions.

Submitted with respect.

DOCUMENT 43. Lt.-Col. St. John Neale to the Japanese Ministers for Foreign Affairs, 6 April 1863.[1]

The Undersigned, Her Britannic Majesty's Chargé d'Affaires, has received the explicit instructions of his Government to demand reparation from the Japanese Government for the murder and outrages committed upon British subjects on the 14th September last on the tokaido, near Kanagawa, by the retainers of the Prince of Satzuma.

The circumstances attending this unprovoked and savage assault, as related by the survivors, and as set forth by the Undersigned in his several communications, written and verbal, with the Japanese Ministers, have never been controverted, attempted to be palliated, or denied.

The statements of indignation with which Her Majesty's Government have learnt the particulars of this outrage are expressed in the following words addressed to the Undersigned by Her Britannic Majesty's Minister for Foreign Affairs:

'The barbarous murder of Mr Richardson, and the murderous assault on two gentlemen and a lady who were in his company, have inspired Her Majesty's Government with great and just indignation. It was to be hoped that the instant trial and condign punishment of the murderers, together with an offer of further reparation, would have shown on the part of the Japanese Government a due sense of the magnitude of the offence which had been committed; but the letter of the Japanese Ministers of Foreign Affairs, dated the 16th of September, dispels this hope. In a tone of helplessness or evasion they say, that in the answer that Saboolo[2] gave to their officer there is something very improper, and that they will have the whole state of the case more accurately inquired into, and inform you of the result.

'There could have been no doubt in the minds of the Ministers of Japan, that a barbarous murder had been committed—no doubt that other murders had at the same time been attempted, and the only course which a Government, sensible of its duties, and able to perform them, could have

---

[1] The text is printed in *Parliamentary Papers 1864*, lxvi. 218–22. The 'Japanese Ministers for Foreign Affairs' were, of course, those Rōjū designated as *gaikoku-gakari*, that is, 'responsible for foreign relations'.

[2] Shimazu Hisamitsu, generally known to contemporaries as Shimazu Saburō.

pursued, was to arrest, try, convict, and execute the murderers; but even the first step of this process does not seem to have been taken.'[1]

Such are the observations of Her Britannic Majesty's Government, which, after mature consideration of the anomalous political rule which prevails in Japan, has instructed the Undersigned to make to the Japanese Government through your Excellencies a peremptory demand for immediate and full redress for the violence and outrage committed. . . .[2]

The Undersigned, in now approaching the specific reparation which is required from the Japanese Government, and which will not be deviated from, modified, or discussed, desires solemnly and earnestly to explain and impress upon your Excellencies as responsible servants of the Tycoon, for the information of His Majesty and the Supreme Council of this Empire, that there is a serious difference between open hostilities, or in other words war, as declared between nations,—and the adoption of such enforced measures of coercion as are necessary to ensure acquiescence to moderate demands should they be indiscreetly refused or attempted to be evaded.

No loss or ruin to Japan is involved by the preliminary measures which are at present contemplated to awaken the Japanese Government to a due sense of its responsibilities, should it refuse or evade to comply with the reparation now peremptorily demanded; but a persistence in such refusal must necessarily lead to a very different and disastrous situation of affairs.

The reparation now demanded for the murders and murderous assaults committed upon British subjects has been affixed by Her Majesty's Government with a considerate regard for the difficult situation of the Japanese Government and its political embarrassment. But the penalty imposed, and the measure of compensation demanded for the sufferers and their families, now computed in thousands, will if the Japanese Government continue to be ill-advised, inevitably expand into millions, to indemnify the costs of armaments which must be employed by Great Britain, should all serious warnings fail to ensure the redress imperatively demanded for these unprovoked and flagrant outrages.

Notwithstanding the evil designs of interested counsellors, the intelligent Ministers of the Tycoon are already aware that the sincere desire of Great Britain is to preserve peaceful relations of friendship and commerce with Japan; but it is of vital interest to Japan that the Tycoon's Government should be guided in its councils by the knowledge that Great Britain will not tolerate even a passive defiance of its power, or refusal of its just demands.

[1] The passage quoted is from Russell to Neale, 24 December 1862 (*Parliamentary Papers 1864*, lxvi. 179–80).
[2] Since the document is a long one, the next passage (*Parl. Pap. 1864*, p. 219, line 24 to p. 220, line 47) is omitted. It cites a number of old grievances, such as the attack on the Tōzenji legation in July 1861, and contrasts unfavourably Japanese attitudes towards Britain with those of the British government and its citizens towards Japan.

If, however, the Ministers of the Tycoon now in office, setting aside all considerations of ordinary prudence, and devoting themselves to devices calculated to gain time, cause Japan to drift into hostilities with a great Power with which it is utterly unable to cope, upon those Ministers will fall the heavy responsibility of all the calamities which may ensue.

Having thus discharged his duty and conscience by the earnest remarks which precede, the Undersigned has the honour to state to your Excellencies that he is instructed to make the following explicit and peremptory demands upon the Japanese Government:—

First. An ample and formal apology for the offence of permitting a
    murderous attack on British subjects passing on a road open by
    Treaty to them.
Secondly. The payment of £100,000 as a penalty on Japan for this
    offence.

The mode, manner, and form of the apology will be regulated in Conferences between the Undersigned and Commissioners appointed by the Japanese Government, as well as the mode and manner of payment of the money reparation demanded.

Twenty days from this date is assigned to the Japanese Government for its reply, which must be of a categorical character, either consenting to or rejecting the demands here made.[1]

At the expiration of the twenty days assigned for the reply of the Japanese Government, should that reply either be a rejection or evasion, or otherwise than a positive acceptance of the reparation demanded, the British Admiral now assembled here with a considerable force will, within twenty-four hours after the receipt of such refusal of these demands, or in the event of no reply whatever being received at the expiration of that period from the Japanese Government, proceed to enter upon such measures as may be necessary to secure the reparation demanded.

The conduct of these measures will thenceforth necessarily be in the hands of the Admiral commanding-in-chief Her Majesty's naval forces.

The Undersigned for his own part is bound to remind the Japanese Ministers that upon the occurrence of the outrage on the 14th of September, in his extreme desire to leave to the Japanese Government the legitimate mode of affording redress, he exercised a discretion, since entirely approved of by Her Majesty's Government, but which obliged him at the same time to bear the burden of much obloquy on the part of the foreign residents of Yokohama.

[1] The Shōgun had already left for Kyōto, his departure having been hurried forward in anticipation of some such ultimatum as this being made by Britain. Edo was thus able to plead that no decision was possible without reference to the senior Bakufu officials, all of whom were with the Shōgun in Kyōto. On these grounds the date for reply to the ultimatum was extended first to 12 May and ultimately to 7 June, on which day the Rōjū gave a written promise of payment.

The Undersigned may even now apprise the Japanese Government that, so strong is his desire, while carrying out the full tenour of his instructions, to avoid the infliction of loss or suffering upon the unoffending inhabitants of Japan, that he will so express his views to the Admiral; but resistance or attempted evasion of the operations of coercion which may be rendered necessary will evidently render all such considerations impracticable.

It becomes, therefore, the imperative duty of the Undersigned earnestly to warn the Japanese Ministers that the slightest molestation, injury, or violence attempted to be offered by the Japanese authorities, the adherents of Daimios, or others, to the persons or property of British subjects at the ports open to foreigners during the continuance of the preliminary measures, should they be rendered necessary, will alter the whole nature of the operations, and result in the immediate exercise of serious hostilities, the extent, duration, and consequences of which cannot be foreseen; but the whole weight and responsibilities of which will rest with the Japanese Government and its advisers. The present demands of the British Government are sufficiently defined and explicit, as are also the first consequences of a refusal to accede to them.

The Undersigned having acquitted himself of his duties in thus earnestly stating and explaining to the Tycoon's Government what is peremptorily required at its hands, and the penalties which must inevitably attend a non-compliance with the same, proceeds to acquaint your Excellencies with the further measures which, under instructions from Her Majesty's Government, will be adopted to enforce a far more important portion of the reparation rendered necessary, and required for the barbarous murder of the 14th of September from the Prince of Satzuma, by whose adherents that deed was perpetrated.

The Japanese Ministers have written, and have stated to the Undersigned on various occasions, and have openly avowed to the Ministers of other foreign States that the Japanese Government could not pursue or arrest malefactors within the domains of the Daimio Prince Satzuma. This is no reason why the adherents of this Prince, who were the actual murderers, should escape condign punishment; and the British Government, taking into mature consideration the difficulties which thus obstruct the Tycoon's Government, is itself constrained to demand satisfaction and redress from the Prince of Satzuma.

A naval force will, therefore, be directed to proceed to a port appertaining to the Prince of Satzuma, where will be demanded from him:—

1. The immediate trial and capital execution, in the presence of one or more of Her Majesty's naval officers, of the chief perpetrators of the murder of Mr Richardson, and of the murderous assault upon the lady and gentlemen who accompanied him.

2. The payment of £25,000 sterling, to be distributed to the relatives of the murdered man and to those who escaped the swords of the assassins on that occasion.

In the event of the refusal, delay, or evasion of the Prince of Satzuma to carry these demands into immediate effect, such measures of coercion will immediately be adopted against him as the Admiral may judge best calculated to obtain the reparation demanded.

The Undersigned, out of courtesy and high consideration for the Tycoon's Government, makes to it the above communication regarding the course to be adopted with the Prince of Satzuma; considering also that the Government of the Tycoon may deem it expedient in the interests of Japan to advise the Prince of Satzuma to comply at once with the demands of the British Government, necessitated by the barbarous outrage committed by his retainers, at the head of whom was his father, Shimadzoo Saboolo,[1] upon an unoffending British subject. With this object, a high officer might be despatched by the Japanese Government charged with averting the consequences of any obstinate or ill-advised conduct on the part of the Prince of Satzuma, in ignorance of the power and determination of the British nation to enforce redress for unprovoked injuries.

The Undersigned, &c.

DOCUMENT 44. Mizuno Tadanori to Inoue Masanao, 20 April 1863.[2]

With reference to the English envoy's recent note demanding payment of an indemnity, you inform me that as it would cause difficulties to approve the request at this time, you have ordered the *gaikoku-bugyō* to undertake negotiations to postpone discussion of the question until the Shōgun returns to Edo. This seems very reasonable. On the other hand, I fear that it might well prove a source of difficulty. There have been a number of attacks made on Englishmen hitherto, and except for a retainer of Matsudaira Tamba-no-kami, who took his own life,[3] we do not know who was responsible for them. This is particularly reprehensible in the case of the Namamugi affair, for although it took place before the eyes of the lord himself, his retainers have been allowed to escape. This is contrary

[1] Shimazu Tadayoshi, at this time head of the Satsuma fief, was the eldest son of Shimazu Hisamitsu (Saburō) and nephew of the former head of the fief, Shimazu Nariakira.

[2] The text is printed in *Ogasawara Iki-no-kami Nagamichi*, pp. 168–70. Inoue Masanao was one of the Rōjū left in charge of affairs in Edo when the Shōgun went to Kyōto.

[3] On 26 June 1862 Itō Gumbei, one of the guards provided by the Matsumoto fief for the British legation at Tōzenji, made a single-handed attack on the minister's quarters, killing a marine and a sailor, and then committed suicide. The head of the Matsumoto fief at this time was the *fudai daimyō* Toda (Matsudaira) Mitsunori, Tamba-no-kami.

to the spirit of friendly treaty relations, and we cannot therefore call it unreasonable of the foreigners to demand an indemnity. Moreover, should our postponement of the issue end in a refusal of the demands, it is we who would be unreasonable. Such action would be to add new difficulties to those we already have. Hitherto, although demands have been made on us every time such attacks have occurred, the foreigners have had to exercise forbearance because it has not been possible to determine with any certainty who was responsible. The Namamugi affair, however, affords them an admirable opportunity for presenting such demands as may be decided by their government. Should the Bakufu refuse their demands, they will be able to seize upon this as a pretext to open hostilities.[1] Thus by failing to keep faith [with the foreigners], the Bakufu would in the end find itself unable to preserve the national prestige [*kokutai*].

We cannot in justice apply this 'expulsion of foreigners' to the Dutch as well, which fact must be made absolutely clear when you go to Kyōto. What is more, even if the Court insists on an expulsion policy, regardless of considerations of honour, it will still be to our advantage to pay this indemnity. Though one may talk about expelling the foreigners without consideration of honour, it is not in fact possible, all in a moment, to drive out those who from every country have already come to Japan, least of all the Dutch. Success will only be possible if the Bakufu gradually takes steps to persuade the foreigners to its views. As the situation stands, moreover, there is only one way to do this, to emphasize that since the opening of the ports there has been a rise in commodity prices which has inflicted great hardship on all classes of our people, and that for this reason the people of Japan, long accustomed to the ways of seclusion, have become more and more unsettled. This is the line of argument which has already enabled the Bakufu to arrange postponement of the opening of the two ports and the two cities.[2] And the present demand for a large indemnity can be turned to advantage. Even though we pay this great sum, there is no likelihood of such attacks ceasing henceforth. Furthermore, if the same situation arises again in the future, it will again be a question of indemnity. Thus the government would be impoverished by the constant need to raise indemnities; the people would become more and more unsettled; and incidents would thereby increase. In that event, friendship would break down on both sides, so providing a basis for the cancellation of treaties. Certainly it would make it impossible for the Bakufu to maintain permanent diplomatic relations. In this way, to the rise in commodity prices and the unsettled state of national opinion which I cited above,

---

[1] The published text actually reads here 'to oppose hostilities', but this must be an error. Presumably the character *somuku* (Ueda *Daijiten*, No. 1116) is printed in error for *oyobu* (Ueda *Daijiten* No. 1111). I have not been able to see the original document.

[2] i.e. Hyōgo, Niigata, Edo, and Ōsaka. See Section IV, The London Protocol.

we should add a further pretext [for returning to a policy of seclusion]. To put it bluntly, it would be as though the Bakufu were purchasing that additional pretext by making the present payment.

It is said that the ships the Bakufu is now buying will cost close to 200,000.[1] Yet while such mechanical contrivances are useful for a time, they eventually wear out. If, by the present payment, we could purchase a pretext that would make possible a permanent solution, that would be much more to our advantage. The expulsion of foreigners cannot with justice be carried out. Yet the Bakufu must somehow correct and adjust, by negotiation, those matters that have impeded its administration since the opening of the ports, notably the rise in commodity prices. And whether the ports be open or closed, it would seem best to pay this indemnity, for it would provide a pretext to be used in these negotiations and would thus be a point of advantage to the Bakufu. I believe the Bakufu should take advantage of the English demand to hand the money over at once.

With Kyōto brought to agreement, opinion generally can also be quieted. Thus our present difficulties would be brought to an end and it would be possible for the Bakufu so to shape its future policy towards the foreigners as might best achieve success. However, if we were to refuse foreign demands on this occasion, a directly contrary result would ensue. It would be as much as to present the foreigners with a pretext for saying that we were lacking in honour and good faith, which would be much to their liking, for it would give them grounds for opening hostilities. And I doubt if in the upshot they would talk of such things as indemnities. They would claim all the advantages they desire, to our incalculable harm.

Even in domestic affairs, nothing can be accomplished if honour and good faith are sacrificed. Still more is this so in our relations with foreign countries. As to the prospects of victory, circumstances might favour us to the extent of achieving a temporary success, but by sacrificing our honour we would run counter both to divine and to human law, and could not therefore hope to achieve lasting victory. Thus the fate and very existence of our country are in jeopardy. I feel that this crisis presses urgently upon us; and because this gives me much concern, I believe that it is essential for the Bakufu, after careful deliberation, to reach a decision and put it into effect.

In that I have written this in haste, working throughout the night till early dawn, I have been unable to prepare a draft and the whole of my report is badly arranged and ill written. I feel I must submit it as it is, however, so I ask that you may overlook these faults and peruse it none the less.

Submitted with respect.

[1] The monetary unit is not stated. The most likely would be 200,000 *ryō* (see Glossary).

DOCUMENT 45. Ogasawara Nagamichi to Bakufu, early May 1863.[1]

In the recent announcement concerning the expulsion of foreigners it was stated that 25 June was the date set for the negotiations in which we should notify all countries that they must withdraw from Japan, closing down their consulates[2] within thirty days and returning their people without exception to their own lands; and that if they refused, we should open hostilities. With this policy I was in general agreement. On mature deliberation, however, I have come to the conclusion that such a course would be most impolitic. Action like this, I believe, would raise difficulties for the Bakufu in a number of ways. To cite the chief objection, when the Dutch have long maintained relations of complete friendship with Japan, it is unreasonable of the Bakufu not to pursue a separate policy towards them; it is unreasonable to talk of effecting the withdrawal of all foreign countries alike, merely on the grounds that our own officials have incurred severe punishment by mishandling foreign affairs in recent years—though in fact not all have yet been punished. This would only give the Bakufu a reputation for injustice. The reason for maintaining relations with the Dutch in the past, I believe, even though privileges of trade and friendship were not extended to other countries, was simply that it afforded means whereby we might 'know our enemy'. 'Know one's enemy and know oneself' is a maxim that the soldier can never afford to ignore, and by extending application of the withdrawal policy to the Dutch, the Bakufu would deprive itself of the means of knowing its enemy. This would in fact, I believe, be to its own disadvantage.

Trade, as I shall show in the summary that follows, is essentially an exchange of goods whereby both the country and its people may be enriched. Moreover, to expel foreigners by force, without regard to considerations of right and wrong, would be contrary at once to natural law and to the principles of humanity and justice. Being an act of violence, it would provide a pretext for all countries to send warships against us. Thus it would become a source of continuing difficulty for our country, and because of it our people would be driven to the depths of misery. Surely he who is both father and mother to our people could not view this with complacency. Furthermore, although military valour might win us temporary success, the sacrifice of honour must in the end bring total defeat. The fact that the Emperor now orders expulsion, on the lines that I have stated above, springs from his desire to ensure the permanent safety

---

[1] The text is printed in *Ogasawara Iki-no-kami Nagamichi*, pp. 159–63. No precise date is given, but it is fitted into the narrative at about 8–10 May 1863.

[2] *Shōkan*: 'consulate' or 'trading factory'. See Document 21, p. 168, note 2.

of our country. For this the Bakufu must feel gratitude. But if the steps taken by the Bakufu are not well judged, the attempt to ensure permanent safety will in fact reduce our people to wretchedness and lead to total national collapse. Thus, while I am aware that it was entirely from such noble motives that the Emperor recently entrusted the Bakufu with the task of preparing plans for the expulsion of foreigners, it is my belief that for the Shōgun, regardless of consequences, to announce the closing of the ports and the expulsion of foreigners at this time, would in fact be a policy diametrically opposed both to national honour and to attaining the desired end of permanent security.

Speaking generally, trade is in accordance with divine will. The exchange of goods brings benefit to all peoples. From ancient times Japan has been in contact with countries overseas, and has derived much advantage from that fact. We have adopted foreign traditions and institutions and have harmonized them with our own; and imperceptibly on this account our national strength has been developed. Our people feel the benefit of this. A study of our history makes it clear that isolation and seclusion were never our national policy in the past. Even when one turns to recent times, to the present line of Shōgun, one finds that the first three of the line, and especially [Ieyasu] the founder, maintained relations with other countries. There are in the Bakufu archives many letters which were exchanged [with foreigners] on account of trade. Foreigners were allowed to send trading vessels constantly into Japanese waters and to found trading stations at will, and were even granted such privileges as that of having places for their recreation and exercise. And because outlaws surviving from the campaigns of the Keichō [1596–1614] and Genna [1615–23] eras infested the seas and attacked foreign ships, orders were issued to the lords of the coastal districts, as a result of the frequent appeals made by the foreigners, instructing them to suppress piracy and prevent damage to the trade. Indeed, trade is of public benefit and must not be destroyed. It is everywhere the duty of a ruler to succour his people, to give them guidance as to their interests in matters of State, to preserve public order and guard the land against harm. I consider, therefore, that in following this course of giving due and lasting importance to trade and friendship, these Shōgun showed their judgement to be far above that of ordinary men. They freely granted every country the goods it sought, even to such things as weapons, and at that time not a single voice was raised in protest. Foreigners even made constant visits to such places as Nara and Sakai. It was the third Shōgun [Iemitsu] who found occasion to change this policy, so that it is only in the last two hundred or so years that we have reversed our previous attitude and come to regard foreigners as our enemies.

In view of these facts, it is my belief that seclusion is not the original ancient law of our country. On the contrary, it is a new ruling. However, if we now tried to change our customs all in a moment, we would be running counter to ideas which the people have come to hold very strongly. Even to the most powerful of rulers that would be impossible. On the other hand, to try permanently to keep our ports closed and foreigners at a distance would be contrary to natural law and would certainly bring national misery and disaster. One might illustrate this by analogy with the flower of the peony when it is about to open. To try to make that slightly opened flower once more into the original bud would be impossible, even to the skill of its maker. Equally, to make this same flower open at once to full bloom is beyond the power even of an emperor. If one considers this principle carefully, one sees that in present conditions both opening the country and seclusion are equally ill advised. This fact is at the root of our interminable disagreements. I believe, first and foremost, that even though the methods of trade between countries have changed from what they were in former times, it is still a fundamental error to ignore such differences as may exist between foreign institutions and our own and to adopt foreign ways indiscriminately; our policy must depend not on foreign practice but on our own interests and position.[1] However, as matters stand I think it desirable that we should open some three or four ports.

The rise in commodity prices since the opening of the ports has inflicted hardship on all, both high and low. The impact of this on the ideas of a people long accustomed to seclusion has led to frequent attacks on foreigners, causing the government many difficulties. I am fully conscious how just is the Emperor's concern about the present situation, for not only are we getting no benefit from the trade, but also there is a possibility that we may suffer great harm from the breakdown of friendly relations. However, the rise in commodity prices springs fundamentally from debasement of the coinage and is not just due to [foreign] trade. I believe that, with our present coinage, prices would continue to rise even if we put a stop to trade.

To ignore the faults in our own domestic organization and indiscriminately to impute the blame to the foreigners, carrying out this ill-advised policy of expulsion and thus, as I have already said, inflicting great hardship on our people, could surely not be described as action becoming in a ruler.[2] Both Court and Bakufu, I fear, would in this be failing in their duty. Still more is it our duty to supply wood, water, food, and other necessities, and to succour the shipwrecked and unfortunate. Thus it is

[1] The translation given for this sentence is the most likely interpretation in the context, but the passage as printed is obscure and almost certainly corrupt. I have assumed that the phrase *yaku ni nazumi-sōrō* should read *kare ni nazumi-sōrō*. I have not been able to see the original document.

[2] Literally, 'action of a man of [Confucian] benevolence'.

my hope that the Shōgun will weigh this question carefully and then urge earnestly and repeatedly on the Court his desire to act in conformity with the ideas I have stated above. I am convinced it would in fact be most disloyal and disrespectful towards the Emperor for the Shōgun to look idly on while the Court's mistaken views brought the people into misery. Simply to obey the Emperor's orders out of blind loyalty, because they are the Emperor's orders, making no attempt to assess their merits and de-merits, would be the action of a woman. I could never believe it to be behaviour appropriate to the office of Shōgun. It is my earnest request that the Shōgun, having considered well the logic of the facts, should remonstrate with the Court at once and with decision. Even should such a course endanger his position, I still think it necessary in present circum-stances that he should disregard this danger and, thinking only of his duty to succour his people and safeguard his country, should act with decision so as to demonstrate by his deeds the sincerity of his loyalty to the Em-peror. I do not say that the expulsion of foreigners is completely im-possible. But I do consider it vital that the Bakufu's plan for achieving it be well considered and appropriate to the circumstances.

It is difficult to put such matters as this in writing, and I have therefore been forced to give here only a summary. I could not but submit this report, despite the extreme pain it causes me to do so, and if you wish to inquire further of me in person, I shall submit an oral statement in greater detail.

DOCUMENT 46. Hitotsubashi Keiki to the Rōjū in Edo, 12 June 1863.[1]

... The date previously set for the expulsion of foreigners was 8 June,[2] though it was always understood that the plan would not be carried out until the Shōgun's return to Edo. The Shōgun accordingly wished to seek Imperial permission to withdraw from the Court. He intended to make this request after accompanying the Emperor upon the Imperial progress, but as the date set for expulsion was drawing near and there would not be time enough [for the Shōgun to reach Edo] even if the Emperor's permission were given, this circumstance was explained to the Emperor, who has decided to set 25 June [as the new date for expulsion]. However, this date, too, does not leave sufficient time. Moreover, a number of fiefs joined in recommending that the Shōgun should make a tour of inspection

---

[1] The text is printed in *Tokugawa Keiki Kō Den*, v. 510–14. The formal greetings (in the first two lines of the printed version) are here omitted.

[2] The original date set was the middle period of the 4th month (28 May–6 June 1863), subse-quently changed, according to both Court and Bakufu records, to 9 June (not 8 June as Keiki states here).

of the Settsu coast defences.[1] The same idea was current also in the Imperial Court. For this reason, and because he was himself uneasy about that area, the Shōgun set out on 7 June to tour the Settsu coast and supervise matters for himself. On his return he will report in detail to the Emperor and then seek permission to return to Edo. Meanwhile, since the date [of expulsion] is already very near, he has ordered me to precede him to Edo, returning there at once and taking charge of the negotiations for the withdrawal of foreigners, which are to begin on 25 June. I left Kyōto on 8 June, therefore, and expect to reach Edo on 23 or 24 June. However, I may be delayed if the river crossings are impassable, and in that event I shall not arrive by 25 June. For this reason I have ordered Takeda Kōunsai,[2] who has long been generally respected in the fiefs, to go on ahead and discuss with you the way in which the negotiations are to be conducted. He will probably reach Edo on 16 or 17 June. I hope, therefore, that you will discuss matters fully with him on his arrival.

In the present position of affairs, it seems that unless the expulsion of foreigners is carried out the Shōgun might even be relieved of office. Indeed, it seems beyond doubt that having formally accepted the Imperial orders to expel the foreigners last year, the Bakufu must sooner or later carry out the expulsion of foreigners if the Shōgun is not to appear neglectful of his duties. Hence we must all make the most strenuous efforts in this matter. It is certain that we must effect the withdrawal of foreigners from Edo and Kanagawa, equally so that we must at the same time close Nagasaki and Hakodate. It was being said at the Imperial Court that withdrawal even of the Dutch and Chinese must be effected. I thought it most unjust to demand the withdrawal of these two peoples now, for they have long maintained relations with us. Yet further consideration showed that other countries could not be expected to agree to these two alone remaining in Japan, so the decision was taken that even they must be made to withdraw.

In the coming negotiations, our main line of argument will be that the treaties were concluded a few years ago solely on the responsibility of the Bakufu; that national opinion has become much unsettled because no report on the subject was made to the Court; that we have now received new and strict orders from the Emperor to effect the withdrawal of foreigners; and that although foreigners have been admitted to friendship and trade hitherto, this must cease henceforth and they must not again set foot in Japanese territory. If, despite all our arguments, the foreigners will not agree to this, we can expect war to break out at once. We must

---

[1] Settsu was the province at the eastern end of the Inland Sea in which the city of Ōsaka was situated.

[2] Takeda Masao, a samurai of the Mito fief in Keiki's service. It seems probable that Takeda had secret oral instructions that the Namamugi indemnity was to be paid, though with the Shōgun still in the Kansai region the Bakufu clearly had to proceed with caution.

therefore be firm in our resolve and at once order all *hatamoto* to make the most desperate efforts in establishing means of defence. The laxity induced by peace has caused all kinds of differences of opinion to appear among us, especially among officials. But we must be firm and unmoved by this; our sole task is to begin this very day preparations for our defence. I do not want time wasted in useless and idle discussion.

I cannot tell how quickly I shall reach Edo, but you must certainly initiate the withdrawal negotiations on 25 June even if I have not arrived by that date. Before I left Kyōto, great anxiety was being expressed there, especially in the Imperial Court, lest action be postponed until after the 25th. The Emperor has again and again issued orders on the subject, while the Shōgun has formally accepted these orders and has indicated in writing his decision to set the date at 25 June. At the time of my departure there came another order from the Palace saying that every effort must be made to ensure that withdrawal be effected without fail on that date. For us to delay now would jeopardize not only my own position but even that of the Shōgun himself. Whatever the objections officials [in Edo] may raise, therefore, you are to explain this to them fully; and if they still disagree, you must act at your own discretion. If there are any who are still hesitant when I arrive, I shall first explain matters fully to them and then, painful as it will be to have to do so, I shall ask the Shōgun's approval for the immediate execution of those who remain obdurate. In these matters I have full authority to act at my own discretion and to deal with the activities of Bakufu officials as I see fit, without seeking special instructions from the Shōgun. I am therefore letting you know this before I reach Edo. You must be firm of purpose and see to it that morale is high. And since there will be no time after I reach Edo to make preparations for defence of the coast and elsewhere, you must put this in hand at once.

There are many matters of which I wanted to inform you, but I have no time to do so while travelling and write now only in outline. I shall make all haste and arrive as soon as possible. Meanwhile I wish the contents of this letter to be kept most secret.[1]

DOCUMENT 47. Jisha-bugyō, machi-bugyō, and kanjō-bugyō to Bakufu, 21 June 1863.[2]

We have given careful consideration to the date recently set for the expulsion of foreigners and to the matter of closing the ports, as announced on

---

[1] In a postscript to this letter Keiki replies to a suggestion, apparently made by the Rōjū, that foreigners be given more than thirty days to quit Japan. Such a proposal, he says, must never come from the Bakufu, though it might be considered if made by the foreigners.

[2] The text is printed in *Zoku saimukiji*, ii. 6–8; and, with small textual variations, in *Kaikoku Kigen*, iii. 2502–4, where the date is given as 17 June 1863.

7 June. Dutch and Chinese have long been permitted to trade with Japan. It seems most unreasonable that we should now order them to leave Nagasaki, where they have long been in residence, at the same time as other foreigners; and equally so that we should allow only thirty days for foreigners to depart, not one being permitted to remain. Such action would jeopardize the safety of the whole Empire and provoke the foreigners into making fresh demands. To enter thus upon an unjust war would be an immense and irretrievable blunder. If we pursue negotiations steadily and in due order, urging our case with reasoned care and exhausting every means of argument to justify us in carrying out the expulsion of foreigners, then, we believe, honour will be preserved and our plans will achieve their purpose. The Bakufu's present plan of closing all three ports at once would make a crisis unavoidable. Our demands would be unreasonable, made without regard for right and wrong. Unless Bakufu policy is framed in the light of the maxim 'know one's enemy and know oneself',[1] war will break out and all countries will seek to seize our territory. In that event, there will be no hope of the future continuance of the Imperial line, nor could the prestige that the Shōgun has inherited from his ancestors be saved from destruction. The results, indeed, would be too terrible to contemplate.

Thus there is no other course open but for the Shōgun to report these circumstances to the Emperor and seek permission to resign his office. Edo is his main stronghold; and moreover, the Princesses Kazunomiya and Tenshōin[2] are there. Once the Shōgun has submitted his resignation, therefore, we believe it best, since it is of the first importance that he act with circumspection, that he should retire at once to Edo and there respectfully await an Imperial decree granting him clemency.

As retainers of the Shōgun, it is assuredly presumption and an offence of the first magnitude for us to advise that he relinquish for a time the 'barbarian-subduing' responsibilities[3] that have been handed down in his line from the days of Ieyasu. But the difficulties we now face are unparalleled since the dawn of our history. We have, therefore, after the fullest consideration, decided to submit this confidential report.

Submitted with the utmost respect.

Bakufu reply, minuted on the above[4]

I am obliged to you for the above report, which I have perused. There are, however, other arguments to be considered. I have accordingly set

---

[1] Cf. Document 45, p. 243, and introduction, p. 7, note 2.
[2] Imperial Princesses who had married Shōgun: Tenshōin was the widow of Iesada and Kazunomiya was the wife of Iemochi.
[3] Cf. Document 3, p. 106, note 3, and Document 40, p. 233, note 2.
[4] This minute is undated and unsigned, but is generally attributed to Ogasawara Nagamichi.

them out below, and ask that you will now reconsider your views on this matter.

You say that it would be unreasonable to demand that Dutch and Chinese withdraw at the same time as other foreigners. At first sight this seems a proper attitude. It appears, however, that there has been a considerable element of bluff in the threats made by the Dutch since the Tempō period [1830–43]. It might be as well, therefore, to expel them in the first instance at the same time as the other foreigners and then take up the question of these two countries subsequently in separate discussions. This, of course, may well depend on the way the negotiations develop.

You speak of 'an unjust war'. We are now to undertake fresh negotiations and urge the withdrawal of foreigners on the two counts of widespread unrest within Japan and our fear of lasting national impoverishment [due to trade]. If the foreigners then open hostilities, surely this cannot be called 'unjust' on our part. And even if we were now temporarily to avert the foreign crisis [in the way you suggest], it seems obvious that this would in fact so agitate national opinion in Japan as to bring total collapse at home. If this were to lead to some incident even more serious than the Tōzenji affair,[1] it would then be we who opened the hostilities. Is it not this, in fact, that would be unjust?

[You say we must observe the maxim 'know one's enemy and know oneself'. It goes without saying that it is necessary to know one's enemy. But in present circumstances, surely failure to recognize the facts of our own position will make it impossible for us to govern the country.][2]

You recommend that the Shōgun resign his office. That is certainly the course least likely to cause disturbance. But in that the Shōgun has these 'barbarian-subduing' responsibilities, it is desirable that as far as it may be possible he should carry them out. Most of the *tozama* lords now seem determined on the expulsion of foreigners. Were the Emperor to accept the Shōgun's resignation, therefore, and issue orders entrusting the task of expulsion to the great fiefs, would not the situation be made many times worse?

DOCUMENT 48. Hitotsubashi Keiki to the Kampaku (Takatsukasa Sukehiro), 9 July 1863.[3]

... Believing myself to be quite unworthy to fulfil my present duties, I submitted to you recently a brief private letter asking that I might be relieved of office.[4] What follows is written to explain why the expulsion of foreigners

---

[1] The attack on the British legation at Tōzenji in July 1861.

[2] This paragraph is omitted from the text given in *Kaikoku Kigen*.

[3] The text is printed in *Tokugawa Keiki Kō Den*, v. 532–7. The formal greetings (in the first line of the printed version) are here omitted.

[4] See Keiki to Takatsukasa Sukehiro, 29 June 1863, in *Tokugawa Keiki Kō Den*, v. 522–3.

could not be carried out and to tell you what has happened since I left Kyōto.

I left Kyōto on 8 June and reached Atsuta[1] on 12 June. The *metsuke* Hori Kunai [Toshitake] arrived there at the same time on his way to Kyōto, so I asked him about the state of affairs in Edo and about the [Namamugi] indemnity. He told me it had been decided to hand over the indemnity. This caused me great concern, for the Shōgun had submitted a number of reports on this matter to the Emperor and had made an announcement concerning it to the Empire at large. It was impossible now for him to change his policy. That such a decision had been reached, I suspected, was due entirely to the actions of officials in Edo, and I therefore sent at once to the Rōjū there to explain that the indemnity must on no account be handed over.[2] Being still uneasy about this, however, I gave one of my retainers detailed oral instructions that the indemnity must not be paid and that the withdrawal negotiations must be started at once, there being not a day to lose, and sent him off post-haste from Hamamatsu-eki as a messenger to convey these orders to [Ogasawara Nagamichi] Tosho-no-kami.

I received no answer to this communication, which fact gave me some concern, so on 23 June, when I stopped in passing at Kanagawa, I sent for the two *bugyō* of that place, Asano [Ujisuke] Iga-no-kami and Yamaguchi [Naotake] Shinano-no-kami. I questioned them about the state of affairs with respect to the English. They said they had earlier handed to the English a written undertaking that the indemnity would be paid on 18 June. However, since orders were twice received from me not to do so, sent while I was travelling, the two men had received urgent instructions from Tosho-no-kami on the morning of 18 June to the effect that the indemnity must not be handed over. The *bugyō* accordingly opened discussions with the English, telling them that the indemnity could not be paid. The English, they said, thereupon became extremely angry, saying that it was an act of gross bad faith for the Bakufu to change its policy now, having once given a written undertaking to pay; and that, seeing now how matters stood, they would thereafter refuse all meetings with us, be it with Rōjū or anyone else Since the English seemed to be putting themselves in a state of readiness for war, the *bugyō* explained, they had sought the help of the French, discussions with whom were still proceeding. I said that notwithstanding all this, the indemnity must not be handed over; but they would not agree, objecting that if this were to be so, war would break out forthwith, and that when it came to the point of war, even if they did not hand the money over themselves, somebody would certainly have to be sent to do so.

[1] Now part of the city of Nagoya.
[2] Keiki's letter to the Rōjū of 12 June 1863 (Document 46), to which this is presumably a reference, in fact contains no mention of the Namamugi indemnity.

Turning to the question of foreign withdrawal, I said that negotiations to this end must also be resolutely pressed. At this the two men looked angry. They asked me why I had accepted the expulsion policy before returning to Edo and advanced all kinds of criticisms. I therefore explained in detail the nature of the Court's wishes. The Shōgun, I told them, could neither provide evidence of his acceptance of the Imperial commands, nor fulfil the proper duties of his office, unless he now carried out the expulsion of foreigners. Moreover, I said, we must bear in mind the personal position of the Shōgun. But they would by no means accept my arguments, insisting that the personal fate of the Shōgun, be it what it may, could not be set against the interests of the Empire. In fact, they said, if I were to continue to insist on a policy of expulsion, I might myself be in danger of assassination. My suspicions were aroused when the two men told me that [Ogasawara] Tosho-no-kami had already left Edo by sea for Kyōto, though he was still in the neighbourhood [of Kanagawa]. I asked why he was going to Kyōto. They said that they did not know any of the details, but that it probably had to do with the indemnity. I subsequently heard that Tosho-no-kami had handed over the indemnity on his own responsibility.

Since I had arrived at Kanagawa at 2 p.m. and this discussion had lasted till after 4 p.m., I now told the two men to withdraw. My general intention had been to reach Edo on 24 June, but I was so disturbed about conditions there that I rode straight through from Kawasaki with only a few men and reached the capital the same night at 10 p.m. The next day I went to the Castle and met all the Rōjū and other officials. I informed them in detail of the nature of the Court's wishes and also gave them full information about the matter of foreign withdrawal. I explained the circumstances in which the Shōgun had stated his formal acceptance of the Emperor's orders, and even showed them in confidence the commission giving me full authority. Yet all the officials agreed in saying that the Bakufu could not accept such orders because it would not be in the country's interests to do so. I accordingly explained once more that this would put them in the position of opposing both the wishes of the Emperor and the orders of the Shōgun, but not one of them would accept my view. They answered that the Bakufu could not accept the Imperial orders, for they did not think it in the best interests of the country to expel the foreigners; though if positive orders were given for the expulsion of foreigners, they said, the matter was out of their hands.

I had heard that at this time many officials, including Rōjū, were beginning to keep to their private residences,[1] and that there were sometimes whole days when not a single one came to the Castle. This put me on my guard. That day, without entering into any heated discussion, I withdrew

---

[1] i.e. were not coming to the Castle to perform their official duties.

from the Castle. According to the talk I heard later, some of the officials were suspicious about what my real intentions might be, and all kinds of rumours were current. I also heard that there was a report, which gave rise to much suspicion, to the effect that I had ulterior motives for insisting on the expulsion of foreigners. Again, the frequent consultations at Yoko-hama about payment [of the indemnity] gave rise to a rumour that some plot was afoot, and it was said that men of spirit[1] were much concerned at this.

Thus there was a complete confusion of reports. Not knowing the real views of the officials, however, I began by summoning [Ogasawara] Tosho-no-kami from Yokohama. I told him that in view of the unanimous recommendations of the officials, I would leave aside the question of Nagasaki and Hakodate for the present, and begin by initiating immediate negotiations for the closing of Yokohama. But the Rōjū and other officials all said that this whole question must be left to Tosho-no-kami; that although I had accepted the important and arduous task of expelling the foreigners, present conditions in fact made it essential to open the country; and that I must therefore go at once to Kyōto and explain this to the Court. If this were so, I told them, then they must send me reports explaining in detail their views and opinions. I would go to Kyōto and report, when a suitable occasion arose and after I had carefully considered their statements, which they must therefore submit at once. They all said, however, that it would be most inconvenient for them to submit such statements. And I doubt if they have any intention of doing so. I charged them strictly that they must submit these statements at once, insisting that I sought their agreement, but so far, from 27 June until this day, not one of them has forwarded a statement.

Why I do not know, but I think all this must be because they do not trust me. It much pains me that in the last year I have become the object of such suspicions. I have carried out my duties till now confident in the Emperor's favour and doing my utmost to carry out his wishes. Yet, as appears from what I have written above, the position is such that the expulsion of foreigners must temporarily be set aside, while it also gives me much concern in respect of the need to pacify national opinion. For this reason, as I said previously, I most earnestly beg that I may be relieved of my official duties. If you announce my dismissal, in accordance with this private request, I shall indeed think myself most fortunate.

Submitted with the utmost consideration and respect.

[1] *yūshi*, a euphemism often used to describe samurai who supported the *sonnō-jōi* movement.

DOCUMENT 49. Ogasawara Nagamichi to Bakufu, 27 July 1863.[1]

I beg to report the circumstances in which, believing that the position was such as to make it inevitable that the [Namamugi] indemnity be paid, I decided to pay it on my own responsibility.

I was from the beginning often urged by the lords of Owari and Mito[2] that we must first hand over the indemnity and then undertake negotiations for the expulsion of foreigners. Notwithstanding my objections that this was most undesirable and that it would therefore be better to pay the indemnity, if at all, only after an attempt had been made to open negotiations for expulsion, they nevertheless insisted that we must first send at least a written bond in promise of payment. Nor could I bring them to agree with me, although I told them several times that this was not a good plan. Moreover, both [Matsudaira Nobuatsu] Buzen-no-kami and [Inoue Masanao] Kawachi-no-kami expressed themselves strongly in favour of paying. In the end, Buzen-no-kami, Kawachi-no-kami, and myself jointly signed and dispatched a written bond.

It was somewhere about the 8th or 9th of June, I think, that the foreigners demanded an initial payment of 40,000 dollars. Thereupon the lords of Owari and Mito again urged that we must pay, and all other officials without exception recommended payment. There was a great clamour, in which I alone expressed disagreement. The lords of Owari and Mito, and indeed everybody else, showed themselves extremely angry because I had summoned the *jisha-bugyō* and others to conference with me and after much discussion had decided to wait for a time and not make payment at once. (I later heard that the lord of Mito had written to Kyōto to say that he had been resolved never to pay the indemnity, but I heard not a word to that effect up to the time of his withdrawal from affairs. I asked Buzen-no-kami and Kawachi-no-kami about it, but they too remembered no such thing.) After this the disputes about whether or not we were to pay the indemnity became daily more fierce. And so matters stood at about the 19th or 20th of June. At about that time, I sent to the English admiral (I cannot remember for certain whether it was only to the English or to all countries) to arrange a meeting at which I would seek to negotiate with him concerning a temporary postponement of the indemnity question and also concerning the expulsion of foreigners. Buzen-no-kami and Kawachi-no-kami refused to sign the letter which I proposed to send at

---

[1] The text is printed in *Ogasawara Iki-no-kami Nagamichi*, pp. 228–30, where it forms section one of the memorandum submitted by Ogasawara at the Bakufu's command. The second section (ibid., pp. 230–3) deals with Ogasawara's actions after paying the indemnity and is not translated here.

[2] As the heads of two senior Tokugawa branch houses, these two lords were in effect the Shōgun's representatives during his absence in Kyōto.

this time, so I had no choice but to send it in my own name alone. However, the English reply confined itself to the statement that the written bond which we had originally sent them had already been sent home and that it was therefore impossible for them to accept any delay. No reference at all was made to appointing a date for negotiations. This put me in a very difficult position, so for the moment I left matters as they were. At this point I fell ill and withdrew to my residence. (With regard to their statement that the written bond had been sent home, I am told that when [the *gaikoku-bugyō*] Kikuchi Iyo-no-kami and Shibata Teitarō went to Yokohama about 8th or 9th June, they unquestionably saw it dispatched by warship.)

I subsequently received orders to effect the withdrawal of foreigners from the three ports, and would at once have begun negotiations to that end—Lord Hitotsubashi, then on his way back to Edo, had sent to inform me that I might open negotiations even before 25 June—had not Takeda Kōunsai refused to agree.[1] He insisted that it would cause difficulties for the Bakufu were this step not left until after the 25th. (His argument was that our preparations for war would not everywhere be completed by the 25th; and that it might therefore be to our own disadvantage to open negotiations before the 25th, for should the negotiations break down, English ships would be sent to such places as the Settsu coast while we were still unprepared.) I accordingly accepted his advice for the moment and postponed negotiations. On further consideration, however, I realized that I had, after all, been entrusted with the duty of negotiating and it would be unpardonable to make no attempt to do so before Lord Hitotsubashi's arrival. I therefore went to Yokohama and sought an interview [with the English]. It was refused. I made several more such requests, but could not in any way get them to agree. This time they said not a word about the indemnity. They said simply that Japan lacked honour and good faith, and I gathered that they had already circulated such reports to all countries. Their reason for publishing abroad our ill repute in this way was that in our written bond we had definitely informed them of the date on which we should hand over the indemnity, but had constantly postponed payment ever since.

Hitherto Japan had been known far and wide, and in all lands, as a country which kept its word. That is why our country has been conspicuous in the East as one which humbled itself before no man. And it seemed to me to be infinitely regrettable that for the sake of this indemnity we should lose that reputation and come to be despised and hated, than which there could be no greater national disgrace. Moreover, the refusal to hold any meetings with us was going to cause us immediate difficulties.

---

[1] Takeda Kōunsai was Hitotsubashi's messenger to the Rōjū. Cf. Document 46, p. 247 and note.

Had the fault lain on their side, we could have had no reason to reproach ourselves. But in the circumstances that I have stated above I felt we had no choice but to pay the indemnity. This I did on 24 June. The decision was taken on my own responsibility, yet it was one which from the beginning all had held to be inevitable.

At the same time I informed the foreigners by letter that I should soon open negotiations [for closing the ports], but to my consternation they sent a most indignant reply. At this point Inoue [Kiyonao] Shinano-no-kami was sent to me by Lord Hitotsubashi with a message of the utmost secrecy. His instructions were that I was to pay the indemnity forthwith, to go at once aboard an English ship, and proceed as an envoy to all foreign countries. Not understanding his meaning, however, I replied without pausing to reflect that it would be impossible for me to go, whereupon he sent a further messenger ordering me to return at once to Edo. I therefore returned at once.

Thus it was throughout a general opinion that payment of the indemnity was inevitable. Even so, in view of Lord Hitotsubashi's orders, I did everything possible to find means of withholding payment. However, after weighing all the circumstances, I came to the conclusion that it would be even less in the national interest to cause our country to be branded faithless and unjust. I therefore had no alternative but to order payment of the indemnity. This in brief is the explanation of my handling of the indemnity question. This, however, is a very short statement, and I could explain the full details only in an oral report, so that I trust that my meaning will be given careful thought. As to events at Kanagawa, I think that inquiries made of Asano [Ujisuke] Iga-no-kami will enable the Bakufu to understand what took place.

The Paris Convention and the Shimonoseki Indemnity, 1863–4

THE action of Chōshū in firing on foreign ships and closing the Straits of Shimonoseki stimulated the anti-Bakufu party into fresh action. By September 1863 they had gained the upper hand at the Imperial Court and were making plans to announce the Emperor's resumption of political power. Their action was premature, however. Many *daimyō* and Court nobles who had previously supported the demand for the expulsion of foreigners were not willing to see the Bakufu destroyed as an institution, and their defection tipped the scales. On the morning of 30 September 1863, with the help of troops supplied by Aizu (Matsudaira Katamori) and Satsuma, the *kōbu-gattai* group effected a *coup d'état*. The leading Chōshū supporters among the Court nobles were forced to withdraw from Kyōto.

Yet this sudden change in the political situation did not end the demand for the expulsion of foreigners. Indeed, it was at once reiterated by the Court. Nevertheless, the Bakufu was encouraged by this development to believe that there was now some hope of settling its more pressing problems, both in home and in foreign affairs. For this, the first essential was time in which to act. The representatives of the Treaty Powers had already made it clear that they would under no circumstances accept the closing of the ports. Nor were they willing to close even the one port of Yokohama, as the Bakufu proposed by way of compromise in October. The latter plan, however, was too attractive to be readily abandoned. It offered a prospect of demonstrating respect for the Emperor's views while avoiding a head-on collision with the foreigners. The Rōjū, therefore, willingly adopted a French suggestion that a mission be sent to Europe to discuss outstanding problems, for there might be better prospects of success for negotiations in Europe than in Japan, as the London Protocol of 1862 seemed to show. At the very least, a mission which was to undertake discussions at several different capitals was bound to last a year or more. Thus even if it failed, it would give the Bakufu time to persuade the Court to other views.

On 7 January 1864 the *gaikoku-bugyō* Ikeda Nagaaki was appointed to head the mission. Neither the Bakufu nor the envoys themselves seem to have been confident of success in the matter of closing Yokohama. The latter, indeed, seem to have regarded their task as being principally to justify Japan's position and gain time—an attitude which the Rōjū did not trouble to correct when commenting on their plans (Document 50).

When the Ikeda mission left Japan on 6 February 1864, the Bakufu had already begun to take steps to reach a new agreement with the Court. Armed now with the argument that no further action could be taken about the expulsion of foreigners until the return of the envoys sent to Europe, it arranged that the Shōgun should once more visit Kyōto in person. He arrived there on 22 February. The leading *daimyō* of the *kōbu-gattai* party (Shimazu Hisamitsu of Satsuma, Yamanouchi Toyoshige of Tosa, Date Muneki of Uwajima, and Matsudaira Keiei of Fukui) had already reached the capital; and the unprecedented step was taken of admitting them formally to the councils both of the Court and the Bakufu. They quickly reached agreement with Hitotsubashi Keiki on the main lines of policy to be pursued in domestic affairs. Yet within a few weeks the party was once more divided. Foreign policy again proved the occasion of disagreement.

On 28 February the Shōgun went to the Palace, where he was handed an Imperial letter enjoining the Bakufu to continue its efforts to secure the expulsion of foreigners, but emphasizing that action was not to be taken 'recklessly' (Document 51). A few days later there was a further letter, vaguer in its wording but similar in tone (Document 52). Both represented a marked change in the nature of Court pronouncements on this subject. The Shōgun's reply of 21 March was equally moderate: the Emperor's wishes would be respected; envoys had been sent to Europe to arrange the closing of Yokohama; and military preparations were being pressed to completion to guard against foreign attack (Document 53). The wording of this reply, however, did not entirely satisfy the Court. It sought a specific promise that expulsion would be carried out even if the mission to Europe failed. It was this request that revealed the dissensions among the *kōbu-gattai* leaders. Shimazu Hisamitsu insisted that the time had come for the Bakufu to tell the Court that expulsion could never be accomplished. Hitotsubashi Keiki, though equally aware of the impossibility of expulsion, preferred not to risk an open breach with the Court when time might make it unnecessary. Moreover, he was suspicious of Satsuma ambitions. For the Bakufu to give way to Chōshū pressure for expulsion one year, he believed, and to Satsuma opposition the next, would inevitably destroy its remaining authority. In this he seems to have had the support of the Rōjū. From the account given by one of Keiki's retainers (Document 54) it is clear that the discussions of the next few days were heated. They were also unexpected. Keiki insisted on having his way, and on 26 March the Shōgun gave the necessary undertaking (Document 55). But it was at the cost of Shimazu's support and of the unity of the *kōbu-gattai* party.

By the concessions he had made to the Court, including the promise to close Yokohama, the Shōgun had succeeded in securing an Imperial decree reasserting Bakufu responsibility for the overall supervision of national affairs. Specifically, permission had been given for military action to be taken against Chōshū. Before the necessary steps to this end could be put in train, however, the representatives of the Treaty Powers, led by Rutherford Alcock, had formed the intention of using force to open the Straits of Shimonoseki if the Bakufu proved unable or unwilling to do so. A joint ultimatum to this effect was finally sent to the Bakufu on 22 July. The Bakufu tried to secure postponement of the expedition, but without avail, and the joint fleet was on the point of sailing when, on 19 August 1864, Ikeda Nagaaki and his colleagues unexpectedly arrived at Yokohama from Paris.

Ikeda had found the French government adamant in refusing his proposals. Far from accepting the closing of Yokohama, France claimed an indemnity for the damage caused by Chōshū and demanded that Yokohama, Nagasaki, and Hakodate should be made free ports as compensation for the Bakufu's failure to observe the terms of the London Protocol. Ikeda soon became convinced that Japan could only avoid disaster by a fundamental change of policy. This, he believed, must envisage far wider contacts with the outside world. More immediately, some, at least, of the French demands must be accepted. On 20 June 1864, therefore, he signed a convention providing for the payment of an indemnity for Chōshū's attack on French ships; for the opening of the Shimonoseki Straits, if necessary with French naval assistance; and for the reduction of duties on certain French goods (Document 56). This action being completely contrary to his instructions, Ikeda then decided to return at once to Japan and report to his government (Document 57).

The mission's return threw the Bakufu into consternation, for it removed the best excuse for avoiding a decision on the question of closing Yokohama. It is probably for this reason that Ikeda and his colleagues were at once dismissed and punished. Moreover, the Bakufu refused to ratify the agreement they had signed, on the grounds that to do so would cause immediate civil war in Japan. This meant that there was no further reason for postponing the naval attack on Chōshū. At the end of August the joint fleet left Yokohama. By 14 September the Shimonoseki batteries had been destroyed and an armistice signed with Chōshū.

On 18 September the four ministers again opened negotiations with the Bakufu. A large indemnity was demanded for the damage sustained and for the costs of the expedition. The Bakufu was warned that failure to demonstrate a more friendly attitude for the future might force the Powers to open direct negotiations with the Emperor, whose ratification of the treaties was in any case desirable. Finally, it was suggested that the claim to an indemnity might be waived if the Bakufu was prepared to open Shimonoseki or some other suitable port in the Inland Sea (Document 58). Conscious of its own weakness, the Bakufu had no choice but to accept these terms. On 22 October 1864 they were embodied in a convention (Document 59). The attempt to satisfy both the foreigners and the expulsion party had again ended in complete failure.

DOCUMENT 50. Ikeda Nagaaki, Kawazu Sukekuni, and Kawada Hiroshi to Bakufu, 19 January 1864.[1]

Having now received orders to proceed abroad as envoys to conduct negotiations for closing the port of Kanagawa, we wish to seek instructions on the following points:

We shall, of course, exert every effort to fulfil the Bakufu's wishes and to bring the negotiations to a successful conclusion, using every argument at our command to convince the foreigners of the inescapable fact that it is impossible for the Bakufu to maintain the treaties, since opposition to them is growing daily in Japan and there is bound eventually to be a complete breakdown of friendly relations if nothing is done. But should it happen that we are unable to achieve success, notwithstanding all our arguments, then there will be no alternative but for the Bakufu to close Kanagawa by force of war. This would be completely to overthrow the treaties. It is for this reason that it has been decided to send envoys far across the seas and make an earnest appeal to foreign countries. Should they refuse our proposals and insist on execution of the treaty provisions, giving no heed to the difficulties that our country faces, then they will be acting contrary to the true spirit of friendship. Thus even if war should then break out, our national honour will be unharmed. We are therefore anxious that the Bakufu should continue to press on with its preparations for war, even after sending us abroad as its envoys. It must not be thought that all will be accomplished by the speeches of an envoy. Rather, we ask that the Bakufu look upon the dispatch of envoys as something done to maintain our honour should it come to war; and that it should devote itself to the establishment of order within Japan, to uniting national opinion, and completing our military preparations. For our part, we who are being dispatched as envoys, crossing many miles of ocean and encountering many hardships, will exert ourselves to the utmost to fulfil the mission entrusted to us and to put our relations with all countries on a permanent footing. That done, we will return and report.

With respect to the negotiations for closing the port of Kanagawa, there

---

[1] The text is printed in *Bakumatsu Ishin Gaikō Shiryō Shūsei*, vi. 19–22. Kawazu and Kawada were next in seniority to Ikeda as members of the mission to Europe.

are two possible plans. Of these, it is our opinion that the second is the more suitable.

Plan 1. Permanent closing of the port

It is very doubtful whether foreign countries would agree to this. Moreover, we do not believe that in present circumstances this would be desirable in Japan's own interests.

Plan 2. Closing the port for a limited term of years

If we propose closing the port for a period of five, seven, or ten years, it may well be that foreign countries would agree. Moreover, we believe that as matters stand limitation to a term of years might also be desirable in Japan's own interests.

Should the foreigners show understanding of our present difficulties and actually agree to the closing of this port, we would, we believe, be failing to keep faith with them if we did not bear the cost of transferring to other ports their merchants and commercial establishments now in Yokohama. However, this will amount to a very large sum of money. We will have to discuss with them how this is to be done, whether by removing import and export duties on the trade at Hakodate and Nagasaki, or by first collecting the duties at the local customs office and then using these to make annual payments. Then again, there are many traders here from all countries. If the above methods are not acceptable, we might borrow the money jointly from wealthy foreign merchants and make annual repayments from the customs receipts. Since this would be to pay them with their own money, we think it might be an acceptable plan. However, it will probably not be possible to achieve this without the payment of interest. And even if we negotiate on the lines indicated above, they may not agree to our proposals unless we are prepared to make a very large initial payment. In this event we will be unable to give them a definite answer, even if they agree to the closing of the port, for there is a limit to Bakufu resources. Should that be the case, therefore, it might be necessary for us to return and submit a report. However, we think it desirable to learn in advance how large a payment it will be possible for the Bakufu to make.

Once one port is closed, trade will still be permitted at the remaining two. Moreover, the foreign envoys will probably still consider it their duty to remain in the capital to supervise the relations between our respective countries, and we may find it impossible to persuade them to leave. It is desirable, however, that we do everything possible to persuade them to retire to Yokohama. Once the envoys are in Yokohama, their warships would also go there and might perhaps stop going to Shinagawa. And as the Bakufu has at present no pretext at all for forbidding the visits of warships [to Edo], we are inclined to think it as well to try persuading them to this course. Yokohama was originally developed for purposes of foreign trade, and once the port is closed it will lose all means of livelihood. There will thus be nothing else for it but to close its shops or transfer them elsewhere. Yet if the supplies of foodstuffs then become inadequate for the foreign envoys and warships, the envoys may well object and insist on returning to Edo. We are therefore of the opinion that if the Bakufu were to put a stop to the examination of junks at Uraga and transfer that operation to Yokohama, we could sufficiently ensure the commercial prosperity of the latter place; while Uraga, since it is a town of long standing, would probably not present such difficulties in ensuring means of livelihood even though it ceased to be the centre for that examination.

Circumstances might arise in which failure to give detailed explanations concerning the disturbed state of national feeling in Japan would make the foreigners suspicious and so perhaps make it impossible for us fully to achieve the Bakufu's purpose. Thus, since there are times when it is necessary to say secretly that which one would not choose to avow openly, we trust that we have your authority to do so.

Unless we can give an assurance that the Chōshū question is being strictly investigated in accordance with our national laws, our government's prestige will suffer. Indeed, it may even be impossible to prevent the dispatch of foreign warships. And should foreign military pressure force the Bakufu to take action, after the arrival of such warships, opinion in Japan will become more and more antagonistic. It is, we believe, very much to our advantage that the Bakufu should prevent any such eventuality by dispatching the present mission. We are therefore anxious that the Bakufu should at once take suitable steps to dispose of this question. Should it be impossible for the Bakufu at this time to take such practical measures as would demonstrate the sincerity of its intentions in this matter, we ask that we may be told, for our own information alone, what steps it is planned to take. Without this, we shall have no explanation to offer to the foreigners, and will thereby be much embarrassed. We therefore ask that we may receive instructions on this point.

With regard to the murder committed at Itogaya village,[1] it would be most unfortunate if this were to involve us in some such indemnity as was paid to England.[2] We therefore think it best that we should inform the French government frankly that we are fully prepared to pay compensation, but only to the immediate family of the victim.

The year before last, when the Bakufu sent envoys to Western countries to arrange postponement of the opening of the two cities and the two

---

[1] On 14 October 1863 Lieutenant Camus, a French army officer stationed at Yokohama, had been murdered at the village of Itogaya, just outside that port. His attackers had not been apprehended.

[2] i.e. for the Namamugi affair. See generally Section V above.

ports,[1] the foreigners claimed a reduction in customs duties. Nothing has been done about this, however. Unless the Bakufu reaches a decision on this point before the present mission sails, its good faith will be brought in question and the impending negotiations will be endangered. We hope, therefore, that an immediate decision will be taken on this. . . .[2]

Apart from the above questions, on which we are seeking instructions in advance, it is probable that the foreigners will themselves raise matters not now foreseen. Since we have been entrusted with this mission, we trust that we have your authority to discuss such points carefully among ourselves and return a definite answer.

Submitted for instructions.

Bakufu instructions with respect to the above[3]

You will negotiate with the object of achieving the permanent closing of the port.

As to the means of paying the costs [of transferring the foreigners in Yokohama to other ports], you may negotiate either of the two methods of payment you have suggested.

Since it is impossible to decide in advance on the amount that can be paid [as an initial payment], you will endeavour, in your negotiations, not to commit us to a heavy outlay; and you will report to us on your return to Edo.

In all other respects you are instructed to proceed as you have proposed in your memorandum.

DOCUMENT 51. Emperor Kōmei to Shōgun Iemochi, 28 February 1864.[4]

Alas! wherever you look, in the conditions that obtain today, you will see that the dangers threatening us are great and imminent indeed. At home, the scene is virtually one of disintegration and collapse: public order has broken down, high and low are disunited, and the people suffer extremes of distress. Abroad, we are subjected to the insults of five arrogant Powers; conquest by them seems certain to be our fate. Thinking of this, I can neither sleep by night nor yet swallow food. And, alas! however one regards these facts, the responsibility is not yours. The fault is mine, and lies in my own want of virtue. What must they say of me, the deities of the universe?

---

[1] See Section IV, The London Protocol.

[2] The next paragraph, which deals only with the question of presents, is here omitted.

[3] This section takes the form of a minute on the foregoing memorandum. There is a further note, dated 3 February 1864, in which the envoys cite and record acceptance of these instructions.

[4] The text is printed in *Zoku saimukiji*, ii. 367-8; and, with small textual variations, in *Kyōto-shugoshoku shimatsu*, Part II, pp. 3-4.

How must they look on me, my forebears in their graves? And for yourself, you must think me the veriest child.

My love for you is as though you were my own son. And you must show affection for me as though I were your father. The Empire's whole hope of recovery depends upon the depth of that affection. How can this be taken lightly? Day and night you must put forth every effort, both of heart and mind, to fulfil the 'barbarian-subduing' duties of your office,[1] so to answer the desires of the Empire's people. The subjugation of the hated foreigner is the greatest of the national tasks that faces us; and it will become possible in the end only if we raise forces with which to chastise them. However, it is not my wish that the expulsion of foreigners be carried out recklessly. You must rather evolve a suitable plan upon deliberation and report it to me. It will be for me to consider its advantages and disadvantages and to determine in detail our fixed and inflexible national policy.

It has long been my wish to accomplish the great task of national revival, which cannot be accomplished without finding suitable men. Now while I see that such men are to be found in some degree among the generality of feudal lords, it is men like the lord of Aizu, the lord of Echizen, Lord Date, the former lord of Tosa, and Lord Shimazu[2] whose depth of loyalty and profundity of thought best fits them at the present time to be entrusted with the direction of state affairs. My love for them is as though they were my children. You must show them affection and make them a party to your counsels.

It is my wish that you and I should together vow to restore the declining fortunes of our country. On the one side we must submit our plans to the spirits of my Imperial predecessors, on the other succour the distress of the people. And if, through idleness, we fail to achieve success, how much the greater will be our crime! The deities of the universe themselves would punish us. Be most diligent, therefore!

DOCUMENT 52. Emperor Kōmei to Shōgun Iemochi, 5 March 1864.[3]

Although unworthy, I early succeeded to the august throne of my fathers[4] and assumed care of this land that has been inviolate through ages eternal.

---

[1] The reference is to the *sei-i* of *Sei-i-tai-shōgun*. See Document 3, p. 106, note 3, and Document 40, p. 233, note 2.

[2] i.e. Matsudaira Katamori of Aizu; Matsudaira Keiei of Echizen; Date Muneki of Uwajima; Yamanouchi Toyoshige of Tosa; and Shimazu Hisamitsu of Satsuma.

[3] The text is printed in *Iwakura Kō Jikki*, i. 781–3; also, with small textual variations, in *Zoku saimukiji*, ii. 380–2, and *Kyōto-shugoshoku shimatsu*, Part II, pp. 5–7.

[4] By Western reckoning, Kōmei was not quite fifteen years old at the time of his accession in March 1846.

And being of little virtue, I fear, I have often failed my Imperial predecessors and my people. Especially is this so with regard to the Western barbarians who since 1853 have come raging to our harbours. Their coming has resulted in a serious rise in commodity prices and the infliction of deep distress on our people, to say nothing of the danger to our national prestige [*kokutai*]. What must they say of me, the deities of the universe? Alas! whose is the blame? Day and night I think on this and cannot cease.

Some time ago I ordered Court nobles and Bakufu officials to give thought to this problem. What are we to do? After more than two hundred years of peace, our military might is not adequate to the task of subjugating the foreigners; and should we seek recklessly to chastise them, I fear, we might instead bring unforeseen disaster upon our country.

The Bakufu has given decisive effect to my wishes and reformed the evil practices that have persisted for over ten generations [of Tokugawa Shōgun]: in the country at large, it has relaxed the requirements concerning the residence of *daimyō* in Edo,[1] has allowed the wives and children of *daimyō* to return [from Edo] to their fiefs, and has issued orders to the fiefs for the completion of military preparations; within the Bakufu itself, it has removed superfluous officials, reduced expenditures, and undertaken the construction of guns and warships on a large scale. By so doing, it has pleased not only myself, but our ancestors and our people. Moreover, it was highly commendable that the Shōgun last spring revived an abandoned custom and came to Kyōto in person. By contrast, Fujiwara Sanetomi[2] and others have given credence rather to the falsehoods of irresponsible *rōnin*. Ignorant of world conditions and heedless of the danger to our country, they misrepresented the instructions I had given and recklessly announced orders for the expulsion of foreigners. Without authority, they sought to raise forces against the Bakufu. Thereupon certain violent retainers of the lord of Chōshū, without cause and in defiance of their lord, opened fire on foreign ships. They murdered the envoy sent to them by the Bakufu and secretly carried off [Sanjō] Sanetomi and others to their own province. There can be no question but that the perpetrators of such violence must be punished. And yet, indeed, all this is due to my own want of virtue. For this I feel unceasing remorse.

To my mind, compared with the ships and guns of the arrogant foreigners, our own ships and guns will not yet suffice to quell their boldness. They will not yet suffice to demonstrate our national might beyond the seas. In fact, it would seem that our weakness makes us despised by the Western barbarian. It is therefore my wish that here at home the Bakufu put forth the whole strength of the Empire in preparing defences for the vital

---

[1] The reference is to the *sankin-kōtai* system. See Glossary.

[2] i.e. Sanjō Sanetomi, who with six other *kuge* fled to Chōshū after the *coup d'état* carried out by the *kōbu-gattai* party on 30 September 1863. The Sanjō family was a branch of the Fujiwara.

harbours of the Settsu coast,[1] thus at once ensuring the safety of the Imperial mausolea and safeguarding our people. Again, the power of the great fiefs must be used to prepare defences for all important harbours in their territories. Looking abroad, numerous warships must be built, to make possible the subjugation of the hated and insatiable foreigner. Thus must be carried out the punishment decreed for them by my Imperial predecessor.

You, the Shōgun, made a long stay in Kyōto last year. This spring you have come again. The *daimyō*, too, are taking an active part in affairs both here and at Edo; and since their wives and children have now been sent back to the fiefs, there is no reason why financial difficulties should prevent them hereafter from making military preparations.[2] You will therefore make every effort to reduce expenditure on peaceful and time-wasting projects. You will unite the strength and will of the whole Empire to effect means of subjugating the foreigners. You will exert yourself to the utmost in fulfilling the duties of your military office and thereby avoid bringing lasting disgrace upon your family name. You, the Shōgun, and the lords of every province, both great and small, are all my children. It is my wish that you join with me in revolutionizing the present position of our country. Without destroying the wealth of our people, equally without encouraging idleness and luxury, you are to make the strictest preparations for the chastisement of the foreigners and exert yourself in the traditional duties of your house. If you should fail in this, not only will you be acting contrary to my own particular desires, but you will also be lacking in obedience to the spirits of my Imperial Ancestors. You would be in conflict with the wishes of your own ancestors. What would they say of you, the deities of the universe?

DOCUMENT 53. Shōgun Iemochi to Emperor Kōmei, 21 March 1864.[3]

I am most profoundly moved that in the Imperial letter which was communicated to me on 5 March the Emperor should have taken upon himself responsibility for all the misfortunes that have befallen our country since his accession. When I reflect upon the mistakes that have been made by the Bakufu hitherto, I am conscious how much there is that merits blame. Not only have I, Iemochi, of my incapacity, disgraced my office, and by my failure to enforce order brought troubles upon my country both

---

[1] i.e. Hyōgo and Ōsaka.

[2] It had long been argued by *tozama* lords that the Bakufu's policy of involving them in heavy expenditure for the upkeep of large establishments in Edo, a policy calculated to keep them poor and therefore quiescent, was in fact hampering their efforts to construct defences.

[3] The text is printed in *Iwakura Kō Jikki*, i. 784–5; and, with small textual variations, in *Zoku saimukiji*, ii. 420–2.

at home and abroad, thus causing the Emperor deep distress; but also, despite the fact that I accepted the Emperor's command to carry out the expulsion of foreigners, when I came to Kyōto last spring, I have proved unable in the end to put that order into effect. Indeed, even in the matter of negotiating the closing of Yokohama, I cannot yet tell when we shall achieve success. With matters standing thus, I have again come to Kyōto at the Emperor's bidding. When I did so, I was convinced that the Emperor would be most incensed and that I should be severely reprimanded. Yet in fact, to my surprise, I have received the Emperor's commendation. More than that, the Emperor, of his surpassing benevolence, has been pleased to express his love for myself and for the feudal lords, both great and small, as though we were his own children. He has given us advice for our future guidance. This is to me personally a matter for the utmost gratitude, such, indeed, as I cannot find words to express.

I shall continue hereafter in all things to carry out the Emperor's stipulations: to reform the long-standing evils in administration and treat the feudal lords with the consideration due to brothers, so uniting all our strength and will in the path of duty as servants of the Emperor; to exert every effort towards reducing unnecessary expenditure on peaceful and time-wasting projects; to intensify military preparations; to establish order in the country and relieve the distress of the people; to complete the defences not only of the Settsu coast, but also of all other provinces, so that we may put an end to Western insults; and to press on with the construction of warships and cannon, thus making it possible at length to accomplish the great task of chastising the foreigners and demonstrate our national might beyond the seas. All this I shall do in the hope that I may set the Emperor's mind at rest. I shall, however, strictly observe the Emperor's injunction that the chastisement of foreigners be not carried out recklessly. I shall make plans that are certain of success. With respect to the closing of Yokohama, I have already sent envoys abroad and am most anxious that success may be achieved; but as we cannot tell what attitude the foreigners will adopt, I continue strictly to fulfil my military duties and to devote serious attention to coast defence. With respect to matters of State in general, I shall in all things submit national policies, once formulated, for Imperial decision. Thus shall the declining fortunes of the Empire be restored. Abroad, we shall quell the boldness of the arrogant barbarian. At home, we shall protect our people. The mind of the Emperor shall be set at rest. I, Iemochi, do most earnestly desire that we may on the one hand revere the will of the Imperial Ancestors, and on the other fulfil the commands of my own forebears. This it is that I, Iemochi, do most devoutly pray. I accordingly submit my formal acceptance of the Imperial commands.

Offered with the profoundest respect.

DOCUMENT 54. Hara Tadanari to Minobe Matagorō and Nomura Teijitsu, Kyōto, 25 March 1864.[1]

I believe that you will already have heard from Umezawa[2] of the course of
events up to 19 March. On the 21st the Shōgun went to the Palace and
submitted his formal acceptance of the Imperial letter of 5 March. He was
then informed that the statement he had made therein concerning the
closing of Yokohama, namely, that it was impossible to tell what attitude
the foreigners would adopt in this matter, was entirely contrary to the
Emperor's wishes. It was not enough, he was told, that the question be
handled in so irresolute a manner: resolute action must be taken to close
the port.

On the 22nd Lord Hitotsubashi, Matsudaira Keiei, and others were
summoned to the Palace, where the *Kampaku* [Nijō Nariaki], Prince
Asahiko, Prince Akira, the *Naidaijin* Konoe [Tadafusa] and the *Udaijin*
Tokudaiji [Kinjun] were in council in the Emperor's presence. Lord
Keiki was first called in alone. The *Kampaku* and Prince Asahiko communicated to him an Imperial pronouncement to the effect that in the
Emperor's view it was necessary to take resolute action for closing the port.
Lord Keiki expressed his deep gratitude for the instructions the Emperor
had issued. That such orders should have been given, he said, conforming
as they did with the Bakufu's original plans and all our most cherished
desires, was a matter for the utmost satisfaction. However, the Emperor
had stated in his earlier letter that he had no desire for the expulsion of
foreigners to be carried out recklessly. The Shōgun had accordingly felt
compelled to moderate his views to some degree and had submitted his
acceptance of these orders in pacific terms. Lord Keiki stated it as his
view, indeed, that the present instructions must be regarded as a great
boon to the Empire. And when it was put to him that no such statement
had appeared in the Imperial letter, he expressed great surprise. The
original had been deposited with the Bakufu, he said, though he could
send for it to show them; but as the draft must be readily available, perusal
of this would clarify the position. It proved, however, that no copy of the
draft was in the Court's possession.

(It was explained to Lord Keiki that on both occasions[3] the draft of

[1] The text is printed in *Tokugawa Keiki Kō Den*, vi. 37–45. Hara Tadanari, Ichi-no-shin, was
a samurai of Mito in the service of Hitotsubashi Keiki. Although writing from Kyōto, his
account of events is regarded as being too highly coloured to be entirely reliable, because of his
sonnō-jōi sympathies. However, it is certain that disagreements did occur on the occasions he
describes, even if they were less extravagantly expressed. Minobe and Nomura were also Mito
samurai and members of the *sonnō-jōi* group.
[2] Umezawa Sontarō, another Mito samurai in Keiki's service.
[3] The passage refers to the letters both of 28 February and of 5 March (Documents 51 and 52),
though it was in the former that the disputed statement appears.

the Imperial letter had been made by Takasaki Itarō,[1] then taken to the Palace and submitted to the Emperor late in the day by Prince Asahiko. It had been approved during the night and issued, by request, first thing the following morning, though still in draft form. For this reason not even the Emperor himself had perused it closely.)

Of course, Keiki was told, it would be most unfortunate if such a statement did prove to be in the letter. It would be necessary to secure Imperial sanction for the issue of a corrected version. The other copy, therefore, should be suppressed. Keiki explained, however, that it was impossible to suppress the letter now, as it had already been announced to the great fiefs that morning. On being told that the Bakufu had acted too quickly, that it would have been better to have held up for a time the announcement to the fiefs, he explained that he had considered this step to be unobjectionable, since the Shōgun's formal acceptance had been in the Court's hands the previous day; and, moreover, that since the Imperial letter, once issued, was of great importance to the State, he had not expected the Court to complain of the speed of Bakufu action. The council agreed that in the circumstances nothing could now be done. However, the Bakufu must at all costs take steps to ensure that the closing of the port be effected with resolution. That being so, Keiki said, he was forced to ask that a further Imperial letter be written, dealing solely with this matter of resolute action to close Yokohama. This would then be announced to the fiefs, together with a fresh statement by the Bakufu.

It having been agreed that this course would be acceptable, Keiei, Ōsumi, and Iyo[2] were summoned into conference and questioned in similar fashion. With one voice, however, the three men declared that while they did not know what answer Hitotsubashi had made, they believed the closing of Yokohama to be quite impossible. The Bakufu must not accept orders to effect it, they said, and they were quite unable to understand the Shōgun's action in submitting his acceptance the previous day. At this, Lord Keiki became very angry. The three men, he said, spoke most unworthily. In the early part of the month, when disputes had arisen in discussing whether or not to close the port, all three had expressed themselves in favour of keeping it open. They had threatened to retire to their fiefs[3] if the Bakufu did not act accordingly. However, since such a split would have been contrary to the Court's expressed desire for unity, they had gradually modified their position and agreed to support the views of the Bakufu. This apart, Keiki said, the fact was that the Shōgun had submitted his formal acceptance of the Emperor's instruc-

---

[1] A samurai of Satsuma, acting here on behalf of Shimazu Hisamitsu.

[2] i.e. Matsudaira Keiei; Shimazu Hisamitsu, Ōsumi-no-kami; and Date Muneki, Iyo-no-kami.

[3] i.e. to withdraw their support from the Bakufu, which would also involve a considerable reduction in the pro-Bakufu military forces available in the capital.

tions on the previous day, and there was therefore no reason for further discussion of the advantages or disadvantages of closing the port. It was the disturbance of commodity prices since the opening of foreign trade, and the suffering thereby inflicted on the people, that had caused the present tumults; and while the Bakufu had, of course, no intention of taking any such drastic action as expelling the foreigners from all three of the ports, since the country's strength was not yet developed and it was thought unwise to invite calamity by acting recklessly, yet it had resolved to close the one port of Yokohama without loss of time. Why then, he asked, did they now suggest that the closing of Yokohama was itself undesirable? No view could be more mistaken than that advanced by these three men. His own feeling, indeed, was that even if orders were issued stating that the Emperor favoured the opening of the country, the Shōgun ought respectfully to decline them.

Prince Akira expressed himself much pleased with this statement. What Hitotsubashi had said, he affirmed, was entirely proper. Certainly it was only thus that the national prestige [*kokutai*] could be maintained and national unity ensured. The *Kampaku* and Prince Asahiko spoke to the same effect. The three miscreants, however, with every appearance of anger, said that if it was intended to adopt such reckless measures, and so destroy the Empire, then their own participation in affairs was useless and they would retire to their fiefs; the Court had better send for the lord of Chōshū and his son, and entrust to them the task of expelling the foreigners.

Lord Keiki said that he had never anticipated that such inexcusable statements could be made. In the first place, the task of expelling foreigners had been entrusted to the Bakufu during the Shōgun's [previous] stay in Kyōto. Even had that not been so, the Imperial instructions which had been received on the present occasion made it impossible to talk of entrusting the task to anyone else. Was it not disgraceful, he asked, to make such inexcusable statements in the presence of the Emperor? Thus questioned, the three men were quite silenced and the council came to an end, the matter being deferred for subsequent discussion. . . .[1]

When Lord Keiki went to Nijō Castle on the afternoon of 23 March, the three miscreants were in the council-chamber used by the Bakufu ministers, at which he was much surprised.

(Their admittance to the council-chamber had been ordered by the Court, but up to this time had been avoided in practice. Keiei, however, had taken advantage of his authority as *Shugoshoku*[2] to decide the

---

[1] A short passage containing Hara's own comments (p. 40, line 14 to p. 41, line 7 in the printed text) is here omitted.

[2] Matsudaira Katamori had just been appointed second-in-command of the Bakufu forces to be sent against Chōshū, and Matsudaira Keiei had become *Kyōto-shugoshoku* in his stead. The

question. From this day one must date the decline of Tokugawa authority.)

Keiki took his seat as if noticing nothing. Ōsumi [Shimazu] and Iyo [Date] explained that in view of what had happened at the Court the previous day, Takasaki Itarō had that morning seen Prince Asahiko. He had been told by the Prince that the whole affair was due to a temporary and unavoidable concatenation of circumstance: that the facts [of the Imperial letter] had been misrepresented and the matter had best be dropped. They also said that Itarō's oral account was not of itself enough to make the position clear, so they planned to call upon the Prince and make further inquiry. They proposed that the council should wait for a while until this discussion had taken place.

Lord Keiki expressed surprise at this. The arrangement would not do, he said; he would himself call upon the Prince and ask about the matter. And orders having been given that they should all go, Keiei called on the others to accompany him and went to Prince Asahiko's residence.

No formal greetings were exchanged.[1] They had been told, Keiki explained, that the Prince had made a statement that morning to Takasaki Itarō, telling him that at the Palace the previous day the Imperial orders had been misrepresented[2] and that he therefore thought the matter had best be dropped. They were calling upon him because they wished to ask exactly what he had said on this occasion. To this the Prince replied that he was not aware of having made any such statement. It was then explained to him that they were making this visit because [Shimazu] Saburō had so reported. The Prince invited them all to be seated to examine into this matter. Shimazu said not a word, except what politeness required. Prince Asahiko explained that Itarō had certainly visited him that morning and had expressed his concern at what had happened the previous day. The Prince had therefore conversed with him for a while, but that was all. Nothing had been said about truth or falsity of representation.

That being so, Lord Keiki said, it was not impossible that the Prince had spoken ambiguously. He had conversed informally about an important matter of State with one who was no more than a sub-vassal. It was thus that the misunderstanding arose. The whole Empire, after all, knew

arrangement lasted only a few weeks, however, and Katamori was then reappointed to his former post.

[1] In reading the account of the meeting that follows, Hara's prejudices have to be borne in mind. Both the records of Matsudaira Keiei (*Zoku saimukiji*, ii. 430–2) and those of Date Muneki (*Date Muneki Zaikyō Nikki*, pp. 340–1) assert that Keiki was drunk on this occasion; and if Hara reports him accurately, his lack of verbal restraint certainly lends colour to this assertion.

[2] This is apparently a reference to the previous day's difference of opinion between Keiki and Asahiko, about whether or not the Imperial letter had contained an injunction that expulsion was not to be carried out 'recklessly'.

the trickery of Satsuma men. The Prince alone trusted them. He must surely perceive that it was because the Prince had himself been deceived that misunderstanding had thus been created between them. The safety of the whole Empire turned on the problems now confronting them. For this reason, Keiki confessed, it had been his intention to seek a full explanation from the Prince, and then, if he continued to talk about 'misrepresentation', to take first the Prince's life and then his own. His sword had been ready. But once the Prince had said that he had no recollection of making any such statement, there was no reason to insist on further inquiries.

However, Keiki continued, Court policy on this question had never been firmly based. It seemed liable to constant change. Incidents such as this would certainly shake the Empire's confidence [in its rulers]. And, he feared, if the Emperor's letters came to be used as instruments whereby men might be deceived, the whole Empire might cease to hold the Throne in awe. Such things compromised its dignity in every way. Notwithstanding what he had said the previous day, therefore, consideration of the existing state of affairs had convinced him that no useful purpose would be served by asking for the issue of a new Imperial letter. He accordingly proposed that a document be submitted next day by the Rōjū, recording formal Bakufu acceptance of a policy of resolute action to close Yokohama. If the Prince agreed that the foregoing statements did not constitute misrepresentation [of the Imperial orders], he would ask him to use his influence to ensure that the Court would pronounce itself satisfied with such a promise of resolute action to close the port. An announcement to this effect would then be made to the fiefs. He no longer asked, Keiki said, that the Imperial letter be revised.

As he said this, Lord Keiki's voice and expression were severe. Prince Asahiko and the other three said not a word. Their faces were ashen. After a time, Prince Asahiko said that he would use all his influence to ensure that the Emperor found this arrangement satisfactory; and he would therefore communicate with Keiki the next day. . . .[1]

DOCUMENT 55. Shōgun to Imperial Court, 26 March 1864.[2]

It is understood that instructions have been communicated privately to

[1] The rest of the letter (from p. 43, line 11 in the printed text) is not translated. It reports a violent and largely incoherent verbal attack by Keiki on Date, Shimazu, and Matsudaira Keiei, after which Keiki left. This is followed by Hara's own comments on the situation. It is clear from other records, however, that Keiki's intoxicated departure did not end the meeting. When he had gone, Asahiko explained to the others that the Court had had no intention of provoking such disagreements. It was concerned only to ensure that the Bakufu was acting in accordance with the advice of the great lords rather than on its own responsibility. This said, it was agreed that the best course, now that the dispute had become public, was for the Bakufu to submit such a statement as Keiki had proposed.

[2] The text is printed in *Ishin-shi*, iii. 688–9; and, with small textual variations, in *Kyōto-shugo-shoku shimatsu*, Part II, pp. 9–10.

[Hitotsubashi] Keiki, stating that the wording of the reference to the closing of Yokohama, contained in the Shōgun's formal acceptance of Imperial orders submitted on 21 March, is not thought by the Court to be sufficiently explicit.

I accordingly wish to submit the following statement. It is my intention eventually to close the port; and as envoys have already been dispatched to foreign countries, I am entirely confident that success will be achieved. I shall, however, respect the instructions, which I have twice received from the Emperor, that the expulsion of foreigners is not to be carried out recklessly. Moreover, I shall continue to take steps to complete the preparation of coast defences.

DOCUMENT 56. The Paris Convention, 20 June 1864.[1]

L'arrangement suivant a été conclu entre le Ministre des Affaires Étrangères et les Ambassadeurs du Japon:

Sa Majesté l'Empereur des Français et Sa Majesté l'Empereur du Japon, désirant consolider par des témoignages d'une mutuelle confiance les relations d'amitié et de commerce qui existent entre les deux pays, ont résolu de régler, d'un commun accord et par arrangement spécial, les difficultés qui se sont élevées entre leurs Gouvernements depuis l'année 1862.

En conséquence, son Excellence M. Drouyn de Lhuys, Ministre Secrétaire d'État au Département des Affaires Étrangères de Sa Majesté l'Empereur des Français; et leurs Excellences Ikeda Tsikougo no Kami, Kawatsou Idzou no Kami, Kawada Sagami no Kami,[2] Ambassadeurs de Sa Majesté le Taicoun, dûment autorisés à cet effet, sont convenus des Articles suivants:

I. En réparation de l'acte d'hostilité commis, au mois de Juillet 1863, contre le bâtiment de la marine impériale le 'Kien Cheng', sur lequel des coups de canon ont été tirés, dans la Province de Nagato, le Gouvernement japonais s'engage à verser entre les mains du Ministre de Sa Majesté l'Empereur des Français à Yedo, trois mois après le retour de leurs Excellences les Ambassadeurs du Taicoun au Japon, une indemnité de 140,000 piastres mexicaines, dont 100,000 piastres seront payées par le Gouvernement lui-même, et 40,000 piastres par l'Autorité de la Province de Nagato.

II. Le Gouvernement japonais s'engage également à faire cesser, dans les

---

[1] The text is printed in *Parliamentary Papers 1865*, vol. lvii, pp. 573–5. Since the agreement was rejected by the Bakufu, of course, the convention never came into operation.

[2] Ikeda Nagaaki, Chikugo-no-kami; Kawazu Sukekuni, Izu-no-kami; and Kawada Hiroshi, Sagami-no-kami.

trois mois qui suivront le retour de leurs Excellences les Ambassadeurs du Taicoun au Japon, les empêchements que rencontrent en ce moment les navires français qui veulent passer le Détroit de Simonoseki, et à maintenir ce passage libre en tout temps, en recourant, si cela est nécessaire, à l'emploi de la force, et, au besoin, en agissant de concert avec le Commandant de la division navale française.

III. Il est convenu entre les deux Gouvernements que, pour favoriser le développement régulier des échanges commerciaux entre la France et le Japon, les réductions de tarifs accordées en dernier lieu par le Gouvernement de Sa Majesté le Taicoun au commerce étranger seront maintenues en faveur des articles importés par des commerçants français, ou sous pavillon français, pendant toute la durée du Traité conclu à Yedo entre les deux pays le 9 Octobre, 1858.

En conséquence, tant que ce Traité demeurera en vigueur, la douane japonaise admettra en franchise les articles suivants destinés à la préparation et à l'emballage des thés — plomb en feuilles, soudures de plomb, nattes, rotins, huiles pour peinture, indigo, gypse, bassines et paniers. Elle percevra seulement un droit de 5 pour cent de la valeur à l'entrée des vins et spiritueux, sucre blanc, fer et fer-blanc, machines et pièces détachées de machines, tissus de lin, horlogerie, montres et chaînes de montres, verreries, médicaments, et un droit de 6 pour cent sur les glaces et miroirs, porcelaines, bijouterie, parfumerie, savons, armes, coutellerie, livres, papiers, gravures et dessins.

IV. Cet arrangement sera considéré comme faisant partie intégrante du Traité du 9 Octobre, 1858, entre la France et le Japon, et il sera immédiatement mis à exécution, sans qu'il soit nécessaire de le soumettre à la ratification des Souverains respectifs.

En foi de quoi, les Plénipotentiaires ci-dessus nommés ont signé le présent arrangement et y ont apposé le sceau de leurs armes.

Fait à Paris, en double original, le vingtième jour du mois de Juin de l'an mil huit cent soixante-quatre.

Document 57. Ikeda Nagaaki, Kawazu Sukekuni, and Kawada Hiroshi to Bakufu, *circa* 18 August 1864.[1]

When we were sent as Bakufu envoys to conduct negotiations with the Treaty Powers concerning the closing of the port of Kanagawa and certain other matters, we went first of all to France. Not only was this the natural

[1] The text is printed in *Bakumatsu Ishin Gaikō Shiryō Shūsei*, vi. 134–7; and, with small textual variations, in *Zoku saimukiji*, iii. 188–99, and *Kaikoku Kigen*, iii. 2665–74. The report itself is dated only Ganji 1, 7th month (2–31 August 1864), but it was submitted to the Bakufu immediately the mission reached Japan, on 18/19 August.

route to travel, but also there were a number of questions outstanding which were of particular concern to that country, such as the Itogaya murder[1] and Chōshū's action in opening fire [on foreign ships]. The intention was, of course, that we should negotiate such an agreement as would prevent the recurrence of difficulties hereafter; but the English and Dutch ministers in Japan, unlike those of other countries, seemed disposed to make difficulties over the Bakufu's plan to close the port. In view of this fact, and because France ranks in importance with England in the world at large, while the present Emperor, Napoleon III, is regarded as outstanding among contemporary European rulers, we considered it probable that if we were able to reach agreement with France, other countries would offer no objections to a similar settlement. For both these reasons, therefore, we made France the first objective of our travels.

We began our negotiations with the Itogaya question and agreed to pay 35,000 dollars from the public finances as compensation to the family of the murdered officer. We then turned to the Chōshū affair. As we had originally proposed,[2] we entered into a number of discussions in which we explained confidentially what action the Bakufu proposed to take in this matter. But the French demanded both an indemnity and the opening of the Shimonoseki Straits to shipping. The opening of the straits was a very reasonable request and we promised that the Bakufu would take appropriate action. The demand for an indemnity, however, seemed less reasonable and we made some demur. At this point Siebold, the former Dutch surgeon in Japan, came to Paris, so we sought his advice. By his account, France sent warships [to Chōshū] after the initial attack on her shipping[3] for the specific purpose of avenging the insult to her flag and only for that purpose; since those warships were dispatched as a consequence of an open and unjustified act of hostility, under the law common to all Western countries Japan would be held responsible for the ensuing expenses. He cited as an example the fact that until recent years France had herself been paying an annual indemnity because her former ruler, Napoleon I, had sent forces to invade other countries. This being so, we could no longer insist that the French demand was unjustified. Furthermore, we realized on reflection that if we offended the French and failed utterly to convince them of the friendly intentions of our own government, it would be quite impossible for us to succeed in negotiating the closing of Kanagawa. We therefore abandoned our former stand and resumed the discussions, resolved that we would pay the indemnity. In the course of discussions further difficulties arose because we differed concerning the

[1] The murder of Lieutenant Camus on 14 October 1863. Cf. Document 50, p. 262 and note.
[2] See Document 50.
[3] On 20 July 1863 two French naval vessels had bombarded the Shimonoseki batteries in retaliation for the attack on the dispatch boat *Kien Cheng* twelve days earlier.

sum to be paid, but since we considered the negotiations that were to follow to be more important, we settled these amicably and reached agreement in general accordance with the French request.

We finally turned our attention to negotiations for the closing of Kanagawa. The French observed that the Bakufu had not yet carried out the stipulations of the agreement made when envoys were sent to arrange postponement of the opening of the two ports and the two cities.[1] This, they claimed, was equivalent to a breach of treaty. They had therefore agreed with the English and Dutch governments that the sole action now to be taken was, as had been laid down during those earlier negotiations, to break off discussions and send warships forthwith to negotiate the immediate opening of the two ports and the two cities. They were aware, however, that this would put Japan in considerable difficulties. By way of alternative, therefore, they proposed that the Bakufu should permit trade duty-free at the three ports already open.

In response to this unforeseen and unreasonable demand we argued that in all the countries of the West there was not one which permitted trade entirely free of duty. Admittedly one might point to one or two places like Hamburg in the German Confederation as examples, but these, we said, had always been known as *freistaaten* and were in no way to be compared with Japan, since they had no monarch and were governed by a council of citizens. Among States which were comparable with Japan, not one such example could be given. Moreover, such a step would be all the more to our disadvantage in that our own commercial organization within Japan itself was undeveloped. It would be different, we argued, if there were any reason to expect that this would bring some immediate benefit to Japan. But that was not so. It was impossible, we urged upon them again and again, for us to take any step that would put our country at such a disadvantage.

At this point it seemed likely that discussions would be broken off. Nor did there seem much prospect of engaging them in negotiations for the closing of Kanagawa. None the less, we made every effort to persuade them to this, insisting on the absolute friendliness of Bakufu intentions. We pointed to the fact that it had sent us specially across the seas as its envoys, while it was itself making plans to pacify national unrest in order that it might preserve friendly relations with foreign countries. They answered, however, that if the Bakufu were really anxious to maintain friendly relations with them, they were on their part, as evidence of friendship, prepared to use the forces they had in Japan to support the Bakufu in suppressing those turbulent elements who were preventing execution of the treaties.

---

[1] The reference is to the arrangements concerning Hyōgo, Niigata, Edo, and Ōsaka made in the London Protocol. See Section IV.

This, we thought, was something very different from what we had meant in speaking of friendship. Yet for the Bakufu to refuse French support, in face of such an offer of joint action, would seem to contradict its claim of friendly intentions. Even if the French had aggressive designs on Japan and were concealing their real purpose, superficially this must seem a gesture of exceptional friendliness. That is how it would sound to the Great Powers. It would make it impossible for us to lay the blame on the French, should our attempt to achieve the closing of Kanagawa end in failure. Moreover, since the Itogaya and Chōshū questions had already been disposed of, only this one matter was left outstanding. It was apparent that if Japan acquired a reputation for injustice and herself broke off the negotiations, this would destroy all hope of securing our main object. In fact, it would be to put ourselves at the foreigners' mercy. Far from there being any question of closing Kanagawa, we should in fact be enabling them to accomplish all their desires, even to the matter of the date for opening the two ports and the two cities.

Then again, close examination of conditions among Western countries reveals that while all of them covet our country and are merely awaiting a suitable opportunity before attacking us, they are aware that they will find it difficult to pursue a long struggle with their forces so far from home across the seas. They are concerned, moreover, lest it prove impossible for them to find means of terminating the conflict should a struggle for advantage develop among themselves. Once the Suez Canal is completed, of course, Western warships will be able to proceed direct to Eastern waters without rounding the Cape of Good Hope and the sea route will be reduced to a third of its present length. Should it then happen that fresh incidents occur in Japan, such as make it difficult for the Bakufu to keep faith with foreign countries and provide the foreigners with occasion for anger, the foreigners, as it seems to us, may well band themselves together and progressively concert their plans for the conquest of the East. Now let us set against this a survey of the present state of affairs in Japan. It was thought that full agreement between Court and Bakufu would follow from the Shōgun's recent visit to Kyōto. Yet it still proves impossible to unite national opinion. Harmony is still to be achieved among our people. Nor are our military preparations yet complete by land or sea. It would be disastrous for us now to incur the enmity of the five [Treaty] Powers and the other foreign countries. To do so might well jeopardize the safety and very existence of our whole country. Such a course, indeed, would be most impolitic.

Having given careful thought and consideration to this state of affairs at home and abroad, we are anxious that the Bakufu should now act as follows: first and foremost, we hope that it will exert itself in plans to maintain our national independence against all countries; that it will make every effort to suppress by force opposition at home and confirm the authority of the government; that it will give the foreigners no pretext for fresh demands nor any opportunity of which they could take advantage; that it will pursue a friendly policy towards them, strictly honouring the treaties and breaking none of their provisions; and that it will take steps at once to complete the equipment of our land and sea forces.

From our careful study of the activities of the Western countries it would seem that they are all seeking opportunities to carry out aggressive designs against each other. As things now stand, it appears likely that all the countries of Europe will be involved in a major war within some three to five years. Once, therefore, the Bakufu has suppressed internal unrest and established law and order in Japan, it will be able to take advantage of the divisions among foreigners in formulating its foreign policy. If, on the other hand, we are at this time guilty of a breach of treaty, it is beyond doubt that all countries would unite against us and that European conflicts would thereby be resolved. This for us would be a national disaster.

While it is with some hesitation that we submit this report, it is based on a close and careful study of the situation. As we have stated above, such study shows that when we sought to explain Bakufu action in proposing the closing of Kanagawa as something unavoidable, a policy undertaken not because it was the wish of our government but because it was forced upon us by national unrest within Japan, the French revealed a kind of friendship for our country which was very different from that we had meant to suggest. Arguing from this to the attitude of Western countries in general, one sees that in fact they despise our country and harbour designs against it. Thus if we insist upon this argument [as an explanation of Bakufu policy], we shall in effect be betraying the weakness of our government. This of itself would lower our prestige. It would, we fear, be the greatest possible dishonour to our country. And should the foreigners claim that our action constituted a breach of treaty, there is no telling what intolerable demands they might make. Were we then to find ourselves with no choice but to break off negotiations, we would, to our grief, be in the position of having committed a blunder of the gravest moment to our country.

In view of these facts, we entered into further detailed explanations with the French. We emphasized the sincerity of our government's intentions; and [since they seemed inclined generally to accept this point][1] we informed them that although we felt compelled to refuse the proposal for duty-free trade, the request might be reconsidered if they in turn would consent to negotiations for the closing of Kanagawa. They replied that no matter how often we broached this subject, they must always reject out-

---

[1] The clause given here in square brackets appears only in the *Bakumatsu Ishin Gaikō Shiryō Shūsei* text.

right the closing of Kanagawa, for England and the other countries had shown themselves unwilling to accept it. However, they said, our envoys had convinced them of the Japanese government's friendliness; and the French Emperor, having heard of late of our country's need for warships, had expressed himself entirely willing, as a mark of the special friendship he bore towards Japan, to hand over to us some ships from his own fleet. No clear statement was made concerning negotiations for the abolition of duties at the three open ports, but we were well satisfied that this question should be separated from that of negotiations for the closing of Kanagawa. We therefore took advantage of this opportunity to bring the talks to an end and sign the agreement. They did inform us that if all the other countries expressed agreement with the closing of Kanagawa, they would then be willing to reopen the question, but this statement was made in the confident expectation that other countries would not express such agreement and is not in any way to be trusted.

As we have already explained, all this has happened despite the fact that France was in general somewhat conciliatory in its approach to the question of closing Kanagawa. It seemed clear to us, therefore, that even if we went next to England, that country would not agree to our request, however much we urged it; and this we had all the more reason to suppose from the fact that when we had an interview in Shanghai with Alcock, the first minister sent by England to Japan, and explained to him the general nature of the Bakufu's wishes, he informed us that his government was already resolved to demand the immediate opening of the two cities and the two ports in certain circumstances and that he thought they would most certainly reject our proposals. Since England and France reacted in this way, it seemed beyond question that other countries would be equally firm. Moreover, even though one or two countries might possibly agree to our proposals, there could be no possibility of accomplishing matters in accordance with the Bakufu's desires so long as these two Powers refused their consent. What was more, where England was concerned there was the additional problem of an attack made on some Englishmen at Nagasaki this spring. Knowing that the Bakufu might not have been immediately able to complete its investigations of this affair, we were unable to determine whether or no it would be possible to keep the two questions quietly apart, as we had done in our discussions with France. Were they to claim, as might well happen, that our proposals constituted a breach of treaty, and were they eventually to exploit this pretext to the point of using military force to put pressure upon Japan, then for all our plea that the Bakufu had had no choice but to act as it did, our negotiations would have ended in failure. Indeed, they would have led to the most regrettable of misfortunes for both parties. Then again, we had been entrusted with an important letter of State. Should this letter by any chance be treated with contempt, our guilt would clearly be beyond all redemption. In a matter so vital to the national prestige [*kokutai*] a settlement could never be reached without recourse to war. And what the outcome would be in that event we have already explained. We would be powerless to prevent the collapse of our country. Moreover, we very much fear that the secret opposition groups within Japan would inevitably seize this opportunity to put their evil schemes into operation.

In view of these facts, we discussed the position fully among ourselves several times and sought the advice of all those with us, even of the subordinate officials attached to the mission. It seemed that it might be wise for either [Ikeda] Chikugo-no-kami or [Kawazu] Izu-no-kami to leave France and return to Japan to submit a report on the whole situation, the other remaining meanwhile to act as envoy. We discussed this fully, but decided that it would not be a justifiable course. Such action would not look well, while for all we could tell the one who was acting as envoy might meanwhile meet with unforeseen difficulties, in that he must continue to urge the Bakufu's views as we had been doing in our negotiations hitherto. We came to the conclusion, therefore, that it would best serve the interests of the country if we were all to return to Edo for the time being and report the situation in full, as we had suggested in our original request for instructions,[1] stating frankly our belief that the Bakufu could commit no greater mistake than to involve Japan in war for the sake of closing Kanagawa.

We arranged [with the French] that once the Bakufu had taken steps to maintain the treaties and establish a basis for permanent friendship, envoys would again be sent to announce this circumstance to foreign countries; and that we would at that time return again to France. Moreover, of the countries to which we had been accredited, it had been expected that we would take this opportunity of discussing the Chōshū question with Holland and America, while we had intended to touch on the Kagoshima question in our discussions with England even though that incident was now closed. To this end, we had been provided with appropriate letters from the Bakufu. We accordingly sent letters to the governments of these three countries, separately and in our own names, explaining our reasons for returning temporarily to Japan.

(When we communicated with the English envoy in these terms, he replied, in accordance with the orders he had received from his country's Foreign Secretary, that to ask the Queen for changes in the treaties would be of no avail and that further discussion of this matter could only be regarded as useless.)

We also sent letters to the Prussian, Russian, and Portuguese ministers resi-

[1] See Document 50.

dent in Paris informing them of our change of plans. It had also been intended that we should go to Switzerland to conclude a treaty, but while this was quite distinct from our business with other countries, there seemed no good reason for going to that country only, when we had decided to abandon our more important negotiations and return temporarily to Japan to seek the Bakufu's instructions. In this case also, therefore, we sent a letter to the Swiss minister resident in Paris informing him of our change of plan. On 20 June we left Paris to await the mail-packet at Marseilles. On 28 June we boarded an English mail boat and set out for Japan.

Speaking generally, for the Bakufu to lay the foundations of national independence it is fundamental that national unity be attained within Japan. Special attention must be paid to the equipment of our land and sea forces, of course, and also to our relations with foreign countries. And the Bakufu must be resolute in performing its engagements. It is thus of the first importance that we study conditions abroad. In our view, therefore, the following steps are desirable:

1. that Resident Ministers be sent to all the countries of Europe;
2. that treaties be concluded not only with European countries but also with all other independent countries; and that we plan in the event of need to ally ourselves with some when in conflict with others;
3. that in order to avail ourselves of Western skills in land and sea warfare, students be sent abroad to study these things;
4. that we subscribe to the various Western newspaper organizations and so inform ourselves of world conditions;
5. that our people be permitted to travel freely to foreign countries, both to trade and to make themselves familiar with conditions overseas.

We have reported separately on these questions,[1] and we trust that the government will give these reports careful perusal. If, as we have recommended, the Bakufu sets aside its plan to close Kanagawa and exerts itself to lay the foundations of national independence, it will be strengthening the national prestige [*kokutai*] and ensuring that our national dignity be not sullied. Should foreign countries then behave in a faithless and dishonest manner, the whole of the blame can be laid upon them. And even though the Bakufu does not achieve thereby the closing of Kanagawa, there could be no course more truly exhibiting respect towards the Emperor. We believe, with all respect, that the Emperor's mind may thus be set at rest. If, therefore, the Bakufu reports in all sincerity to

[1] A separate report was devoted to each of these five points. See *Bakumatsu Ishin Gaikō Shiryō Shūsei*, vi. 141-50, and *Zoku saimukiji*, iii. 199-217.

Kyōto what we have here set down as the result of direct and careful observation, it is our belief that the Emperor will express himself completely satisfied.

We forward herewith the minutes of the discussions we held while in France; the text of the agreement we have concluded;[1] the original and translation of the receipt for the [Itogaya] indemnity; copies of the letters we sent to the Resident Ministers of other countries when we left Paris and their replies to these; copies of our letters to the Foreign Ministers of England, America, and Holland; and newspaper articles which we had published to ensure that there be no misunderstanding with respect to our activities.

Submitted with respect.

DOCUMENT 58. Minutes of a conference between the Ministers in Japan of Great Britain, France, the United States and the Netherlands, and the *gaikoku-bugyō* Takemoto Masao, held at Yokohama, 18 September 1864.[2]

The British Envoy informed the Japanese officials that Her Majesty's ship 'Perseus' arrived, as he had anticipated, only a few hours after Takemoto had taken his leave yesterday. By this vessel despatches had been received from the senior naval officers by his colleagues and himself, acquainting them that in two days the whole of the batteries of the Prince of Nagato had been silenced, and the force collected for their defence defeated and entirely dispersed. . . .[3]

From all which the British Envoy observed there was this conclusion to be drawn, that the Prince of Choshiu, notwithstanding all his vaunted power and long preparation, in a position of great natural strength, had been utterly unable to defend his batteries against the allied forces, and in three days all his troops having been defeated and dispersed, not a gun was left in any of his forts, and he himself had found it necessary to sue for peace. But there was another conclusion brought out by that which followed these events. The Prince declared that hitherto he had only acted under the orders of the Mikado and Tycoon, that he had no enmity himself against foreigners, but was perfectly willing to enter into friendly relations.

---

[1] See Document 56.

[2] This text is printed in *Parliamentary Papers 1865*, vol. lvii, pp. 670–3, and is signed by the ministers of the four Western Powers, namely Rutherford Alcock, Léon Roches, R. H. Pruyn, and D. de Graeff van Polsbroek. The Japanese officials present, in addition to Takemoto Masao, Kai-no-kami, included the *gaikoku-bugyō* Shibata Masanaka, Hyūga-no-kami.

[3] The joint naval attack on the Shimonoseki batteries had been completed by 14 September and a truce signed with Chōshū. The details given are here omitted. Here and elsewhere in this document, the *daimyō* of Chōshū is variously referred to as 'the Prince of Nagato' and 'the Prince of Choshiu'.

Such being the substance of the news brought by the 'Perseus' and the result of the operations against the Prince of Choshiu, who had held the Straits closed by batteries for fifteen months, it was now necessary to advert more especially to the Prince's alleged justification of this long violation of Treaties. The Prince not only declared that, as a Daimio of Japan, he had acted under the orders both of the Mikado and of the Tycoon in all that he had done, but he further produced certified copies in Japanese of those orders.[1] The foreign Representatives, under these circumstances, desired to know what answer the Tycoon's Government had to make to this direct charge of complicity.

Takemoto no Kami replied that he would shortly have something to say on this subject, but would be glad first to hear anything which the Representatives might further have to communicate.

The French Minister said he was of opinion, in concert with all his colleagues, that the present was a very critical moment in the relations between foreign countries and Japan, and that the time had arrived for a total change in those relations. Hitherto the foreign Representatives had suspected that the Tycoon, under the pressure of many difficulties, had been led to play a double part, which, however calculated in one point of view to secure his safety, was, on the other, full of peril to the foreigners in Japan, and, as they conceived, not without some danger to himself. He had often seemed to be playing into the hands of the Daimios most hostile to the maintenance of foreign relations, and to be seriously preparing to put a stop to these, while at the same time he professed to the several Treaty Powers a very earnest desire to maintain intact all the rights conferred by existing Treaties; but now it was no longer a matter of suspicion but of certainty, and the documents placed in the Admiral's hands prove that the whole of these outrages and flagrant violations of Treaties by the Prince of Nagato were really the acts of the Mikado and Tycoon, since done under orders which might easily be interpreted to sanction if not to prescribe the exact order of proceedings adopted by the Prince. The time, therefore, had come for dropping all mask and adopting a totally different policy; and unless the Tycoon, strengthened and materially aided as he must be by this complete victory over the Prince of Nagato, and by such support as the foreign Representatives were in a position to render him, would undertake without further temporizing to put himself in accord with the superior authority of the Mikado in this matter of the Treaties, obtain his sanction and give entire execution to all their stipulations, an opportunity, not likely to occur again, would be lost in the Tycoon's interest not less than theirs.

Takemoto Kai no Kami, in reply, stated that he fully agreed with the

---

[1] i.e. the orders issued by the Court and Bakufu in June 1863, the texts of which are given in *Ishin-shi*, iii. 406. See generally Section V,

opinions just expressed that this was a very critical moment, and that it behoved the Tycoon's Government to take advantage of it in the way indicated. In regard to the charge made by the Prince of Choshiu and the written orders he produced in justification, he, Takemoto Kai no Kami, had to remark:

1st. That the order, such as it was, had been transmitted, not by the Tycoon, but by an act of treachery on the part of persons about the Mikado, and without competent authority.

2ndly. That it did not order the Prince to fire upon foreign ships, and the proof that such was not its proper meaning might be found in the fact that although a similar order was communicated to all the other Daimios, he alone had put that interpretation upon it, because it suited his own designs.

To this the American Minister replied that, although it was true the order was not in express terms to fire, yet as it declared the intention of the Tycoon to cease all intercourse with foreigners on the 20th of June, 1863, the Prince might naturally draw the inference that he was expected to treat them as enemies.

Takemoto replied, that such acts were contrary to the Tycoon's wish was further established by his sending down an Aide-de-camp at once to cause the Prince to stop firing; and this emissary was murdered in the territories of Choshiu.

As to the appearance of double dealing on the part of the Tycoon's Government, on the one side concerting measures for the closing of the port of Yokohama, and on the other for maintaining the Treaties in their integrity, the Tycoon had hitherto been, as the Representatives well knew, in a position to make something of this kind unavoidable, in the interest of foreigners as well as for his own sake; since had he openly refused to carry out the orders received from the Mikado for the expulsion of foreigners, he was liable to be deposed, and his dynasty might be destroyed. Now, however, that the Prince of Nagato had been defeated by the allied expedition, there was certainly a great opportunity for putting an end to whatever was ambiguous in the position of the Tycoon, as regarded the foreign Powers. But in furtherance of such end it was essential that the allied squadron should be recalled to prevent all chance of collision with other Daimios, and new complications arising.

The American Minister then observed that it was evident from the tenor and urgency of this demand, which Takemoto had been no doubt instructed to make, that the Tycoon was still inclined to pursue the policy of conciliating the hostile party; whereas he now occupied a vantage ground, secured for him by the action of the Treaty Powers, which relieved him from such subservience. He was no longer under the necessity, which it was pleaded had hitherto controlled his free action, of presenting one face to the Treaty Powers, and another to his own subjects. The power of the hostile party was now broken, and the Tycoon was able to act with security. He would accordingly be expected to prove his good faith, by strictly observing the engagements entered into by Treaties, and no longer holding out expectations of their modification. The Tycoon must know by this time that such modifications as the hostile party contemplated would never be acceded to. So far as the Tycoon was concerned, the Representatives present had indeed the assurance that they were only asked for the purpose of gaining time, and not with any hope of ultimate concession. The temporizing policy hitherto followed, however, had greatly aggravated the evils which the Tycoon professed to be desirous of remedying; and the safest course, as well as the wisest, would now be found in a faithful observance of Treaties, without pretence at negotiations for their modification, or apparent concessions to those who only sought their entire nullification.

Takemoto said, that believing with foreign Representatives the present time very favourable for efforts at Kioto [Kyōto] to place the relations of Japan with foreign countries on a better footing, he was all the more anxious that the fleet should immediately return, and especially that no troops should be left to occupy any post in the Inland Sea, lest new complications or collisions should arise, which might seriously interfere with the success of efforts now to be made.

The British Minister replied that it had been determined by common consent to keep an effective hold upon the Straits until satisfactory arrangements were entered into by the Tycoon's Government, both as to the navigation of the Inland Sea and the better maintenance of Treaty rights generally. Either the Tycoon must find the means of bringing the Mikado and hostile party of Daimios in accord with him for the maintenance of Treaties, or the Western Powers might find themselves compelled to go beyond the Tycoon, and enter into relations with the Mikado. It had been already suggested that a new order of things might at once be established if the Tycoon would take advantage of the recent blow dealt to the Sako party,[1] in the person of Choshiu. Advantage might also be taken of the intimation now conveyed, that unless some agreement could be come to on the subject of Treaties between the various conflicting Powers in Japan, foreign States might, however reluctantly, find themselves compelled in self-defence to take steps which would bring them in more or less direct relation with the Mikado and those Daimios who had hitherto supported him in a hostile course of action. Hitherto the Tycoon had always been considered as the Treaty-making Power in Japan, and the

---

[1] The *jōi* ('expel-the-foreigners') party was also known variously as the *sakō* ('close-the-ports') and the *sakoku* ('close-the-country') party.

sole Representative of Government in relation with foreign States. But if it continued to be demonstrated that the Tycoon had not the necessary authority, and was so completely overruled by a superior power in the State as to be unable to prevent or resist orders for the rupture of Treaties, however well-disposed he might be to maintain them, foreign Powers would sooner or later have no alternative but to seek this superior Power in the State, and make their own terms.

Takemoto Kai no Kami observed, that agreeing in much which had been suggested, he was, nevertheless, not in a position to make any definite answer in so grave a matter. He would, therefore, at once proceed to Yeddo [Edo] to report all that had been said. In the meantime he must still urge the importance of immediately recalling the fleet, to prevent all chance of new collisions.

The French Minister wished to ask Takemoto two or three questions. And first, if the Tycoon could now obtain the full concurrence and support of the Mikado in the maintenance of foreign relations and existing Treaties, would the Tycoon then find it possible to give them full effect, and to deal with any recalcitrant or rebellious Daimios, now especially that Satsuma and Choshiu, two of the most powerful, having tried their strength against foreign Powers and failed, were no longer hostile?

Takemoto answered without hesitation yes, certainly.

The French Minister then asked whether it would not be very inconvenient to the Mikado to receive the foreign Representatives in Kioto?

Takemoto smiled and said, undoubtedly it would be very inconvenient.

Then, continued the French Minister, would it not be much better for the Tycoon to profit by this opportunity, so happily afforded by the recent defeat of the Prince of Nagato, and the great discouragement it must be to the Sako party, and prevent any necessity arising for such a step?

To which Takemoto replied also in the affirmative, observing that such indeed would be the desire of the Tycoon, and he, Takemoto, would immediately hasten to Yeddo, that the Gorogio [Rōjū] and Tycoon might be informed without delay of all that had passed, and of the whole bearing of the important events which had taken place in the Straits.

The British Minister summed up by saying it was desirable the high officers now present should return to Yeddo impressed with two leading facts: First, that the time had arrived for a total and radical change of policy on the part of the Tycoon in respect to the Sako party and the foreign Powers; abandoning all attempts to temporize with and conciliate the former by seeming to consent to measures for the expulsion of foreigners one day, or by the stoppage of the trade another. . . .

And, secondly, the British envoy then continued, he trusted they would leave this Conference with the conviction that it was impossible for foreign Powers any longer to let their Treaty rights and material interests in the country be perpetually damaged and sacrificed between the two conflicting authorities of the Mikado and Tycoon. It followed, therefore, that either the Tycoon must find means to reconcile the two, and successfully assert his power to execute the Treaties fully, or measures must be taken into the consideration of foreign Governments for arriving at a satisfactory result by other means than representations to the Tycoon, courteously listened to always, but wholly inoperative.

In the meanwhile, anxious to give every support to the Tycoon in his efforts tending to this end, desirous of avoiding any cause of embarrassment that might interfere with his action in this direction, willing even to strengthen Takemoto's hands in the arduous work on which he had now been employed, he might go back to the Tycoon with the assurance that the Admirals would speedily return with the greater part of the force, and no permanent position would at present be taken on shore to command the Straits. On the other hand, having at no slight cost obtained such important results as the removal of all the impediments to the free navigation, and the submission of the Prince of Nagato, it was out of the question their immediately relinquishing these material and political results, or exposing them to any jeopardy. A certain number of ships, therefore, would remain in the vicinity of Shimonosaki to secure the free passage and strict maintenance of the terms on which peace would be granted to the Prince.

The American Minister observed, further, that it would be a question now whether, after the past experience, it was not essential to prevent the liability of the Straits being closed at the caprice of any single Daimio.

To do this effectually, it might be necessary that so much of the territories of the Prince as should be required to secure foreign trade henceforth from any such contingency should be imperialized, and made over to the Tycoon's keeping. Whether also Shimonosaki, or some other port in its vicinity, should not be made a port for foreign trade, was matter now for deliberation. As some indemnity for the sacrifices made by the four Treaty Powers to secure the removal of the long existing obstruction, and the injury done to foreign trade during the past fifteen months, the four Treaty Powers might reasonably require it from the Tycoon; and the Tycoon himself might be disposed to make this arrangement of his own accord, and the more willingly that there was reason to believe this concession, if now insisted upon by the Admirals, could be at once obtained from the Prince of Choshiu, as Daimio of the province.

The British Minister observed, in conclusion, that it would be necessary for the Representatives then present to confer, in person, with the Gorogio on this and other important matters connected with the present aspect of affairs. These subjects were distinctly mentioned now, therefore, that when the meeting took place the members of the Gorogio might not be taken by surprise, and require time for deliberation, but be prepared at once to enter into the discussion of the proper measures to be taken.

Takemoto Kai no Kami said he perfectly understood all that had been said, and, with his colleagues, he would hasten back to Yeddo to render an account of his mission.

The Conference was then closed.

DOCUMENT 59. Convention concerning the Shimonoseki indemnity, signed at Yokohama, 22 October 1864.[1]

The Representatives of Great Britain, France, the United States, and the Netherlands, in view of the hostile acts of Mori Daizen, Prince of Nagato and Suwo,[2] which were assuming such formidable proportions as to make it difficult for the Tycoon faithfully to observe the Treaties, having been obliged to send their combined forces to the Straits of Shimonasaki,[3] in order to destroy the batteries erected by that Daimio for the destruction of foreign vessels and the stoppage of trade; and the Government of the Tycoon, on whom devolved the duty of chastising this rebellious Prince, being held responsible for any damage resulting to the interests of Treaty Powers, as well as the expenses occasioned by the expedition;

The Undersigned Representatives of Treaty Powers, and Sakai Hida no Kami, a member of the Second Council, invested with plenipotentiary powers by the Tycoon of Japan, animated with the desire to put an end to all reclamations concerning the acts of aggression and hostility committed by the said Mori Daizen, since the first of these acts, in June 1863, against the flags of divers Treaty Powers, and at the same time to regulate definitively the question of indemnities of war, of whatever kind, in respect to the allied expedition to Shimonasaki, have agreed and determined upon the four Articles following:

ARTICLE I

The amount payable to the four Powers is fixed at 3,000,000 dollars. This sum to include all claims, of whatever nature, for past aggressions on the part of the Prince of Nagato, whether indemnities, ransom for Shimonasaki, or expenses entailed by the operations of the allied squadrons.

ARTICLE II

The whole sum to be payable quarterly in instalments of one-sixth, or

---

[1] This document was signed by the *wakadoshiyori* Sakai Tadasuke, Hida-no-kami (for Japan); Rutherford Alcock (for Great Britain); Léon Roches (for France); Robert Pruyn (for the United States); and van Polsbroek (for Holland). The text is printed in *Parliamentary Papers 1865*, vol. lvii, p. 686.

[2] Mōri Yoshichika, Daizen-daibu, *daimyō* of Chōshū (Nagato) and Suō.

[3] The place-name Shimonoseki was also known to foreigners at this time as Shimonosaki and Shimonasaki.

500,000 dollars, to begin from the date when the Representatives of said Powers shall make known to the Tycoon's Government the ratification of this convention and the instructions of their respective Governments.

ARTICLE III

Inasmuch as the receipt of money has never been the object of the said Powers, but the establishment of better relations with Japan, and the desire to place these on a more satisfactory and mutually advantageous footing is still the leading object in view, therefore, if His Majesty the Tycoon wishes to offer in lieu of payment of the sum claimed, and as a material compensation for loss and injury sustained, the opening of Shimonasaki, or some other eligible port in the Inland Sea, it shall be at the option of the said foreign Governments to accept the same, or insist on the payment of the indemnity in money under the conditions above stipulated.

ARTICLE IV

This Convention to be formally ratified by the Tycoon's Government within fifteen days from the date thereof.

In token of which the respective Plenipotentiaries have signed and sealed this Convention in quintiplicate, with English and Japanese versions, whereof the English shall be considered the original.

Imperial Ratification of the Treaties, 1865

AFTER the Shimonoseki bombardment and the resulting convention of 22 October 1864, Japan's relations with the Treaty Powers underwent important changes. The representatives of Britain, France, Holland, and the United States, especially after the arrival of the new British minister, Sir Harry Parkes, in July 1865, became more and more aware of the critical position of the Bakufu in Japan's domestic politics; and they urged increasingly that if the Shōgun could not redress their grievances (or give effect to their demands), then they must enter into direct communication with the Court at Kyōto. Indeed, in the diplomatic crisis of November 1865 they transferred the scene of negotiations from Yokohama to Ōsaka, whence the repercussions of their actions on the Imperial Court were more immediate and direct. The Bakufu was thereby denied the advantages of time and distance by which it had profited hitherto.

At the same time, to the leaders of the anti-Bakufu party, at least, opposition to the Shōgun's foreign policy was becoming as much a matter of political expediency as of principle, for the bombardments of Kagoshima and Shimonoseki had helped to convince the men of Satsuma and Chōshū of the reality of Western power. This change was gradual, however, and did not in any case serve to decrease the government's difficulties. Of more immediate importance was the new political alignment that resulted from the Bakufu's attempts to punish Chōshū.

As early as June 1864 the Bakufu had secured an Imperial edict authorizing punitive measures against Chōshū. In August, in an attempt to reverse this decision, some contingents of Chōshū samurai and *rōnin* had made an armed attack on the capital; and though few in number, they had only been driven from Kyōto after bitter fighting. As a result, Chōshū was declared rebellious and a punitive expedition was announced. For various reasons the Shōgun's army was not ready to begin operations until December, and even then fighting was prevented by the mediation of Satsuma, whose leaders negotiated an agreement between the two contestants. By the end of January 1865 the Bakufu forces had been disbanded, to the great satisfaction of the many *daimyō* who believed that both Bakufu and Chōshū were carrying the dispute to extremes, but in other respects the agreement was not honoured by either side and the situation again deteriorated rapidly. In May a new expedition was announced, though this did not in fact take place until the following year.

Meanwhile the effective leadership of the Satsuma fief was slipping from the hands of Shimazu Hisamitsu. The men who now began to control the fief's policy—Ōkubo Toshimichi and Saigō Takamori—gradually began to draw closer to Chōshū. Throughout the second half of 1865 secret negotiations were in progress between the two fiefs, and in March of the following year these resulted in a formal alliance aimed at the overthrow of the Bakufu and the restoration of Imperial authority. Thus by the autumn of 1865, when a new diplomatic crisis occurred, the Bakufu's position was already worsening. It could no longer count on Satsuma's influence at Court. Nor did it retain any semblance of initiative in foreign affairs. In its preoccupation with the question of Chōshū it had again allowed this to be seized by the Treaty Powers. .

In April 1865, already recognizing that its first attempt to subdue Chōshū had failed, the Bakufu informed the foreign representatives that, under the terms of the October convention (Section VI, Document 59), it was unable to open a new port and would therefore pay the first instalment of the Shimonoseki indemnity. At the same time it asked that payment of the second instalment might take place one year later, instead of three months as originally provided. This question was referred to the governments concerned, but as they could not reach agreement, chiefly because of differences between Britain and France, a final decision was left to the ministers in Japan. Instructions to this effect reached them in October. Parkes now brought forward again an earlier British proposal, that the Powers should agree not merely to postpone the second instalment of the indemnity but even to waive altogether the remaining two-thirds ($2,000,000) in return for the following concessions by Japan: (i) early opening of Hyōgo and Ōsaka; (ii) Imperial ratification of existing treaties; (iii) reduction of Japanese import duties to a basic rate of 5 per cent. The French minister, Léon Roches, at first opposed the British proposals. After some discussion, however, he gave way. On 30 October the ministers of Britain, France, Holland, and the United States met in Yokohama and drew up a memorandum offering a settlement on these terms (Document 60). In it they also announced their intention of transferring the negotiations to Ōsaka, since the Shōgun and most of the Rōjū were then in that city.

On 4 November a fleet of nine warships brought the foreign representatives to Hyōgo. Three days later they communicated their offer to Ogasawara Nagamichi, giving him seven days in which to reply. The Bakufu, despite having received warning from Edo, was thrown into confusion; and on 13 November its council decided to accept the foreign terms for fear of a direct approach by foreign envoys to the Imperial Court. This decision was at once reversed, however, at the urging of Hitotsubashi Keiki, who reached Ōsaka from Kyōto the same night. Next day the Bakufu asked for more time to reply to the proposals in view of the need for prior consultation with the Court. The final date for reply was fixed at 24 November.

News of the arrival of a foreign fleet had meanwhile reached Kyōto, and rumour was rife that the Bakufu planned to open Hyōgo forthwith. Satsuma brought pressure to bear on the Court to summon a conference of feudal lords to discuss the situation (Document 61), hoping thereby to settle also the question of Chōshū. On 17 November the Court itself took an unprecedented step. It ordered the dismissal of the two Rōjū (Abe Masatō and Matsumae Takahiro) who had been foremost in urging the Shōgun to open Hyōgo. At Ōsaka this order caused consternation. To his advisers the Shōgun's position seemed now to be untenable. Next day he submitted his resignation to the Emperor, recommending Keiki as his successor, while in a memorandum accompanying his letter of resignation he urged the need for immediate Imperial ratification of the treaties (Document 62).

Reports of these events inevitably found their way to the foreign representatives at their anchorage off Hyōgo. On 21 November Sir Harry Parkes wrote in strong terms to warn the Bakufu of the dangers of refusal or delay (Document 63). This, together with the shock of the Shōgun's resignation, rallied the Bakufu's supporters in Kyōto. The Shōgun was brought to the capital. (His resignation had not been and was not to be accepted.) Hitotsubashi Keiki joined with the senior Bakufu officials in urging the Emperor to ratify the treaties (Document 64) and lengthy conferences were held at the Palace. The Satsuma leaders had meanwhile been asked whether they would themselves undertake the task of negotiating with the foreigners; but despite their willingness to do so and their insistence that no sanction must be given to the treaties or to the opening of Hyōgo until the *daimyō* had been consulted, the arguments of Keiki and Prince Asahiko prevailed (Document 65). On 22 November the Emperor announced his decision to ratify the treaties (Document 66).

The Imperial decree had ordered that no action be taken about the opening of Hyōgo, but this was glossed over in the Bakufu's reply to the foreign envoys (Document 67). The negotiations, in fact, had been a signal success for the Treaty Powers. They had secured Imperial ratification of the treaties and a promise of tariff revision; and since Hyōgo was not to be opened, the Bakufu agreed to continue the indemnity payments. Politically and economically, the Bakufu alone had suffered by the crisis. Thereafter it virtually abandoned its attempts to resist foreign demands.

DOCUMENT 60. Memorandum by the Ministers in Japan of Great Britain, France, the United States, and Holland, Yokohama, 30 October 1865.[1]

En vertu de la Convention signée le 22 Octobre, 1864,[2] le Gouvernement Japonais s'est engagé à payer aux Gouvernements d'Angleterre, de France, des Etats Unis d'Amérique et des Pays Bas une somme de 3,000,000 de dollars comme indemnité des dépenses nécessitées par l'expédition de Shimonasaki.

Les Représentants des quatre Puissances susnommées, désireux de témoigner auprès du Gouvernement Japonais les sentiments désintéressés de leurs Souverains, et de leur unique désir d'améliorer leurs relations avec le Japon, laissèrent à Sa Majesté le Taikoun la faculté de remplacer le paiement de cette indemnité par l'ouverture d'un nouveau port au commerce étranger.

Sommé par les Représentants des dites Puissances d'avoir à déclarer s'il voulait, ou non, user de cette faculté, le Gouvernement Japonais déclara, il y a six mois environ, qu'il préférait payer l'indemnité, attendu que l'état du pays lui faisait considérer comme impolitique l'ouverture d'un nouveau port. Mais, en même temps, il demandait un délai d'une année pour opérer le second versement de l'indemnité.

Les Représentants des quatre Puissances, tout en reconnaissant au Gouvernement Japonais le droit d'opter entre les deux conditions, ne se crurent pas autorisés à accorder le délai demandé et durent en référer à leurs Gouvernements respectifs. Les instructions qu'ils ont demandées à ce sujet sont parvenues aux Soussignés.

Le droit du Taikoun d'opter entre le paiement de l'indemnité aux termes fixés par la Convention du 22 Octobre, et l'ouverture d'un port dans la Mer Intérieure, est naturellement reconnu par chacune des dites Puissances, mais elles diffèrent d'opinion au sujet du délai demandé par le Gouvernement Japonais.

Les Cabinets de St. James et de la Haye exigent ou l'exécution rigoureuse des Articles de la Convention du 22 Octobre à cet égard, ou bien consentent à ce délai, et même à l'abandon des deux tiers de l'indemnité aux trois conditions suivantes:

1. Que le Gouvernement Japonais ouvre le port de Hiogo et la ville d'Osaca le 1 Janvier, 1866.

---

[1] The text of this memorandum, which is signed respectively by H. S. Parkes, Léon Roches, A. L. C. Portman, and D. de Graeff van Polsbroek, is printed in *Parliamentary Papers 1866*, vol. lxxvi, pp. 497–8. It was communicated to Mizuno Tadakiyo, the Rōjū whom the Bakufu had left in charge of affairs in Edo.

[2] See Section VI, Document 59.

2. Que le Mikado ratifie les Traités conclus avec les Puissances étrangères.

3. Enfin que le Tarif des droits d'entrée soit fixé pour la plupart des marchandises à 5 pour cent et ne puisse en aucun cas dépasser 10 pour cent.

Le Cabinet de Paris ne verrait, au contraire, pas d'obstacle à accorder un délai au Gouvernement Japonais, si ce dernier agissait de bonne foi à l'égard des Puissances signataires des Traités, et il verrait un danger à lui imposer l'ouverture d'Osaca avant l'époque fixée par la Convention Additionnelle de 1862.[1] Le Cabinet de Paris déclare en outre formellement, ce qui est également admis par les Cabinets de St. James et de la Haye, que le Taikoun étant libre d'opter entre le paiement de l'indemnité et l'ouverture d'un port, nous ne serions pas en droit, si ce Prince exécute l'une de ces conditions, d'exiger l'ouverture anticipée de Hiogo et d'Osaca.

Le Ministre de l'Empereur ajoute, en résumé, dans la dépêche que son Excellence adresse aux Cabinets de Londres, de la Haye, ou de Washington, en date du 22 Juillet, 1865, que le Gouvernement Impérial est d'avis que la solution de cette question soit remise aux Représentants des quatre Puissances au Japon.

En réponse à cette communication, Lord Cowley a fait connaître à M. Drouyn de Lhuys que le Gouvernement de Sa Majesté Britannique consentait à cette dernière proposition.

Le Représentant des Etats Unis d'Amérique n'a pas reçu d'instructions de son Gouvernement, mais les mesures arrêtées par le présent memorandum n'étant que la conséquence de la politique qui a été inaugurée entre les quatre Puissances signataires des Traités, M. Portman, Chargé d'Affaires *ad interim*, n'hésite pas à cette occasion de s'unir à ses collègues.

M. le Graeff van Polsbroek a reçu des instructions identiques de son Gouvernement.

En l'état, les Représentants soussignés d'Angleterre, de France, des Etats Unis d'Amérique et de Hollande ont jugé nécessaire de se réunir à l'effet de s'entendre:

1. Sur les moyens de concilier entre elles les instructions de leurs Gouvernements respectifs, tout en conservant intacte l'union et l'entente commune qui leur ont déjà donné tant de force. Et

2. Sur la marche à suivre afin de tirer le meilleur parti possible de la situation actuelle.

Après avoir examiné la question sous toutes ses faces:
Considérant, d'un côté, que les propositions du Gouvernement de Sa

---

[1] The London Protocol. See Section IV, Document 37. By this agreement both Hyōgo and Ōsaka were to be opened on 1 January 1868.

Majesté Britannique relativement à l'abandon d'une partie de l'indemnité :
1. De l'ouverture anticipée du port de Hiogo et de la ville d'Osaca ; 2. De
la ratification des Traités par le Mikado ; et 3. De la révision du Tarif des
Douanes, — sont conformes à l'esprit de la Convention du 22 Octobre,
1864 ;

Considérant, d'un autre côté, que le Gouvernement de Sa Majesté
l'Empereur ne s'écarte des propositions du Cabinet de St. James qu'en
ce qu'elles auraient d'inopportun, vu l'état des partis au Japon ;

Considérant que les conditions réclamées par l'Angleterre et la Hollande, si elles étaient accordées spontanément par le Gouvernement Japonais, n'offriraient plus les dangers que redouteraient la France si ces conditions étaient imposées, et seraient préférables pour tous les intéressés au
paiement des deux tiers de l'indemnité, et que dès lors la France n'aurait
plus d'objection à opposer à ce nouvel arrangement, qui, on le répète, est
tout à fait conforme à l'esprit de la Convention du 22 Octobre ;

Considérant que l'intérêt bien entendu des Puissances signataires des
Traités et du Japon lui-même exige une prompte solution aux questions
pendantes, et que l'abandon des deux tiers de l'indemnité pourrait faciliter
et hâter la ratification des Traités par le Mikado, ratification qui est la
meilleure garantie, à l'avenir, des bonnes relations des Puissances étrangères avec le Japon, et que, du reste, le Gouvernement du Taikoun s'est
engagé à l'obtenir du Mikado ;

Considérant que l'absence du Taikoun et de ses principaux Ministres
rend toute négociation à Yédo, si non impossible, du moins illusoire ; qu'il
importe pourtant d'affirmer notre droit d'obtenir, en son temps, l'exécution d'un engagement et d'une Convention solennels, et de convaincre
le Gouvernement Japonais, ainsi que le Mikado et les Daimios, que les
Puissances étrangères sont irrévocablement décidées à exiger l'ouverture
de Hiogo et d'Osaca à l'époque fixée par les Traités, s'ils ne l'obtiennent
pas avant, par suite d'un accord mutuel ;

Les Représentants soussignés sont convenus, d'un commun accord, de
transporter momentanément à Osaca le siège des négociations.

Cette mesure, qui est parfaitement conforme à l'esprit des Traités,
puisque les dits Représentants sont accrédités auprès de la personne du
Taikoun, aura, en outre, aux yeux des amis et des ennemis du Taikoun
une signification qui pourra singulièrement influer sur l'heureuse issue des
événements qui se préparent.

En effet, les Soussignés ont été informés que le Taikoun, cédant aux instances du Mikado et des Daimios qui l'entourent, a consenti à recevoir
le Prince de Nagato à résipiscence moyennant des conditions que ce
Daimio rebelle avait acceptées, il y a huit mois environ, du Prince d'Ouari,
Généralissime de l'armée Taikounate, mais qu'il n'a pas remplies sous
divers prétextes. Or, le Taikoun se méfiant, avec raison, des dispositions

réelles de son sujet, a fixé une époque (le 15 Novembre) passé laquelle il considérera comme non avenues les conditions favorables qu'il a bien voulu accorder au Daimio rebelle, et procédera immédiatement à son châtiment.

L'arrivée à Osaca des Représentants des Puissances signataires des Traités venant à ce moment décisif, suivis d'une force navale respectable, traiter amicalement avec les Ministres du Taikoun, empêcherait, il y a lieu de le croire, le commencement des hostilités qui seraient peut-être le signal de la guerre civile, dont les conséquences, quelles qu'elles fussent, ne pourraient que nuire aux intérêts politiques et commerciaux des Puissances étrangères au Japon. En tout cas cette arrivée ne peut manquer de donner au Gouvernement Japonais l'appui moral qui doit lui faciliter le résultat de ses démarches à l'effet d'obtenir du Mikado la ratification des Traités.

En conséquence, les Soussignés sont convenus de s'adresser immédiatement aux commandants des forces navales de leur nations respectives afin de leur faire connaître la situation politique et de les inviter à les transporter à Osaca, où ils séjourneront le temps nécessaire pour mener à bonne fin l'importante négociation qui les y appelle.

Les Soussignés prennent cette détermination avec la conviction intime qu'elle peut amener de très heureux résultats, et qu'en aucun cas elle n'est de nature à compromettre la politique sage et conciliante que leurs Gouvernements respectifs leur ont ordonné de suivre à l'égard du Japon.

Fait à Yokohama, en quadruple exemplaire, le 30 Octobre, 1865.

DOCUMENT 61. Uchita Naka-no-suke to Kampaku (Nijō Nariaki), Kyōto, 16 November 1865.[1]

It has been reported that foreign ships arrived recently at Hyōgo. Although not fully informed about the situation, we have heard privately that when Abe [Masatō] Bungo-no-kami and Matsumae [Takahiro] Izu-no-kami negotiated with the foreigners some days ago, they agreed to open the port [of Hyōgo]; and that as a decision must be effected within the space of ten days, the Shōgun is to come at once to Kyōto and submit a report on this matter to the Emperor.

Since Hyōgo is close to the Imperial capital and is, moreover, an Inland Sea port of great importance, we deem it quite impossible that the Emperor should sanction its opening. We know that for many years, ever

---

[1] The text is printed in *Iwakura Kō Jikki*, i. 943. Uchita Naka-no-suke, who was the Satsuma fief *rusui* in Kyōto, here writes as the fief's official spokesman, but it is clear that he is expressing the views of Ōkubo Toschimichi rather than of Shimazu Hisamitsu. In fact, another copy of the letter, printed in *Kaikoku Kigen*, iii. 2757–8, is there attributed to Ōkubo himself—though wrongly so, for Ōkubo was at this time visiting Matsudaira Keiei at Fukui.

since the original incursion of the Americans, the Emperor has been inflexibly resolved on this point. Hence, though this is in no way a matter with which we should concern ourselves, we feel that were the Emperor to sanction Bakufu action in conformity with the foreign demands, the Empire's safety would inevitably be threatened; our country would suffer such unparalleled disgrace as even a thousand years might not afford opportunity to repair. We believe, indeed, that this single action would of itself influence the trend of national opinion and bring the greatest of future calamities upon us. It is therefore our desire that the Emperor should immediately summon the feudal lords and require them to submit their advice, that the Imperial prestige might thus be made manifest. [To do so will consume some time and may therefore make the foreigners more unyielding.][1] If they should then have recourse to reckless action, it is our desire that the Emperor should give orders for their immediate expulsion. In that event, though there be but few of us now in our fief residence here, it is our wish to be placed in the van of the battle, where we shall fight with the utmost desperation in the attempt to repay the debt we owe our country, for so we have been instructed by Shūri-daibu and Ōsumi-no-kami.[2] It is therefore our desire that the Emperor be pleased to summon the lords.

This request I submit with respect, on the instructions of the senior officials of the fief.

DOCUMENT 62. Shōgun Iemochi to Emperor Kōmei, Ōsaka, 18 November 1865.[3]

I, Iemochi, am young and lacking in ability. I have exerted myself hitherto unsparingly and without cease in performing the duties of the great office of *Sei-i-tai-shōgun* that I bear; but in the crisis that now threatens us both at home and abroad, I am alike incapable of relieving the Emperor's anxieties and of succouring my people. Nor have I the capacity to enrich our country and increase its military strength, so to make the Imperial prestige resound beyond the seas. And thus, to my great grief and distress, I must at last confess myself unworthy of my office.

Of the members of my house, I believe that Keiki,[4] who has been long at Court and is well versed in public business, is fully capable of filling this great office. I, Iemochi, therefore, hereby resign that office and name

[1] This sentence appears only in the *Kaikoku Kigen* text.

[2] The head of the Satsuma fief, Shimazu Tadayoshi, Shūri-daibu; and his father, Shimazu Hisamitsu, Ōsumi-no-kami.

[3] The text is printed, with minor textual variations, in *Iwakura Kō Jikki*, i. 955–7; *Kaikoku Kigen*, iii. 2759–62; and *Zoku saimukiji*, iv. 298–301.

[4] Hitotsubashi Keiki, next in line of succession.

Keiki as my successor. It is my wish to hand over the task of administration to him, and I petition the Emperor that he may entrust Keiki with the supervision of all State affairs, just as he did myself.

I enclose separately a report to the Throne on the immediate problem facing us. I ask that instructions concerning this may be issued to Keiki.

Enclosure

I, Iemochi, have given the fullest thought to the present state of world affairs. Conditions have been steadily changing in recent years. It has become customary for countries to make friendly agreements, to exchange goods, and to work together to increase their wealth and strength. This development I believe to be inevitable and in conformity with the natural order of things. Hence, for Japan alone to refrain from diplomatic intercourse would be to show ourselves cowardly and suspicious. It might well make it impossible, in fact, to preserve our national dignity and prestige.

Some years ago we concluded a treaty of friendship with the American envoy at Shimoda; and in view of this, the facts were reported to the Emperor and Imperial sanction obtained. Thereafter we steadily abandoned the old practices of seclusion and began gradually to lay the foundations of national wealth and strength. Subsequently, however, the Emperor ordered us to withdraw from foreign intercourse. We sought, as far as we could, to respect the Emperor's wishes. But he also ordered us not to carry out expulsion recklessly. It is certainly impossible to carry out chastisement of the foreigners unless we first lay plans for increasing our wealth and military strength; and I therefore considered that our most urgent immediate task was to follow the example of the foreigners in using the profits from trade to construct many ships and guns, adopting the strategy of using the barbarian to subdue the barbarian.

I was exerting all my efforts to this end when there arose the problem of the punishment of Chōshū, which finally brought me here to Ōsaka Castle. Then foreign ships arrived without warning at the port of Hyōgo. The foreigners demanded that the Emperor should again give his sanction to the treaty provisions. They insisted that if I, Iemochi, should be unable to arrange this, they would go to the Court and make their demands directly to the Emperor; and although we advanced every possible argument in negotiation with them, we could by no means persuade them [to abandon their demands]. Yet if we were recklessly to resort to arms, we should have not the least hope of victory. Even if we obtained a temporary success, our country, surrounded on all sides by sea, would be attacked night and day, from east and from west, from north and from south; and through ceaseless war our people would thenceforth be plunged in misery. In a ruler there could be no greater injustice and inhumanity than this. I very much fear, indeed, that not only the existence of my house would be imperilled, but even the safety of the Throne itself. To act thus would be a matter of the greatest moment. It might even be thought contrary to that benevolence with which an Emperor should cherish his people. And by acting thus I should myself be failing in my duties. It is therefore my desire that the Emperor may give this matter the most careful thought and, unmoved by the pressure of popular opinion, may demonstrate his judgement and foresight by again affirming his sanction of the treaties, making it clear that they were negotiated in a just and realistic manner. Once this is done, I shall exert all my endeavours, in foreign affairs to effect such measures as will bring the foreigners under control, in home affairs to achieve the punishment of Chōshū. Thus shall I on the one hand relieve the Emperor of anxiety and on the other ease the lot of our people, thereby fulfilling the wishes of my ancestors.

However great our national valour, I am convinced that if foreign war and domestic revolt break out together, if all the countries of the West become our enemies, then the Emperor's safety will inevitably be threatened and our people will be plunged into the depths of misery. And being by virtue of my office responsible for the government and administration of the country, it very much grieves me to say that I do not see how I could give effect to any such Imperial commands [as might lead to this result]. Thus, as I have said above, nothing could better ensure the permanence of the Throne and the happiness of our people than for the Emperor at once to issue orders sanctioning the treaties. This is my most earnest entreaty, bitterly as I regret the necessity for it.

It would be most unfortunate were the foreigners to decide to go to the Imperial Court. So we have exerted every effort in negotiation and persuaded them to give us until 24 November to send a reply to Hyōgo. I am therefore anxious that the Emperor should issue his commands as soon as may be possible.

Submitted to the Throne.

DOCUMENT 63. Sir Harry Parkes to Shōgun Iemochi, 'Princess Royal', off Hyōgo, 21 November 1865.[1]

The official declarations made by your Majesty's Ministers to the foreign Representatives have led the latter to conclude that the difficulties which obstruct the faithful fulfilment of the Treaties are occasioned by the opposition of the Mikado and certain of the Daimios.

In the hope, therefore, of removing a source of dispute which is highly prejudicial to our interests and, at the same time, most dangerous to the tranquillity of Japan, I and my colleagues, the Representatives of France, the United States of America, and the Netherlands, have taken advantage

[1] The text is printed in *Parliamentary Papers 1866*, vol. lxxvi, p. 517.

of the presence of your Majesty at Osaca to urge the necessity of an immediate settlement of these unfortunate differences. By giving their approval to the engagements contracted by your Majesty with foreign Powers, the Mikado and the Daimios have it in their power to put an end to the difficulties which are at present felt, and to avert those evils by which the future is threatened.

With the view, also, of facilitating the execution of the Convention of the 22nd October, 1864,[1] my colleagues and myself have proposed to your Majesty to abandon two-thirds of the indemnity, due to our Governments under the said Convention, on the following conditions:

1. The sanction of the Treaties by the Mikado.
2. The opening of Hiogo and Osaca at a date to be agreed upon.
3. The revision of the Tariff.

On the 14th instant your Majesty's Ministers applied to us to give them ten days to reply to these proposals; and, although we had already been detained here for that length of time, we agreed to this additional delay.

Seven of these ten days have since elapsed, and we now learn that the Minister sent by your Majesty to meet us at Hiogo[2] has been dismissed from office.

In view of a proceeding which bears so unfriendly a construction, we consider it incumbent upon us to state that it is on your Majesty that the duty of settling these difficulties devolves. A happy accord between the Mikado, your Majesty, and the Daimios would ensure the maintenance of satisfactory relations between your people and foreigners, without prejudice to the interests or the independence of Japan. But disunion must bring upon your country the most grave disorders, as our Governments are firmly resolved to insist upon the faithful and complete observance by all parties, whether our enemies or our friends, of every condition of the Treaties concluded with your Majesty.

It remains, therefore, with your Majesty to take the proper steps for securing, by peaceful means, the execution of these Treaties.

Under any circumstances, it is necessary that I and my colleagues should receive from your Majesty, within the ten days which we have consented to wait, a categorical reply to the above-mentioned proposals. This reply, whether favourable or not, should be made to us in writing; and if not received by us within the time named, we shall consider that its absence denotes a formal refusal of our conditions on your Majesty's part, and we shall, in that case, be free to act as we may judge convenient.

[1] Section VI, Document 59.

[2] The first discussions were conducted by Ogasawara Nagamichi, but the reference here is to Abe Masatō, who assumed responsibility for the negotiations on 11 November, having returned to Ōsaka from Kyōto the previous day. The Imperial decree ordering his dismissal was issued on 17 November.

DOCUMENT 64. Bakufu officials to Imperial Court, Kyōto, 22 November 1865.[1]

Foreign ships recently arrived without warning at the port of Hyōgo. The foreigners demanded that the Emperor should again give his sanction to the treaties; and if the Bakufu could not arrange this, they insisted, they would go to the Court and make their demands directly to the Emperor. And although, by exhausting every resource of negotiation, we have persuaded them to wait until 24 November for our reply, they positively will not depart without the Emperor's sanction of the treaties. If we were recklessly to resort to arms, we should have not the least hope of victory. Even if we gained a temporary success, all the Western countries would become our enemies; and once this occurred, not only would the existence of the Bakufu be imperilled, but even the safety of the Throne itself. Our whole people would be plunged in misery. To act thus would be a matter of the gravest moment. It would be contrary to that benevolence with which the Emperor cherishes his people. And being by virtue of our official functions responsible for the government and administration of the country, we do not see how we could give effect to any such Imperial commands [as might lead to this result]. It is therefore our desire that the Emperor may give this matter the most careful thought and grant immediate sanction to the treaties. If he does so, we will make every effort to ensure that the foreign ships depart.

DOCUMENT 65. Ōkubo Toshimichi to Saigō Takamori and Minoda Dembei, Kyōto, 24 November 1865.[2]

21 November. I waited upon the *Naidaijin*, who informed me that he had received a letter from Lord Nijō.[3] It said that Hitotsubashi rode back to Kyōto this morning and reported that the Shōgun arrived at Fushimi at dawn today. Hitotsubashi and Aizu[4] had conferred with him and explained their views, whereupon it had been decided that the Shōgun

---

[1] The text is printed in *Iwakura Kō Jikki*, i. 958–9; *Kaikoku Kigen*, iii. 2763–4; and *Tokugawa Keiki Kō Den*, vi. 317–18. The letter was signed by Ogasawara Nagamichi (*Rōjū*), Matsudaira Sadataka (*Kyōto-shoshidai*), Matsudaira Katamori (*Kyōto-shugoshoku*), and Hitotsubashi Keiki. The wording of the letter, though less ceremonious, follows closely that of some passages in the Shōgun's memorandum (Document 62).

[2] This letter, the text of which is printed in *Ōkubo Toshimichi Monjo*, i. 325–32, takes the form of a journal of events in Kyōto after Ōkubo's return from Fukui on 20 November 1865. Only the section dealing with the events of 21 and 22 November is here translated (p. 327, line 5, to p. 330, line 10, in the printed text). Both Saigō and Minoda were at this time in Satsuma, of which fief they, with Ōkubo, were now the most important leaders.

[3] The *Naidaijin*, Konoe Tadafusa, was Satsuma's chief ally among the Court officials. Nijō Nariaki was at this time the *Kampaku*.

[4] Matsudaira Katamori of Aizu, *Kyōto-shugoshoku*.

should come to Kyōto today and go to Nijō Castle. This news the *Kampaku* had hastened to send. The *Naidaijin* therefore went to Court at 6 p.m. today. Hitosubashi, Aizu, Kuwana,[1] Ogasawara,[2] and others also attended there.

At midnight orders came from the Palace that our intermediaries were to be sent to the *Naidaijin*, so we sent Fujii Kunai and Inoue Yamato to the Hikurōdo chamber, where the *Naidaijin* met them. He informed them that he had been much disturbed by the evening's conference. Of the foreigners' demands, that for the opening of Hyōgo took second or third place. Their chief desire was for Imperial sanction of the opening of the three ports [already opened]. It had been argued at the conference that a meeting of the feudal lords should be summoned and a firm policy worked out in accordance with the general opinion; and that negotiations should accordingly be undertaken with the foreigners to arrange postponement of any decision until such a meeting could take place. But the Hitotsubashi faction stated that even if such negotiations were held there was no possibility that the foreigners would consent. And if hostilities were to commence, they said, our country would in a moment be reduced to ashes. It would suffer indescribable hardships. Hitotsubashi himself had insisted that negotiations for postponement were quite impossible. The *Naidaijin* had argued with him at length and had made every effort to make him change his mind, but as matters stood he had been unable to do so. He therefore instructed our intermediaries to tell him whether Satsuma might not agree to undertake such negotiations. They explained that it was impossible for them to give a definite answer there and then. They would consult with the principal officials of the fief and then give the *Naidaijin* our answer. So saying, the two men returned to us.

This was a matter on which we had already held private consultations, so, after some discussion, we replied as follows:

> The opening of Hyōgo and the granting of Imperial sanction for the opening of the three ports are difficult questions vital to our Empire. Lightly to give Imperial approval would cause disunity throughout the land and endanger the Imperial prestige. That being so, the Court should summon the most powerful of the lords and take a decision in accordance with their advice. If the Court will dispatch a suitable person to negotiate with the foreigners for matters to be delayed until such a meeting can take place, and will order the Satsuma fief to join itself with this mission, we will put forth all our efforts and endeavours in this task. And it is our belief that there would be good prospects of success.[3]

[1] Matsudaira Sadataka of Kuwana, *Kyōto-shoshidai*.
[2] The *Rōjū* Ogasawara Nagamichi.
[3] Literally 'eight or nine chances in ten of success'.

Instead of sending an oral message we wrote a letter to this effect, which Inoue Yamato took to the Palace and presented to the *Naidaijin*. Consultations then took place, and it was decided in general terms that Lord Ōhara [Shigenori] should be appointed as the Imperial envoy. Yamato returned to us very early on the morning of 22 November, therefore, with orders that Satsuma was to make the necessary preparations with all possible haste. It was decided that [Iwashita] Sajiemon and I should be attached to the mission. Then word came from the Palace that I was to wait upon the *Naidaijin*. I went to him at once.

He told me that he had suggested a meeting with Lord Ōhara so as to submit our views to him. A general explanation of our ideas had found him most resolute. And he had just received private notification from His Excellency[1] asking that our fief might carry out the whole affair, since it seemed that we had first made the proposal. However, the *Naidaijin* said, discussions were still in progress and it seemed possible that some objections might yet be raised. Since a decision would soon be reached, his instructions were that I should wait till then.

I accordingly waited until after four o'clock, when the *Naidaijin* returned to tell me that it would be quite impossible to carry out our plan. He had just had a heated argument with Hitotsubashi, he said, who had proved completely stubborn. Hitotsubashi insisted that he would not stir from his place until the Imperial sanction had been given. He had even gone so far as to say that if the fiefs should object to Imperial sanction being given, he would himself undertake to deal with the matter. Thus there was no help for it, the *Naidaijin* said. Much as he regretted it, a private decision had been taken that Imperial sanction would be accorded to the treaties, so far as concerned the three ports [already open]. This, I gathered, had been brought about by the intrigues of Prince Asahiko. There was no help for it.

I urged strongly that it was of the utmost importance that the lords be summoned and that there be no wavering about the opening of Hyōgo. I then withdrew. I understand that Lord Ōhara, too, had a fierce dispute with Hitotsubashi. He pointed out that in so important a matter the Bakufu should have reported earlier. Had it done so, the lords could have been summoned and full consultations held. It was most reprehensible, he said, for the Bakufu to have reported only the previous night and sought an immediate decision. Hitotsubashi, I hear, replied contemptuously that the responsibility was entirely his own and he was prepared to accept whatever punishment might follow.

---

[1] Presumably the *Kampaku*, though this is not entirely clear from the text.

DOCUMENT 66. Imperial Court to Bakufu, 22 November 1865.[1]

Foreign ships came recently to Hyōgo. Yesterday, 21 November, the Shōgun submitted a further report on the situation through the persons of the *Chūnagon* Hitotsubashi, Matsudaira [Katamori] Higo-no-kami, Matsudaira [Sadataka] Etchū-no-kami, and Ogasawara [Nagamichi] Iki-no-kami. Discussions went on all night and have continued until this evening. Today, when representatives of the fiefs were summoned and asked their views, it transpired that nearly all[2] agreed in recommending that it would be proper to grant Imperial sanction [for the treaties]. This is indeed unavoidable.

The Imperial instructions are announced in the enclosure herewith.

Enclosure

The Imperial consent is given to the treaties and appropriate action is to be taken accordingly.

Separate.[3]

With reference to the instructions given in the enclosed announcement, there are various unsatisfactory provisions in the treaties previously concluded. They do not conform to the Emperor's wishes. They are therefore to be re-examined and fresh arrangements are to be made after consultation with the fiefs.

With regard to Hyōgo no action is to be taken.

DOCUMENT 67. Bakufu to the British Minister in Japan, 24 November 1865.[4]

We have lately received from you several despatches to which we should have sent separate answers, but the great pressure of our national affairs has caused a delay, for which we must express our regret. However, we now reply to them all together, and hope that this answer will be to your satisfaction.

---

[1] The texts printed in *Zoku saimukiji*, iv. 307–8, and *Kyōto-shugoshoku shimatsu*, Part II, pp. 191–2, show only minor textual variations. Those given in *Kaikoku Kigen*, iii. 2764–5, and *Iwakura Kō Jikki*, i. 960, are both in some degree incomplete.

[2] Literally 'eight or nine out of ten'.

[3] It seems that the brief announcement above was intended to be public, while the comments added in this separate section were for the private information of the Bakufu. Cf. Document 67.

[4] This translation is taken from *Parliamentary Papers 1866*, vol. lxxvi, p. 518, and follows closely the Japanese text given in *Kaikoku Kigen*, iii. 2769–70. Identical notes were sent to the ministers in Japan of the United States, the Netherlands, and France. They were signed by three Rōjū: Matsudaira (Honjō) Munehide, Hōki-no-kami; Matsudaira Yasunao, Suō-no-kami; and Ogasawara Nagamichi, Iki-no-kami. The Bakufu subsequently tried, without success, to repudiate the promises made in this letter on the grounds that they were made privately by the three Rōjū and not formally by the government.

With regard to the Treaties, our Tycoon has made such strenuous efforts in his representations to Kioto, that the imperial consent has been given, as you will see from the inclosure.[1]

With regard to the opening of Hiogo, we are unable to discuss that at present. However, though we intend to open it at the expiry of the time fixed by the London Convention, we will open it earlier if the state of affairs should permit of it. But as we cannot decide to do so at present, we will send orders to Yeddo to pay the third instalment of the Shimonasaki indemnity during the 12th Japanese month, as is provided for by Convention. And we will carry out the remainder of the Convention of the 22nd October, 1864, according to its stipulations.

We fully consent that the Tariff shall be amended, and will send immediate orders to Midzuno Idzumi no Kami and Sakai Hida no Kami[2] to conduct as satisfactorily as possible the necessary discussions at Yeddo.

We beg to communicate the above.

A respectful and humble communication.

---

[1] This was the enclosure given with Document 66 above, a simple statement that the treaties had received Imperial consent and appropriate action was to be taken.

[2] The *Rōjū* Mizuno Tadakiyo, Izumi-no-kami, and the *Wakadoshiyori* Sakai Tadasuke, Hida-no-kami, who were responsible for affairs in Edo in the absence of the Shōgun and other members of the Council.

The Opening of Hyōgo, 1867

BETWEEN the autumn of 1865 and the spring of 1867 there occurred no major crisis in Japan's foreign relations. Tariff reform could be effected by the Bakufu without reference to the Court, so the agreement of June 1866 occasioned no fresh disputes. The Chōshū question, in fact, continued to dominate politics. In March 1866 the Bakufu defined the terms on which it would accept settlement, including a reduction of the Chōshū territories by 100,000 *koku* and the enforced retirement of both the head of the fief and his son. These terms the Court approved. But many of the leading *daimyō* thought them too severe. A Bakufu ultimatum was ignored by Chōshū and late in July Bakufu forces moved to the attack. Nowhere were they successful. By mid-September, indeed, they were in retreat; and when the Shōgun Iemochi died (19 September 1866), the Court took advantage of this event to order the cessation of hostilities.

Defeat at the hands of a single *daimyō* robbed the Bakufu of what little prestige remained to it. Hitotsubashi Keiki, who now became Shōgun, still faced the problem of settling the Chōshū dispute, though now the punishment of that fief had necessarily to be more formal than real. He also faced new difficulties in foreign affairs. In March 1867 the French minister, Léon Roches, in an audience at Ōsaka Castle, reminded him that the Bakufu was still committed to the opening of Hyōgo on 1 January 1868 under the terms of the London Protocol. He gave warning that if the port were not opened as promised, the Treaty Powers might resort to force, or alternatively might enter into direct relations with the *daimyō* and the Court. Early in April the British minister, Harry Parkes, proposed discussions preliminary to the opening of Hyōgo. This persuaded Keiki that he could not afford to wait for the advice of the great lords, though he had already requested it. On 9 April he submitted a memorial to the Court seeking Imperial sanction to open the port, on the grounds that this was both necessary as a means of avoiding national disaster and desirable as a step towards strengthening the country (Document 68). The Court refused outright (Document 69). A further request a few days later, again stimulated by a letter from Parkes, met with no better reception (Documents 70 and 71).

The fact was that the Bakufu now faced the powerful opposition of Satsuma, which since March 1866 had been in secret alliance with Chōshū. Their immediate aim was to secure Chōshū's restoration to favour at

Court. But ultimately the two fiefs sought to overthrow the Tokugawa, though it was still uncertain what political system they proposed to institute instead. Satsuma was represented in Kyōto by Ōkubo Toshimichi, who worked closely with the *Naidaijin* Konoe Tadafusa. Between them they were able to organize both the fiefs and the Court in opposition to Bakufu proposals. Ōkubo's first concern, as he told the former *Kampaku* Konoe Tadahiro, was to ensure that no decision be taken about Hyōgo without an opportunity being given for the great lords to express their views (Document 72). The point of this was not to prevent the opening of the port. It was rather to provide an occasion for the discussion of other issues, notably that of Chōshū. When Shimazu Hisamitsu reached the capital on 15 May, Ōkubo explained to him that this was an opportunity for Satsuma to assume leadership of the anti-Bakufu group and unite the great fiefs behind her (Document 73).

By 3 June 1867 Date Muneki, Matsudaira Keiei, and Yamanouchi Toyoshige had all arrived in Kyōto. These three were the *daimyō* whose support was most important both to Shimazu and to the Shōgun, and the five men were in constant consultation during the next few weeks. By 23 June it seemed that they might reach agreement. All were convinced that Hyōgo must be opened. But as their price for accepting this, the four *daimyō* insisted on a settlement with Chōshū. Keiki eventually agreed to waive Bakufu demands for a reduction of the fief's territory. Only the head of the fief was to be retired and his son was to succeed. But there was further dispute over the timing. The four lords, under the prompting of the Satsuma leaders, demanded that the Chōshū decision be announced first, partly because they feared that the opening of Hyōgo would enable the Bakufu to strengthen itself considerably with French help, and partly because some of them felt that they now had the opportunity to score a decisive victory. Keiki continued to argue that Hyōgo was much the more urgent problem of the two. Keiei eventually proposed a compromise, that there should be a simultaneous announcement of both decisions, and this was at first agreed. It was planned that the four *daimyō* should accompany the Shōgun to the Palace on 25 June to urge this action on the Court. At the last minute, however, the Satsuma leaders persuaded them to reverse this decision and reject all compromise. On the morning of 25 June, therefore, Shimazu, Date, Yamanouchi, and Matsudaira Keiei wrote jointly to the Shōgun reiterating their demand that the Chōshū decision be taken before the announcement that Hyōgo was to be opened.

Keiki decided to force the issue. The same day he went to the Court and sought Imperial sanction both for the opening of Hyōgo and for the new policy towards Chōshū. Shimazu absented himself entirely from the discussions that followed, while Date and Keiei attended only with reluctance. For nearly two days the debate raged at Court. As Saga Sanenaru's diary shows (Document 74), there was still much opposition to the opening of Hyōgo among the *kuge*. Keiki, however, had secured the support of Prince Asahiko and some of the senior Court officials. When the Sesshō, Nijō Nariaki, proved hesitant, these men forced his hand (Document 75). On 26 June 1867 the Court issued orders approving both the opening of Hyōgo and the new 'lenient' policy towards Chōshū (Document 76).

Keiki's victory was by no means final. This evidence of the Bakufu's continuing ability to coerce the Imperial Court shocked the opposition into further action. Shimazu, Date, Yamanouchi, and Matsudaira Keiei now informed the Court that they had not in fact been in favour of the Bakufu's proposals, thus putting the disagreement officially on record (Document 77). Thereafter the political crisis continued to grow until in November Keiki resigned and the Tokugawa Bakufu came to an end. It is primarily in this context that the Hyōgo dispute is of importance. By the middle of 1867 there was no longer any essential difference, among the men whose influence was greatest, about the necessity for smoother relations with the Treaty Powers. But foreign policy was still an issue on which the Bakufu could effectively be attacked. Thus the four great lords had withheld their support until they forced the Bakufu into concessions about Chōshū. In the last resort, foreign policy had become no more than a field for political manœuvre.

DOCUMENT 68. Shōgun Keiki to Imperial Court, 9 April 1867.[1]

When the Emperor gave his sanction to the treaties, during November of the year before last, he issued instructions that no action was to be taken with regard to Hyōgo. The Bakufu should have informed the foreigners of this at once. But to have done so would have led to immediate ruin and brought to nothing the Emperor's earnest desire for peace. Moreover, to make changes in the treaties, once concluded, was quite impossible, for it would serve only to lose us the confidence of other countries. This matter caused us much anxiety. But since the Emperor had, in view of the nature of the crisis, sanctioned the treaties and even overlooked the Bakufu's action in submitting such reports, we felt it incumbent on us to accept his orders as they stood and to give the matter further thought. Then there arose the Chōshū question and following it the death of the Shōgun Iemochi. Now it is getting very near the date fixed for the opening of Hyōgo and the foreign countries are making frequent demands on us. I have therefore once again been giving long and careful thought to these questions. It is clear that for us to enforce changes in the treaties would

---

[1] The text is printed, with some small and unimportant textual variations, in *Tokugawa Keiki Kō Den*, vii. 40–42; *Kaikoku Kigen*, iii. 2900–2; *Zoku saimukiji*, vi. 110–13; and *Iwakura Kō Jikki*, ii. 42–43.

call our honesty into question. It would put us in serious difficulties and would in the end plunge all our people into misery and endanger the safety of our country. Once that point was reached we would have no choice but to give effect to the treaties. This would indeed be to destroy at once our national honour and prestige, and for me would be a betrayal of my duty. Our particular need at present is for powerful warships and equipment. It is to build up our national wealth and strength by adopting foreign methods. To do this effectively we must at all costs open our ports. If we were for any reason to refuse to do so now, our means of increasing our wealth and strength—already a matter of some difficulty—would immediately disappear. What is more, treaties are the basis of international relations. If there were to be no permanent and lasting rules, the large would in the end overcome the small, the weak would be dominated by the strong.[1] Among the countries of the West there are both great and small, both strong and weak. But they lay great stress on keeping faith. They show respect for treaties. Thus they do not suffer from annexation and aggression and all preserve their national independence. A country's very existence depends on the observance of treaties. Therefore, I believe, we must at all costs carry out the provisions of the treaties we have once concluded. It is desirable that the Court, too, should give these facts full consideration. Should it have any doubts about the advantages and disadvantages of what I propose, I will submit detailed explanations orally when I come to the Palace.

As I have often reported, world conditions have changed. Yet if you study those conditions closely, both past and present, you will find that while there are differences both of territory and of customs among nations, all experience the same process of evolution, all experience alike the span of life from birth to death. In this there is no difference between one and another. All are born of the same womb. Thus to keep faith with one another is to conform to divine justice. Moreover, as an island Japan holds a vital position in the world, in the eyes both of East and of West. At this time other countries are making steady progress. Distance is no obstacle to them and they communicate freely with each other. If we alone, at such a time, cling to outworn customs and refrain from international relations of a kind common to all countries, our action will be in conflict with the natural order of things. We will, I think, soon find ourselves in great difficulties. Now is our opportunity, therefore, to change this state of affairs. It is desirable that the Court should guide itself by the ancient saying, 'since all men are brothers treat all with the same benevolence', that Court and Empire together should begin afresh. By so doing we shall exert all our efforts to wipe out the evil practices of the past.

---

[1] I here follow the *Kaikoku Kigen* text. The others read 'the strong would in the end overcome the weak, the weak would be dominated by the strong'.

Before many years are out our wealth and strength will be assured, our military prestige will have expanded and increased. And so the Emperor's mind will be set at rest.

This I report to the Throne.

DOCUMENT 69. Imperial Court to Shōgun, 23 April 1867.[1]

You have recently urged once again the opening of the port of Hyōgo, though it was forbidden the year before last by an Imperial command which the Shōgun then accepted. This is a question of the utmost difficulty and importance. It would be impossible to justify to our Imperial predecessor[2] the issue of fresh orders on this subject. Moreover, the views of the feudal lords are to be sought at once. The Shōgun will therefore carefully reconsider his attitude.

DOCUMENT 70. Shōgun Keiki to Imperial Court, 26 April 1867.[3]

Some days ago I submitted a memorial putting forward my views concerning the opening of Hyōgo and the fulfilment of treaty obligations. I now have the honour to acknowledge receipt of Imperial instructions to the effect that the matter is one of great difficulty and importance in which the Emperor would find it impossible to justify to his Imperial predecessor the issue of new orders; and that, moreover, the views of the feudal lords are to be sought at once and I must therefore carefully reconsider my attitude.

I, Keiki, have long been in attendance at the Court. Since the time of the Emperor Kōmei I have most respectfully sought to learn the Emperor's desires. It is not easy for me, therefore, to recommend the opening of Hyōgo, especially in view of the Imperial instructions that were issued the year before last. But after giving the most careful consideration to the interests of our country and to the advantages and disadvantages that might ensue, I realize that it is only by acting as I recommended several days ago that we can prevent permanent harm to the national prestige [*kokutai*]. Inexcusable though my action is, after weighing the gravity of the matter again and again I cannot but report as I do.

Moreover, it is completely impossible to effect changes in the treaties once they have been concluded. When the foreign countries present their

---

[1] The text is printed in *Iwakura Kō Jikki*, ii. 44, and *Tokugawa Keiki Kō Den*, vii. 43–44.

[2] The Emperor Kōmei had died at the end of January 1867 and had been succeeded by the young Emperor Meiji. The argument is often used in the documents that follow, that to open Hyōgo would be to show disrespect for the wishes of the Emperor Kōmei, who had consistently opposed this course.

[3] The text is printed, with small and unimportant textual variations, in *Tokugawa Keiki Kō Den,* vii. 44–45; *Kaikoku Kigen*, iii. 2902–3; *Zoku saimukiji*, vi. 126–7; and *Iwakura Kō Jikki*, ii. 44–45.

demands, therefore, we must answer them in accordance with the views I expressed in my report the other day. Even at a time when a multitude of State affairs crowd in upon us this is of the utmost importance. It can by no means be neglected. Somehow it must be carried through. That I should have put this matter off until I am now forced to make a report like this makes me approach the Court with a sense of the deepest shame. Yet these issues are vital to the safety of our country. I must therefore submit this report, however greatly I thereby incur the Imperial displeasure. It is my hope that the Court will take full cognizance of these facts and will now seek further consultations on this matter.

This I request, again submitting my report to the Throne.

DOCUMENT 71. Imperial Court to Shōgun, 3 May 1867.[1]

In the memorial which you submitted the other day giving your further ideas [concerning Hyōgo], you state that it is completely impossible to effect changes in the treaties once they have been concluded; and that when the foreign countries present their demands, therefore, we must answer them in accordance with the views expressed in your previous report. Such statements are open to question. The *Sesshō* [Nijō Nariaki] has been instructed to inform the Bakufu that under no circumstances must permission be given for the opening of Hyōgo until Imperial orders have been issued.

The Bakufu is to transmit to the Court its formal acceptance of this command.

DOCUMENT 72. Ōkubo Toshimichi to Konoe Tadahiro, early May 1867.[2]

The policy to be pursued with regard to the opening of Hyōgo is, I believe, a most grave question, of vital importance to our country. It is in every way necessary, therefore, that discussion of the desirability of opening this port be set aside for the time being and that policy be determined in accordance with the general advice when the views of the leading feudal lords of the Empire have been ascertained.[3] It is clear that if our policy should fail, not only would unrest be created through the Empire but also

---

[1] The text is printed in *Tokugawa Keiki Kō Den*, vii. 45–46, and *Iwakura Kō Jikki*, ii. 45.

[2] The text is printed in *Ōkubo Toshimichi Monjo*, i. 456–8. The letter is there dated Keiō 3, 4th month (4 May–2 June 1867), but was presumably written not later than Shimazu Hisamitsu's arrival in Kyōto on 15 May.

[3] On 28 April the Court had in fact called upon some twenty-four fiefs to submit their views on this question. Assuming that the date given for this letter is correct, Ōkubo is presumably reiterating here the importance of waiting for the results before taking further action, regardless of Bakufu impatience. What he really sought was a delay until the great lords could reach the capital.

the safety of the country would itself be jeopardized. Moreover, to grant Imperial sanction all in a moment, without seeking the views of the feudal lords of the Empire, would be an act of the greatest irreverence which it would be impossible to justify to the Emperor's predecessor.[1] And if such action gave occasion for the outbreak of civil disorder the position would be still more serious. The Court, therefore, should first secure general agreement and then determine a sound and enduring policy such as will pacify opinion throughout the Empire. It must make distinction between one and another[2] and issue such orders as will not lower the Imperial prestige. Only thus can the matter be handled properly. As to the opening of Hyōgo, it will, I fear, be necessary to announce a policy consistent with the present situation. But I think it desirable, since this is truly a matter of the greatest importance to the country, that the Court should issue instructions stating that the feudal lords of the Empire are to submit their advice and that a decision will be taken by the Court after general agreement has been reached.

Document 73. Ōkubo Toshimichi to Shimazu Hisamitsu, *circa* 15 May 1867.[3]

Your arrival in Kyōto at this time comes at a moment of grave importance, when both the safety and the existence of our country are at stake. It is especially important because the Bakufu is observing your actions and the great fiefs are waiting to see what move you will make. It is no light matter that the trend of national affairs should depend upon the actions of a single province. Yet faced as we are by an emergency in both domestic and foreign affairs, the abasement of the Court's prestige on the one hand and the misery of the people on the other make it impossible for you to stand idly by.

It is my hope that that true loyalty which makes you so unsparing in your efforts on our country's behalf may spread throughout the Empire. We must hereafter engage all our ardour in the task of establishing the Empire. We must act with humanity and justice. And since it is on this that success will depend, we must at all costs take steps to inspire the great fiefs through the example of your loyalty. This must be the root and basis of our action. In past years you have become known for your righteous

---

[1] The Emperor Kōmei. See Document 69, p. 310, note 2.

[2] The meaning of this is not clear. It may imply that the Court should listen to the views of its supporters rather than those of its critics. On the other hand, it may mean no more than that the Court should study the situation carefully before issuing its orders.

[3] The text is printed in *Ōkubo Toshimichi Monjo*, i. 468–71. It is there dated only Keiō 3, 4th month (4 May–2 June 1867), but it was clearly written at about the time of Shimazu Hisamitsu's arrival in Kyōto on 15 May 1867.

and loyal attitude. Now that you are at last in Kyōto, there are many, both in the Court and among the fiefs, whose views are sound and who desire to rally behind you; but they have been unable to move because not all the fiefs have the same ideas and because there is among them a tendency to hesitation and vacillation. These are trifling difficulties, but I think it desirable that you should consult with the leading feudal lords, even including such men as Owari, Aki, Yanagawa, and the rest,[1] discussing matters impartially with them all, whether they are in agreement with us or not; and that you should then send out messengers on their various tasks.[2]

As you are generally aware,[3] it was earlier decided that the urgent need is to secure the appointment of men of ability at the Court. As to the opening of Hyōgo, it seems that no other course is now possible but for the Imperial council to act resolutely in the light of the situation both at home and abroad, instituting an enduring policy such as will preserve our national prestige from harm and making the treaties once for all the responsibility of the Imperial Court.[4]

As to Chōshū, it is desirable that this, like the previous question, be handled by a special Imperial command. Orders should be issued acknowledging that the lords of Chōshū, father and son, acted out of a sincere desire to maintain the interests of the whole country and continuing them in their family territories of Nagato as before, so that all their retainers may be set at rest and their loyalty assured. However, the head of the fief himself should be retired on account of his negligence.

To change the Imperial orders with respect to the opening of Hyōgo is a great and unpardonable crime. It is desirable, therefore, that the Shōgun's territories should be reduced and that he should then be summoned to join the ranks of the feudal lords as one of themselves. This, I realize, is a very serious matter; but it is my belief that as matters now stand the general opinion leaves the Court no choice but to make this decision.

I submit above, in outline only, a general statement of my views.

[1] The senior Tokugawa branch house of Owari; Asano, the great *tozama* lord of Aki (Hiroshima); and Tachibana, the *tozama* lord of Yanagawa (Chikugo).

[2] Presumably with the intention of rallying support among those lords who were not present in the capital.

[3] This is an attempt (offered with great diffidence, especially as I have not been able to see the original document) to extract some meaning from the statement *tairyaku on-ori ainarisōrō tokoro nite*, which does not otherwise seem capable of interpretation. Certainly Satsuma did later, during June, try to force the appointment of its friends to offices at Court, though it failed through the opposition of Nijō Nariaki; and this fact weakens the possibility that the passage could read 'It was earlier decided . . . at the Court, which has in the main been achieved', though the Japanese might just possibly bear this construction.

[4] This is presumably a reference to the Satsuma plan for negotiating fresh treaties with the West in the name of the Emperor rather than that of the Shōgun (as Komatsu explained at the time to Satow; see Satow, *A Diplomat in Japan*, p. 190).

DOCUMENT 74. Diary of Saga Sanenaru, 25 and 26 June 1867.[1]

25 June. Clear and cloudy by turn. Sultry. . . .

About 1 p.m. I was told to go to the Palace as there was to be a discussion of State affairs. The Shōgun was to attend, it was said, together with Matsudaira Ōkura-tayū, Shimazu Ōsumi-no-kami, and Date Iyo-no-kami. When the time came, however, the three fiefs[2] were not there. They were sent for, and Keiei and Date came to the meeting. The *Sesshō*, the Princes In-no-miya and Hitachi-no-miya, the two former *Kampaku*, the *Naidaijin*, the *Sadaishō*, the two *dainagon* Kujō and Takatsukasa, the *gisō* and *buke-densō*[3] all took their places in the conference room. Also present were the Shōgun, the three fiefs [*sic*], *Rōjū*, the *Shoshidai*, *Wakadoshiyori*, &c.

The Shōgun stated that the leaders of the four fiefs of Echizen, Satsuma, Tosa,[4] and Uwajima had come recently to the capital and urged the desirability of lenient treatment for Chōshū and the need for opening the port of Hyōgo. The Bakufu was of the same opinion on both matters. He was therefore reporting this and seeking the Imperial sanction, he said. It was put to him, however, that while it was of course proper to pursue a lenient policy towards Chōshū, yet there were considerable differences between the views of the Bakufu and the ideas of the four fiefs about how this was to be carried out. Hence, he was told, action should only be taken when the two parties had reconciled their views; while with respect to Hyōgo a definite answer would be made when differences of opinion among various people had been removed. But the Shōgun urged that a definite answer be given at once.

The discussions at this council did not lead to a decision, though when the long day ended negotiation and debate continued by lamplight till the short night gave place to dawn and all were weary to the point of exhaustion. . . .

26 June. Cloudy and sultry, like yesterday. Occasional heavy rain.

After all-night discussions, a further council today like that of yesterday. But still no agreement was reached. There was nowhere any disagreement,

[1] The text is printed in *Saga Sanenaru Nikki*, ii. 69–71. The first and last parts of the entry for 25 June, which deal with other matters, are omitted.

[2] This expression is used to describe the three feudal lords: Matsudaira Keiei, Ōkura-tayū, of Echizen; Date Muneki, Iyo-no-kami, of Uwajima; and Shimazu Hisamitsu, Ōsumi-no-kami, of Satsuma. In this and the following document I refer to them as Keiei, Date, and Shimazu respectively, though the texts use variously their names, titles, or fiefs.

[3] The *Sesshō* Nijō Nariaki; the Princes Asahiko and Akira; the former *Kampaku* Takatsukasa Sukehiro and Konoe Tadahiro; the *Naidaijin* Konoe Tadafusa; the *Sadaishō*, apparently Ichijō Saneyoshi; the two *dainagon* Kujō Michitaka and Takatsukasa Sukemasa. Saga Sanenaru was one of the *gisō*. The office of *Sesshō*, when filled, superseded that of *Kampaku*.

[4] Yamanouchi Toyoshige of Tosa, though still in the capital, took no part in these final conferences.

I stated, about the lenient policy towards Chōshū. As to the opening of Hyōgo there would certainly be objections. Moreover, I added, the Court officials generally had long been consulted about questions of foreign affairs and their views sought; still more, therefore, since the question before us was of vital importance, concerning as it did the opening of a port near the capital, was it proper that action be taken only after these officials had been consulted. The *Sesshō* summoned such officials as the *Sanbansho-tōkin* and *Koban-gomen* and asked their views. Some put forward objections. Others remained silent. The circumstances made them hesitant and most did not state their views. It is the greatest of pities that men should be so temporizing.

These questions were so complicated and took so much time that in the end the sun set once again on our discussions. The Shōgun, meanwhile, persisted obstinately in his demands. But myself and others would not let him dictate to us. However, both the former *Kampaku* Takatsukasa [Sukehiro] and his son Sukemasa advanced arguments against us. The Imperial Princes, the great ministers, and the *sekke*[1] conferred together and decided to withdraw from affairs. The discussions collapsed. Their action was quite inexplicable and most infuriating. They were mere sycophants of the Bakufu, giving no heed to the country's danger. Most hateful behaviour. But everyone blindly followed their lead and we could exert no control. Yanagiwara, Hase, and myself put forward our views; but we were told in confidence that it was because a rift had opened between Court and Bakufu, due to the failure of the appropriate officials[2] in their duties of mediation, that these men felt unable to stand idly by and had therefore proposed this withdrawal from affairs [to force the issue]. When Yanagiwara, Hase, and myself accordingly offered to resign our posts, the *Sesshō* dissuaded us.

We being silenced for a time, the Bakufu seized this opportunity to press its arguments. The *Sesshō* became flustered. Taking advantage of this, the men listed above urged him to act in complete accordance with the Bakufu demands. This time we could not prevent it and it was finally decided to conform to the Bakufu's ideas in every particular. The Shōgun was notified of this in writing. Thus the trouble we had for so long taken about the lenient policy towards Chōshū and the granting of permission for the opening of Hyōgo had ended in vain. Only heartfelt sighs could express our indignation.

At 10 p.m. we withdrew from the Palace. . . .[3]

[1] Members of the five families (Konoe, Takatsukasa, Kujō, Nijō, and Ichijō) from which alone the office of *Sesshō* could be filled.

[2] i.e. the *gisō* and *buke-densō*, who were the official channels of communication between Court and Bakufu. Yanagiwara, Hase, and Saga were all *gisō*.

[3] The translation ends at p. 71, line 3, of the printed text. The rest of the day's entry deals with less important matters.

DOCUMENT 75. Diary of Prince Asahiko, 25 and 26 June 1867.[1]

25 June. Cloudy. Much rain in the afternoon. . . .

Hara [Tadanari] Ichi-no-shin came to me as messenger from the Shōgun. He told me the latter was making a private request today for Imperial sanction to be given at once in both matters [of Chōshū and Hyōgo]. He added that Takatsukasa[2] thought this desirable. I answered that I was also in agreement. I proposed writing to the former *Kampaku* to let him know this. He agreed.

Sometime after 2 p.m. I received a summons to go to the Palace. The Shōgun was there, but we learned that the three fiefs[3] had not come. Keiei had sent his apologies through the *buke-densō.* He was sent for and came to the Palace in the evening. The other two lords were also sent for. About 9 p.m. Shimazu sent word that he was indisposed and could not come. Date came about midnight.

While we were waiting for Date to come, the Shōgun and Keiei, with Etchū-no-kami, Iga-no-kami, Mino-no-kami, and others,[4] held a conference with the *Sesshō* and all Court officials down to the *gisō* and *buke-densō.* They were told that the three fiefs sought the issue of Imperial orders authorizing a lenient policy towards Chōshū and wished Hyōgo to be opened subsequent to this. The Shōgun urged that both matters be dealt with at the same time. This was discussed [by the Court officials] after withdrawal to another room, when it appeared that there were all kinds of conflicting opinions among us. However, it was decided that the Court should first state its readiness to issue orders authorizing a lenient policy towards Chōshū. As to Hyōgo, it seemed best that a reply be given later.

There was then a conference with the Shōgun, Keiei, Date, &c. They were informed that orders would be issued authorizing a lenient policy towards Chōshū, but that as there remained some differences of opinion concerning this, the action to be taken would in the first place be left to the Shōgun. As to the opening of Hyōgo, this would be dealt with later. But the Shōgun urged that, as time was limited, both questions ought certainly to be settled together.

There was a slight earthquake about 2 p.m.

---

[1] The text is printed in *Asahiko Shinnō Nikki,* ii. 386–91. The first part of the entry for 25 June (up to p. 387, line 5) is here omitted. Most of the text is also printed in *Tokugawa Keiki Kō Den,* vii. 95–99, where there are slight differences of detail but some useful editorial notes.

[2] The former *Kampaku* Takatsukasa Sukehiro.

[3] Matsudaira Keiei, Date Muneki, and Shimazu Hisamitsu, hereafter referred to as Keiei, Date, and Shimazu respectively. See Document 74, p. 314, note 2.

[4] The *Kyōto-shoshidai* Matsudaira Sadataka, Etchū-no-kami; the *Rōjū* Itakura Katsukiyo Iga-no-kami; and the *Rōjū* Inaba Masakuni, Mino-no-kami.

26 June. Rainy.

Continuing the above.

A further conference was held about dawn. It was decided to try sending for Shimazu again and that either Keiei or Date be sent as messenger to him. The *buke-densō* Hino was sent with orders to this effect, but Keiei and Date made their excuses. When the Court insisted, they said that that being so they would send for one of Shimazu's retainers and let him know of the position. This was left at their discretion. We were told that the Satsuma retainer Komatsu Tatehaki was coming; but during the morning it turned out that Shimazu had made his excuses.

While a Satsuma retainer was still being sought, proposed that the Court should authorize a lenient policy towards Chōshū and approve the opening of Hyōgo. The *Sesshō* and the two former *Kampaku*[1] discussed this privately. They reached a decision in general terms and showed their draft reply to myself and others in confidence. Some changes were made in the text, though the *Naidaijin*[2] still did not seem to approve. This decision was taken about noon. During the morning the two Arisugawa princes and Prince Shikibu had been summoned. Prince Akira and I offered Prince Shikibu's apologies, which were accepted by the *Sesshō* and the rest. The feudal lords were also sent for. About noon people began to arrive at the Palace. About 2 p.m. Prince Takahito of Arisugawa and others were shown the draft reply. They all said they had no objections to it. The *gisō* and *buke-densō* said the same.

About 4 p.m. the feudal lords began arriving at the Palace. Ōgimachi Sanjō[3] told the *Sesshō* and other officials that there were objections [to the Bakufu proposals]. There were no doubts about the lenient policy towards Chōshū, he said. The objections were simply to the opening of Hyōgo. Since the previous Emperor had seen fit to forbid this, it was not right for the Court to decide upon it now. The year before last the Shōgun had stated that he would not open Hyōgo in addition to the three ports already open; and for the Bakufu now to make a proposal of this kind was a complete breach of Imperial orders. He said he wanted the Court to issue orders closing the ports and expelling the foreigners, in accordance with the wishes of the previous Emperor. The *gisō* proposed that no reply should be made by the Court today.

This morning I learned that matters were to be explained to the feudal lords. This I accepted, but the Court nevertheless asked me for my views.

In conversation with me this morning Takatsukasa Sukemasa made the point that if objections were raised when the feudal lords were at the Palace it was going to make it difficult to persuade them to our view. He

[1] The two former *Kampaku* Takatsukasa Sukehiro and Konoe Tadahiro.
[2] The *Naidaijin* Konoe Tadafusa, who was in close touch with the Satsuma leaders.
[3] The *gisō* Saga Sanenaru (Jitsuai). For his account of these events see Document 74 above.

asked if anything could be done about this. Being, as I told him, of the same mind, I immediately interviewed the *gisō* Ōgimachi Sanjō and Yanagiwara and put the point to them. They answered that in the view of the *gisō* no such step [as informing the feudal lords] should be taken at all; the first step of all was to settle the differences of opinion among the Court nobles themselves. They all insisted that this was not the matter to discuss.

When evening came the Shōgun still showed every sign of determination. To his grief, he said, he considered that the country was now facing real disaster. Takatsukasa Sukemasa repeatedly urged the *Sesshō* to issue the reply drafted earlier. But the *Sesshō* made no answer. He was at his wit's end.

The former *Kampaku* Takatsukasa now said to me that it seemed we were quite powerless to act; and disrespectful though it was to the new Emperor, he feared we must make up our minds to withdraw from participation in public business and retire from the Court. We accordingly went to the room called Jakō-no-ma. The former *Kampaku* Takatsukasa, Kujō [Michitaka], Takatsukasa Sukemasa, and I were soon agreed, and I proposed that we should at once inform the *Sesshō*. Prince Akira also expressed agreement with us. As we were going along the corridor we met the former *Kampaku* Konoe, so we told him of our decision. He too expressed agreement. We moved into the room called Hakkei-no-ma, where I first explained to the Court that believing ourselves quite powerless to act in public affairs we now proposed to end our participation in the business and discussions at Court and to withdraw at once. We then retired to another room. The *gisō* all came to that room to reason with us. The two former *Kampaku* had at once gone back to the Jakō-no-ma, where I believe the *gisō* went to them. Apparently they wanted to discuss the situation in detail and at length with the two former *Kampaku*; similarly with myself. I contented myself with saying that they must certainly have noticed the concern felt by the two former *Kampaku* during the last two days and the confusion existing among the officials; we felt quite powerless, so were submitting a statement of the position. Hino also came to reason with us in the same way. When we had all agreed to delay our withdrawal for the moment, the *Sesshō* came to the Jakō-no-ma and expressed his regrets to the two former *Kampaku*. Similarly to Prince Takahito and myself. He asked that we delay our withdrawal and we consented. Later we again proposed to withdraw. The same happened. So we waited. Later, when Hino brought us a letter of some kind,[1] the two former *Kampaku* had already withdrawn. It was shown to me, but I said we could not partici-

[1] Presumably a copy of the Court's reply to the Bakufu. See Document 76. It is not clear whether this is the same reply as had been drafted by the senior officials earlier in the day, but it seems probable that it was.

pate in State affairs. Later I looked at it and said I approved. Prince Takahito and the rest all withdrew. I withdrew after consultation with the *Sesshō*. This was about 9 p.m. . . .[1]

DOCUMENT 76. Imperial Court to Bakufu, 26 June 1867.[2]

With respect to Chōshū, various fiefs that came to the capital last year and the four fiefs[3] that have come this year have all recommended that we issue orders authorizing a lenient policy. The Shōgun has also recommended a lenient policy. Since the Court is of the same opinion, a lenient policy is to be instituted at once.

As to the opening of Hyōgo, this has long been a matter of difficulty. It was, moreover, forbidden by the last Emperor. However, the Shōgun has reported that circumstances make it inevitable. Such views have also been expressed by various fiefs, and the four fiefs present in the capital have reported in like terms. We have therefore decided that there is indeed no other course open but to grant the Imperial sanction. Steps are accordingly to be taken to effect this.

Orders were issued that the port of Hyōgo was to remain closed and that the treaties were to be revised. These orders are hereby cancelled.

DOCUMENT 77. Date Muneki, Shimazu Hisamitsu, Yamanouchi Toyoshige, and Matsudaira Keiei to Imperial Court, 28 June 1867.[4]

It is our belief that the two questions of opening the port of Hyōgo and handling Chōshū are the most difficult and important facing us in foreign and domestic affairs at the present time. The Bakufu quite unjustifiably launched troops in a second attack on Chōshū, seeking to subdue that fief by force, though entirely without success. This caused tumult throughout the country, alienating opinion in all the fiefs and provoking criticism [of the Bakufu].

It was always our conviction that the establishment of national stability,

[1] The rest of the day's entry is omitted as being comparatively unimportant.

[2] There seems to be some doubt about the exact form of this Imperial pronouncement. As issued by the Bakufu (*Kaikoku Kigen*, iii. 2915–7) it took the form of two separate documents, one dealing with Chōshū and one with Hyōgo. *Iwakura Kō Jikki*, ii. 47, gives it as a single item, though omitting the part that makes the last paragraph of this translation. *Tokugawa Keiki Kō Den*, vii. 85–86, gives three separate items, corresponding to the three paragraphs of the translation but in reverse order. The wording of these texts, however, does not differ.

[3] The leaders of the fiefs; namely, Matsudaira Keiei of Echizen, Shimazu Hisamitsu of Satsuma, Date Muneki of Uwajima, and Yamanouchi Toyoshige of Tosa.

[4] The text is printed in *Ishin-shi*, iv. 646–7; and with small textual variations in *Zoku saimukiji*, vi. 304–5, and *Iwakura Kō Jikki*, ii. 49.

which is at present the urgent task, could only be achieved if the whole country were shown that affairs were being handled in a just and straightforward manner; and that the first step should therefore be taken in the matter of Chōshū, by issuing Imperial orders to restore the lords of that fief, father and son, to their regular and original rank and thereby give concrete evidence of a reversal of Bakufu policy. Once such clear and open evidence had been manifested, we felt, opinion throughout the country would for the first time be set at rest. It would then be proper, as the second step, to take appropriate measures for the opening of Hyōgo.

A short time ago the Court was pleased to seek our views on this subject. Before returning a reply to this inquiry we made repeated representations to the Bakufu concerning the order to be observed and the distinctions to be made in treating these two questions. Yet the day before yesterday, 26 June, we received written notification that the Court had issued orders authorizing, with respect to Chōshū, the adoption of a lenient policy; and stating, with respect to the opening of Hyōgo, that as the four fiefs then present in the capital[1] had expressed agreement there was indeed no other course open but to grant the Imperial sanction. This was a most unexpected and disturbing development. To question instructions issued by the Court is no light matter, and we are most conscious of our presumption in so doing, but errors of fact in a matter of such importance to the State cannot be passed over in silence. We therefore feel compelled to make some reference to the matter.

Submitted.

---

[1] i.e. Shimazu, Date, Yamanouchi, and Keiei, the four signatories of this letter. They are here citing the text of the Imperial pronouncement (Document 76 above).

Glossary of Administrative and Other Technical Terms

BAKUFU 幕府 Shogunate: the term used to describe the *de facto* central government of Japan under a *Sei-i-tai-shōgun* (q.v.). The Shōgun's officials (collectively, the Bakufu) carried out the actual duties of administration and the Imperial Court retained only a nominal authority.

BUGYŌ 奉行 Bakufu officials in the middle and upper levels of the administrative hierarchy as organized in the Tokugawa period (1603–1868). Some belonged to the central government in Edo (see *jisha-bugyō*, *machi-bugyō*, and *kanjō-bugyō*). Important new creations of this kind at the end of the period included the office of *gaikoku-bugyō* (q.v.). Other *bugyō*, usually of slightly lower rank, represented the Shōgun as governors of the more important cities under Bakufu control, especially Nagasaki, Shimoda, Hakodate, Kanagawa (Yokohama), and Hyōgo (see separately).

BUKE 武家 'Military houses': collective term for members of the feudal class as a whole, up to and including the Shōgun. Normally used to distinguish the Bakufu or feudal lords on the one hand from the Imperial Court or Court nobles (cf. *kuge*) on the other.

BUKE-DENSŌ 武家傳奏 Officials of the Imperial Court whose duty it was to receive communications from the *buke*, usually from the Bakufu, and submit them to the Emperor. Of relatively high rank, slightly lower than that of *gisō* (q.v.).

CHŪNAGON 中納言 Imperial Court title, held as a rule by Court nobles ranking immediately below the great ministers; in the Tokugawa period often bestowed also on members of the *sanke*.

DAIMYŌ 大名 Feudal lords, i.e. those who held fiefs with a rice revenue rated at 10,000 *koku* or more a year. In the Tokugawa period they were divided into two categories, namely *fudai daimyō* and *tozama daimyō* (q.v.).

EDO MACHI-BUGYŌ 江戸町奉行 See *machi-bugyō*.

FUDAI DAIMYŌ 譜代大名 Those *daimyō* (q.v.) whose ancestors

had supported Tokugawa Ieyasu before the battle of Sekigahara (1600), by which he established his supremacy; sometimes referred to as hereditary vassals of the Tokugawa. In the Tokugawa administrative system only *fudai daimyō* were eligible for the senior offices, i.e. those of *jisha-bugyō* and above. Cf. *tozama daimyō* and *hatamoto*.

GAIKOKU-BŌEKI-TORISHIRABE-GAKARI 外 國 貿 易 取 調 掛 A group of Bakufu officials 'responsible for the study of foreign trade'; first appointed 17 November 1856. Included most of those with special knowledge of foreign affairs, headed by the Rōjū HOTTA Masayoshi, and formed an *ad hoc* committee which was to decide the terms on which Japan should open her ports to trade.

GAIKOKU-BUGYŌ 外 國 奉 行 Bakufu officials, first appointed 16 August 1858, whose duty it was to advise the Bakufu on foreign affairs and to conduct negotiations with foreign diplomats both in Japan and abroad; sometimes referred to by English contemporaries as 'Under-Secretaries for Foreign Affairs'. It was an office of fairly high rank, ranking approximately with that of *kanjō-bugyō*, i.e. just below those of *daimyō* status, and was often held concurrently with that of *kanjō-bugyō* or that of *bugyō* of one of the great ports (Nagasaki, Kanagawa, &c.). Numbers varied from 5 (in 1858) to a maximum of 13 later, with considerable fluctuations in between.

GAIKOKU-GAKARI 外 國 掛 'In charge of [relations with] foreign countries': prefix used with the titles of some Bakufu offices in the late Tokugawa period to designate those who bore a special responsibility for the conduct of foreign affairs, e.g. *gaikoku-gakari-ōmetsuke*. Cf. *kaibō-gakari*.

GISŌ 議 奏 Officials of the Imperial Court, usually 4 or 5 in number, whose duty it was to act as advisers to the Emperor and especially to transmit his orders to the Court and Bakufu. Ranked immediately below the great ministers of the Court.

GUNKAN-BUGYŌ 軍 艦 奉 行 Bakufu officials with special responsibility for naval matters. The office was created on 28 March 1859 as part of the administrative changes consequent on the opening of the ports and ranked approximately with that of *kanjō-bugyō*.

HAKODATE BUGYŌ 箱 館 奉 行 Bakufu officials responsible for the administration of the port of Hakodate and the neighbouring territory of Ezo (Hokkaidō) and for the conduct of relations with foreigners there; hence often known in English as 'Governors of Hakodate'. The office was created in 1802 and was held by two men, one normally being at any given time in Hakodate, the other in Edo.

HATAMOTO 旗本 Direct vassals of the Tokugawa, holding fiefs with a rice revenue rated at less than 10,000 *koku* a year, who had the right of audience with the Shōgun. Those who did not have the right of audience were known as *gokenin* 御家人 Most of the lesser Bakufu officials were drawn from the ranks of the *hatamoto* and *gokenin*. Cf. *fudai daimyō*.

HYŌGO BUGYŌ 兵庫奉行 Bakufu officials responsible for the administration of the port of Hyōgo (modern Kōbe) and hence often known in English as 'Governors of Hyōgo'. The office was created in December 1864, there being only one *bugyō* until December 1865, when the office lapsed until August 1867. Thereafter there were always two *bugyō*.

HYŌJŌSHO 評定所 Highest feudal court of Tokugawa Japan, dating from the seventeenth century, which consisted of the 'three ranks of *bugyō*', i.e. *jisha-bugyō*, *machi-bugyō*, and *kanjō-bugyō* (q.v.). Sometimes used as a collective term of address for those senior Bakufu officials, below the rank of *wakadoshiyori*, who were consulted on important questions of policy.

ICHIBU 一分 Japanese silver coin of the late Tokugawa period. See under *ryō*.

JISHA-BUGYŌ 寺社奉行 Bakufu officials with special responsibility for the supervision of shrines and temples. Office open only to *fudai daimyō*, the lowest in the administrative hierarchy that was so restricted; ranked below *wakadoshiyori* but higher than all other *bugyō*.

JŌI 攘夷 'Expel the barbarian': slogan of those groups which opposed the treaties made with the West in 1854–8; later became associated with the movement to overthrow the Tokugawa (cf. *sonnō*). See Introduction, pp. 8–15.

KAIBŌ-GAKARI 海防掛 'In charge of maritime defence': prefix used with the titles of some Bakufu offices after 1845 to designate those who bore a special responsibility for coast defence and, by implication, for foreign relations, e.g. *kaibō-gakari-ōmetsuke*. In the latter connexion later superseded by the term *gaikoku-gakari* (q.v.).

KAIKOKU 開國 'Open the country': slogan of those groups which favoured the conclusion of treaties with the West in 1854–8; later associated with support for the Bakufu against its enemies at home. See Introduction, pp. 5–8.

KAMON 家 門 The 'Related Houses': junior branches of the Tokugawa line, other than *sanke* and *sankyō* (q.v.). They were not in the line of succession to the Shōgun and bore the family name of Matsudaira.

KAMPAKU 關 白 In normal times, the senior official of the Imperial Court; replaced by the *sesshō* (q.v.) when the Emperor was a minor. The office was confined to the five Fujiwara branch families of Ichijō, Nijō, Kujō, Konoe, and Takatsukasa.

KANAGAWA BUGYŌ 神奈川奉行 Bakufu officials responsible for the administration of the port of Kanagawa (Yokohama) and foreign trade and relations there; hence often known in English as 'Governors of Kanagawa'. The office was created on 3 July 1859, when 5 men were appointed to it; numbers varied thereafter up to 9. Often held concurrently with the office of *gaikoku-bugyō*.

KANJŌ-BUGYŌ 勘定奉行 Bakufu officials with a special responsibility for finance; usually 5 or 6 in number during the late Tokugawa period. This was one of the higher posts open to those who were not *daimyō*, ranking immediately below that of *machi-bugyō* (q.v.).

KANJŌ-GIMMIYAKU 勘定吟味役 Bakufu officials of lower rank, subordinate to the *kanjō-bugyō*.

KANSAI 關西 Japan 'west of the barrier': that part of the country which lay west of the road barrier established by the Tokugawa Bakufu (on the Tōkaidō road in the Hakone mountains) to control entrance to and exit from the neighbourhood of Edo; most often used of the more limited area at the eastern end of the Inland Sea, including Kyōto, Ōsaka, and Hyōgo; hence sometimes used loosely as a term for the Imperial Court or the Imperial capital. Cf. *Kantō*.

KANTŌ 關東 Japan 'east of the barrier': cf. *Kansai*. Most often used as a term for Edo and its neighbourhood; hence sometimes used loosely for the Bakufu.

KAPITAN. The head of the Dutch trading factory at Deshima (Nagasaki), i.e. the Dutch East India Company's *opperhoofd* there up to the end of the eighteenth century. In the nineteenth century the same term was used by Japanese for the Dutch government representative, later the Dutch minister, as long as he continued to reside at Deshima.

KŌBU-GATTAI 公武合體 'Court-Bakufu unity': slogan adopted by those groups of feudal lords and Court nobles who in the late Tokugawa period sought to obtain a greater share of political authority without actually destroying the Bakufu. See Introduction, pp. 45–47.

KŌKEN 後見 See *Shōgun-kōkenshoku.*

KOKU 石 Measure of capacity, standardized at 4·96 English bushels; used before 1868 to assess the rice revenue of fiefs and the size of ships.

KOKUJI-GOYŌ-GAKARI 國事御用掛 Officials of the Imperial Court designated to advise the Emperor on national affairs. The office was created on 28 January 1863 in an attempt to moderate the political action of *sonnō-jōi* extremists by providing a new channel through which those other than the great nobles could express their views; in some senses, therefore, a consultative council (of 29 members in the first instance). It never really succeeded in its object, though it continued in existence until 1868.

KOKUTAI 國體 Term originally meaning 'national prestige' and apparently so used in the late Tokugawa period. Subsequently used widely in the context of modern nationalism, when it is translated 'national polity' or 'fabric of the State'. It invariably has favourable connotations, through which it makes an appeal to national or nationalist prejudice.

KUGE 公家 or 公卿 'Court families' or 'Court nobles': term used to distinguish the nobles of the Imperial Court from the feudal nobility (cf. *buke*).

KYŌTO-SHOSHIDAI 京都所司代 Bakufu official: the Shōgun's representative in Kyōto, responsible for supervising the Imperial Court and capital, especially for controlling the access of feudal lords to the Court and the relations between Court and Bakufu. The office was invariably held by one of the more important *fudai daimyō.* Cf. *Kyōto-shugoshoku.*

KYŌTO-SHUGOSHOKU 京都守護職 Bakufu official: had essentially the same functions as the *Kyōto-shoshidai* (q.v.) but was the senior of the two. The office, which was held only by members of the *kamon* houses, was created on 24 September 1862 as part of the attempt to strengthen the *kōbu-gattai* party.

MACHI-BUGYŌ 町奉行 Bakufu officials: specifically, those responsible for the administration of the Shōgun's capital of Edo (*Edo machi-bugyō*), always two in number. This was the senior administrative post open to those who were not *daimyō* (cf. *jisha-bugyō*). *Machi-bugyō* were also appointed at Kyōto, Ōsaka, and elsewhere, but these were appreciably lower in rank.

METSUKE 目 附 Bakufu officials, of slightly lower rank than *bugyō*, responsible for supervising the activities of officials and members of the feudal class below *daimyō* status, with the special duty of detecting maladministration or disaffection; hence often translated 'censor', sometimes 'spy'. Cf. *ōmetsuke*.

MIKADO 帝 The Emperor: term normally used by foreigners in the nineteenth century, especially to distinguish the Emperor from the Shōgun (cf. *Tycoon*).

NAGASAKI BUGYŌ 長 崎 奉 行 Bakufu officials responsible for the administration of the port of Nagasaki and the foreign trade carried on there; usually known in English as 'Governors of Nagasaki'. The office was created in the seventeenth century and was held concurrently by two men, one normally being at any given time in Nagasaki, the other in Edo.

NAIDAIJIN 內 大 臣 'Minister of the Centre': one of the highest offices of the Imperial Court, ranking with those of *Sadaijin* and *Udaijin* (q.v.). It was always held by a Court noble; but in addition the title *Naidaijin* was also bestowed on the Shōgun, who took rank at Court accordingly.

NAIRAN 內 覽 Senior official of the Imperial Court, ranking immediately after the *Kampaku* and often combined with that office.

ŌMETSUKE 大 目 附 Bakufu officials responsible especially for supervising the activities of officials and feudal lords of *daimyō* status and detecting maladministration and disaffection (cf. *metsuke*). Ranked approximately with *kanjō-bugyō*.

ŌSAKA-JŌDAI 大 坂 城 代 Bakufu official responsible for the administration of the city of Ōsaka; a senior post, held always by one of the *fudai daimyō*.

ŌSETSU-GAKARI 應 接 掛 'In charge of discussions': term applied to those Bakufu officials appointed specially to negotiate with foreign envoys coming to Japan, the appointment in each case being made *ad hoc*. The description was usually completed by prefixing the name of the country from which the foreign envoy came, e.g. the *America ōsetsu-gakari* in 1854 were the officials appointed to treat with Perry.

RI 里 Measure of distance: 1 *ri* = 2·44 miles.

RŌJŪ 老 中 In normal times the most senior of Bakufu officials, usually 4 or 5 in number and often called members of the Council of State in Edo. They had general powers of supervision over the administration and were especially concerned with the control of *daimyō* and the conduct of Court-Bakufu relations. Appointments were made from *fudai daimyō* whose fiefs were rated at 25,000 *koku* or more a year; but in practice, in the late Tokugawa period, *Rōjū* were only chosen from those with fiefs of 50,000 *koku*. Cf. *Tairō*.

RŌJŪ-KAKU 老中格 Bakufu officials ranking as *Rōjū* (q.v.) but not actually appointed as such.

RŌNIN 浪人 'Wave men': samurai who no longer owed fealty to a lord, either by force of circumstance (e.g. the transfer or disgrace of their lord) or by choice. In the late Tokugawa period, especially, many samurai who favoured extreme measures in politics abandoned their fiefs and became *rōnin* in order not to implicate their lords in 'illegal' activities. Others acted similarly from economic motives.

RUSUI 留守居 'Steward': in a feudal context, a retainer who was put in charge of an establishment in the absence of his lord; used especially of those who supervised the establishments maintained by the fiefs in Edo, Kyōto, and Ōsaka.

RYŌ 両 Unit of currency, equal to 4 *ichibu*. The silver *ichibu* was minted in Japan from 1837 to 1868 and remained in use until the currency reforms of 1874. Under the terms of the 1858 treaties it was exchanged by weight for Western silver coins, the standard rate being 311 silver *ichibu* to 100 Mexican dollars. There were, however, two kinds of silver *ichibu* in use at the same time, equal in weight but differing in intrinsic value, and this fact caused a number of disputes with the Western Powers. The Tempō *ichibu*, minted 1837–54, consisted of gold 0·21 per cent., silver 98·86 per cent., and copper 0·93 per cent. This was the coin on which the treaty stipulations had been based. But in 1859 the Bakufu began to mint the Ansei *ichibu*, debasing the coinage with the object of reducing the drain on precious metals which was expected to result from foreign trade. The Ansei *ichibu* consisted of gold 0·06 per cent., silver 89·35 per cent., and copper 10·59 per cent. The weight of the *ichibu* remained constant at 2·31 *momme* (1 *momme* = 58 Tr. grains).

SADAIJIN 左大臣 'Minister of the Left': one of the highest offices of the Imperial Court, ranking with those of *Udaijin* and *Naidaijin* (q.v.) and immediately after the *Kampaku* and *Nairan*.

SAKOKU 鎖國 'National seclusion', i.e. the policy pursued by the Tokugawa Bakufu before 1853. It is sometimes translated 'close the country' and taken (though inaccurately) to be an equivalent of *jōi* (q.v.).

SAMURAI 侍 Any member of the feudal (military) class, irrespective of rank; commonly used for the lower ranks of that class, i.e. the retainers of feudal lords.

SANKE 三 家 The 'Three Houses': the three senior branch houses of the Tokugawa family, descended from the younger sons of Tokugawa Ieyasu; known from their fiefs as the Owari, Kii (Kishū), and Mito houses. The head of each branch bore the family name of Tokugawa. With the *Sankyō* (q.v.), they formed the group from which the Shōgun's successor was chosen if the direct line failed.

SANKIN-KŌTAI 参 勤 交 代 Feudal custom enforced by the Toku-gawa Bakufu as a means of retaining control over the great lords. Each *daimyō* was normally required to spend 4 or 6 months of every year in Edo, where his family remained as hostages when he was resident in his fief. The regulations varied slightly from time to time and were greatly relaxed in the autumn of 1862.

SANKYŌ 三 卿 The 'Three Lords': branch houses of the Tokugawa family; those of Tayasu and Hitotsubashi being descended from the eighth Tokugawa Shōgun, Yoshimune, and that of Shimizu from the ninth Shōgun, Ieshige. With the *Sanke* (q.v.), they formed the group from which the Shō-gun's successor was chosen if the direct line failed.

SEI-I-TAI-SHŌGUN 征 夷 大 将 軍 'Barbarian-subduing generalis-simo': title first used for the commander of the Imperial forces in the cam-paigns against the Ainu and taken in 1192 by the Minamoto as that under which they became *de facto* rulers of Japan. It became hereditary and was used thereafter by successive families who ruled Japan (tracing their descent in some way from the Minamoto), the Tokugawa being the last of these. It was normally used in the abbreviated form *Shōgun*. The Shōgun ruled in the Emperor's name but was entirely outside the control of the Imperial Court and worked through his own administrative system. Cf. *Bakufu*.

SEIJI-SŌSAISHOKU 政 事 総 裁 職 Bakufu official: new office created on 4 August 1862 as part of the attempt to increase the power of the *kōbu-gattai* group; lapsed in the summer of 1864. His authority was equivalent to that of a *Tairō* (q.v.), but the office differed in that it was held not by a *fudai daimyō* but by one of the *kamon*.

SESSHŌ 摂 政 'Regent': an official acting in the Emperor's name when the Emperor was a minor. This was the highest appointment at the Imperial Court, replacing that of *Kampaku* (q.v.) during the period of a minority; con-fined to the five Fujiwara branch families of Ichijō, Nijō, Kujō, Konoe, and Takatsukasa.

SHIMODA BUGYŌ 下田奉行 Bakufu officials responsible for the administration of the port of Shimoda and foreign trade there: hence usually known in English as 'Governors of Shimoda'. The office was created in 1842 and was held by two men, one normally being at any given time in Shimoda, and the other in Edo.

SHŌGUN 将軍 See *Sei-i-tai-shōgun*.

SHŌGUN-KŌKENSHOKU 将軍後見職 'Guardian to the Shōgun': post usually filled only during the minority or incapacity of a Shōgun. The appointment of Hitotsubashi Keiki in 1862, however, was a political move designed to strengthen the position of the *kōbu-gattai* group, the Shōgun then being old enough to dispense with any personal substitute.

SHOSHIDAI 所司代 See *Kyōto-shoshidai*.

SHUGOSHOKU 守護職 See *Kyōto-shugoshoku*.

SONNŌ 尊王 'Honour the Emperor': slogan of those who in the late Tokugawa period sought in some degree a restoration of Imperial prerogatives and prestige; subsequently developed into a demand for the complete abolition of the Bakufu. See Introduction, pp. 36–38.

SONNŌ-JŌI 尊王攘夷 'Honour the Emperor, expel the barbarian': slogan of the anti-Bakufu movement after 1858. See separately *sonnō* and *jōi*.

TAIRŌ 大老 'Regent': highest office in the Bakufu; an appointment was made only in time of crisis, but when made the Tairō took precedence over the *Rōjū* and in effect conducted all important State business. The office was restricted to *fudai daimyō* with fiefs of 100,000 *koku* or more; in practice to the four families of Doi, Hotta, Sakai, and Ii (and usually to the last two of these).

TAMARI-NO-MA 溜間 One of the chambers in the Shōgun's palace. *Daimyō* visiting the palace were ranked according to the chamber which they used, those of the *tamari-no-ma* being a few of the more powerful *fudai daimyō* and a number of the *kamon*.

TOZAMA DAIMYŌ 外様大名 Those feudal lords of *daimyō* status (see *daimyō*) whose ancestors had not submitted to Tokugawa rule until after Ieyasu's victory at Sekigahara (cf. *fudai daimyō*). They were always regarded by the Tokugawa as possible rivals and were permanently excluded from all Bakufu offices. Sometimes referred to in English as the 'outside feudatories'.

TYCOON. Anglicization of the title *Taikun* 大 君 and used generally by foreigners in the late Tokugawa period to describe the Shōgun (to distinguish him from the Emperor or 'Mikado' in Kyōto).

UDAIJIN 右 大 臣 'Minister of the Right': one of the highest offices of the Imperial Court, ranking with those of *Sadaijin* and *Naidaijin* (q.v.).

URAGA BUGYŌ 浦 賀 奉 行 Bakufu officials responsible for the administration of Uraga, which was a port of inspection for Japanese coastal vessels, especially those proceeding to Edo; usually known in English as 'Governors of Uraga'. The office was established in 1721 and was held by one or two men (always by two after 1844).

WAKADOSHIYORI 若 年 寄 Bakufu officials, ranking below the *Rōjū* and above the *jisha-bugyō*, with the special duty of supervising the activities of members of the feudal class below *daimyō* status; usually 6 or 7 in number. They were sometimes known in English as members of the 'Second' or 'Junior' council.

ZOKURON-HA 俗 論 派 The 'conventional party': a group of *fudai daimyō* and Bakufu officials who in the late Tokugawa period sought to preserve their own (and by extension the Bakufu's) traditional prerogatives against the encroachment of the Mito and other opposition factions.

Biographical Notes

[These notes are selective in that they outline the official careers of those Japanese who played an important part in the conduct or discussion of foreign affairs in the late Tokugawa period, but omit posts held before or after that period as well as those of minor consequence; no attempt is made to provide a narrative of events or activities. Dates are given where available, the date after a title being that on which it was assumed and dates under the heading *Fief* being those between which the individual in question was head of the fief.]

ABE MASAHIRO 阿部正弘 (1819–57). Feudal lord (*fudai daimyō*) and Bakufu official. *Title*: Ise-no-kami 伊勢守 (1837). *Fief*: Fukuyama 福山 ; *fudai*; 100,000 *koku* (110,000 from 1853) (1837–57). *Office*: Rōjū (Nov. 1843–Aug. 1857).

ABE MASATŌ (Seigai) 阿部正外 (1828–87). Bakufu official, later feudal lord (*fudai daimyō*). *Titles*: Echizen-no-kami 越前守 (1859); Bungo-no-kami 豊後守 (1864). *Fief*: Shirakawa 白河 ; *fudai*; 100,000 *koku* (1864–6). *Offices*: (before succeeding to fief) Kanagawa bugyō (Dec. 1861–Sept. 1862); Gaikoku-bugyō (Sept. 1862–June 1863); Machi-bugyō (June 1863–Apr. 1864); (after succeeding to fief) Rōjū (July 1864–Nov. 1865).

ANDŌ NOBUMASA 安藤信正 (1820–71). Feudal lord (*fudai daimyō*) and Bakufu official. *Titles*: Ise-no-kami 伊勢守 (1836); Nagato-no-kami 長門守 (1843); Tsushima-no-kami 對馬守 (1856). *Fief*: Iwaki-taira 磐城平 ; *fudai*; 50,000 *koku* (60,000 from 1862) (1847–62). *Offices*: Jisha-bugyō (Jan. 1852–Sept. 1858); Wakadoshiyori (Sept. 1858–Feb.1860); Rōjū (Feb. 1860–May 1862).

ARAO NARIMASA 荒尾成允 Bakufu official. *Titles*: Tosa-no-kami 土佐守 (by 1852); Iwami-no-kami 石見守 (by 1859). *Offices*: Metsuke (as *kaibō-gakari*, July 1852–June 1854); Nagasaki bugyō (June 1854–Oct. 1859).

ASAHIKO, PRINCE 朝彦親王 (1824–91). Imperial prince. *Titles*: Nakagawa-no-miya 中川宮 (1863); In-no-miya 尹宮 (by 1867).

DATE Muneki (Munenari) 伊達宗城 (1819–92). Feudal lord (*tozama daimyō*). *Titles*: Tōtomi-no-kami 遠江守 (1844); Iyo-no-kami 伊豫守 (1858). *Fief*: Uwajima 宇和島 ; *tozama*; 100,000 *koku* (1844–58).

HARA Tadanari 原忠成 also known as Ichi-no-shin 市之進 (1830–67). Samurai of Mito in the service of HITOTSUBASHI Keiki; regarded as the most able of Keiki's retainers.

HAYASHI Noboru 林昇 also known as Gakusai 學齋 (1833–1906). Confucian scholar and Bakufu official. *Title*: Daigaku-no-kami 大學頭

HITOTSUBASHI Keiki. *See* TOKUGAWA Keiki.

HONJŌ Munehide 本莊宗秀 also known as MATSUDAIRA 松平 Munehide (1809–73). Feudal lord (*fudai daimyō*) and Bakufu official. *Titles*: Hōki-no-kami 伯耆守 (1840); Tango-no-kami 丹後守 (1868). *Fief*: Miyazu 宮津 ; *fudai*; 70,000 *koku* (1840–66). *Offices*: Jisha-bugyō (Nov. 1858–Feb. 1861); Ōsaka-jōdai (Feb. 1861–July 1862); Kyōto-shoshidai (July–Sept. 1862); Rōjū (Sept. 1864–Sept. 1866).

HOTTA Masayoshi 堀田正睦 also known as Masahiro 正篤 (1811–64). Feudal lord (*fudai daimyō*) and Bakufu official. *Titles*: Sagami-no-kami 相模守 (1826); Bitchū-no-kami 備中守 (1834). *Fief*: Sakura 佐倉 ; *fudai*; 110,000 *koku* (1825–59). *Office*: Rōjū (Nov. 1855–Aug. 1858).

IDO Satohiro 井戶覺弘 (d. 1858). Bakufu official. *Title*: Tsu-shima-no-kami 對馬守 (by 1849). *Offices*: Metsuke (Dec. 1842–Dec. 1845); Nagasaki bugyō (Dec. 1845–Sept. 1849); Machi-bugyō (Sept. 1849–Dec. 1856); Ōmetsuke (Dec. 1856–May 1858).

IEMOCHI, Shōgun. *See* TOKUGAWA Iemochi.

IESADA, Shōgun. *See* TOKUGAWA Iesada.

IEYOSHI, Shōgun. *See* TOKUGAWA Ieyoshi.

II Naosuke 井伊直弼 (1815–60). Feudal lord (*fudai daimyō*) and Bakufu official. *Titles*: Gemban-no-kami 玄蕃頭 (1847); Kamon-no-kami 掃部頭 (1850). *Fief*: Hikone 彦根 ; *fudai*; 350,000 *koku* (1850–60). *Office*: Tairō (June 1858–Mar. 1860).

IKEDA Nagaaki 池田長發 also 長顯 (1837–79). Bakufu official. *Title*: Chikugo-no-kami 筑後守 (1863). *Offices*: Metsuke (June 1862–June 1863, as *gaikoku-gakari*; and again Sept.–Oct. 1863); Gaikoku-bugyō (Oct. 1863–Aug. 1864).

IKEDA Yoshinori (Keitoku) 池田慶德 (1837–77). Feudal lord (*tozama daimyō*); son of TOKUGAWA Nariaki; brother of HITOTSUBASHI Keiki. *Titles*: Sagami-no-kami 相模守 (1851); Inaba-no-kami 因幡守 (1865). *Fief*: Inaba 因幡; *tozama*; 325,000 *koku* (1850–71).

INOUE Kiyonao 井上清直 (d. 1868). Bakufu official; brother of KAWAJI Toshiaki. *Title*: Shinano-no-kami 信濃守 (by 1858). *Offices*: Shimoda bugyō (May 1855–Mar. 1859); Gaikoku-bugyō (Aug. 1858—Mar. 1859; again Sept. 1862–Jan. 1863; again Oct.–Dec. 1864); Gunkan-bugyō (Nov. 1859–Sept. 1862); Kanjō-bugyō (Dec. 1864–Oct. 1866); Machi-bugyō (Jan.– Sept. 1863; again July 1866–Jan. 1868).

INOUE Masanào 井上正直 Feudal lord (*fudai daimyo*) and Bakufu official. *Title*: Kawachi-no-kami 河内守 (1852). *Fief*: Hamamatsu 濱松; *fudai*; 60,000 *koku* (1847–71). *Offices*: Jisha-bugyō (Apr. 1861–Nov. 1862); Rōjū (Nov. 1862–Aug. 1864; and again Jan. 1866–July 1867).

ITAKURA Katsukiyo (Katsushizu) 板倉勝靜 (1823–89). Feudal lord (*fudai daimyō*) and Bakufu official. *Titles*: Suō-no-kami 周防守 (1849); Awa-no-kami 阿波守 (1864); Iga-no-kami 伊賀守 (1865). *Fief*: Matsuyama 松山; *fudai*; 50,000 *koku* (1849–68). *Offices*: Jisha-bugyō (Sept. 1857–Mar. 1859; and again Mar. 1861–Apr. 1862); Rōjū (Apr. 1862–July 1864; and again Dec. 1865–Feb. 1868).

IWAKURA Tomomi (Tomoyoshi) 岩倉具視 (1825–83). Court noble. *Offices*: only held minor Court appointments before 1868, but was in the confidence of the Emperor Kōmei and was one of the leaders of the anti-Bakufu movement; after 1868, one of the inner circle of Meiji statesmen.

IWASE Tadanari 岩瀬忠震 (1818–61). Bakufu official. *Titles*: Iga-no-kami 伊賀守 (c. 1854); Higo-no-kami 肥後守 (by 1858). *Offices*: Metsuke (as *kaibō-gakari*, Feb. 1854–Aug. 1858); Gaikoku-bugyō (Aug.–Oct. 1858).

IZAWA Masayoshi 伊澤政義 Bakufu official. *Title*: Mimasaka-no-kami 美作守 (by 1842). *Offices*: Nagasaki bugyō (May 1842–Dec.

1845); Uraga bugyō (Jan.–Apr. 1854); Shimoda bugyō (Apr. 1854–Sept. 1855); Ōmetsuke (as *kaibō-gakari*, Oct. 1856–Feb. 1858; and again, as *gaikoku-gakari*, Nov. 1858–Oct. 1863); Machi-bugyō (Feb.–Nov. 1858).

KAWADA Hiroshi 河田 熙 also known as Kandō 貫堂 (1835–1900). Bakufu official. *Title*: Sagami-no-kami 相模守 (1864). *Offices*: Metsuke (Jan.–Aug. 1864); Ōmetsuke (from Mar. 1868).

KAWAJI Toshiaki 川路聖謨 (1797–1868). Bakufu official; brother of INOUE Kiyonao. *Title*: Saemon-no-jō 左衛門尉 (by 1851). *Offices*: Ōsaka machi-bugyō (July 1851–Oct. 1852); Kanjō-bugyō (Oct. 1852–June 1858); Gaikoku-bugyō (June–Nov. 1863).

KAWAZU Sukekuni 河津祐邦 Bakufu official. *Titles*: Izu-no-kami 伊豆守 (*c.* 1863); Suruga-no-kami 駿河守 (1864). *Offices*: Gaikoku-bugyō (Nov. 1863–Aug. 1864); Kanjō-bugyō (Mar.–Sept. 1867); Nagasaki bugyō (Sept. 1867–Feb. 1868); Wakadoshiyori (from Mar. 1868).

KEIKI, Shōgun. *See* TOKUGAWA Keiki.

KŌMEI, Emperor 孝明天皇 (1831–67). Succeeded to the throne Jan./Feb. 1846.

KONOE Tadafusa 近衛忠房 Court noble. *Offices*: Naidaijin (Jan. 1864–Oct. 1867); Sadaijin (Oct.–Dec. 1867); Kokuji-goyō-gakari (Jan. 1863–Jan. 1868).

KONOE Tadahiro 近衛忠熙 (1808–98). Court noble. *Offices*: Naidaijin (July 1824–July 1847); Udaijin (July 1847–Jan. 1857); Sadaijin (Jan. 1857–Apr. 1859); Nairan (Oct.–Nov. 1858; and again July 1862–May 1863); Kampaku (July 1862–Mar. 1863); Kokuji-goyō-gakari (Jan. 1863–Jan. 1868).

KUJŌ Michitaka 九條道孝 (1839–1906). Court noble; eldest son of KUJŌ Naotada. *Offices*: Kokuji-goyō-gakari (June 1864–May 1867); Sadaijin (Dec. 1867–June 1869).

KUJŌ Naotada (Hisatada) 九條尚忠 (1798–1871). Court noble; father of KUJŌ Michitaka. *Offices*: Udaijin (Feb. 1824–July 1847); Sadaijin (July 1847–Jan. 1857); Nairan (Sept. 1856–Oct. 1858; and again Nov. 1858–July 1862); Kampaku (Sept. 1856–July 1862).

KURIMOTO Sebei 栗本瀨兵衛 also known as Joun 鋤雲 (1822–97). Bakufu official. *Title*: Aki-no-kami 安藝守 (*c.* 1866). *Offices*: Metsuke (Aug. 1864–July 1865); Gaikoku-bugyō (Dec. 1865–Mar. 1866; and again from Dec. 1866); Kanjō-bugyō/Hakodate bugyō (from July 1867).

KUZE Hirochika 久世廣周 (1819–64). Feudal lord (*fudai daimyō*) and Bakufu official. *Titles*: Yamato-no-kami 大和守 (1837); Izumo-no-kami 出雲守 (1844); reverted to Yamato-no-kami from 1848. *Fief*: Sekiyado 關宿 ; *fudai*; 58,000 *koku* (68,000 from 1861) (1830–62). *Offices*: Jisha-bugyō (Nov. 1843–Nov. 1848); Rōjū (Jan. 1852–Dec. 1858; and again Apr. 1860–June 1862).

MANABE Akikatsu 間部詮勝 (1802–84). Feudal lord (*fudai daimyō*) and Bakufu official. *Title*: Shimōsa-no-kami 下總守 (1819). *Fief*: Sabae 鯖江 ; *fudai*; 50,000 *koku* (40,000 from 1862) (1814–63). *Office*: Rōjū (Aug. 1858–Jan. 1860).

MATSUDAIRA Chikanao 松平近直 Bakufu official. *Title*: Kawachi-no-kami 河內守 (*c.* 1844/5). *Offices*: Metsuke (Dec. 1841–Oct. 1844); Kanjō-bugyō (Oct. 1844–Sept. 1857).

MATSUDAIRA Katamori 松平容保 (1836–93). Feudal lord (*kamon*) and Bakufu official. *Titles*: Wakasa-no-kami 若狹守 (1847); Higo-no-kami 肥後守 (1852). *Fief*: Aizu 會津 ; *kamon*; 230,000 *koku* (1852–69). *Office*: Kyōto-shugoshoku (Sept. 1862–Mar. 1864; and again May 1864–Jan. 1868).

MATSUDAIRA Keiei (Yoshinaga) 松平慶永 also known as Shungaku 春嶽 (1828–90). Feudal lord (*kamon*) and Bakufu official. *Titles*: Echizen-no-kami 越前守 (1839); Ōkura-tayū 大藏大輔 (1864). *Fief*: Fukui 福井 ; *kamon*; 320,000 *koku* (1838–58). *Offices*: Seiji-sōsaishoku (Aug. 1862–May 1863); Kyōto-shugoshoku (Mar.–May 1864).

MATSUDAIRA Keitoku 松平慶德 *See* IKEDA Yoshinori (Keitoku).

MATSUDAIRA Munehide. *See* HONJŌ Munehide.

MATSUDAIRA Nobuatsu 松平信篤 also known as Nobuyoshi 信義 Feudal lord (*fudai daimyō*) and Bakufu official. *Titles*: Tajima-no-kami 但 馬 守 (1843); Kii-no-kami 紀 伊 守 (1843); Buzen-no-kami 豊 前 守 (1852). *Fief*: Kameyama 亀 山 ; *fudai*; 50,000 *koku* (1843–66). *Offices*: Jisha-bugyō (Nov. 1848–Dec. 1858); Ōsaka-jōdai (Dec. 1858–Feb. 1861); Rōjū (Feb. 1861–Oct. 1863).

MATSUDAIRA Noriyasu 松 平 乗 全 Feudal lord (*fudai daimyō*) and Bakufu official. *Title*: Izumi-no-kami 和 泉 守 (1840). *Fief*: Nishio 西 尾 ; *fudai*; 60,000 *koku* (1840–63). *Offices*: Jisha-bugyō (Mar. 1843–Jan. 1845); Ōsaka-jōdai (Jan.–Apr. 1845); Rōjū (Nov. 1848–Sept. 1855; and again Aug. 1858–June 1860).

MATSUDAIRA Sadataka (Sadanori) 松 平 定 敬 (1846–1908). Feudal lord (*fudai daimyō*) and Bakufu official. *Title*: Etchū-no-kami 越 中 守 (1859). *Fief*: Kuwana 桑 名 ; *fudai*; 110,000 *koku* (1859–68). *Office*: Kyōto-shoshidai (May 1864–Jan. 1868).

MATSUDAIRA Tadakata 松 平 忠 固 also known as Tadamasa 忠 優 Feudal lord (*fudai daimyō*) and Bakufu official. *Title*: Igano-kami 伊 賀 守 (1830). *Fief*: Ueda 上 田 ; *fudai*; 53,000 *koku* (1830–59). *Offices*: Jisha-bugyō (Jan.–Apr. 1845); Ōsaka-jōdai (Apr. 1845–Nov. 1848); Rōjū (Nov. 1848–Sept. 1855; and again Oct. 1857–Aug. 1858).

MATSUDAIRA Yasunao 松 平 康 直 later known as MATSUI Yasuhide 松 井 康 英 (1830–1904). Bakufu official, subsequently feudal lord (*fudai daimyō*). *Titles*: Iwami-no-kami 石 見 守 (1860); Suōno-kami 周 防 守 (1865). *Fief*: Tanakura 棚 倉 ; transferred to Kawagoe 川 越 from Dec. 1866; *fudai*; 60,400 *koku* (80,400 from Dec. 1865) (1864–9). *Offices*: (before succeeding to fief) Kanagawa bugyō (Jan. 1860–Feb. 1863); Gaikoku-bugyō (Jan.–Oct. 1860; and again May 1861–Sept. 1863); Kanjō-bugyō (Sept. 1863–July 1864); Ōmetsuke (July–Aug. 1864); Machi-bugyō (Aug.–Dec. 1864); (after succeeding to fief) Jisha-bugyō (Feb.–May 1865); Rōjū (May–Dec. 1865; and again Jan. 1866–Feb. 1868).

MATSUI Yasuhide. *See* MATSUDAIRA Yasunao.

MATSUMAE Takahiro 松 前 崇 廣 Feudal lord (*tozama daimyō*) and Bakufu official. *Titles*: Izu-no-kami 伊 豆 守 (1848); Shima-no-kami 志 摩 守 (1849; not often used). *Fief*: Matsumae 松 前 ; *tozama*; 10,000 *koku* (1849–66); in addition, Yanagawa 梁 川 ; *tozama*;

30,000 *koku* (1854–66; but usually referred to as ·being of Matsumae). *Offices*: Jisha-bugyō (June–Sept. 1863); Rōjū-kaku (Aug.–Dec. 1864); Rōjū (Dec. 1864–Nov. 1865).

MEIJI, EMPEROR 明 治 天 皇 ; given name Mutsuhito 睦 仁 (1852–1912). Son of Emperor Kōmei; succeeded to Throne 13 Feb. 1867.

MINOBE MATAGORŌ 美 濃 部 又 五 郎 also Shigesada 茂 定 (1818–64). Samurai of Mito; member of *sonnō-jōi* faction.

MINODA DEMBEI 簑 田 傳 兵 衛 (1812–70). Samurai of Satsuma; worked closely with Saigō Takamori and Ōkubo Toshimichi in the anti-Bakufu movement.

MIZUNO TADAKIYO 水 野 忠 精 also Tadatsune 忠 經 Feudal lord (*fudai daimyō*) and Bakufu official. *Title*: Izumi-no-kami 和 泉 守 (1855). *Fief*: Yamagata 山 形 ; *fudai*; 50,000 *koku* (1845–66). *Offices*: Jisha-bugyō (Dec. 1858–Jan. 1861); Wakadoshiyori (Jan. 1861– Apr. 1862); Rōjū (Apr. 1862–July 1866).

MIZUNO TADANORI 水 野 忠 德 (1810–68). Bakufu official. *Titles*: Chikugo-no-kami 筑 後 守 (*c.* 1853); Shimōsa-no-kami 下 總 守 (1862). *Offices*: Uraga bugyō (June 1852–June 1853); Nagasaki bugyō (June 1853–Feb. 1855; and again May 1857–Jan. 1858); Kanjō-bugyō (Feb. 1855–Jan. 1858; and again Sept.–Nov. 1859); Gaikoku-bugyō (Aug. 1858–Sept. 1859; and again June 1861–Aug. 1862); Kanagawa bugyō (July–Sept. 1859); Gunkan-bugyō (Sept.–Nov. 1859); Hakodate bugyō (Aug.–Oct. 1862).

MŌRI YOSHICHIKA 毛 利 慶 親 also Katachika 敬 親 (1819– 71). Feudal lord (*tozama daimyō*). *Title*: Daizen-daibu 大 膳 大 夫 (1837). *Fief*: Chōshū 長 州 (Nagato 長 門); *tozama*; 369,000 *koku* (269,000 after June 1866) (1837–69).

MORIYAMA TAKICHIRŌ 森 山 多 吉 郎 Bakufu interpreter in Dutch and English. Interpreted for Tsutsui and Kawaji in negotiations with Poutiatine at Nagasaki in 1853. Thereafter chief Bakufu interpreter. Accompanied Alcock to London in 1862 to join Takeuchi mission. Retired from public life after 1868.

NAGAI NAOMUNE 永 井 尚 志 (1816–91). Bakufu official. *Titles*: Iwa-no-jō 岩 之 丞 (by 1853); Gemba-no-kami 玄 蕃 頭 (by

1858). *Offices*: Metsuke (as *kaibō-gakari*, Nov. 1853–Jan. 1858); Kanjō-bugyō (Jan.–Aug. 1858); Gaikoku-bugyō (Aug. 1858–Mar. 1859; and again Nov. 1865–Apr. 1867); Gunkan-bugyō (Mar.–Sept. 1859); Kyōto machi-bugyō (Aug. 1862–Mar. 1864); Ōmetsuke (Mar. 1864–May 1865; and again Nov. 1865–Apr. 1867); Wakadoshiyori-kaku (Apr. 1867–Jan. 1868); Wakadoshiyori (Jan.–Mar. 1868).

NAITŌ NOBUCHIKA 內 藤 信 親 also known as Nobukoto (Shinshi) 信 思. (1812–74). Feudal lord (*fudai daimyō*) and Bakufu official. *Title*: Kii-no-kami 紀 伊 守 (1827). *Fief*: Murakami 村 上 ; *fudai*; 50,090 *koku* (1825–64). *Offices*: Jisha-bugyō (Jan. 1844–Nov. 1848); Ōsaka-jōdai (Nov. 1848–Oct. 1850); Kyōto-shoshidai (Oct. 1850–Jan. 1852); Rōjū (Oct. 1853–June 1862).

NIJŌ NARIAKI (Naritaka, Nariyuki) 二 條 齊 敬 (1816–78). Court noble. *Offices*: Naidaijin (Apr. 1859–Feb. 1862); Udaijin (Feb. 1862–Jan. 1864); Kokuji-goyō-gakari (Jan. 1863–Jan. 1868); Nairan (Oct. 1863–Jan. 1868); Sadaijin (Jan. 1864–Oct. 1867); Kampaku (Jan. 1864–Feb. 1867); Sesshō (Feb. 1867–Jan. 1868).

NOMURA TEIJITSU 野 村 鼎 實 (1824–88). Samurai of Mito; member of *sonnō-jōi* faction.

OGASAWARA NAGAMICHI 小 笠 原 長 行 (1822–91). Bakufu official; eldest son of feudal lord (*fudai daimyō*). *Titles*: Tosho-no-kami 圖 書 頭 (by 1862); Iki-no-kami 壹 岐 守 (by 1865). *Fief*: eldest son and heir of lord of Karatsu 唐 津 ; *fudai*; 60,000 *koku* (never succeeded). *Offices*: Wakadoshiyori (Oct.–Nov. 1862); Rōjū-kaku (Nov. 1862–July 1863; and again Oct.–Nov. 1865); Rōjū (Nov. 1865–Nov. 1866; and again Dec. 1866–Mar. 1868).

ŌGIMACHI SANJŌ SANENARU. *See* SAGA Sanenaru.

OGURI TADAMASA 小 栗 忠 順 (d. 1868). Bakufu official. *Titles*: Bungo-no-kami 豊 後 守 (*c.* 1860); Kōzuke-no-suke 上 野 介 (*c.* 1865). *Offices*: Metsuke (as *gaikoku-gakari*, Oct. 1859–Dec. 1860); Gaikoku-bugyō (Dec. 1860–Aug. 1861); Machi-bugyō (Oct. 1862–Jan. 1863); Kanjō-bugyō (Jan.–June 1863; and again Sept. 1864–Jan. 1865); Gunkan-bugyō (Jan.–Mar. 1865).

ŌHARA SHIGENORI 大 原 重 德 (*c.* 1810–79). Court noble. *Office*: Kokuji-goyō-gakari (Jan.–Apr. 1863).

ŌKUBO Toshimichi 大 久 保 利 通 also known as Ichizō 市 蔵 (1832–78). Samurai of Satsuma; one of the most able leaders of the anti-Bakufu movement and after 1868 one of the inner circle of Meiji statesmen.

SAGA Sanenaru (Jitsuai) 嵯 城 實 愛 also known as ōGIMACHI sanjō Sanenaru 正 親 町 三 條 實 愛 (1816–1909). Court noble. *Offices*: Gisō (Aug. 1860–Mar. 1863; and again Feb. 1864–Nov. 1866); Kokuji-goyō-gakari (Jan. 1863–Jan. 1868).

SAIGŌ Takamori 西 鄉 隆 盛 (1828–77). Samurai of Satsuma; one of the outstanding figures of the anti-Bakufu movement and after 1868 one of the inner circle of Meiji statesmen.

SAKAI Tadashige 酒 井 忠 績 Feudal lord (*fudai daimyō*) and Bakufu official. *Title*: Uta-no-kami 雅 樂 頭 (1861). *Fief*: Himeji 姬 路 ; *fudai*; 150,000 *koku* (1861–7). *Offices*: Rōjū (Aug. 1863–July 1864); Tairō (Feb. 1865–Jan. 1866).

SAKAI Tadasuke (Tadamasu) 酒 井 忠 毗 Feudal lord (*fudai daimyō*) and Bakufu official. *Titles*: Ukyō-no-suke 右 京 亮 (1833); Hida-no-kami 飛 驒 守 (1862). *Fief*: Tsuruga 敦 賀 ; *fudai*; 10,000 *koku* (1833–67). *Office*: Wakadoshiyori (Oct. 1853–July 1862; again June–Sept. 1863; and again Aug. 1864–Jan. 1866).

SAKAI Tadayoshi 酒 井 忠 義 (1813–73). Feudal lord (*fudai daimyō*) and Bakufu official. *Titles*: Shūri-daibu 修 理 大 夫 (1834; and again 1850); Wakasa-no-kami 若 狹 守 (1841); Ukyō-daibu 右 京 大 夫 (1862). *Fief*: Obama 小 濱 ; *fudai*; 103,558 *koku* (93,558 from 1862) (1834–62). *Office*: Kyōto-shoshidai (Dec. 1843–Sept. 1850; and again Aug. 1858–July 1862).

SANJŌ Sanetomi (Saneyoshi) 三 條 實 美 (1837–91). Court noble; son of SANJŌ Sanetsumu. *Offices*: Gisō (Nov. 1862–Oct. 1863); Kokuji-goyō-gakari (Jan.–Sept. 1863).

SANJŌ Sanetsumu 三 條 實 萬 (1802–59). Court noble; father of SANJŌ Sanetomi. *Offices*: Gisō (Oct. 1831–Mar. 1848); Buke-densō (Mar. 1848–May 1857); Naidaijin (June 1857–May 1858).

SHIMAZU Hisamitsu 島 津 久 光 also known as Saburō 三

郎 after 1862 (1817–87). Feudal lord; brother of SHIMAZU Nariakira; father of SHIMAZU Tadayoshi. After the latter became lord of the fief in 1859, Hisamitsu was the effective leader of Satsuma in national affairs (until late in the 1860's). *Title*: Ōsumi-no-kami 大 隅 守 (1864).

SHIMAZU NARIAKIRA 島津齊彬 also known as Saburō 三 郎 (1809–58). Feudal lord (*tozama daimyō*). *Titles*: Hyōgo-no-kami兵 庫 頭 (1825); Bungo-no-kami豊 後 守 (1832); Shūri-daibu修理大夫 (1843); Satsuma-no-kami 薩 摩 守 (1851). *Fief*: Satsuma 薩 摩 ; *tozama*; 770,000 *koku* (1851–58).

SHIMAZU TADAYOSHI 島 津 忠 義 also Mochihisa 茂 久 (1840–97). Feudal lord (*tozama daimyō*); eldest son of SHIMAZU Hisamitsu. *Title*: Shūri-daibu 修 理 大 夫 (1859). *Fief*: Satsuma 薩 摩 ; *tozama*; 770,000 *koku* (1859–71).

TAKATSUKASA MASAMICHI 鷹 司 政 通 (1789–1868). Court noble; father of TAKATSUKASA Sukehiro; brother-in-law of TOKUGAWA Nariaki. *Offices*: Nairan (Apr. 1823–Sept. 1858); Kampaku (Apr. 1823–Feb. 1846; and again Mar. 1846–Sept. 1856); Sesshō (Feb.–Mar. 1846).

TAKATSUKASA SUKEHIRO 鷹 司 輔 煕 (1807–67). Court noble; son of TAKATSUKASA Masamichi. *Offices*: Naidaijin (Apr. 1848–Mar. 1857); Udaijin (Mar. 1857–Apr. 1859); Kokuji-goyō-gakari (Jan. 1863–Jan. 1868); Nairan (Mar. 1863–Jan. 1864); Kampaku (Mar. 1863–Jan. 1864).

TAKEMOTO MASAO 竹 本 正 雅 Bakufu official. *Titles*: Tosho-no-kami 圖 書 頭 (by 1859); Kai-no-kami 甲 斐 守 (1861/2); Awaji-no-kami 淡 路 守 (1863). *Offices*: Gaikoku-bugyō (Nov. 1859–July 1862; and again Jan. 1863–Dec. 1864); Kanagawa bugyō (Dec. 1859–Oct. 1860; and again Aug. 1861–Dec. 1862); Ōmetsuke (Dec. 1862–Aug. 1863).

TAKEUCHI (also TAKENOUCHI) YASUNORI 竹 内 保 德 (b. 1806/7). Bakufu official. *Title*: Shimōzuke-no-kami 下 野 守 (by 1861). *Offices*: Hakodate bugyō (July 1854–Mar. 1861); Kanjō-bugyō (Mar. 1861–Sept. 1864); Gaikoku-bugyō (May 1861–Sept. 1864).

TOKI TOMOAKI 土 岐 朝 昌 Bakufu official. *Titles*: Buzen-no-kami 豊 前 守 (by 1854); Settsu-no-kami 攝 津 守 (c. 1858);

Shimōzuke-no-kami 下 野 守 (*c.* 1859). *Offices*: Uraga bugyō (June 1854–Mar. 1857); Kanjō-bugyō (Sept. 1857–Apr. 1859); Sumpu-jōdai (i.e. Governor of Shizuoka Castle) (Apr. 1859–Feb. 1863).

TOKI YORIMUNE 土 岐 賴 旨 (*c.* 1814–84). *Hatamoto* and Bakufu official. *Title*: Tamba-no-kami 丹 波 守 (by 1843). *Offices*: Shimoda bugyō (Nov. 1843–Mar. 1844); Uraga bugyō (Mar. 1844–Apr. 1845); Ōmetsuke (as *kaibō-gakari*, Apr. 1845–Apr. 1846; and again Sept. 1855–June 1858).

TOKUGAWA IEMOCHI 德 川 家 茂 earlier known as Yoshitomi 慶 福 (1846–66). Feudal lord (*sanke*) and Shōgun. *Title*: (before succeeding as Shōgun) Sachūshō 左 中 將 (1851). *Fief*: Kii 紀 伊 (Kishū 紀 州); *sanke*; 550,000 *koku* (1849–58). *Office*: Sei-i-tai-shōgun (Nov. 1858–Sept. 1866) as 14th of Tokugawa line.

TOKUGAWA IESADA 德 川 家 定 (1824–58). Shōgun; son of TOKUGAWA Ieyoshi. *Office*: Sei-i-tai-shōgun (Nov. 1853–Aug. 1858) as 13th of Tokugawa line.

TOKUGAWA IEYOSHI 德 川 家 慶 (1793–1853). Shōgun. *Office*: Sei-i-tai-shōgun (Oct. 1837–July 1853) as 12th of Tokugawa line.

TOKUGAWA KEIKI (Yoshinobu) 德 川 慶 喜 earlier known as HITOTSUBASHI Keiki 一 橋 慶 喜 (1837–1913). Feudal lord (*sankyō*) and Shōgun; son of TOKUGAWA Nariaki. *Titles*: Keibu-kyō 刑 部 卿 (1848); Chūnagon 中 納 言 (1862). *Fief*: Hitotsubashi 一 橋 ; *sankyō*; 100,000 *koku* (1847–59; and 1862–7). *Offices*: Shōgun-kōkenshoku (from Aug. 1862); Sei-i-tai-shōgun (Jan. 1867–Jan. 1868) as 15th and last of the Tokugawa line.

TOKUGAWA NARIAKI 德 川 齊 昭 (1800–60). Feudal lord (*sanke*). *Title*: Chūnagon 中 納 言 (*c.* 1830). *Fief*: Mito 水 户 ; *sanke*; 350,000 *koku* (1829–44).

TOKUGAWA YOSHIATSU 德 川 慶 篤 Feudal lord (*sanke*); son of TOKUGAWA Nariaki. *Title*: Gon-chūnagon 權 中 納 言 (1851). *Fief*: Mito 水 户 ; *sanke*; 350,000 *koku* (1844–69).

TOKUGAWA YOSHINOBU. *See* TOKUGAWA Keiki.

TSUTSUI MASANORI 筒井政憲 (1778–1859). *Hatamoto* and Bakufu official. *Title*: Hizen-no-kami 肥前守 (by 1854). *Offices*: Ōmetsuke (as *kaibō-gakari*, Aug. 1854–Feb. 1857).

UCHITA NAKA-NO-SUKE 内田仲之助 also Masakaze 政風 (1815–93). Samurai of Satsuma; fief representative first in Edo, later in Ōsaka.

UTSUKI ROKU-NO-JŌ 宇津木六之丞 (1809–62). Samurai of Hikone; secretary to II Naosuke.

YAMANOUCHI TOYOSHIGE 山内豊信 also known as Yōdō 容堂 (1827–72). Feudal lord (*tozama daimyō*). *Title*: Tosa-no-kami 土佐守 (1853). *Fief*: Tosa 土佐 ; *tozama*; 242,000 *koku* (1849–59).

BIBLIOGRAPHY

A FULL bibliography for the study of the relationship between foreign policy and domestic politics in the late Tokugawa period would not differ greatly from a bibliography of the period as a whole. Certainly its scope is too great for a work of this kind. Some useful books on the subject are listed in E. H. Norman's *Japan's Emergence as a Modern State* (New York, 1940), which might be supplemented by the references given in the first chapter of R. A. Scalapino's *Democracy and the Party Movement in Prewar Japan* (Berkeley, 1953). All I seek to give here is an introductory note on the nature of the materials available, with a special emphasis on foreign affairs, and a list of those works which have been found most directly of use.

The largest manuscript collection is to be found in Tōkyō University's Shiryō-hensanjo (Institute for the Compilation of Historical Materials). It includes not only Japanese government archives for the period, but also papers or copies of papers from private depositories. Much of this has already been published in the *Dai Nihon Komonjo* series, in the section entitled *Bakumatsu Gaikoku Kankei Monjo*, of which 22 volumes and a 4-volume appendix have so far appeared (covering the years 1853–9). In it are printed private letters and extracts from journals, in addition to official memoranda, government correspondence, and the texts of treaties, and it is planned to continue the series for the rest of the late Tokugawa period. There are also a number of documents remaining in the Gaimushō (Foreign Office) in Tōkyō. The task of publishing them was begun in the series *Bakumatsu Ishin Gaikō Shiryō Shūsei*, but this was discontinued after six volumes had appeared. For the most part the papers that were published deal with details of protocol and finance, with a selection of materials also on the missions sent abroad by Japan between 1859 and 1867.

Until publication of the *Bakumatsu Gaikoku Kankei Monjo* is completed, which will not be for a number of years yet, documentary material on foreign affairs for the period after 1859 has to be sought item by item in the enormous bulk of published work dealing with the mid-nineteenth century. Of this only the briefest account can be given. Turning first to published papers from private sources, the largest and most valuable collection is undoubtedly to be found in the *Nihon Shiseki Kyōkai* series. This series, comprising 187 volumes in all and consisting of over seventy separate works, includes the diaries and family papers of almost every important figure of late Tokugawa and early Meiji history: feudal lords, Court nobles, leaders of the anti-Bakufu movement, and many more. Frequently these works contain the text of documents which are not available elsewhere in print, or even, at times, in manuscript. Of particular relevance are the papers of Ōkubo Toshimichi (*Ōkubo Toshimichi Monjo*) and those of Matsudaira Keiei (*Sakumu kiji; Saimu kiji*; and *Zoku saimukiji*).

Other works, of equal importance for the material they contain, are the earlier studies of Bakumatsu history compiled during the Meiji period. These consist often of collections of documents, printed *in extenso*, only loosely strung together with narrative. The best known of these are *Iwakura Kō Jikki* and Katsu Awa's

z 2

Kaikoku Kigen, while at least two others, *Kyōto-shugoshoku shimatsu* and *Shimazu
Hisamitsu Kō Jikki*, are of almost equal value. The method of compilation which
they use has been followed in some degree by many later historians. The
biography of Ogasawara Nagamichi (*Ogasawara Iki-no-kami Nagamichi*), for
example, contains a number of previously unpublished documents, and Shibusawa's *Tokugawa Keiki Kō Den* brings together a useful collection of material in
volumes v–vii.

Modern historical work in Japan has tended to treat Bakumatsu political
and foreign problems separately. This is true even of general histories, at least
as regards their internal arrangement. The most detailed and reliable survey
of the period is the 6-volume *Ishin-shi*, while the shorter (one-volume) *Gaikan
Ishin-shi* is similar in plan and serves as a useful summary. The work of individual historians, even within the field of foreign affairs, usually has a specialized
approach or emphasizes particular aspects of the problem. Inobe, for example,
is indispensable for the study of Japanese ideas concerning foreign relations
generally, a type of work in which he is followed, rather less convincingly, by
Akao. Honjō and Tsuchiya also concentrate (in this context) on the history of
ideas, the former being primarily concerned with economic motivation. Of
those who are specialists in diplomatic history, Tabohashi is generally regarded
as an expert on relations with Russia and Ōtsuka on France. Ishii has proceeded from the discussion of foreign trade to a more general consideration of
the economic aspects of international relations, his later work being characterized by a strong interest in the clash between the capitalist economy of the West
and the feudal economy of Japan. So far, none of the younger historians has
emerged as a specialist in the field.

Although it is not the purpose of these remarks to serve as a guide to materials
on Western attitudes or policies towards Japan, there are a number of English
and American works, especially, which throw light on Japanese activities in this
period. Chief among them are Hawks's account of the Perry expedition,
Townsend Harris's journal, and Alcock's *The Capital of the Tycoon*. Somewhat
later in date is Satow's *A Diplomat in Japan*; while British *Parliamentary Papers*
and the U.S. Congress 'Foreign Relations' series contain some translations of
Japanese documents in addition to official correspondence dealing with Japan.
British and Foreign State Papers is a useful work of reference for the texts of treaties
and other formal agreements.

The list which follows gives more detailed bibliographical data on the works
which have been referred to above and in the footnotes to the earlier sections of
this book.

LIST OF WORKS USED

[*Note*: Much Japanese historical work has been produced by
ad hoc societies or committees, which fact often leaves the actual
authorship in doubt. Unless a book can be clearly attributed
to an individual, therefore, it is listed here under its title.]

AKAO, Tōji, 'Harris raichō tōji ni okeru taigai shisō ni tsuite' [Ideas concerning
foreigners at the time of Harris's arrival], *Shirin*, xxiii (1938), pp. 794–843.

Tōji, 'Nichi-bei kari tsūshō jōyaku chōin mondai wo meguru Ii Tairō to Mito-han ippa to no kōsō' [The struggle between Ii Tairō and the Mito party concerning the question of signing the draft Japanese-American commercial treaty], *Shirin*, xxvi (1941), pp. 426–44.

—— 'Perry torai zengo ni okeru taigai kokumin shisō no kōsatsu' [An inquiry into popular ideas concerning foreigners at about the time of Perry's arrival], *Shirin*, xxii (1937), pp. 529–54, 753–82.

Alcock, Sir Rutherford, *The Capital of the Tycoon: a Narrative of a Three Years Residence in Japan*, 2 vols., London, 1863.

Asahiko Shinnō nikki [Diary of Prince Asahiko], Nihon Shiseki Kyōkai series, 2 vols., Tōkyō, 1929. Covers the period from Aug. 1864 to Oct. 1867, omitting the months of Dec. 1864 and Jan. 1865.

Bakumatsu gaikoku kankei monjo. See under *Dai Nihon Komonjo*.

Bakumatsu Ishin gaikō shiryō shūsei [Collected materials on late-Tokugawa and Restoration diplomatic history], 6 vols., Tōkyō, 1942–4. Chiefly material on the details of finance and protocol; some also on missions sent abroad, 1859–67.

Beasley, W. G., *Great Britain and the Opening of Japan: 1834–1858*, London, 1951.

Coleman, H. E., 'The life of Shoin Yoshida, being a translation from the Japanese life of Shoin Yoshida by Mr Iichiro Tokutomi', *Trans. Asiatic Soc. Japan*, xlv (1917), pp. 119–88. Does not include some passages which appear in the (revised) Japanese version (q.v. under Tokutomi, Iichiro).

Dai Nihon Komonjo—Bakumatsu gaikoku kankei monjo [Old Japanese documents—Documents on late-Tokugawa foreign relations], 22 vols. and 4-vol. appendix, Tōkyō, 1911– in progress. A very full collection of public and private papers on foreign affairs, arranged chronologically.

Date Muneki zaikyō nikki [The Kyōto diary of Date Muneki], Nihon Shiseki Kyōkai series, Tōkyō, 1916. Covers the periods Dec. 1862 to June 1864 and Oct. 1866 to Mar. 1868, when Date was in Kyōto.

Gaikan Ishin-shi [Short history of the Restoration], Tōkyō, 1944.

Greene, D. C., 'Osada's life of Takano Nagahide', *Trans. Asiatic Soc. Japan*, lxi (1913), pp. 379–492.

Gubbins, J. H., *The Progress of Japan 1853–1871*, Oxford, 1911. Prints the texts of a number of treaties, &c.

van Gulik, R. H., '*Kakkaron*, a Japanese echo of the Opium War', *Monumenta Serica*, iv (1939–40), pp. 478–545.

Harris, Townsend, *The Complete Journal of Townsend Harris, First American Consul General and Minister to Japan*, ed. M. E. Cosenza, New York, 1930. Covers the period up to Feb. 1858, with some scattered entries for May and June of that year. Useful notes based on Harris's unpublished letters.

Hawks, F. L., *Narrative of the Expedition of an American Squadron to the China Seas and Japan, performed in the Years 1852, 1853, and 1854, under the Command of Commodore M. C. Perry*, 3 vols., Washington, 1856.

Holtom, D. C., *The National Faith of Japan: a Study in Modern Shintō*, London, 1938.

Honjō, Eijirō, 'Leon Roches to Bakumatsu·no shosei kaikaku' [Leon Roches and Bakumatsu administrative reform]; first published in *Keizaishi Kenkyū*, xiii (1935); reprinted in Honjō's *Bakumatsu no shin-seisaku* [New policies of the Bakumatsu period],

Tōkyō, 1935, pp. 178–214. Footnote references are to the latter. A shorter version, in English, was published under the title 'Leon Roches and administrative reform in the closing years of the Tokugawa regime' in *Kyōto University Economic Review*, x, 1 (July 1935), pp. 35–53.

HONJŌ, EIJIRŌ, *Nihon keizai shisō-shi gaisetsu* [Outline history of Japanese economic thought], Tōkyō, 1946. Some of the relevant material is given, in English, in Honjō's 'A survey of economic thought in the closing days of the Tokugawa period', *Kyōto University Economic Review*, xiii. 2 (Oct. 1938), pp. 21–39.

INOBE, SHIGEO, 'Ansei jōyaku chokkyo sōsei ni kansuru ichi-kōsatsu' [An inquiry concerning the petition for Imperial sanction of the Ansei treaties], *Shigaku Zasshi*, xlii (1931), pp. 469–90. The 'Ansei treaties' are so called after the Ansei year-period in which they were concluded (1854–8).

—— 'Mito gaku-ha no jōi-ron' [The expulsion ideas of the Mito school], *Shirin*, v (1920), pp. 125–53.

—— 'Perry torai no sai ni okeru kokuron no kisū' [The trend of national opinion at the time of Perry's arrival], *Shirin*, xiii (1928), pp. 343–70.

—— 'Sakuma Shōzan no taigai iken' [Sakuma Shōzan's views on foreign affairs], *Kokugakuin Zasshi*, xxx (1924), pp. 455–86, 608–37.

ISHII, TAKASHI, *Bakumatsu bōeki-shi no kenkyū* [A study in the history of Bakumatsu period trade], Tōkyō, 1942.

—— 'Bakumatsu ni okeru Eikoku kaigun no Nihon engan fūsa keikaku' [The British navy's plan for blockading the Japanese coast in the Bakumatsu period], *Rekishi Chiri*, lxxvi (1940), No. 1, pp. 35–44, No. 2, pp. 111–23.

—— *Bakumatsu no gaikō* [Bakumatsu period diplomacy], Tōkyō, 1948.

—— 'Gokai saretaru Ii Naosuke' [Ii Naosuke the misunderstood], *Rekishigaku Kenkyū*, viii, pp. 532–3, 556–7.

Ishin-shi [History of the Restoration], 6 vols., Tōkyō, 1939–41.

Iwakura Kō Jikki [Authentic records of Lord Iwakura], 3 vols., Tōkyō, 1927 (first published in 2 vols. in 1906).

Iwakura Tomomi kankei monjo [Papers concerning Iwakura Tomomi], Nihon Shiseki Kyōkai series, 8 vols., Tōkyō, 1927–35.

Kaikoku Kigen. See under KATSU, AWA.

KANNO, KAZUTARŌ, 'Shokō to gaikoku bōeki' [Feudal lords and foreign trade], in *Bakumatsu keizaishi kenkyū*, ed. Honjō Eijirō (Tōkyō, 1935), pp. 375–419.

KATSU, AWA, *Kaikoku kigen* [Origins of the opening of the country], 3 vols., Tōkyō, 1893. Prints many documents on politics and foreign affairs, 1853–68.

Kawakatsu-ke monjo [Kawakatsu family papers], Nihon Shiseki Kyōkai series, Tōkyō, 1930. Collection of documents, largely concerning Japan's foreign relations, 1862–8.

KEENE, D., *The Japanese Discovery of Europe: Honda Toshiaki and Other Discoverers, 1720–1798*, London, 1952.

KOBAYASHI, SHŌJIRŌ, *Bakumatsu-shi* [Late-Tokugawa history], Nihon Jidai-shi series, vol. xi, rev. ed., Tōkyō, 1927 (1st ed., 1907).

Kyōto-shugoshoku shimatsu [Account of the Kyōto-shugoshoku], compiled by Yamagawa Hiroshi, published posthumously, rev. ed., Tōkyō, 1912 (1st ed., 1911). Account of Matsudaira Katamori's activities as Kyōto-shugoshoku, including the text of many documents, for the period Sept. 1862 to Jan. 1868. One volume in two parts, with separate pagination.

Meiji Ishin-shi kenkyū [Studies in the history of the Meiji Restoration], Tōkyō, 1929.

MURDOCH, J. (and YAMAGATA, I.), *A History of Japan*, 3 vols., London, 1903–26.

NORMAN, E. H., *Japan's Emergence as a Modern State*, I.P.R. Inquiry series, New York, 1940.

Ogasawara Iki-no-kami Nagamichi, Tōkyō, 1943. A biography which includes a number of hitherto unpublished documents.

OKA, YOSHITAKE, 'Ishin-go ni okeru jōi-teki fūchō no zanson' [The survival of expulsion tendencies after the Restoration], *Kokka Gakkai Zasshi*, liii (1939), pp. 289–313, 652–88, 761–85.

Ōkubo Toshimichi monjo [The Ōkubo Toshimichi papers], Nihon Shiseki Kyōkai series, 10 vols., Tōkyō, 1927–9.

OLIPHANT, L., *Narrative of the Earl of Elgin's Mission to China and Japan in the Years 1857, '58, '59*, 2 vols., Edinburgh and London, 1859.

ŌTSUKA, TAKEMATSU,.*Bakumatsu no gaikō* [Bakumatsu period diplomacy], Iwanami kōza *Nihon Rekishi* series, Tōkyō, 1934.

—— 'Fukkoku kōshi Leon Roches no seisaku kōdō ni tsuite' [The policy and actions of the French Minister Leon Roches], *Shigaku Zasshi*, xlvi (1935), pp. 809–50, 982–1001.

Saga Sanenaru nikki [The diary of Saga Sanenaru], Nihon Shiseki Kyōkai series, 3 vols., Tōkyō, 1929–31. Covers the period Aug. 1864 to Feb. 1872.

Saimu kiji, Nihon Shiseki Kyōkai series, Tōkyō, 1922. Records of Matsudaira Keiei of Fukui, with connecting narrative, for the period May–Sept. 1862, preceded by a brief account of national affairs between Aug. 1858 and May 1862. Cf. *Sakumu kiji* and *Zoku saimukiji*.

Sakumu kiji, Nihon Shiseki Kyōkai series, 4 vols., Tōkyō, 1920–1. Records of Matsudaira Keiei of Fukui, with connecting narrative, for the period July 1853 to Aug. 1858. Cf. *Saimu kiji* and *Zoku saimukiji*.

SATOW, E. M., *A Diplomat in Japan. The Inner History of the Critical Years in the Evolution of Japan when the Ports were opened and the Monarchy restored*, London, 1921. Chiefly an account of the years 1862–8, based on the journals kept by Satow as an interpreter in Japan.

SHIBUSAWA, EIICHI, *Tokugawa Keiki Kō Den* [Biography of Lord Tokugawa Keiki], 8 vols., Tōkyō, 1918. Vols. v–vii consist entirely of printed documents, assembled from a number of different sources.

Shimazu Hisamitsu Kō Jikki [Authentic records of Lord Shimazu Hisamitsu], 8 vols., Tōkyō, 1910. Largely documentary material, with connecting narrative.

TABOHASHI, KIYOSHI, *Kindai Nihon gaikoku kankei shi* [History of modern Japanese foreign relations], rev. ed., Tōkyō, 1943 (1st ed., 1930). Account of Japan's foreign relations, especially with Russia, from the late eighteenth century to 1854.

Tokugawa Keiki Kō Den. See under SHIBUSAWA, EIICHI.

TOKUSHIGE, ASAKICHI, 'Bakumatsu no taigai sensō shōri-ron' [Ideas about the prospects of victory in foreign war in the Bakumatsu period], *Rekishi to Chiri*, xxxiii (1934), pp. 257–65, 347–57.

TOKUTOMI, IICHIRŌ, *Yoshida Shōin*, rev. ed., Tōkyō, 1934 (1st ed., 1908). More detailed than Coleman's English edition.

TSUCHIYA, TAKAO, 'Bakumatsu dōranki no keizaiteki bunseki' [Economic analysis of unrest in the Bakumatsu period], *Chūō Koron*, xlvii, No. 11 (Oct. 1932), pp. 75–91.

—— 'Bakumatsu shishi no mita Shina mondai' [The China question as seen by loyalists of the Bakumatsu period], *Kaizō*, xx, No. 7 (July 1938), pp. 154–67.

WAGENER, G., 'Aus dem Tagebuche Hendrik Heuskens', *Mitteilungen der Deutschen Gesellschaft für Natur- und Volkerkunde Ostasiens*, iii, No. 29 (June 1883), pp. 372–90. German summary, with some extracts from the French original, of the diary of Townsend Harris's secretary; covers the period Aug. 1856 to June 1858 and the month of Jan. 1861.

WATANABE, SEIYŪ (Yosuke), 'Ishin no henkaku to Chōshū-han' [Restoration changes and the Chōshū fief], in *Meiji Ishin-shi kenkyū* (q.v.), pp. 625–83.

WATANABE, TETSU, 'Shimonoseki shōkin no shi-harai ni tsuite' [Concerning the payment of the Shimonoseki indemnity], *Shien*, iv (1930), pp. 1–17.

Zoku saimukiji, Nihon Shiseki Kyōkai series, 6 vols., Tōkyō, 1921–2. Records of Matsu daira Keiei of Fukui, with connecting narrative, for the period Sept. 1862 to Oct. 1867. Cf. *Sakumu kiji* and *Saimu kiji*.

Index

Abe Masahiro, biographical note, 331; negotiations with Perry, 21–25, 230; relations with Tokugawa Nariaki, 25–27.

Abe Masatō, 81–82, 296, 300 n.; biographical note, 331.

Aizawa Seishisai (Hakumin), *jōi* views of, 8–9, 10–11.

Aizu fief, 59, 105. *See also* Matsudaira Katamori (of Aizu).

Aki fief, 313.

Akira, Prince, 268, 270, 314–15, 317, 318.

Alcock, Rutherford, at Tōzenji, 47; his views on Japanese policy, 50–51, 211–16; and negotiation of the London Protocol, 54–58, 195–7, 208; his memorandum concerning same, 211–16; his views on the closing of Kanagawa, 279; and the Shimonoseki dispute, 74–77, 282–8; text of convention signed by (1864), 288–9; succeeded by Parkes, 79.

America. *See* United States.

Andō Nobumasa, biographical note, 331; appointment of, 52; policy of, 52–54, 58, 230; his letter to Court concerning London Protocol negotiations, 204–6; his letter to Alcock concerning same, 208–11; fall of, 60.

Arai Hakuseki, 9.

Arao Narimasa, biographical note, 331; and negotiation of the Dutch supplementary treaty, 29; his memoranda concerning same, 139–45; text of treaty, signed by, 149–55.

Arisugawa, Princes of, 317.

'Arrow' War, its effect in Japan, 27–28.

Asahiko, Prince, biographical note, 331; his part in Court discussions, 73–74, 90, 268–72, 303, 314–15; extract from diary of (1867), 316–19.

Asano Ujisuke, 251–2, 256.

Ashikaga period, 115.

Awa province, 109.

Bakufu (see also *Sei-i-tai-shōgun*), glossary entry, 321; its administration and the formulation of policy, 18–21, 36; traditional seclusion policy of, 3–4, 105–6, 117, 137–9, 209, 244–5; expulsion policy of, 45, 53–54, 62–64, 66, 71, 74; and document references thereto, 194, 202–3, 206–7, 225–34, 243–53, 255–6, 264, 266, 267, 268–72, 282–8, 298; trade policy of, 25, 30–31, 34, 50–51, 54, 73, 74, 78–79; and document references thereto, 132–9, 149–55, 244–5; negotiates London Protocol, 54–58, 204–6, 208–11; its policy in

Namamugi dispute, 65–68, 240–2, 250–6; seeks closing of Yokohama, 71–77, 260–3; sends mission to France (1864), 71–72, 75–76, 260–3, 273–82; its policy in Shimonoseki dispute, 75–77, 282–9; its relations with Roches, 78–79, 82–83; secures Imperial ratification of the treaties, 80–83; and documents relating thereto, 297–305; its policy concerning Hyōgo (1865–7), 80–83, 87–90; and documents relating thereto, 308–20; its financial difficulties, 48–51, 76–77, 241–2; political dangers to, 32, 105, 110, 115, 136, 199, 235, 280, 301; its relations with Imperial Court, 36–42, 44–45, 52–54, 58–64, 65–68, 70–74, 81–82, 87–90; and documents referring thereto, 181–2, 183, 189–93, 198–204, 225–34, 235, 246, 248, 252–3, 266–7, 284, 298–9, 301, 303, 304, 308–11, 314–20; relations with *kōbu-gattai* leaders, 62–63, 65–68, 227–34, 250–3, 268–72, 301–3, 314–20; relations with Chōshū, 70, 80, 85–86, 87–90; and documents referring thereto, 295–6, 298–9, 308, 312–20; relations with feudal lords generally, see under *daimyō*.

Batavia, Governor-General of, 109, 134.

Belgium, negotiations with, 53, 205.

Bellecourt, M. de, 56.

Bonin Islands, 17, 112 n.

Bowring, Sir John, 27, 29, 133, 164.

Britain. *See* Great Britain.

bugyō, glossary entry, 321; administrative functions of, 19–20, 181.

buke, glossary entry, 321.

buke-densō, glossary entry, 321; their part in Court discussions, 38 n., 314, 316, 317.

Cachon, Mermet de, 78.

California, 99, 100, 160.

Camus, Lieut., murder of, 262, 275 n.

Canton, British attack on, 130, 136.

Castaways, treatment of, 100, 101, 107–8, 116, 118, 120–1, 123–4, 245.

China, events in, Japanese reactions to, 4, 7, 8–9, 27–28, 103, 126, 130, 144, 160–4, 166, 178, 179, 181, 192, 207.

Chinese, trade of, at Nagasaki, 3, 105, 134, 247, 249, 250.

chōnin, 48, 87.

Chōshū, and the *jōi* movement, 45, 61–62, 64, 70–71, 228, 230, 232, 270; and the Shimonoseki dispute, 69–70, 74–77, 83–84, 257–60, 262, 265, 275–6, 282–8, 288–9; Bakufu operations against, 80, 85–86, 295–6, 298–9,

Chōshū (contd.)
319; alliance with Satsuma, 84-86, 88-90; documents concerning pardon of, 311-20.

Christianity, Japanese views on, 3, 103-4, 119, 137, 147, 170-1; treaty provisions concerning, 154, 155 n., 187.

Chūnagon, glossary entry, 321.

Chusan Islands, 115.

Coal, American request for, 100, 108, 111, 114, 118, 120, 121, 124.

Commerce. See Trade.

Commercial treaties. See Treaties.

'Company' trade, Dutch, 140.

Consuls, provisions of Perry Convention concerning, 25, 122, 127; legal jurisdiction of, 34, 186-7, 187-8.

Court, Imperial (see also Emperor), influence of, 36-38; its views on foreign policy, 38, 40-42, 52-54, 61-62, 71, 72-74, 87-90; its instructions to Bakufu concerning same, 180-1, 193-4, 263-4, 264-6, 304, 310, 311, 319; its relations with Bakufu, see under Bakufu; influence of unrest on, 49-50, 52, 61-62; its discussions concerning Harris treaty, 39-42, 44-45, 180-1, 189-94; agrees to Kazunomiya marriage, 52-54; sends envoys to Edo, 60-62, 63; drops demand for immediate expulsion, 72-74, 263-6; ratifies the treaties, 81-82, 301-5; agrees to opening of Hyōgo, 87-90, 314-19.

Cowley, Lord, 294.

Currency, arrangements concerning, 51, 120, 121, 151, 154, 155 n., 186.

Curtius, Donker, negotiations with Bakufu (1857), 27, 28-31, 128-30, 139-49; text of supplementary treaty concluded by, 149-55.

Customs duties, establishment of, 34, 48, 150, 185-6; Japanese views on, 28, 134, 135; revision of, 57, 80, 82-83, 217, 220, 261, 274, 276, 294, 295, 300, 305.

daimyō (see also fudai daimyō and tozama daimyō), glossary entry, 321; their relations with the Bakufu, 23, 24, 25, 26, 35, 39, 42, 62, 72-74, 87-90; and documents referring thereto, 181, 227, 228, 229, 235, 264, 265, 266, 267, 269, 270-1, 282-7, 297, 302, 310, 311-12; economic difficulties of, 48-49, 191; trade of, 49, 84, 133-4, 135, 217; their views on foreign policy, 21-23, 35-36, 42, 214; their memoranda on foreign policy in 1853-4, 102-7, 112-14, 114-17, 117-19; their memoranda on foreign policy in 1857-8, 165-8, 168-9, 176-9, 179-80.

Date Muneki, biographical note, 332; member of Hitotsubashi party, 38, 46; and the kōbugattai party, 58-59, 66, 72-74, 264, 268-72;

supports Shimazu Hisamitsu, 72-74, 88-90, 314-15, 316-19; his letter to Court concerning Hyōgo and Chōshū (1867), 319-20.

Defence, Japanese preoccupation with, 5-6, 8; document references to, 105-7, 109-10, 113, 116, 117, 165-6, 178-9, 180, 182-3, 191-2, 230, 235, 265.

Deshima. See under Dutch.

Diana, Russian frigate, 11, 172 n.

Dutch, their trade at Nagasaki (Deshima), 3, 29, 104, 105, 134, 140-1, 192 n.; propose opening of Japan, 109, 112; negotiations with Bakufu in 1857, 21, 27-31, 128-30, 139-49, 174; text of supplementary treaty concluded by, 149-55; proposed as intermediaries for Japan, 107 n., 111-12, 118; relations with Japan after 1858, 47, 69-70, 74-77, 241, 243, 247, 249, 250, 275, 280, 282-9, 293-6.

Echizen (Fukui): fief of Matsudaira Keiei (q.v.).

Edo (Yedo), opening of, 34, 172-4, 174-6, 178-9, 189, 202; postponement of opening of, 54-58, 62-63, 87; and documents relating thereto, 204-6, 208-21, 225-6, 247.

Edo Bay, American survey of, 103, 108-9, 115, 125, 126.

Edo machi-bugyō. See machi-bugyō.

Eikoku Sakuron, 84.

Elgin, Lord, 50.

Emperor (see also Kōmei and Meiji), his views on foreign policy, 41, 44, 52-53, 72, 225; his letters to Shōgun (1864), 263-6; his status a diplomatic issue, 79-80, 213-14; ratification of treaties by, 55, 79-83, 290-2; and documents referring thereto, 283, 285-7, 293-6, 297-9, 301-5.

England. See Great Britain.

Expansion, Japanese ideas concerning, 16-17, 37.

Expulsion (see also jōi), Japanese ideas concerning, 8-18, 33, 51 n., 105-7, 297; decision to carry out (1863), 58-64, 222-4; and documents relating thereto, 225-36, 241, 243-56; Chōshū attempt to carry out, 69-70; Kyōto discussions concerning (1864), 72-74, 264, 266, 267, 268-72; declining support for, 83, 85.

Extraterritoriality, 34, 186-7, 187-8.

Ezo (Hokkaidō), 4, 106, 141, 161, 169.

Feudal lords. See daimyō.

Fillmore, Millard, U.S. President, letter to Japan, 99-101

Foreigners, attacks on, 47-48, 64, 69-70, 236-40, 245, 279.

Formosa, 162.

France, and the Shimonoseki dispute, 69–70,
74–77, 282–8, 288–9; negotiates Paris Convention, 71–72, 75–76, 257–60, 273–82;
offers naval support for Bakufu against
Chōshū, 274, 276–7, 279, 296; pro-Bakufu
policy of Léon Roches, 78–79, 86 n., 87; and
Imperial ratification of the treaties, 290–2,
293–6.
fudai daimyō (see also *daimyō*), glossary entry,
321; political activities and importance of,
18, 19, 22, 23, 25, 26, 35 n., 43, 52, 58, 59,
60, 62, 68, 199, 227; their memoranda on
foreign policy, 117–19, 130–1, 131–4, 165–8,
176–9, 243–6 254–6.
Fujii Kunai, 302.
Fujita Tōko, *jōi* views of, 8–9, 10–11.

gaikoku-bōeki-torishirabe-gakari, glossary entry,
322; appointment of, 27–28.
gaikoku-bugyō, glossary entry, 322; duties of,
20–21, 240; memorandum concerning London Protocol, 57, 218–21.
gaikoku-gakari, glossary entry, 322; duties of,
20–21.
gisō, glossary entry, 322; political activities of,
38 n., 90, 314–15, 316, 317, 318.
Glover, Thomas, 84, 85.
Gongen-sama (*see also* Tokugawa Ieyasu), 214.
Gorogio. See *Rōjū*.
Gotenyama, British legation at, 212, 225, 226.
Great Britain, as an influence on Japanese
policy, 4, 27, 29, 32; and documents relating
thereto, 132–3, 136, 144, 145, 160–5, 171,
178–9, 179–80, 181–2, 192; early treaties
with Japan, 25, 50; negotiates London Protocol, 54–58, 195–7, 216–17; and the Namamugi dispute, 64–69, 222–4, 236–40, 251–2,
254–6; opposes closing of Yokohama, 279,
280; and the Shimonoseki dispute, 69–70,
74–77, 282–9; later relations with Satsuma
and Chōshū, 83–84, 88; demands Imperial
ratification of the treaties, 79–83, 290–2,
293–6, 299–300, 304–5; demands opening
of Hyōgo, 87–88, 306–8.
gunkan-bugyō, glossary entry, 322.

Hachijō-jima, 117.
Hakodate, opening of, 25, 29, 33, 62; and
documents relating thereto, 120–2, 124–5,
135, 139, 141, 149–55, 184, 186, 187, 204,
225–6, 261; proposed closing of, 247, 253.
Hakodate bugyō, 19, 27 n., 130; glossary entry,
322.
Hamburg, 276.
Hara Tadanari, biographical note, 332; political activities of, 73 n., 316; letter of (1864),
268–72.

Harikawa Seigan, 40.
Harris, Townsend, concludes Shimoda Convention, 31, 188; negotiates treaty with
Bakufu (1857–8), 27, 31–34, 36, 43; and
documents referring thereto, 131–4, 139–40,
141, 156–9, 181–3, 298; text of statement to
Hotta (1857), 159–65; text of treaty concluded by (1858), 183–9.
Harris Treaty, text of, 183–9; documents concerning negotiation of, 159–83.
Hase Nobuatsu, 315.
Hashimoto Sanai, 40.
hatamoto, 248; glossary entry, 323.
Hayakawa Hisatake (Shōjirō), 204.
Hayashi Noboru, biographical note, 332;
text of Perry Convention, negotiated by,
119–22; report on Perry negotiations, 122–7.
Hayashi Shihei, 8 n.
Heusken, Hendrik, 47.
Hikone fief, 18, 105.
Himeji fief, 18.
Hino Sukemune, 317, 318.
Hitachi-obi, 10.
Hitotsubashi, Tokugawa branch house of,
18–19, 38.
Hitotsubashi Keiki. See Tokugawa Keiki.
Hitotsubashi party, 38–41, 43–44, 46, 51,
58.
Hokkaidō. See Ezo.
Holland. See Dutch.
Honda Tadamoto, 39, 204 n.
Honda Tadanori, 181.
Honda Yasuhide, 107 n.
Honjō Munehide, biographical note, 332;
official letter to Parkes (1865), 82, 304–5.
Hori Kunai, 251.
Hotta Masayoshi, biographical note, 332; appointment to office, 26–27; *kaikoku* policy of,
22; memorandum on foreign policy (1857),
131–4; and negotiations with Harris, 32–34,
131–4, 159–65, 182; memorandum concerning Harris negotiations, 165–8; seeks Imperial approval of Harris treaty, 36–42,
180–1, 198, 225; and the succession dispute,
39, 42; dismissal of, 44, 51.
Hyōgo (Kōbe), opening of, 34, 184, 187; postponement of opening of, 54–58, 62–63; and
documents relating thereto, 204–6, 208–21,
225–7; renewed demand for opening of
(1865), 80–83, 84; and documents relating
thereto, 293–7, 300, 302, 303, 304, 305;
final negotiations for opening of (1867), 86–
90, 306–8; and documents relating thereto,
308–20.
Hyōgo-bugyō, glossary entry, 323.
Hyōjōsho, glossary entry, 323; consulted on
policy, 130, 170.

ichibu, glossary entry, 323.

Ichijō Saneyoshi, 314.

Ido Satohiro, biographical note, 332; text of Perry Convention, negotiated by, 119–22; report on Perry negotiations by, 122–7.

Iemitsu, Shōgun. *See* Tokugawa Iemitsu.

Iemochi, Shōgun. *See* Tokugawa Iemochi.

Iesada, Shōgun. *See* Tokugawa Iesada.

Ieyasu, Shōgun. *See* Tokugawa Ieyasu.

Ieyoshi, Shōgun. *See* Tokugawa Ieyoshi.

Ii, family of, 18, 22, 42.

Ii Naosuke, biographical note, 332; his views on foreign policy in 1853, 8, 22; memorandum concerning same, 117–19; policy in Harris negotiations, 35, 43, 44–45, 181–3, 230; memorandum concerning same, 176–9; and the succession dispute, 38–39, 42–44; policy às Tairō, 43–45, 51; assassination of, 51–52, 199, 207.

Ikeda Nagaaki, biographical note, 333; *kaikoku* views of, 20; negotiates Paris Convention, 21, 71–72, 75–76; his memorandum seeking instructions concerning same, 260–3; text of same, signed by, 273–4; his report on negotiation of same, 274–82.

Ikeda Yoshinori (Keitoku), 11 n.; biographical note, 333.

Iki, island of, 192.

Inaba Masakuni, 316.

Indemnities: for the Tōzenji attack, 47, 56; for the Namamugi (Richardson) affair, 64–69, 222–4, 238, 240, 241–2, 251–2, 254–6; for the Itogaya murder, 262, 275; for the Shimonoseki attacks, 76–77, 79–80, 83, 257–60, 275–6, 282–9, 293–6, 300, 305.

India, British position in, 144, 161, 162, 171.

Inoue Kiyonao, biographical note, 333; his negotiations with Harris, 31, 33–34, 181–2; text of Harris treaty, signed by, 183–9; other activities of, 24 n., 256.

Inoue Masanao, biographical note, 333; and the Namamugi negotiations, 65, 240, 254.

Inoue Yamato, 302, 303.

Ise province, ports in, 172–3.

Ise shrine, 119, 190, 193, 194, 201.

Ishikawa Tokugorō, 40.

Itakura Katsukiyo, biographical note, 333; political activities of, 63, 316.

Itō Gumbei, 240.

Itogaya murder, 262, 275, 282.

Iwakura Tomomi, biographical note, 333; political activities of, 41, 52–53, 61, 88; his memorandum on the Kazunomiya marriage, 198–200.

Iwase Tadanari, biographical note, 333; political activities of, 24 n., 26, 27 n., 38, 40, 51; his views on foreign policy, 20, 28, 33; his

memorandum on foreign policy (1857), 134–6; his negotiations with Curtius, 21, 28–31; his memoranda regarding same, 139–45; text of Dutch supplementary treaty, signed by, 149–55; his negotiations with Harris, 33–34, 181–2; his memorandum concerning same, 174–6; text of Harris treaty, signed by, 183–9.

Iwashimizu shrine, 119.

Iwashita Sajiemon, 69, 303.

Izawa Masayoshi, biographical note, 333; text of Perry Convention, signed by, 119–22; his report on Perry negotiations, 122–7; his memorandum on foreign policy in 1857, 134–6.

Izu Islands, 109–10, 192.

Izu province, 120, 124.

Izumi province, 225, 226.

Japan, Emperor of. *See* Emperor.

Japan, foreign relations of. *See separately under names of foreign countries concerned.*

Japan, government of. *See* Bakufu.

jisha-bugyō, glossary entry, 323; political activities of, 19, 65, 254; their memorandum concerning Perry negotiations, 107–12; their memoranda on expulsion (1863), 234–6, 248–50.

jōi ideas (*see also* Expulsion), glossary entry, 323; general account of, 8–15; comparison with *kaikoku* ideas, 15–18, 165–6; relationship to *sonnō* ideas, 36–38, 45–47; and the Imperial Court, 40–42, 44–45, 53–54, 61–62, 63–64, 70–71, 81–82; effects of economic distress on, 49–51, 61, 245; effect of Kagoshima and Shimonoseki bombardments on, 83, 85; documents illustrating, 102–7, 114–17, 168–9.

Kagoshima, dispute leading to bombardment of, 64–69, 280; proposed opening of, 87.

kaibō-gakari, glossary entry, 323; administrative position of, 5, 20–21; memoranda by, 134–6, 137–9.

kaikoku ideas, glossary entry, 323; general account of, 5–8, 25, 28, 43; comparison with *jōi* ideas, 15–18, 165–6; become associated with support for Bakufu, 45–47; effect of economic distress on, 20, 49–51; documents illustrating, 117–19, 134–6, 137–9, 165–8, 274–82.

kamon, glossary entry, 324; political activities of, 19, 47, 58; memoranda by, 114–17, 176–9, 179–80, 225–7, 227–34.

Kampaku, glossary entry, 324; position of, 38 n.; *see also variously* Konoe Tadahiro; Kujō Naotada; Nijō Nariaki; Takatsukasa Masamichi; Takatsukasa Sukehiro.

Kanagawa (Yokohama), opening of, 34, 62; and documents referring thereto, 124, 171–2, 173, 174 n., 175–6, 184, 186, 187, 204, 225–6; proposed closing of, 71–77; and documents referring thereto, 247, 253, 260–3, 267, 268–82; French school at, 78.

Kanagawa, treaty of. *See* Perry Convention.

Kanagawa bugyō, glossary entry, 324; position of, 19; and the Namamugi indemnity, 251–2.

kanjō-bugyō, glossary entry, 324; status and activities of, 19–20, 30, 31, 32, 65; their memorandum concerning Perry negotiations, 107–12; their memorandum on trade (1857), 137–9; their memoranda concerning expulsion (1863), 234–6, 248–50.

kanjō-gimmiyaku, glossary entry, 324.

Kansai, glossary entry, 324.

Kantō, glossary entry, 324.

Kapitan, Dutch (*see also* Curtius, Donker), glossary entry, 324; document references to, 109, 123, 130, 132, 134, 136, 140, 141, 143, 146–8.

Karatsu, 173.

Kashima shrine, 119.

Kawada Hiroshi, biographical note, 334; his memorandum seeking instructions (1864), 260–3; text of Paris Convention, signed by, 273–4; his report on negotiation of same, 274–82.

Kawaji Toshiaki, biographical note, 334; political activities of, 24, 26, 27 n., 38, 40, 42 n., 51, 107 n., 145, 146, 147; *kaikoku* views of, 20, 28; his memorandum on foreign policy (1857), 137–9.

Kawazu Sukekuni, biographical note, 334; his memorandum seeking instructions (1864), 260–3; text of Paris Convention, signed by, 273–4; his report on negotiation of same, 274–82.

Kazunomiya, Princess, marriage of, 52–54, 195–7; and documents relating thereto, 198–204, 206–8, 249.

Keiki, Shōgun. *See* Tokugawa Keiki.

Kido Kōin, 85.

Kien Cheng, French ship, 273, 275 n.

Kii (Kishū), Tokugawa branch house of, 18, 38–39, 42, 44.

Kii province, ports in, 172–3, 175.

Kikuchi Ryūkichi, Iyo-no-kami, 255.

kinritsuki, 232, 233 n.

Kishū. *See* Kii.

koban-gomen, 315.

Kōbe. *See* Hyōgo.

kōbu-gattai party, glossary entry, 324; formation of, 45–47; its activities in 1862–3, 58–64, 70–71; and the dispute over closing Yokohama, 72–74, 268–72; its estrangement from

Bakufu, 85–86, 88–90; documents illustrating views of, 225–7, 227–34.

kōkenshoku. See *Shōgun-kōkenshoku*.

koku, glossary entry, 325.

Kokugakusha, influence on *jōi* movement of, 9, 36–38.

kokuji-goyō-gakari, glossary entry, 325.

kokutai, glossary entry, 325; discussion of, 2–3; document references to, 103, 181, 241, 265; 270, 280, 281, 310.

Komatsu Tatehaki, 88, 317.

Kōmei, Emperor, biographical note, 334; his views on foreign policy, 41, 44, 52–53, 72, 225; and the Kazunomiya marriage, 52–54, 200; his letters to Shōgun Iemochi (1864), 263–4, 264–6; death of, 310 n.

Konoe Tadafusa, biographical note, 334; political activities of, 268, 301–3, 314–15, 317.

Konoe Tadahiro, biographical note, 334; political activities of, 39, 61 n., 64, 311, 314–15, 316–19.

Korea, 55, 162, 213.

kuge (*see also* Court), glossary entry, 325; political activities of, 40, 52, 54, 61, 64, 70, 71, 73, 88; views on foreign policy of, 40–42, 58, 66, 81–82, 90.

Kujō Michitaka, biographical note, 334; and the Hyōgo dispute (1867), 314, 318.

Kujō Naotada, biographical note, 334; political activities of, 39, 41, 189, 200 n.

Kuper, Vice-Admiral, 65.

Kurile Islands, 4, 106 n., 141, 169 n.

Kuroda family, 105.

Kuze Hirochika, biographical note, 335; appointment of, 52; policy of, 52–54, 58, 230; his letter to Court concerning London Protocol negotiations, 204–6; his discussions with Alcock concerning same, 56; his letter to Alcock concerning same, 208–11; fall of, 60.

Kyōgoku Kōrō, text of London Protocol, signed by, 216–17.

Kyōto, proposed opening of, 220; as centre of anti-Bakufu activities, 40–41, 49–50, 61–62, 63–64, 225, 228.

Kyōto-shoshidai, glossary entry, 325; position of, 18, 232, 233 n.; political activities of, 39, 53–54, 66, 82; his memorandum to the *Kampaku* (1861), 206–8.

Kyōto-shugoshoku (*see also* Matsudaira Katamori), glossary entry, 325; position and activities of, 60, 82, 225, 227, 270–1.

Lagoda, American ship, 101.

Lawrence, American ship, 101.

Lhuys, Drouyn de, 273, 294.

London Protocol, negotiation of, 54–58, 195–7;

London Protocol (*contd*.)
and documents relating thereto, 204–6, 208–16, 218–21, 305; text of, 216–17; threatened revocation of, 75, 77, 276, 294.

Loochoo. *See* Ryūkyū.

machi-bugyō, glossary entry, 325; duties of, 19; their memorandum concerning Perry negotiations, 107–12; oppose expulsion policy (1863), 65; their memoranda concerning same, 234–6, 248–50.

Makino Tadamasa, memorandum of (Harris negotiations), 176–9.

Manabe Akikatsu, biographical note, 335; his mission to Kyōto (Harris treaty), 44–45, 52, 53; his memorandum to the Court, 189–93; the Court's reply to same, 193–4; later references to the mission, 198, 206, 225.

Matsudaira Chikanao, biographical note, 335; appointed as one of the *gaikoku-bōeki-torishi-rabe-gakari*, 27 n.; his memorandum on foreign policy in 1857, 137–9.

Matsudaira Katamori, biographical note, 335; appointment as *Kyōto-shugoshoku*, 60, 270 n.; and the *kōbu-gattai* party, 70–71, 72, 229, 232–3, 234, 264, 301–2; views on foreign policy (1862), 62–63; and memorandum concerning same, 225–7; signs Bakufu promise of expulsion, 234; urges Imperial ratification of treaties (1865), 301, 304.

Matsudaira Keiei, biographical note, 335; *jōi* views of, 13–14, 22; his memorandum concerning Perry negotiations, 114–17; change in views of (Harris treaty), 35; and memorandum concerning same, 179–80; his part in succession dispute, 38–44; and the *kōbu-gattai* party, 46, 58–59, 62–64, 66, 72–74, 264, 268–72; signs Bakufu promise of expulsion, 234; his letter of protest concerning Hyōgo and Chōshū, 319–20.

Matsudaira Keitoku. *See* Ikeda Yoshinori.

Matsudaira Munehide. *See* Honjō Munehide.

Matsudaira Nobuatsu, biographical note, 335; and the Namamugi indemnity, 254.

Matsudaira Nobuyoshi, 65.

Matsudaira Noriyasu, biographical note, 336; leader of *zokuron-ha*, 26; memorandum of (Harris negotiations), 176–9.

Matsudaira Sadamichi, memorandum of (Harris negotiations), 176–9.

Matsudaira Sadataka, biographical note, 336; as *Kyōto-shoshidai*, 302, 304, 316; urges Imperial ratification of treaties, 301.

Matsudaira Tadakata, 26, 44, 182; biographical note, 336.

Matsudaira Tadanori, memorandum of (Harris negotiations), 176–9.

Matsudaira Yasunao (Matsui Yasuhide), biographical note, 336; negotiates London Protocol, 54–58; text of same, signed by, 216–17; his letter to Parkes (1865), 304–5.

Matsudaira Yoritane, memorandum of (Harris negotiations), 176–9.

Matsudaira Yoritoshi, memorandum of (Harris negotiations), 176–9.

Matsui Yasuhide. *See* Matsudaira Yasunao.

Matsumae fief, 120, 124, 169.

Matsumae Takahiro, biographical note, 336; and the negotiations of 1865, 82, 296.

Meiji, Emperor, biographical note, 337; letters in name of (1867), 310, 311, 319.

metsuke, glossary entry, 326; position of, 19–20; *kaikoku* views of, 30, 31; memorandum illustrating same (1857), 134–6.

Mikado (*see* Emperor), glossary entry, 326.

Ministers, resident, establishment of, 32–34; and document references thereto, 160, 162, 168–79, 183–4.

Minobe Matagorō, 268; biographical note, 337.

Minoda Dembei, 301; biographical note, 337.

Mito (*see also* Tokugawa Nariaki), and *jōi* ideas, 8–15; influence of, 18–19, 254; Bakufu suspicions of, 26, 42, 60; alliance with *sonnō* party, 36–38, 40–41; attacks on foreigners by, 47–48; assassination of Ii Naosuke by *rōnin* of, 51, 202.

Mizuno Tadakiyo, 293 n., 305; biographical note, 337.

Mizuno Tadanori, biographical note, 337; political activities of, 26, 27 n., 51; his views on foreign policy, 20, 28, 33, 65; his memorandum on foreign policy in 1857, 137–9; negotiates Dutch supplementary treaty, 21, 28–31; his memoranda regarding same, 139–49; text of same, signed by, 149–55; his memorandum concerning negotiations with Harris, 170–4; his letter concerning the Namamugi indemnity (1863), 240–2.

Mōri Yoshichika, 45, 288; biographical note, 337.

Moriyama Takichirō, 57; biographical note, 337.

Morrison, American ship, 101.

Morrison, G. C., 212.

Musashi province, 175.

Nabeshima family, 105.

Nagai Naomune, 24 n., 51; biographical note, 337.

Nagano Shuzen, 40.

Nagasaki, British frigate at, 4; Dutch (Deshima) and Chinese trade at, 3, 29, 105, 134, 149–55, 247, 249, 250; opening of, 28, 29, 34, 62, 124,

Nagasaki (*contd.*)
139, 149–55, 184, 186, 187, 204, 225–6, 261; proposed closing of, 247, 249, 253.
Nagasaki bugyō, 19, 27 n., 130; glossary entry, 326; memoranda of (1857), 139–45.
Nagasaki Treasury (*Nagasaki Kaisho*), 142–3, 150, 151, 152, 153, 154, 155 n.
Nagato province. *See* Chōshū.
Naidaijin, 38 n.; glossary entry, 326.
Nairan, glossary entry, 326.
Naito Nobuchika, 204 n.; biographical note, 338.
Namamugi incident, 64–69, 222–4; and documents relating thereto, 236–42, 250–6.
Nara, 244.
Navy, British, as threat to Japan, 27–28, 32, 64–65, 164, 178–9, 237–40; plan for blockade of Japan by, 64; bombardment of Kagoshima by, 69.
Neale, St. John, his policy in Namamugi dispute, 64–65, 67–69; his letter to Bakufu concerning same, 236–40.
Netherlands. *See* Dutch.
Niigata, opening of, 34, 184, 187; another port to be substituted for, 87, 184; postponement of plans for, 54–58; and documents relating thereto, 204–6, 208–21.
Nijō Castle, 73, 270, 302.
Nijō Nariaki, biographical note, 338; appointment as *Kampaku*, 72; and the closing of Yokohama, 268, 270; and Imperial ratification of the treaties, 296, 301–2, 303; and the disputes of 1867, 90, 311, 313 n., 314–15, 316–19.
Nikkō, 119.
Nomura Teijitsu, 268; biographical note, 338.

Ogasawara Nagamichi, biographical note, 338; his memorandum concerning expulsion policy (1863), 243–6; further minute concerning same, 249–50; pays Namamugi indemnity, 66–68, 251–2; his memorandum justifying same, 254–6; urges Imperial ratification of the treaties, 80, 82, 300 n., 302, 304; his letter to Court concerning same, 301; his letter to Parkes concerning same, 304–5.
Ōgimachi Sanjō Sanenaru. *See* Saga Sanenaru.
Ōhara Shigenori, biographical note, 338; political activities of, 41, 60, 82, 228, 303.
Okabe Nagatsune, 234.
Okazaki fief, 39.
Oki, island of, 192.
Ōkubo Tadahiro, 27 n.
Ōkubo Toshimichi, biographical note, 339; accompanies Ōhara mission to Edo, 60; opposes Imperial ratification of the treaties, 81–82; his letter concerning same, 301–3;

and Satsuma's anti-Bakufu policy, 83–86; his letter concerning same (1867), 312–13; opposes opening of Hyōgo, 88–90; his letters concerning same, 311–13.
Oliphant, L., 50, 212.
ōmetsuke, glossary entry, 326; functions of, 19–20; their views on foreign policy, 30; their memorandum on same (1857), 134–6.
Opium, its import to Japan, 152, 162–3, 186.
Opium War, its influence on Japanese policy, 4, 7, 104, 161, 179.
Oregon, 99.
Ōsaka, opening of, 28, 34, 45, 135, 172, 175, 185; postponement of opening of, 54–58, 62–63, 87; and documents relating thereto, 204–6, 208–21, 225–7; negotiations at, 21, 80–83, 295, 299–300; renewed demand for opening of, 293–6, 300.
Ōsaka-jōdai, glossary entry, 326.
ōsetsu-gakari, 20–21, 131; glossary entry, 326; report by (Perry negotiations), 122–7.
Ōshima, 117.
Ōu province, 219.
Ouari. *See* Owari.
Owari, Tokugawa branch house of, 18, 60, 254, 295, 313.

Paris Convention, negotiation of, 21, 71–72, 75–76, 257–60; and documents relating thereto, 260–3, 267, 272–3; text of, 273–4; Japanese negotiators' report concerning, 274–82.
Parkes, Harry S., secures Imperial ratification of the treaties, 79–83, 290–2; his memorandum demanding same, 293–6; his letter to Bakufu concerning same, 299–300; the Bakufu's reply thereto, 304–5; his relations with Satsuma and Chōshū, 83–84, 86 n., 88; and the opening of Hyōgo, 87–88, 306–8.
Perry, Commodore M. C., his negotiations with Japan, 21–25, 97–99, 230; text of President's letter, brought by, 99–101; his letter to Bakufu, 101–2; text of Convention negotiated by, 119–22; Japanese report on negotiations with, 122–7.
Perry Convention, documents concerning negotiation of, 99–119, 122–7; text of, 119–22; superseded by Harris treaty, 188, 189.
Perseus, H.M.S., 282, 283.
Polsbroek, D. de Graeff van, and the Shimonoseki dispute, 282–8; text of indemnity convention, signed by, 288–9; his memorandum concerning Imperial ratification of the treaties, 293–6.
Portman, A. L. C., his memorandum concerning Imperial ratification of the treaties, 293–6.

Ports, opening of. *See separately* Edo; Hakodate; Hyōgo; Kanagawa; Ōsaka; Nagasaki; Niigata; Shimoda.

Portugal, 155 n., 280.

Poutiatine, Admiral E., his negotiations of 1853–5, 11, 24, 145, 146, 147, 172 n.; his negotiations of 1857, 29–30, 129–30, 144–9.

Princess Royal, H.M.S., 299.

Prussia, proposed treaty with, 53, 204–8, 211, 280.

Pruyn, R. H., and the Shimonoseki dispute, 282–8; text of indemnity convention, signed by, 288–9.

Rangakusha, and foreign policy, 5–8, 104.

Rezanov, Nicolai, 4.

ri, 125, 187; glossary entry, 326.

Richardson, murder of. *See* Namamugi incident.

Roches, Léon, and the Shimonoseki dispute, 74–77, 282–8; text of indemnity convention, signed by, 288–9; his memorandum concerning Imperial ratification of the treaties, 293–6; his policy of supporting the Bakufu, 78–79, 87.

Rōjū, glossary entry, 326; policy and activities of, 18, 21, 59, 62–63, 66, 72, 73, 168, 229, 232–3, 246–8, 252–3; their memoranda on foreign affairs, 130–1, 200–4, 204–6.

Rōjū-kaku, glossary entry, 327.

rōnin, glossary entry, 327; anti-Bakufu activities of, 48, 58, 67, 77, 90, 199, 225, 228, 232, 265.

Russell, Lord, and the London Protocol, 55, 57; text of same, signed by, 216–17; his instructions concerning the Namamugi dispute, 64–65; his instructions concerning the Shimonoseki dispute, 74–75; his instructions concerning Imperial ratification of the treaties, 80.

Russia, in the Kuriles and the north, 4, 106 n., 141, 161, 169; as an influence on Japanese policy, 4, 24, 55, 129–30, 144–5, 146–9, 161, 171, 178, 179, 215, 219–20; treaties of, 21, 25, 29–30, 129–30, 144–5, 146–9, 175.

rusui, glossary entry, 327.

ryō, glossary entry, 327.

Ryūkyū (Loochoo) Islands, 112, 124.

Sadaijin, 38 n.; glossary entry, 327.

Sadaishō, 314.

Sado island, 192.

Saga Sanenaru, biographical note, 339; and the Hyōgo dispute, 90 n., 317, 318; extract from diary of, 314–15.

Sagami province, 109, 172.

Saigō Takamori, 85, 88 n., 301; biographical note, 339.

Sakai, city of, 117, 118, 244.

Sakai family, 18, 42.

Sakai Tadasuke, 305; biographical note, 339; text of Shimonoseki indemnity convention, signed by, 288–9.

Sakai Tadateru, of Himeji, his memorandum concerning Harris negotiations, 176–9.

Sakai Tadayoshi, biographical note, 339; as *Kyōto-shoshidai,* 189, 194, 200 n., 204 n.; his letter to Court concerning London Protocol negotiations, 206–8.

Sakashita-mon, attack on Andō Nobumasa at, 56 n., 60.

sakoku, glossary entry, 327.

Sakuma Shōzan, views on foreign policy of, 7–8.

Sakurada-mon, murder of Ii Naosuke at, 51, 199, 207.

samurai, glossary entry, 327; anti-Bakufu and anti-foreign ideas of, 48–50, 58, 61–62, 67, 77, 86, 90.

sanbansho-tōkin, 315.

Sandwich Islands, 160.

Sanjō Sanetomi, biographical note, 339; as imperial envoy, 62, 63, 231–2, 234; *jōi* activities of, 265.

Sanjō Sanetsumu, 39, 41; biographical note, 339.

sanke, glossary entry, 328; position and activities of, 18–19, 39, 44, 58, 68, 181; memoranda by, 102–7, 168–9.

sankin-kōtai, glossary entry, 328; revision of, 62, 265.

sankyō, 18–19; glossary entry, 328.

Satō Shinen, 16.

Satow, E. M., 83 n., 84, 88.

Satsuma (*see also* Shimazu Hisamitsu and Shimazu Nariakira), and the *kōbu-gattai* party, 58–62, 64, 72–73, 85, 86; its dispute with Britain (Namamugi incident), 64–69, 222–4; and documents relating thereto, 236–40, 286; its growing friendship with Britain, 83–84; anti-Bakufu activities of, 81–82, 86–90, 228, 230, 232, 296–7, 301–3; its alliance with Chōshū, 84–86; urges pardoning of Chōshū, 88–90, 311–20.

Seclusion policy. *See under* Bakufu.

Sei-i-tai-shōgun (*see also* Bakufu), glossary entry, 328; status of, 18, 36–38, 75, 77–78, 235, 246, 247, 252, 284–7, 313; proposals for resignation of, 63, 67, 82, 88, 231–2, 249, 250, 297–8, 313; audiences of foreign diplomats with, 31, 87; his visits to Kyōto, 60, 62, 63, 65, 68, 72, 75, 89–90; and document references thereto, 227, 228, 234, 235, 238 n., 246–7, 265, 266,

Sei-i-tai-shōgun (contd.)
267. 301–2; his letters to the Emperor (1864), 266–7, 272–3, 297–9; commands expedition against Chōshū, 85; resignation of, 90.
Seiji-sōsaishoku, glossary entry, 328; Matsudaira Keiei appointed as, 60, 227, 234 n.
sekke, 315.
Sesshō (*see* Nijō Nariaki), glossary entry, 328.
Settsu province, 225, 226, 247, 255, 266, 267.
Shibata Masanaka (Teitarō), 255, 282 n.
Shikibu, Prince, 317.
Shikoku, 219.
Shima province, ports of, 172–3, 175.
Shimazu Hisamitsu, biographical note, 339; and the *kōbu-gattai* party, 46, 58–59, 60–62, 64, 66, 72–74, 264; his disputes with Tokugawa Keiki, 66, 72–74, 88–90, 268–72; and the Namamugi dispute, 64–66, 236, 240; opposes closing of Yokohama, 72–74; opposes Bakufu in Hyōgo dispute (1867), 88–90, 312, 314–15, 316–19; his letter to Court concerning same, 319–20.
Shimazu Nariakira, biographical note, 340; his views on foreign policy, 23; his memorandum concerning same (1853), 112–14; supports Hitotsubashi party, 38–39; death of, 46 n.
Shimazu Tadayoshi, 46 n., 297; biographical note, 340.
Shimizu, Tokugawa branch house of, 18–19.
Shimoda, opening of, 25, 120–2, 124–5, 126, 139, 155 n., 171–2, 226; closing of, 33, 132, 173, 184.
Shimoda bugyō, glossary entry, 329; views and activities of, 19, 27 n., 31, 130, 131, 139–40, 141, 142.
Shimoda Convention, 31, 188.
Shimonoseki, attacks on foreign shipping at, 69–70, 262, 265; bombardment of, and negotiations preceding same, 59, 74–76; negotiation of indemnity agreement concerning, 75–77, 79–80, 83, 257–60, 273–6, 280, 282–8, 293–6, 305; text of same, 288–9; effects of bombardment of, 77, 83–84, 282–8; proposal for opening of, 77, 87, 287, 289.
Shinagawa, 47, 261.
Shinron, 10.
Shipwrecked seamen. *See* Castaways.
Shōgun. See *Sei-i-tai-shōgun*.
Shōgun-kōkenshoku, glossary entry, 329; Tokugawa Keiki's appointment as, 60, 231.
Shoshidai. See *Kyōto-shoshidai*.
Shugoshoku. See *Kyōto-shugoshoku*.
von Siebold, 275.
Smuggling, regulations against, 152–3.
sonnō ideas, glossary entry, 329; their influence on foreign policy, 36–38, 45–47.

sonnō-jōi, 45–46, 49–50; glossary entry, 329. *See also separately sonnō* and *jōi*.
Stirling, Sir James, 161.
Succession dispute, of 1858, 38–39, 41–44.
Suez Canal, 277.
Switzerland, proposed treaty with, 53, 205, 281.

Taikun (Taikoun; Taicoun). *See* Tycoon.
Tairō (*see also* Ii Naosuke), glossary entry, 329; appointment of, 42.
Takahito, Prince, 317, 318, 319.
Takasaki Itarō, 269, 271.
Takasugi Shinsaku, 85.
Takatsukasa Masamichi, 39, 41; biographical note, 340.
Takatsukasa Sukehiro, biographical note, 340; as *Kampaku*, 64, 72, 250; supports Shōgun in Hyōgo dispute (1867), 90, 314–15, 316–19.
Takatsukasa Sukemasa, 314, 315, 317–18.
Takeda Masao (Kōunsai), 247, 255.
Takemoto Masao, biographical note, 340; and the Shimonoseki indemnity discussions, 76, 282–8.
Takeuchi (Takenouchi) Yasunori, biographical note, 340; negotiates London Protocol, 54–58; text of same, signed by, 216–17.
Tamari-no-ma, glossary entry, 329; memorandum by *daimyō* of (1858), 176–9.
Tariff. See Customs duties.
Tayasu, Tokugawa branch house of, 18–19.
Tempōrin. See Sanjō Sanetomi.
Tenshōin, Princess, 249.
Toba, proposed opening of, 172–3.
Toda (Matsudaira) Mitsunori, 240.
Toki Tomoaki, 146, 148; biographical note, 340.
Toki Yorimune, biographical note, 341; views and activities of, 27 n., 28, 38, 42 n., 176; his memorandum on foreign policy (1857), 134–6.
Tokudaiji Kinjun, 268.
Tokugawa government. *See* Bakufu.
Tokugawa Iemitsu, 244.
Tokugawa Iemochi, biographical note, 341; his nomination as Iesada's heir, 38–39, 42–44; his marriage to Princess Kazunomiya, 52–54; his letters to Emperor in 1864, 266–7, 272–3; his letter urging Imperial ratification of the treaties, 297–9; attempted resignation of, 82, 297–8; death of, 86, 308.
Tokugawa Iesada, 38–39, 43–44, 193; biographical note, 341.
Tokugawa Ieyasu, 3, 181, 199, 214, 231, 235, 244, 249.
Tokugawa Ieyoshi, 123 n.; biographical note, 341.
Tokugawa Keiki (Hitotsubashi Keiki), biographical note, 341; attempt to nominate as

Tokugawa Keiki (*contd.*)
Iesada's heir, 38–44; his relations with *kōbu-gattai* party, 58–60, 63–64, 72–74, 227–34; his relations with Bakufu officials, 60–63, 67–68, 72, 81, 246–8, 250–3; accepts expulsion policy (1863), 63–64, 66; his letter to Court avowing same, 234; his instructions to *Rōjū* concerning same, 246–8; his letter to *Kampaku* concerning same, 250–3; and the Namamugi dispute, 66–68, 250–3, 255–6; and the closing of Yokohama, 72–75; his disputes with Shimazu Hisamitsu, 66, 72–74, 88–90, 268–74, 314–19; and Imperial ratification of the treaties, 81–82, 297–8, 301–3, 304; his memorandum urging same, 301; and Bakufu policy towards Chōshū, 85, 87–90; becomes Shōgun, 86; urges the opening of Hyōgo, 87–90, 314–19; his letters to Court concerning same, 308–10, 310–11; resignation of, 90.

Tokugawa Nariaki, biographical note, 341; influence of, 11; *jōi* views of, 11–15; and the Perry Convention, 22, 23–25; his memorandum concerning same, 102–7; his relations with Abe Masahiro, 25–27; made responsible for defence, 26, 113; and the Harris treaty, 35, 42; his memorandum concerning same, 168–9; and the succession dispute, 37, 38, 39, 40; death of, 45.

Tokugawa Yoshiatsu, 11 n.; biographical note, 341.

Tokugawa Yoshimune, 18.

Tokugawa Yoshinobu. *See* Tokugawa Keiki.

Tokugawa Yoshitomi. *See* Tokugawa Iemochi.

Tosa fief (*see also* Yamanouchi Toyoshige), activities of retainers of, 61–62, 64, 228.

tozama daimyō (see also *daimyō*), glossary entry, 329; position and activities of, 22, 47, 58, 60, 61, 72, 77, 225, 227; retainers of, in Osaka, 80; views of, 23, 250; memoranda by one of, 112–14.

Tōzenji, attack on British legation at, 47, 55–56, 64, 212, 237 n., 250.

Trade, foreign requests concerning, 99–100, 125–6, 160, 164; regulations concerning, 25, 27, 140–1, 143, 149–55, 175, 185, 188, 189, 216–17; Bakufu restrictions on, 50–51, 74; Bakufu views on, 25, 30–31, 34, 50–51, 54, 73, 78–79; and document references thereto, 108, 110–12, 132–41, 143, 167, 201, 218–19, 244–5; *kaikoku* views on, 6–8, 118, 134–41, 143, 167, 179; *jōi* views on, 9–10, 104, 169; effects of, in Japan, 49–51; of Satsuma and Chōshū, 83–84.

Treasury. *See* Nagasaki Treasury.

Treaties and agreements: with Britain (1854–8), 25, 50; with Russia (1854–8), 21, 25,

29–30, 129–30; with Perry, negotiation of, 21–25, 97–99, 122–7; Perry Convention, text of, 119–22; with Dutch (1856), 143 n., 149; with Dutch (1857), negotiation of, 21, 27–31, 128–30, 139–49; Dutch supplementary treaty (1857), text of, 149–55; with Harris (Shimoda Convention, 1857), 31, 188; with Harris (commercial treaty, 1858), negotiation of, 31–35, 38–43, 156–9, 159–65, 181–3; Harris treaty, text of, 183–9; with Britain (1862), negotiation of, 54–57, 195–7; London Protocol, text of, 216–17; with France (1864), negotiation of, 71–72, 75–76, 257–60, 274–82; Paris Convention, text of, 273–4; concerning Shimonoseki indemnity, negotiation of, 76–77, 282–8; Shimonoseki Indemnity Convention (1864), text of, 288–9; all treaties, Imperial ratification of, 55, 79–83, 283, 285–7, 290–2, 293–305.

Tsuda Masamichi, memorandum by (1857), 134–6.

Tsūkō Ichiran, 170–1.

Tsushima, foreign threat to, 55 n., 192, 219–20; proposed opening of, 57, 213, 217, 219–20.

Tsutsui Masanori, 24, 26; biographical note, 342.

Tycoon, glossary entry, 330.

Uchita Naka-no-suke, biographical note, 342; memorandum by (1865), 296–7.

Udaijin, 38 n.; glossary entry, 330.

Udono Chōei, text of Perry Convention, signed by, 119–22; report concerning same, 122–7.

Umeda Umpin, 40.

Umezawa Sontarō, 268.

United States, letters to Japan (1853), 99–102; negotiations with Japan (1853–4), 21–25, 122–7; text of agreement with Japan (1853), 119–22; concludes Shimoda Convention with Japan (1857), 31, 188; negotiations with Japan (1858), 31–34, 43, 156–65, 181–3; text of commercial treaty with Japan (1858), 183–9; and the Shimonoseki dispute, 69–70, 74–77, 282–9; and Imperial ratification of the treaties, 290–6; and the opening of Hyōgo, 97–99.

Uraga, opening of, 124, 172–3, 174 n.; defence of, 105, 109–10, 113, 115; and Yokohama, 262.

Uraga bugyō, 97; glossary entry, 330.

Utsuki Roku-no-jō, biographical note, 342; extract from journal of, 181–3.

Uwajima fief. *See* Date Muneki.

wakadoshiyori, 18; glossary entry, 330.

Wakamatsu fief. *See* Aizu.

waki-ni trade, 140 n.

Winchester, Mr., 80.
de Wit, 56.

Yamaguchi Naotake, 251–2.
Yamanouchi Toyoshige, biographical note, 342; supports Hitotsubashi party, 38–39, 41; and the *kōbu-gattai* party, 46, 58–59, 63, 66, 72, 264; signs Bakufu promise of expulsion (1863), 234; and the Hyōgo dispute, 88–90, 314; protests against decision regarding same, 319–20.

Yanagawa fief, 313.
Yanagiwara Mitsunaru, 315.
Yedo (Yeddo). *See* Edo.
Yezo. *See* Ezo.
Yokohama. *See* Kanagawa.
Yokosuka, naval dockyard at, 78.
Yoshida Shōin, 16–17, 45.
Yoshimune, Shōgun. *See* Tokugawa Yoshimune.

zokuron-ha, 26, 42; glossary entry, 330.

REPRINTED LITHOGRAPHICALLY IN GREAT BRITAIN
AT THE UNIVERSITY PRESS, OXFORD
BY VIVIAN RIDLER
PRINTER TO THE UNIVERSITY